HEDGING
Principles, Practices, and Strategies
for the Financial Markets

Joseph D. Koziol

WILEY

JOHN WILEY & SONS
New York • Chichester • Brisbane • Toronto • Singapore

Library of Congress Cataloging in Publication Data:

Koziol, Joseph D.
  Hedging: principles, practices, and strategies for the financial markets / by Joseph D. Koziol.
    p. cm.
  Bibliography: p.

  1. Hedging (Finance) 2. Financial futures. 3. Options (Finance)
I. Title.
HG6024.A3K683   1990
332.64'5—dc20   89-8963
                                                         CIP

ISBN 0-471-63560-X

Printed in the United States of America

10 9 8 7 6 5 4 3 2 1

Dedicated to my Mother and Father

Preface

The rapid growth in futures, options, and derivative products trading has increased the demand for hedging programs. Simple and advanced hedging programs depend on the same principles; an understanding of the principles and the process will guide the hedger in establishing and monitoring these programs.

The purpose of this text is to prepare the reader for hedging by presenting the foundations of hedging theories, illustrating hedging practices, and showing how to develop strategies. The following chapters demonstrate that, regardless of industry, many financial and physical hedging situations share common attributes and objectives. Suitable hedges can significantly improve an organization's performance.

In this book, the theories of hedging and cross hedging are conceptually developed through the presentation of a variety of examples. Comparative approaches are used to describe the principles and highlight potential pitfalls. The cash-and-carry or ''repo'' programs are described as the foundations of the hedging process, then the text shows how they can be destabilized when there are inadequate provisions for cash flow considerations. This is a practical problem for any hedger: Although a ''perfect hedge'' can work on the last day, the prior sequence of events can overwhelm and destroy a hedge. Under some conditions, favorable basis action may be insufficient to maintain the integrity of the hedge, which gives rise to a "hedging paradox." Arbitrage and program trading transactions are also prone to the same debilitating forces because they are essentially multiple asset actions derived from the single asset cash and carry.

The emergence of options markets has increased the hedging solution horizon. Swings in volatility can be beneficial to hedgers, provided that they know how to respond; otherwise, wide disparities in volatility assessments can produce serious stresses on the overall hedge. This book identifies a number of these situations and offers insights on how to minimize their adverse impacts.

As with any market strategy, the hedger must be able to adapt to changing circumstances. The adaptive process, while predicated on statistical procedures, requires creativity. If hedgers have a knowledge of techniques used for markets other than their own, they have an advantage in constructing desirable hedges and adjustment procedures.

Part I introduces terms and concepts that will be examined repeatedly in subsequent chapters. It provides the analytical framework and various empirical techniques.

Chapter 1 defines contractual agreements, futures, forwards, and options contracts. Long and short hedges are described. The concepts of correlation, economic validity, convergence, and consistency are analyzed.

Chapter 2 describes the basis and its crucial bearing on the success or failure of a hedge program. It presents a step-by-step description of how price-level risks are transformed into more narrowly definable basis risks. This mathematical simplification readily reduces two or more factors into a single variable that reflects a relationship between the hedging instruments and hedgeable positions.

Chapter 3 presents quantitative approaches that are necessary to analyze the basis from several perspectives: minimum and maximum boundaries, expected values versus theoretical ones, oscillatory movements, decay versus appreciation, stable versus unstable, and degrees of protection.

Chapter 4 examines the comparative advantages and disadvantages of the more common adaptive processes. It indicates the crucial assumptions made for many models and their underpinnings, while highlighting potentially serious flaws. In particular, this book presents alternative solutions for beta- and delta-type hedges, which share many strengths and weaknesses. The material methodically demonstrates dynamic monitoring, updating, and trading strategies.

Part II is comprised of four chapters. Chapter 5 presents concerns about and advantages for hedging grains, meats, metals, tropical products, and the energy complex. It goes through the mechanics of cash-and-carry and reverse cash-and-carry transactions, and then relates this procedure to the securities markets. It focuses on attempts to secure enhanced rates of return, and diverse prices and wide basis relationships are addressed. The material highlights circumstances where ratio hedging is more appropriate: Crush and reverse crush, crack and reverse crack, and feed spread strategies are explained. Within this framework, program trading and portfolio insurance techniques are evaluated.

Chapter 6 examines debt hedging for both borrowers and lenders. Taxables and exempts are treated across the maturity horizon and appropriate techniques are presented for fixed-rate and variable-rate securities.

Chapter 7 focuses on the capital, income, and expense flow characteristics for asset and liability management. Macro gap analysis for financial institutions is developed by presenting several statistical methods that delineate the data. The concept is refined by imparting additional time periods to the analysis through the application of micro gap considerations. Duration analysis and its interrelationship with yield-curve fluctuations generate guidelines for dynamic solutions to the previously static gap descriptions. Trend and cyclic statistical tools are used to identify patterns in the flows.

Chapter 8 details the mechanics of equity hedging and its clearly separate and distinct role in locking in rates of return or protecting stock holding values versus portfolio diversification techniques. It demonstrates that ordinary portfolio diversification methods are vulnerable to the existence of highly interdependent returns and, thus, that the assumption of independence of returns and the intended reduction of mutually occurring disastrous rates of return is statistically incorrect and inappropriate. Evidence is cited that supports the high likelihood of mutually occurring outlier risks. This recurring situation is formally developed as conditional states recognition. Diversification is statistically compared to hedging, and the text describes more suitable protective techniques.

Part III deals with the underlying factors of a hedge program. The four chapters discuss the mechanisms that justify the economic existence of the futures and options markets.

Trading the basis is examined in Chapter 9. This important aspect of a program illustrates additional benefits that can occur when the basis is carefully analyzed and acted upon. The chapter shows why arbitrage efforts are predicated on the basis, and, finally, it demonstrates whether it can be in the deliverer's or recipient's interests to effectuate a delivery, hence paper or cash.

Chapter 10 distinguishes and develops the concepts of deliveries, settlements, and other offsets. It shows how AAs, EFPs, and against-cash techniques complement both hedging and cross-hedging strategies.

Chapter 11 presents evaluative procedures to determine optimum futures or options hedging applications. These procedures show that conditionalized information can improve results (many fair value models are statistically one-dimensional). A solution set is developed by infusing Bayesian analysis into the decision-making process, which identifies conditionalized states for preferred strategies. The chapter also addresses the issue of delta neutrality: Although many would agree on the textbook definition, they would not necessarily have a consensus on its applications.

The design and implementation of a hedging program is outlined in Chapter 12. Objectives, constraints, selectivity, and opportunities are assessed in terms of what is at risk, what are the implied benefits, how to organize the trading decision group, and how to evaluate the hedging results against early and revised expectations.

Hedging is an evolutionary process. With standardized terms, corporate treasurers, controllers, and hedge managers in any industry can implement and monitor various physical or financial hedging programs. Standardization is especially valuable because many times the policies and guidelines established by the chief financial officer or hedging committee are then implemented by other staff members.

JOSEPH D. KOZIOL

Bedford, New York

Acknowledgments

The following people and organizations deserve special acknowledgment: the Chicago Board of Trade, the Chicago Mercantile Exchange, the New York Mercantile Exchange, the New York Cotton Exchange, the Coffee, Sugar, & Cocoa Exchange, the Kansas City Board of Trade, the Commodity Research Bureau, Inc., COMEX and Municipal Market Data, Inc., Tom Walker, Hugh Sigmon, Gerald Becker, Maurice Girardi, Dana Kellerman, Leslie Wurman, and Dick Dobbins. All were helpful during the preparation of the manuscript. I am particularly grateful to Ralph A. Musil. His wisdom and dedication to the financial industry served as a valuable inspiration to my efforts here.

The people at John Wiley & Sons deserve a special thank you for their patience, editing, and production. Tom Gilmartin and Rich Moses were very helpful in attending to the many details. Mary Cavanagh proved to be an exceptional copy editor. Karl Weber was an understanding and very reliable professional editor.

Marjorie and Christine Koziol were excellent and devoted proofreaders and indexers.

Finally, I extend my appreciation to my colleagues, friends, family, and staff for their helpful criticisms and comments, typing, graphics, and proofreading efforts.

Contents

List of Tables and Figures

TABLES

FIGURES

PART I
PRINCIPLES

1

Introduction

Hedging is a multivariate process for managing risks and achieving objectives. Among many other functions, it can price marketings, offer acquisition alternatives, provide portfolio insurance, stretch or shorten financial maturities, and improve working capital management.

Hedging is multidisciplinary. Accounting, production, marketing, financing, taxation, legal aspects, and other areas must be considered in order to arrive at a comprehensive hedging program.

Hedging is a dynamic process that manages specified risks with a suitable offset mechanism over time. This mechanism must have the capacity to generate financial responses that occur inversely to those for the underlying hedge items, be they portfolios, commodities, or indices. For example, if the underlying portfolio decreased by $100, then the hedge account should have generated an offsetting increase of $100. If an underlying futures position advanced by $500, then the options hedge should have declined by $500.

Hedging is *not* the simple buying or selling of futures and options against physicals. It is the prudent selection process whereby regulatory, financial, operational, supply and demand, and other factors must be continually evaluated in order to derive the maximum benefits from the program.

INSIGHT

All successful hedging programs have a common trait—insight. Although they carefully apply quantitative analysis, they are not formula approaches. Insight is the ability to penetrate the hedging problem, recognize the essential variables, and effectively place the appropriate hedge position. This book provides numerous examples for a variety of markets. By broadening your understanding, you can develop insight.

CONDITIONAL ASPECTS

Any hedging program has many conditional aspects. Awareness of them allows the hedge director to choose a better strategy, which can make a substantial difference in performance. This is analogous to another method of risk management—insurance. How much coverage is needed? For whom? For what? How large are the deductibles? These are important questions to answer in the final resolution of an insurance coverage program.

Similar principles apply here. One can effectively secure coverage, but to do so to the extreme may reduce hedging performance. The introduction of too many moving parts and adjustment processes can be operationally and financially onerous. As Chapter 11 illustrates, this is particularly true for some options oriented tactics.

METHODS

The four basic methods by which hedges can be established are:

1. Contractual arrangements
2. Forward contracts
3. Futures contracts
4. Options contracts

Contractual Arrangements

Contractual arrangements occur when two parties agree to a legally enforceable set of terms. For most organizations, they are common occurrences during the ordinary course of business. Examples are an agreement to sell refined gold at a certain price, the sale of heating oil against a specified benchmark, or the receipt of computers for dollars or yen.

These are *nonstandardized* arrangements, in which *terms* are likely to vary for each situation. *Performance* risks are borne by both parties. In these cases, the amounts of the transactions and the conveyance of goods, securities, or services are to take place according to a specified schedule of delivery, payment for which is to precede, coincide with, or follow the transfer of funds. There can be substantial penalties for any modifications or failure to comply. These transactions are not readily amenable to early offset or contractual adjustments.

Forward Contracts

Forward contracts call for the transfer of commodities, securities, or currencies at a specified time in the future. Often the payment is to be made at that time. Although there is no explicit standardization as in futures and options contracts, forward contracts tend to follow certain conventions. For example, the settlement (payment) procedures for conducting foreign exchange transactions at banking institutions are fairly well known, as are security payment practices. Usually, there are no requirements for good faith deposits—margining—for which futures and options positions are mandatory. Sometimes, letters of credit are necessary to conduct transactions, and significant penalties for premature or late offset may be assessed. The marketplace for currency transactions is very broad, and performance depends on the trading partners. They may need to shop around because they are not conducting trades through a recognized exchange.

Futures Contracts

Futures contracts are *standardized* instruments. The standards include: specific size or quantity of contract; stipulated grades, acceptable securities, or underlying index; premium and discount structure (conversion factor process) when applicable; and invoicing, delivery, and settlement procedures. The rules for trading, hedging, and margining positions are regulated by the particular exchange and the relevant regulatory bodies.

Futures contract performance risks here are borne by the appropriate *clearinghouses*, not the trading partners. There is no stipulated penalty for premature or late offset. Unlike contractual arrangements and forward contracts, future contracts allow greater flexibility for opening and closing positions.

Options Contracts

Options are unilateral contracts on an underlying futures contract, an underlying security or currency, or a physical commodity. The buyer of an option acquires the right, not the obligation to exercise; the seller of the option incurs the obligation to satisfy the terms of the option should an exercise occur.

There are two types of options: puts and calls. A *call* gives the purchaser of the option the right but not the obligation to exercise. In the case of an option on a futures contract, an exercise would give the owner a long position in the underlying futures contract, and the seller would be *assigned* the offsetting short position in the futures contract. The purchaser of a *put*, upon exercise, would receive a short position in the underlying futures, whereas the seller or grantor of the put would be *assigned* a long position in the underlying futures. No stipulated penalty is imposed for premature or late offset. Options allow flexibility for opening and closing positions.

CONCEPTS AND FRAMEWORK

Three concepts capture a substantial portion of the hedging framework: *time, interest,* and *volatility*. They interact and modify one another, and they are fundamental building blocks for many financial models.

Figure 1.1 shows a hedger at point D, his departure point for three subsequent time paths and outcomes: DO_1, DO_2, and DO_3. The DO_2 line represents a flat and stable path. DO_1 represents a positive return and DO_3 represents a negative return to the hedger. Distances from DO_2 reflect the variability of outcomes. These distances represent profits and losses or rewards and risks.

As Figure 1.1 illustrates, time increases the potential opportunity/risk outcome range. In this diagram, interest rates or volatilities govern the slopes of the DO lines.

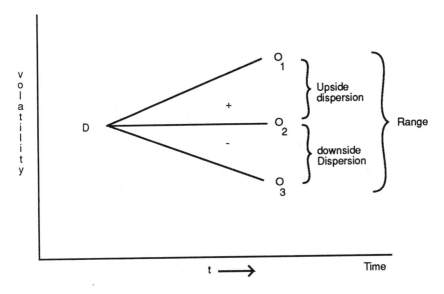

FIGURE 1.1   Three outcomes.

Time

Time can be the temporal distance to expiration for an options contract, to the first notice day or the last trading day, or time can represent an operational period or cycle. Depending on the circumstances, time can refer to the expected holding period, the required holding period, the expected growing period, the minimum processing period, the maximum marketing period, or whatever interval specification is appropriate for the hedge. In all these cases, *time* identifies the length of temporal distance between two decision or action points.

Given appropriate substitutions for interest or volatility, these alternative lines represent time values for either futures or options. For futures, the primary factor would be interest rates multiplied by time, whereas for options their time value would be predicated upon the interaction of time and volatility. Regardless of a program's sophistication, lines similar to these identify opportunities and costs, both of which are addressed by hedging. Specification and action affect hedging performance. In practice, these critical variables influence the time value of money, carrying charges, time value of options, expected price changes or levels, selection of hedge instrument contract months, and other decision criteria.

Interest

Positions cost or earn interest. Hedging strategies evaluate costs (financial carrying charges) and opportunities (time values). Interest rates can be federal funds, short-term Treasury bills, Eurodollar rates, or whatever rates of interest are relevant to the situation. The rate of interest can also be an imputed opportunity cost. The multiplicative interaction between time and interest rates presents carrying charges and the time value of money. By substituting volatility for interest rates, one can see a similar multiplicative interaction between time and volatility.

Volatility

For the moment, we will view volatility as variability. In terms of volatility, changes or fluctuations constitute risks. Many factors influence volatility: for agricultural commodities these can include weather, transportation, pests, or blights; for financials, monetary or fiscal policies and actions. Volatility considers the potential of change. The greater the potential change, the greater the potential volatility and the greater the need for protection. Time compounds this risk factor. For example, a gold producer or jeweler may not be alarmed when gold is trading at $450 per ounce and its expected variation is ± $15 per ounce for one year. However, concern would be heightened if the outlook were for a potential variation of ± $150 per ounce for the same time period. Hedging recognizes the danger of change and attempts to neutralize it.

Volatility is frequently considered as the variance or the statistical variation about a mean. A derivative statistic is the standard deviation or square root of the variance. Risk measurement statistics are easy to compute; interpreting them properly is more difficult. These statistics look at both sides of the mean, the pluses and the minuses; in so doing, they place a symmetrical framework around the interpretation of risk. But this does not necessarily reflect reality. An unhedged portfolio manager is at risk when declining prices prevail, not in a time of higher prices. Likewise, a farmer is better off when prices are rising and he has not sold or hedged his crop. For these two examples, higher prices do not increase risk; it is lower prices that do so.

Conversely, a user or consumer of commodities would be at risk if prices advanced when the cost of input had not been covered. For example, a metal fabricator sold finished goods, such as aluminum cans, assuming a comparatively favorable cost of input. Similarly, a financial institution extended credit (a mortgage), and subsequently prices of credit instruments fell (mortgage rates rose), placing the interim liquidation value of the mortgage portfolio at risk. Subsequently, higher interest rates would lower the market value of the mortgage portfolio. Also, the financial institution would have locked in a competitively lower and disadvantageous rate for its income stream. The asymmetrical characteristic of risk can be approached with broader solution sets.

Interactions and Simulations

Time, volatility, and interest interact with one another. Depending on their relative dominance, different outcomes occur. By introducing other variables into financial modeling functions, one can obtain expressions for futures and options pricing models. Chapter 2 examines the development of futures pricing models. Chapter 11 presents an option evaluation model. Depending on the hedger's input of needs, constraints, and modifications, these generalized models become dedicated ones. A hedger can simulate results by generating what-if scenarios and outcomes. This approach is very valuable because simulations isolate more desirable strategies against widely ranging conditions and highlight potential trouble spots.

DEFINITIONS

Time Value of Money

The time value of money is an integral part of a hedging program. It injects a comparative framework into the solution process. Notationally, the time-value-of-money concept views the situation as:

$$TVM = M(1 + i)^t$$

where TVM = time value of money
      M = money
      i = rate of interest
      t = time interval

This analytical perspective dictates the financial feasibility of various basis trades, arbitrage situations, the selection of delivery months, and whether the programs should lean toward futures, options, forward contracts, leasing arrangements, or even cash. It establishes the criteria for cash-and-carrys, reverse cash-and-carrys, repos, and reverse repos. The better the ability to identify the discounting, compounding, and financing processes, the greater the likelihood of superior hedge performance.

Carrying Charges

Carrying charges are an extension of the concept of the time value of money. These charges consider storage, insurance, and handling in addition to the financing (or opportunity) costs. By including an h term that reflects storage and insurance in the TVM expression, we arrive at TVM $= M(1 + i - h)^t$. This shows that additional carry expenses trim time value returns. For precious metals such as gold and silver, the costs of storage and insurance are other expenses for maintaining (carrying) an inventory. The major expense is the financial cost of holding physical inventory. The other expenses are typically modest. For gold, an average monthly storage charge would be approximately $7.00 per lot deliverable against a 100-ounce futures contract.

For many commercial or institutional hedgers, the cost of storage and handling charges can be minimal or even approach zero versus other hedgers or traders. Hedgers who lack the infrastructure to conduct such transactions must rely on outside parties to effectuate a cash-and-carry program.

Time Value for Options

Time value for options is related to that for futures and physicals. The major distinction is that volatility (in its many forms) plays the dominant role and interest rates are of secondary importance. Essentially, option premiums reflect the market's consensus valuation of the implied variability for the option. The hedger must compare this fair market value with his needs and thus determine whether the option has acceptable *expected* value.

Notationally, the time-value-of-money concept is altered for options yielding:

$$TVO = M(1 + v)^t$$

where TVO = time value of an option
  M = money
  v = volatility and
  t = time interval

By simply substituting v for i, we have moved toward an elementary, though enlightening, option-pricing expression. Intuitively, we see that higher vs imply higher time values and higher option premium values. By reintroducing i into this simple expression as a discounting variable, we obtain a model that calculates a terminal financial value for an option.

Futures Contract Equivalency

Futures contract equivalency serves two key purposes. First, it converts hedgeable positions into standardized units, which then serve as building blocks. This technique permits the hedger to evaluate comparable units. For example, 200 ounces of 12 karat (12K) gold is one futures contract equivalent of COMEX gold, because each COMEX gold contract specifies 100 ounces of highly refined gold. (Here we assumed that 12K is 50 percent pure and 24K is 100 percent pure.) The 200 ounces of 12K gold do not reflect two COMEX futures contract equivalents. Pursuing this example a bit further, the relationship of ore to refined product requires considerable metallurgical and economic analyses. One does not simply hedge unprocessed ore at its gross weight but, rather, at its value-adjusted weight. Here, value adjusted considers the cost of producing gold or other extractable resource in relationship to prevailing prices, to determine the feasibility of mining, selling, and hedging.

The initial equivalency criterion for Treasury bonds is the conversion factor. This factor equates $100,000 par value of a specified Treasury bond of terms other than twenty years and coupons other than 8 percent into a comparable standardized 8 percent, twenty-year maturity issue. Conversion factors are published numbers that transform term to maturity and coupon rate into one statistic.

Defining the Basis Versus Spread

The *basis* is a mathematical relationship between a hedgeable item and the hedge instrument. This relationship is frequently presented as the difference between the cash price and the futures (hedge instrument) price. For example, spot gold at $400 and December futures (one year out) at $424 indicates a basis of $24 ($424 − $400 = $24) futures over cash. Depending on the participant, this differential is also known as a *spread*. To distinguish cash versus futures and futures versus futures transactions, we will use the term *basis* to refer to cash versus futures (futures contract equivalents) relationships, and *spreads* to refer to futures versus futures relationships. Other relationships, such as processing, profit, crushing, feeding, and crack spreads, will be specifically identified.

Two Basic Risks

There are many kinds of risk. Hedging programs attempt to control two basic types: price-level risk and basis-level risk. Generally, the broader risk is price level. Often price-level risk is viewed from a prehedge perspective, whereas basis-level risk is viewed from a posthedge perspective.

Price-Level Risk. Prices vary over time, and these changes are risky since there is no certain outcome. This can place an organization in jeopardy. Consider a gold refiner who maintains an inventory of 1,000 ounces of pure gold. If the current cash price is $500, then the inventory has a market value of $500,000. Starting at the $500 level, this refiner would be at risk in the extreme for $500 per ounce. Expressed differently, each dollar change per ounce varies the inventory valuation by $1,000. If the outlook was for a 10 percent variation in prices over the year, this refiner would be subject to a $50,000 (10% × $500,000) loss or gain over the course of a year. A wider range in variability would imply greater risk but also greater opportunity. Table 1.1 shows different outcomes for 10, 20, and 30 percent variability

Table 1.1   Comparative Impact for 1,000 Ounces

	Illustrative Gold Example		
Variability (percent)	Cash change	Futures change	Basis
10	$ 50,000	$ 52,500	$2,500
20	$100,000	$105,000	$5,000
30	$150,000	$157,500	$7,500

in prices. It also shows the impact of selling 10 futures contracts (which reflect the 1,000 ounces) at $525 per ounce.

As can be seen, there *were* compensatory swings of ±$52,500, ±$105,000, and ±$157,500 for the 10, 20, and 30 percent variability environments. The offsetting swings were somewhat larger than the underlying swings (±$50,000, ±$100,000, and ±$150,000). This is attributable to the assumption that spot and futures prices here both varied by the same percentages, not the same dollar figures. (Later we will see how to make adjustments for this condition.)

Basis-Level Risk. Continuing with the forgoing example, we will examine basis-level risk and compare it to price-level risk in Table 1.2. The hedger used our earlier definition of basis (the relationship between the cash and the futures) and placed a sell or short hedge since there was a sale of futures against a long underlying position. The transaction was conducted at a basis of $25 (per ounce) futures over cash.

The variation in the basis describes its risk. The dollar changes due to basis-level risk are significantly smaller than those for price-level risk. This dampening of financial risk is a major determinant of the hedge's effectiveness. By evaluating price-level risk against basis-level risk, one can quantify the degree of efficiency for the hedge.

Table 1.2 Comparative Basis-Level Risk

				Illustrative Gold Example		
Time	Dollar cash price	Dollar cash change	Dollar futures price	Dollar futures change	Dollar basis	Dollar basis change
1	500		525		25	
2	505	5	531	6	26	1
3	505	0	530	−1	25	−1
4	502	−3	525.5	−4.5	23.5	−1.5
5	500	−2	524	−1.5	24	0.5
6	490	−10	515	−9	25	1
7	502	12	525.5	10.5	23.5	−1.5
8	495	−7	518	−7.5	23	−0.5
9	498	3	522	4	24	1
10	500	2	524	2	24	0

Primary Process

The primary process converts price-level risk into the more narrowly defined basis-level risk, as shown in Figures 1.2 and 1.3. Through this transformation, hedgers convey onto the marketplace what had been broadly distributed price-level risks. By so doing, hedgers now have the substantially tighter boundaries of the more manageable basis-level risks.

It is this risk transformation process and not the simple passing on of risks from hedgers to speculators that underlies the process. Many times, according to the Commitment of Traders reports, large traders and hedgers account for the majority of open positions. How can this be? Hedgers can be both *buyers* and *sellers*, not just one-sided hedgers. That is, hedgers are not always short or long. Nevertheless, the role of speculators and trading organizations can not be dismissed, as these parties often supply the liquidity and breadth needed for a viable hedging mechanism for a given marketplace.

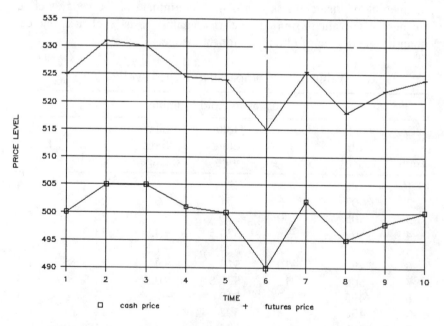

FIGURE 1.2a Cash and futures price simultaneous plot.

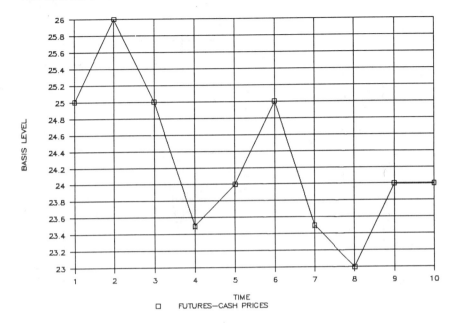

FIGURE 1.2b Basis differential.

Many variables influence the hedge. Individual circumstances can determine any one of several solutions. Mathematically, the task is the optimization of a multivariate problem.

MULTIPLE BASIS RELATIONSHIPS

In Table 1.3, the introduction of additional futures contract months expands the basis listing. The inclusion of other grades, delivery points, and so on of the underlying item also generates multiple basis relationships. The increase in complexity provides broader opportunities as well as risks. Selection of the appropriate relationships is vital.

Describing Basis Behavior

By shifting the emphasis from monitoring two variables (futures prices and cash prices) to one variable—the basis—the hedger can readily analyze the

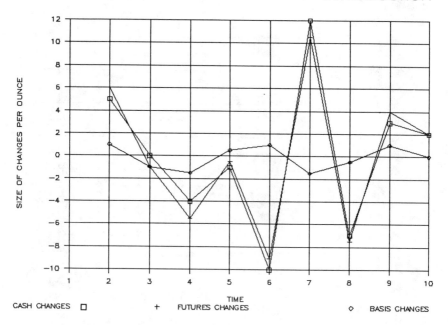

FIGURE 1.2c   Price versus basis changes: comparative evaluation.

impact of the marketplace on the hedge. Several terms that are particularly helpful are: over, under, narrowing, widening, weakening, and strengthening.

The first two terms, *over* and *under*, state the relationship between the futures and the underlying cash. Futures can be over cash or under cash; that is, futures prices can be higher than cash prices or below cash prices. Once this relationship is established, the hedger can quickly determine the net financial impact of the hedged position by monitoring its basis behavior. If the hedger sold futures at a premium to cash (futures over/cash under), then a subsequent *narrowing* or reduction in the basis differential would be considered as favorable basis behavior for him ($25 futures over cash narrows to $15 futures over cash). A *widening* in the basis would not be favorable for him from a basis perspective ($25 to $35 futures over cash).

Weakening and *strengthening* refer to the ability of the underlying cash market to gain or deteriorate relative to the futures. For example, grain located at a port is trading 12 cents a bushel under the futures. Subsequently, it was quoted at 8 cents under futures. This movement of 4 cents

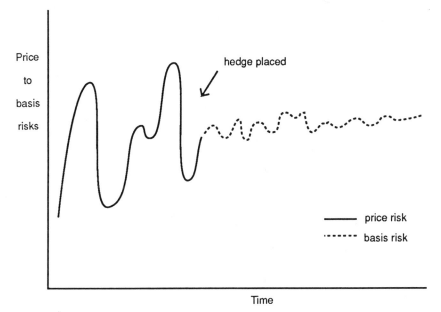

SOURCE: Barkley International Inc.

FIGURE 1.3. Transformation plot of price to basis risk.

reflected a strengthening since cash quotes improved relative to futures. Still later, the grain was quoted at 3 cents over the futures board. This further strengthening (another 11 cents) saw the cash market shift from a discount to the futures board to a premium over the board. If cash proceeded to slip 2 cents so that it was quoted one cent over futures, the relationship then weakened by 2 cents.

These terms operate under a variety of conditions. Figure 1.4 shows how a basis relationship may widen when the underlying market is advancing (up), declining (down), or in the midst of sideways action.

The hedger must evaluate the impact of various market conditional states and the associated potential fluctuations in the basis, to establish expected values for the central point (average) and its dispersion. The research should identify what events motivated the responses as they can prove to be significant determinants for the interpretation of market and basis behavior. This additional information "conditions" the analysis and actions. Statistically, the improvement to a program occurs because it modifies the situation from an unconditional to a conditional case; if specific

Table 1.3   Multiple Basis Relationship Listing When Additional
Futures Months Are Considered

	Gold: Cash & Futures			Futures		
Date	Cash	Nov	Dec	Feb	Cash– Nov	Cash– Dec	Cash– Feb
11/ 1	410.90	411.60	414.00	418.90	−0.70	−3.10	−8.00
11/ 2	414.75	421.80	424.20	429.30	−7.05	−9.45	−14.55
11/ 3	423.40	421.50	423.70	428.80	1.90	−0.30	−5.40
11/ 4	421.00	421.50	423.50	428.60	−0.50	−2.50	−7.60
11/ 7	420.60	422.80	424.70	429.90	−2.20	−4.10	−9.30
11/ 8	419.70	419.10	421.20	426.30	0.60	−1.50	−6.60
11/ 9	420.80	423.10	424.70	429.80	−2.30	−3.90	−9.00
11/10	419.10	419.00	420.50	425.50	0.10	−1.40	−6.40
11/11	420.30	421.60	423.10	427.80	−1.30	−2.80	−7.50
11/14	419.30	423.90	425.20	429.90	−4.60	−5.90	−10.60
11/15	424.00	424.40	425.60	430.30	−0.40	−1.60	−6.30
11/16	423.85	424.50	425.60	430.50	−0.65	−1.75	−6.65
11/17	422.00	420.10	421.10	426.00	1.90	0.90	−4.00
11/18	417.75	417.40	418.10	423.00	0.35	−0.35	−5.25
11/21	415.95	415.80	416.50	421.30	0.15	−0.55	−5.35
11/22	418.40	417.70	418.10	422.90	0.70	0.30	−4.50
11/23	419.25	420.00	420.10	424.80	−0.75	−0.85	−5.55
11/28	424.25	423.30	423.30	427.90	0.95	0.95	−3.65
11/29	423.10		421.90	427.10		1.20	−4.00
11/30	422.60		424.80	429.60		−2.20	−7.00

SOURCE: Barkley International Inc.

information has operational value, it should be used. (This approach is
recognized as conditional or Bayesian analysis. These areas are discussed
in the many statistical texts available.)

TYPES OF HEDGES

There are two types of hedges, the long hedge and the short hedge, also
known as buy and sell hedges. All hedging strategies revolve around these
two types. Complexity arises from the implementation of complicated

Market Conditions

	Up	Sideways	Down
Widening	0_1	0_2	0_3
Sideways	0_4	0_5	0_6
Narrowing	0_7	0_8	0_9

B
a
s
i
s

0s are outcomes, probabilities, or expected values.

FIGURE 1.4   Widening, narrowing, and sideways basis behavior versus market conditions.

weighting strategies, evaluative techniques, and derivative product hedging instruments.

Long Hedge

The *long* or *buy* designation refers to the status of the open futures (contract equivalent) position. If the hedger is *long* futures, then it is implied that he is doing so against a short cash (physical) position. When permitted, this cash position can be anticipatory as well as actual. For example, a corporate treasurer may confidently await the arrival of a periodic influx of funds several days, weeks, or even months hence, but during the interim may find prevailing currency rates, interest yields, or security prices at particularly attractive levels and may desire to hedge the awaited inflow now.

Short Hedge

The *short* or *sell* hedge refers to the status of the open futures (contract equivalent) position. Typically, organizations that maintain inventories, such as securities trading firms, refiners, or commodity producers, tend to be short hedgers. They sell futures or enter sale agreements to protect inventory or portfolio values.

EXAMPLES

The following four examples describe the technique of placing a futures position as protection. Two of the situations are futures against actual positions; the other two describe anticipatory futures hedges. In all these cases, hedging provided protection, either through price level or through interest rate. All of the examples list the basis for comparison.

Physical Long Hedge

The Mini Oil Refining Company requires 48,000 barrels of crude oil for the year, so it evaluates three alternatives. It can:

1. Buy 48,000 barrels on the spot market, store, and eventually refine them.
2. Buy 4,000 barrels each month of the year.
3. Buy what it immediately needs on the cash market, and price the remaining input via the futures.

By purchasing futures contracts, Mini Company places a long hedge. As it purchases actual crude oil or enters into more sophisticated exchange transactions, Mini lifts that portion of the outstanding long hedge. Each NYMEX oil futures contract represents 1,000 barrels. Therefore, the maximum coverage would require the purchase of 48 contracts, or 4 for each month prior to the purchase of actual crude. The market is in inverted form, with the near months at a premium relative to the deferreds. The refiner from a cost of input perspective would find its interests better served by matching the futures to the deferred production months rather than carrying much, if any, additional crude. This aspect is better approached from an inventory modeling perspective, whereby the hedger can assign penalties, if any, for becoming dry or for being out of crude or oil products. Carrying crude oil under these circumstances would entail higher financing costs due to actual out-of-pocket charges or foregone opportunities.

This example shows that the cost of the input can be protected, although the refiner is still faced with protecting the value of the products. Therefore, the refiner would probably engage in selling hedges of the products (gasoline and heating oil) as well.

Table 1.4 lists three different basis relationships for nearby, six-month and one-year-out futures. The table also lists three different basis relationships for the same futures but different locations of crude oil. As this simple example shows, the permutations become quite large. In order to search for optimum solutions, a transportation network structure is a viable approach.

Physical Short Hedge

A farmer decides to plant 1,000 acres of corn. Historically, yields have averaged 120 bushels per acre with a 10 percent variation (108–132 bushels per acre). Rather than subjecting his entire crop and financial outcome to heavy seasonal sales pressure at harvest, he intends to hedge the statistically expected production. In essence, he is substituting futures contract sales commitments for his crop prior to the physical sale.

Each Chicago Board of Trade (CBOT) corn futures contract represents 5,000 bushels of grain. Therefore, the initial solution set ranges from 21 to 26 futures contracts and is centered on 24 contracts (120,000/5,000 = 24). The next steps involve an analysis of costs, prices, and timing.

Table 1.5 lists possible outcomes given $1.25 and $1.75 per bushel for the variable and the fixed and variable costs as well as other cost structures. From a marginal perspective, the farmer must capture at least $1.25 per bushel; otherwise, every bushel planted and harvested negatively impacts him. Any price above $1.25 covers the variable and helps defray the fixed component of the total cost structure.

Assuming the worst prices at harvest means that any other prices would have to be higher. Since hedging does not necessarily mean doing everything at the same price and doing the maximum as well, but is rather a flow and an adaptive process, the farmer can time his futures sales. Doing so alters the financial outcomes and improves his expectations.

Table 1.4 Different Futures Delivery Months and Different Locations

Crude Oil Cash and Futures

Date	Futures Nearby	Futures 6 months	Futures 1 year	Contract Grade	Cash Loc A	Cash Loc B	Contract grade basis			Location basis		
							CG—Nrby	CG—6 MF	CG—1 YRF	Nrby—CG	Nrby—Loc A	Nrby—Loc B
1	15.00	14.75	14.70	15.10	14.90	15.25	0.10	0.35	0.40	-0.10	0.10	-0.25
2	15.25	14.95	14.80	15.40	15.20	15.60	0.15	0.45	0.60	-0.15	0.05	-0.35
3	15.15	14.90	14.85	15.40	15.20	15.55	0.25	0.50	0.55	-0.25	-0.05	-0.40
4	15.05	14.90	14.70	15.10	14.80	15.30	0.05	0.20	0.40	-0.05	0.25	-0.25
5	15.25	14.75	14.50	15.20	15.00	15.40	-0.05	0.45	0.70	0.05	0.25	-0.15
6	15.25	14.85	14.65	15.25	15.05	15.45	0.00	0.40	0.60	0.00	0.20	-0.20
7	15.50	15.25	15.00	15.75	15.60	16.00	0.25	0.50	0.75	-0.25	-0.10	-0.50
8	15.40	15.10	14.90	15.60	15.40	15.75	0.20	0.50	0.70	-0.20	0.00	-0.35
9	15.20	15.00	14.70	15.50	15.30	15.65	0.30	0.50	0.80	-0.30	-0.10	-0.45
10	15.00	14.70	14.40	15.25	15.05	15.40	0.25	0.55	0.85	-0.25	-0.05	-0.40

SOURCE: Barkley International Inc.

Key
Loc A = Location A
Loc B = Location B
CG   = Contract grade
Nrby = Nearby
6 MF = 6-month future
1 YRF = 1-year future

Table 1.5 Net Profits for Given Variable and Fixed Costs

Market price	108 Bu/Acre Variable cost results	108 Bu/Acre Fixed & variable cost results	120 Bu/Acre Variable cost results	120 Bu/Acre Fixed & variable cost results	132 Bu/Acre Variable cost results	132 Bu/Acre Fixed & variable cost results
$1.20	($5,400)	($59,400)	($6,000)	($66,000)	($6,600)	($72,600)
$1.25	$0	($54,000)	$0	($60,000)	$0	($66,000)
$1.50	$27,000	($27,000)	$30,000	($30,000)	$33,000	($33,000)
$1.75	$54,000	$0	$60,000	$0	$66,000	$0
$1.80	$59,400	$5,400	$66,000	$6,000	$72,600	$6,600
$2.00	$81,000	$27,000	$90,000	$30,000	$99,000	$33,000
$2.25	$108,000	$54,000	$120,000	$60,000	$132,000	$66,000

Key
Variable costs = $1.25/bu
Fixed & variable costs = $1.75/bu
Table based on 1000 acres

Consider the results if all 24 futures were sold in October versus the sale of 24 contracts in July. Many studies have shown a seasonal pattern for grain prices, which typically peak during the summer. The highs tend to coincide with the beginning of the most potentially stressful period although this often depends on the crop. Subsequently, if there is little or no stress, the market discounts the price structure to reflect this (other variables being equal).

The hedger has many choices. The sales can be weekly for 24 weeks. Here, one contract is sold each week from April through September. (Remember that here the potential crop averages 24 futures contract equivalents.) Or he can sell one contract each week from May to October. Timing sales this way means that the crop's value approaches an average prevailing price prior to harvest; which would tend to exceed autumn prices.

There are many variations to this theme. It should be noted that this periodic selling arrangement gives the farmer the flexibility to adjust the hedge according to his growing conditions. If conditions are poor, he can reduce the selling pace of futures since the expected production is likely to be less. If conditions are favorable, he can accelerate the pace somewhat to account for greater than normal production. Either way, the process is adaptive. If all the futures sales were conducted prior to or at planting, and a drought or other significant problem occurred, then the farmer would have to adjust the hedge mix radically in order to reduce excessive hedge coverage. By carefully timing the sales, the farmer can *optimize* returns, though not necessarily *maximize* them. Efforts to maximize often entail exceptionally high timing and other risks.

The hedger is not selling futures blindly; he is constantly aware of prices and relationships between his grain and the futures. Otherwise, he can lock-in an unfavorable price and basis.

Financial Long Hedge

A money manager anticipates a moderate decline in interest rates (a rally in bond prices). The manager knows that a $20 million fund influx is due to arrive within three weeks. However, her outlook calls for the rally to occur within that time frame. By establishing a long futures hedge, the money manager in Table 1.6 can construct a hedge position that will behave

Table 1.6   Illustrative Money Manager Using a Buy Hedge

| | Financial Short Hedge | |
	Cash	Futures
Anticipated	20 million influx within 3 weeks. Intends to buy the 8's of 1996–01 92–05	Buys 200 contracts of Treasury Notes 92–10
Realized	Receives $20 million influx Buys $20 million par of 8's of 1996–01 95–21	Sells 200 contracts of Treasury Notes 95–24
Net	Cash market advanced 3¹⁶/₃₂ or $700,000 increase in cost for intended position	Realized 3¹⁴/₃₂ gain per contract or $687,500 for long hedge position
Overall Impact	Hedge provided $687,500 coverage of $700,000 move.	

NOTE: The futures contract is predicated on an 8 percent coupon. There was no conversion factor adjustment here.

in similar fashion to the intended actual position. Upon the receipt of funds, the money manager liquidates the long futures and purchases the actual bonds. Depending on her prevailing outlook, she could adjust the timing of this hedge response.

Financial Short Hedge

An underwriter protects inventory values by establishing a short futures position hedge against his actual holdings. The inventory is no longer subject to the vagaries of the interest rate market. The sale of futures effectively precludes widely fluctuating inventory values. (See Table 1.7, which lists the changes in inventory and hedge values.) Now the government securities dealer can focus on the behavior of the basis.

Alternatively, the hedgers could have used the options markets to protect their positions. Again, the basis must be determined. The sale of calls or the purchase of puts would provide varying degrees of protection. The former strategy could enhance underwriting returns though only partially immunizing the underwriter from major declines in prices, whereas the latter strategy could provide greater protection at the expense of trimming returns. To help identify the better strategies, which vary according to conditions, the book provides a framework for quantifying the decision-making process. The above examples stress that circumstances vary from hedger to hedger and different techniques may be required by each.

FLEXIBILITY

Hedging can provide flexible protection. It can secure raw materials, configure maturities for assets and liabilities, fix portfolio valuations, or place a floor under mineral reserves, crop production, or currency balances, among many other uses. An organization confronted with open or exposed positions can alter the risk climate in order to attain stability and lessen the degree of uncertainty by dispensing with particular risks and thus improving the likelihood of success.

PROPERTIES OF A GOOD HEDGE

The following four properties are important to a good hedge:

1. Economic validity

Table 1.7   Illustrative Government Security Dealer/Underwriter
Protecting Inventory with a Sell Hedge

	Financial Short Hedge		
	Cash	Futures	Basis
Initial Position	Long 10 MM par @ 96–12 or $9,637,500	Sells 100 futures @ 96–10 which represents a market value of $9,631,250	Cash over futures 2 ticks or ²⁄₃₂
Position Terminated	Sells 10 MM par @ 94–12 or $9,437,500	Buys 100 futures @ 94–02 which represents a market value of $9,406,250	Cash over futures 10 ticks or ¹⁰⁄₃₂
Net	Realized a loss of $200,000 in cash security account	Realized a gain of $250,000 in hedge account	Here, cash strengthened relative to futures despite downward move in both prices
Overall Impact	Hedge generated an additional $50,000 of coverage due to favorable basis response.		

Alternatively, by monitoring the basis, the 1/4 point change indicated an improvement of $250 per futures contract equivalent or $25,000 (100 contracts × $250).

NOTE: In Tables 1.6 and 1.7 the Conversion Factor was 1.0 since the notes were 8 percent coupons.

2. Reasonable correlative movements
3. Convergence
4. Consistent basis behavior

These are fundamental guidelines for the implementation and reporting of hedge operations. (See Financial Accounting Standards Board Publication No. 80, "Statement of Financial Accounting Standards: Accounting for Futures Contracts," August 1984.)

Economic Validity

Economic validity means that the organization can manage risk by suitable hedges that are based on sound fundamental factors and not spurious relationships. There must be economic justification and need for the placement of hedges, and there must be analysis to identify the appropriate instruments.

Correlation

The three perspectives for reasonable correlative movements over time are:

1. The degree of correlation between the absolute prices or yields
2. The degree of correlation between the first differences in absolute prices or yields
3. The degree of correlation between the dollar swings in the actual portfolio versus the hedge position

Perspective 1 tracks the degree of association between the two variables: the item to be hedged and the hedge instrument. This correlation tends to be the strongest at the outset, since it compares overall levels.

Perspective 2 recognizes that there can be important operational disparities between the hedge item and the hedge instrument *on a net change basis*. This disparity can have significant impact on the need for additional funding to maintain the integrity of the hedge program. Often it can be seen that although the *levels* are near each other, the *net changes* do not as neatly match up together. This is not necessarily an insurmountable problem, but it is a very important consideration because it distinguishes programs for their ability to be responsive to aberrant basis behavior, albeit temporarily.

Perspective 3 identifies the degree of inverse correlation or extent of compensatory offset. This analysis determines how well in a statistical sense the hedge program offsets swings in the underlying cash market. In the event that this point produces initially weak results, further analysis and adjustments in the hedge mix may be necessary.

Reasonable correlative movements refer to the inverse correlative financial offsets. That is, when the portfolio goes down in value, the hedge account goes up in value. The more nearly the two movements approximate each other in dollar values, the tighter the hedging basis. A consistent basis does not imply strictly predictable, constant, or certain behavior. It does mean that the basis can fluctuate within preestablished or comfortable boundaries.

Convergence

Convergence is the property that relates the physical market or cash index to the predicated futures. The futures contract's specifications stipulate the underlying commodity, security, or index that is the delivery or settlement grade, while the numerical basis defines the mathematical relationship between the cash and the board. At expiration, the convergence should be complete because the spot futures market's prices approximate the underlying cash market's prices, given the premium-discount structure. For markets satisfied by cash settlement and not a deliverable security or commodity, this convergence is complete. Therefore, futures gain parity by losing either their premium or discount to the cash. Figures 1.5 and 1.6 illustrate this concept.

Convergence can pertain to the affinity of one futures contract delivery month toward another. Again the passage of time generates behavior such that the intramonth spread differentials move in a reasonably expected manner. Figures 1.7 and 1.8 illustrate convergence movements.

Consistency

The basis behavior should be consistent. This means that the time path of the basis can be relied on to behave in an acceptable manner. Though related to convergence, the consistency feature is more indicative of fluctuations in the actual basis about the stipulated theoretical basis. Aside from the last-day final settlement, at which time the *convergence* attribute finalizes itself, especially for cash settlement futures contracts, the consistency feature makes the hedge trades viable.

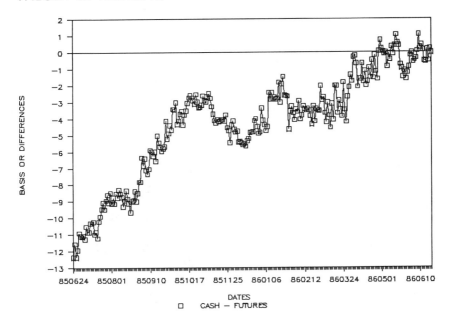

FIGURE 1.5   S&P 500 cash and futures: cash-futures; the convergence between cash and futures contract (futures stated at a premium to cash).

THEORY OF HEDGING

Hedging establishes economically sound techniques that generate compensatory offsets to valuation fluctuations. Ideally, the hedges would produce identical offsets; but identical offsets are not necessary for a hedge to be suitable.

The procedure is predicated on a principle of risk transformation whereby the larger value swings in interest rates or price levels are exchanged for the more tightly defined basis-level value swings. This is accomplished by the transfer of the opportunities of speculative gains and losses to counterparts in the marketplace which need not be solely speculative trading interests. A long hedge and a short hedge in the marketplace can accommodate each other's requirements by the placement of futures positions that are bona fide hedge positions and that will be terminated upon the occurrence of a cash market transaction. One example of this would be

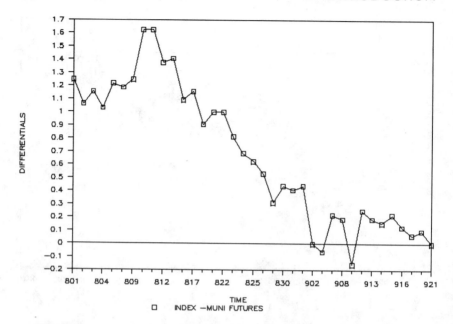

FIGURE 1.6 Illustrative convergence: decimal equivalents; cash versus futures discount convergence (futures stated at a discount to cash).

a producer of grain selling short against his anticipated production, while a miller would purchase futures to establish raw material input costs. Similarly, crude oil producers can set selling prices while refiners set processing margins. An issuer of variable rate debt protects against rises in interest charges by selling futures. A potential buyer is a money manager who wants to lock in today's levels of interest rates (anticipating subsequent declines in rates between inflows of periodic funds). The money manager would benefit from current acceptable rates for subsequent investments, thus influencing overall performance.

Capital requirements, regulatory and internal constraints and directives, market-oriented activities, and competitive pressures impact the hedging–trading operations. The evolution of standard business practices can warrant the implementation of hedging programs not only for risk management, but for maintaining marketing competitiveness. If one's clients are accustomed to using the futures for AAs or EFPs, then the firm should try to accommodate those needs.

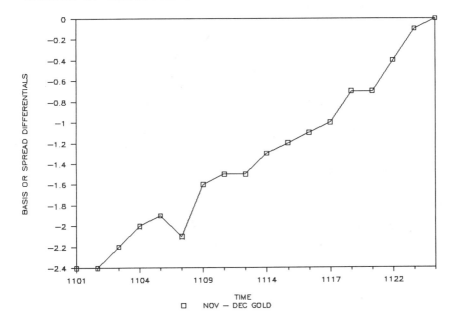

FIGURE 1.7   Futures-futures: nearby under next month; nearby futures stated at a discount to subsequent futures month.

There are any number of hedging problems with their own circumstances, constraints, and goals, and, reassuringly, there are any number of potential solutions to these problems.

THEORY OF CROSS HEDGING

A modification of the hedging process is the cross hedge. The principles and properties that govern suitable hedging relationships apply here too. The absence of a futures or options market to accommodate a commodity such as brass, or a security such as corporate bonds, does not categorically prevent a hedging problem. Most hedges are actually cross hedges because of the multitude of grades, delivery specifications, maturities, coupons, and call features that do not completely comply with *good delivery stipulations* as required by the exchanges. A degree of protection can be attained by using a cross hedge.

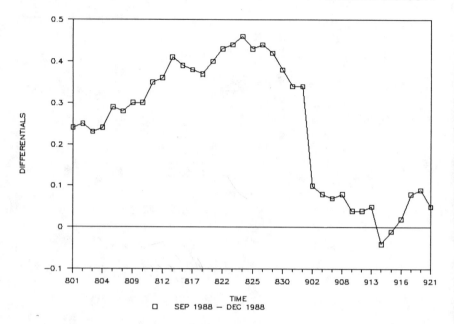

FIGURE 1.8 Illustrative convergence: futures-futures example; futures versus futures discount convergence (nearby futures stated at a premium to subsequent futures month).

Cross hedges occur when there are variations from the futures contract deliverable specifications such as grade of corn and its location, or security coupon rates and outstanding maturity, which, though not deliverable, are still amenable to hedging purposes. Should the actual physical transfer of a position be desired, then the application of an EFP-type transaction could be arranged. This would allow for conveyance of the nondeliverable (in the futures sense) yet transferable, goods or securities. The process for eventual physical transfers is conducted by a preestablished trading basis in order to convey goods or securities that are not proscribed as acceptable for delivery purposes but are exchangeable (given the ex-pit trading provision and provided the transaction satisfies other exchange regulations).

Cross hedging is not to be confused with hedging stocks via the platinum market, corn with wheat, or other unrelated markets, although there may be statistics that temporarily appear to justify the notion. The hedge must be constructed prudently, with consideration for the concluding offset as well as for maintaining the integrity of the basis.

Cross Hedge Examples

Twenty-year zero coupon bonds may not be hedged readily via the T-bond futures market, because the basis point and dollar equivalency characteristics are substantially distinct for each instrument. A more complex hedging program is required to account for the proportionately wider swings in the early years for zero coupon issues relative to their parentage— the long-term Treasury bond.

Cottonseed oil may be better hedged via the soybean oil market than through the cotton market. In many of these cases, the basis is preestablished in terms of so many points or cents per pound over (or under) cottonseed oil over soybean oil futures.

Collateralized mortgage obligations (CMOs) are popular instruments that can be amenable to Treasury security cross hedges rather than hedges with Ginnie Maes (GNMAs). Mortgage transfers can be done by an EFP when allowable. An EFP can be structured to take into account the variations of the mortgage obligations.

Careful analysis, not similarity of names, is crucial here. Preferred stock that is variable in terms of dividend policies can be more suitable to hedging purposes via debt market instruments such as Eurodollar or T-bill futures rather than the Standard and Poors (S&P) or Major Market Index (MMI) futures. This is especially true if the variation in dividend payout is related (the basis is previously established) to some relationship percentage or absolute points over or under a stipulated Treasury security. At other times, such securities may be better hedged via the stock index futures or a combination of stock indices and debt futures. The decision depends on the underlying characteristics of the instruments.

DISTINGUISHING CHARACTERISTICS

Traditionally, the futures markets were linked to the underlying commodity markets through the delivery mechanism. If the short position holder (from a futures contract perspective) decided to deliver the commodity, he could do so provided it satisfied the contractual requirements of grade, quantity, location, and other specifications. In a clear sense, the futures contract could be offset only by the subsequent buy-back (short covering) or the physical delivery of commodity against the open futures position.

Deliveries are not to be confused with sales. While all futures deliveries consummate futures sales, not all sales are completed with deliveries in the futures markets. Consider the case of gold. Although there is a slight adjustment for fineness and a moderate adjustment for weight, there is no allowance for bullion that is too heavy or too light pursuant to exchange regulations. Physical transfers of bullion for futures in these cases is conducted by an exchange for physical transaction, not a delivery in the strict sense of the term.

Other Risks

There are other risks, or hazardous conditions, that can have a debilitating effect on hedge programs, including:

1. Changes in exchange regulations and margining requirements
2. FCM regulations and margining requirements
3. Sudden shifts and structural departures in basis relationships
4. Governmental or regulatory body policies and actions
5. Unanticipated and dramatic changes in the organization's operations
6. Lack of provision for sufficient funding
7. Application of strategies that require stable conditions during turbulent markets
8. Application of various delta-neutral oriented options strategies

Risk 1. Changes in exchange regulations and margining requirements can influence an organization's ability to sustain or even to implement various hedge strategies. Exchanges have required 100 percent margining of spot positions in order to rectify disruptive situations. The exchanges can and do place size limitations for futures and options positions even though the trades are hedges. For large-scale hedging operations, this means that the organization may have to obtain an exemption. Although exemptions are usually granted upon application and review, these exemptions are not automatically approved. Essentially, bona fide hedges can be placed to the extent that they reflect justifiably hedgeable risks (positions). The exchanges modify these limitations on a case-by-case basis, but they are still authorized to use emergency powers, if necessary, to maintain the overall integrity of the system.

Risk 2. Futures commission merchants (FCMs) can impose their own limitations on position sizes and margining. The FCMs' requirements must be equal to or more restrictive than those of the exchange. Often, sudden changes in policies occur during dramatic and volatile markets. In a way, at times of the greatest need, the hedging programs can be forced to comply with smaller position limits or more stringent financing.

Subtleties such as the number of outstanding options or net options positions can influence a hedge program, since these limitations do not currently distinguish on the grounds of futures contract equivalents or a delta orientation, but only on quantity. For example, 2,500 deep-out-of-the-money options are viewed identically to 2,500 deep-in-the-money options as far as position size is concerned, although obviously not for margining, internal equity, or hedging purposes.

Risk 3. Sudden or structural shifts in basis relationships can cause financial problems. These shifts are more likely in cross hedge operations than in outright deliverable situations. For example, hedging Eurobonds with U.S. Treasury note or bond futures contracts may be working satisfactorily until there is a declaration of change in tax status and no grandfather provision. This can prompt dramatic swings in basis levels, with serious impacts on a hedge program. Even markets that permit redeliveries may experience difficulties. This occurs when the physical position experiences an abrupt and large decline in value while the hedging instruments (futures or options) have exchange-imposed price change limits, thereby precluding immediate and even similar offsets.

Risk 4. Governmental or regulatory body policies and activities can influence hedge program performance. Groups such as the insurance or banking industries can impose trading limitations or even preclude full hedging programs with their regulations.

The imposition of embargoes, quotas, war act powers, and drastic monetary and fiscal actions can have serious repercussions on outstanding or contemplated hedges.

Risk 5. An organization can find itself facing a major disruptive strike, holding securities that have been lowered in credit, or being notified that an important client just closed his account or canceled a very large order. Farmers and ranchers could face a major crisis due to drought, crop failure, livestock quarantine, or foreclosure proceedings. A firm may not be able to satisfy its commitments in actuals or futures when production has been unexpectedly slashed or prevented.

Firms may find that their access for inventory funding or working capital credit has been revoked or slashed. During the early 1980s many significant commercial banks declined to extend any additional credit to metals firms—trading houses, producers, or manufacturers—thereby forcing metals firms to dramatically alter their hedge plans. The October 1987 stock market crash unsettled many firms until the Federal Reserve supplied the financial system with vast amounts of liquidity to keep market makers, securities firms, and other financial institutions from going under as a result of the meltdown of equity values.

Risk 6. The lack of provision for funding is more an internal problem than an external constraint. Management must allocate funds and credit to initiate and maintain hedge positions. The fact that a hedge is placed does not remove the financing obligation but, rather, may necessitate it. If the hedge instrument's market moves in the direction of the hedge for futures or options writes, then positive cash flow can be generated. In the event of an option purchase program, the value of the purchased option may appreciate to offset the swing in the underlying physical position. The resultant appreciation funds are not immediately available; rather, that position must be liquidated or rolled over in order to gain access to the compensatory cash flow.

Futures, options, and some forward contracts require initial and variation financing. The organization must be aware that funds can be demanded to maintain these hedges, not just for their initiation.

Risk 7. The application of futures-options strategies commonly requires smooth pricing scenarios such as pricing on openings or closings. Depending on how the hedge is constructed, unstable conditions at those times or others may pose severe problems. It must be recognized that the futures and options markets are continually moving, and trades that could have been done at particular prices a moment ago may not be possible again or for quite a while. This may not be a serious obstacle, although hedge programs must be flexible enough to price or execute at other than absolutely maximum or singular levels. The hedge placed at price level x may not be an optimal way of hedging; rather, the hedger should determine the threshold level and work around it from an expected-value perspective.

Risk 8. Ratio writes, delta neutrality, and other options-oriented strategies depend on adaptive processes to maintain the hedges' intended integrity level such as delta neutrality or 100 percent coverage. Yet in operation, despite many realignments, the actual performance can be less than superior or desirable as a result of transactions and monitoring costs, lack of price continuity during erratic market times, or inability to readjust the hedge smoothly. For example, the placement of delta-neutral hedges for stock portfolios can be quickly impaired. A dynamic gap or structural change in prices due to a specified event may generate a sharp advance in prices. The ratio writes now transform into *overwrites* whereby the hedger is now overcovered and is actually assuming speculative positions, which are at odds with the underlying market behavior. Conversely, the sale of puts can quickly become a fiasco during an abrupt market break. Prices tend to rupture during such times and not to trickle lower.

These states of affairs will produce actual losses. Even an adjustment at the first opportunity will produce a loss because the overnight position was delta-neutral, but adjusted at an unfavorable delta relationship. Should the position be pared down, given a state of pronounced price trends, the participant could still face serious financial problems. He will not have the same ability to place hedge positions should price behavior emerge that would have a more positive effect on his financial situation. Practically speaking, neither the hedger nor the trader has the luxury of multiple trials and errors to break even on an expectation basis. Although this assumption is accurate for the statistical population, it is not so for each participant.

An approach responsive, not reactionary, to market conditions, which can be evaluated with a small sample and which can produce acceptable results, is needed. A suitable hedge performance is analogous to insurance coverage: It does not restore life, excellent health, or an exact replacement of a work of art, home, factory, or equipment; but it does give financial restitution equal to the insured value.

COMMON ASSUMPTIONS

Many hedging studies cite several critical assumptions, which though not always accurate, are good starting points for analysis. Seven important assumptions are:

1. Independent observations
2. (Log) normally distributed changes
3. Indifference to up, down, or neutral market environments
4. Outlier occurrences that are extremely remote and independent
5. Market changes that are predominantly very small and continuous
6. Trendless behavior for basis and price levels
7. The need for large sample statistics

Numerous techniques alleviate some of the problems associated with these assumptions, including: data transformations and tests for statistical independence for ordered series. Better performing hedge programs rely on the hedger's qualitative and quantitative abilities to distinguish between important decision variables and conditions.

ORGANIZATIONAL COMMITMENT

Simply proclaiming a hedging program does not guarantee that it will reduce the risks of doing business. It requires a dedicated effort to identify risks accurately and the commitment to follow through with a suitable program. Hedges are not hit or miss; they are quantifiable management tools to be employed by experienced personnel. Depending on the size of the organization and the number of departments that will benefit from hedging, the firm may have to allocate managers, traders, and accountants to direct, conduct, and monitor the program.

2
Identifying and Selecting the Basis

Hedging is an interactive process with the *basis* at its core. A hedging program's success depends on identification of the relevant basis relationships. Chapters 2, 3, and 4 focus on the dimensions of the basis, which are determined by answering the following questions: What has it been? Where is it? What should it be? Where can it be expected to be?

THREE BASIS DETERMINATIONS

The basis defines the quantitative relationship that exists between the physical position and the hedge instrument. Three ways of determining basis value are:

1. Subtraction (cash − futures, or futures − cash)
2. Ratio   (cash/futures or futures/cash)
3. Stipulation (cash ± a predetermined factor, or
               futures ± a predetermined factor)

Subtraction of cash from futures, or the reverse, is the method most commonly used. It results in the broadest relationship between the physical (commodity or security) product and the hedge instrument, and, for debt issues, it adjusts the simple differences through a conversion factor. Tables 2.1 and 2.2 list data for Figures 2.1, 2.2, and 2.2a, which illustrate simple basis determination for gold and for bonds.

Ratio orientation can be used when there are substantial value or grading differences between the physical position and the contractual specifications of the selected hedge vehicle. In the financial markets, ratios are used with beta- (ratio-) oriented stock and bond portfolios. Table 2.3 and Figure 2.3 highlight a stock portfolio.

In the easiest method, *stipulation,* two hedging parties predetermine the basis and then conduct their transactions. This technique is the backbone

Table 2.1   Simple Differences

		Gold Cash and Future Prices in Dollars Per Ounce	
Date	Cash	November futures	Cash–November basis
1101	410.90	411.60	−0.70
1102	414.75	421.80	−7.05
1103	423.40	421.50	1.90
1104	421.00	421.50	−0.50
1107	420.60	422.80	−2.20
1108	419.70	419.10	0.60
1109	420.80	423.10	−2.30
1110	419.10	419.00	0.10
1111	420.30	421.60	−1.30
1114	419.30	423.90	−4.60
1115	424.00	424.40	−0.40
1116	423.85	424.50	−0.65
1117	422.00	420.10	1.90
1118	417.75	417.40	0.35
1121	415.95	415.80	0.15
1122	418.40	417.70	0.70
1123	419.25	420.00	−0.75
1128	424.25	423.30	0.95
1129	423.10		
1130	422.60		

SOURCE: Barkley International Inc.

Table 2.2 Treasury Bond Cash Futures and Basis Series

Date	7¼s	12⅜s	T-Bond Futures	7¼s Decimal Equivalent	12⅜s Decimal Equivalent	Futures Decimal Equivalent	Futures CF Adjusted Decimal Equivalent 7¼s	Futures CF Adjusted Decimal Equivalent 12⅜s	7¼s Raw Basis Decimal Equivalent	7¼s CF Adjusted Basis Decimal Equivalent	12⅜s Raw Basis Decimal Equivalent	12⅜s CF Adjusted Basis Decimal Equivalent
881101	83.31	129.16	91.02	83.97	129.50	91.06	83.51	125.78	−7.09	0.46	38.44	3.72
881102	83.20	129.07	90.20	83.63	129.22	90.63	83.11	125.17	−7.00	0.51	38.59	4.05
881103	83.31	129.20	91.06	83.97	129.62	91.19	83.63	125.95	−7.22	0.34	38.44	3.68
881104	82.19	128.02	89.24	82.59	128.06	89.75	82.31	123.96	−7.16	0.28	38.31	4.10
881107	82.04	127.17	89.08	82.13	127.53	89.25	81.85	123.27	−7.12	0.27	38.28	4.26
881108	82.12	127.22	89.10	82.38	127.69	89.31	81.91	123.36	−6.94	0.47	38.38	4.33
881109	82.02	127.09	89.02	82.06	127.28	89.06	81.68	123.01	−7.00	0.38	38.22	4.27
881110	81.31	127.04	89.08	81.97	127.13	89.25	81.85	123.27	−7.28	0.12	37.88	3.85
881111	81.21	126.25	88.21	81.66	126.78	88.66	81.31	122.45	−7.00	0.35	38.13	4.33
881114	81.27	127.00	89.01	81.84	127.00	89.03	81.65	122.97	−7.19	0.19	37.97	4.03
881115	81.24	126.27	88.31	81.75	126.84	88.97	81.59	122.88	−7.22	0.16	37.87	3.96
881116	81.03	126.04	88.05	81.09	126.13	88.16	80.85	121.76	−7.06	0.25	37.97	4.36
881117	80.20	125.10	87.20	80.63	125.31	87.63	80.36	121.03	−7.00	0.26	37.69	4.28

(Continued)

Table 2.2 *(continued)*

881118	80.22	125.18	87.30	80.69	125.56	87.94	80.65	121.46	−7.25	0.04	37.63	4.10
881121	80.30	125.23	88.02	80.94	125.72	88.06	80.76	121.63	−7.13	0.18	37.66	4.09
881122	80.27	125.21	88.01	80.84	125.66	88.03	80.73	121.59	−7.19	0.11	37.62	4.07
881123	81.01	125.28	88.03	81.03	125.88	88.09	80.79	121.68	−7.06	0.24	37.78	4.20
881125	80.11	125.01	87.11	80.34	125.03	87.34	80.10	120.64	−7.00	0.24	37.69	4.39
881128	80.20	125.13	87.23	80.63	125.41	87.72	80.45	121.16	−7.09	0.18	37.69	4.25
881129	80.26	125.20	87.30	80.81	125.63	87.94	80.65	121.46	−7.12	0.17	37.69	4.17
881130	81.09	126.06	88.15	81.28	126.19	88.47	81.13	122.19	−7.19	0.15	37.72	3.99

CF = Conversion Factor
CF = .9171 for 7¼s
CF = 1.3812 for 12³⁄₈s
SOURCE: Barkley International Inc., © copyright 1989.

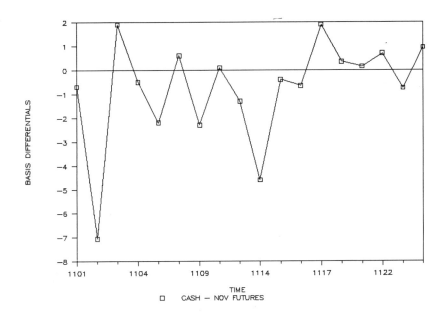

FIGURE 2.1 Cash-Futures: cash under futures; gold cash versus futures.

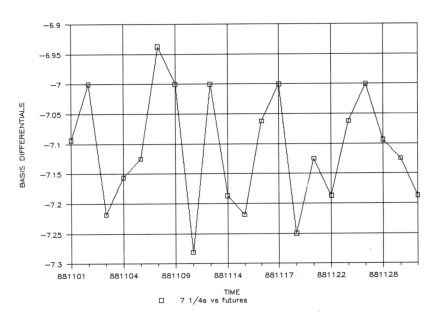

FIGURE 2.2 Raw basis: decimal equivalents; raw basis given simple differences.

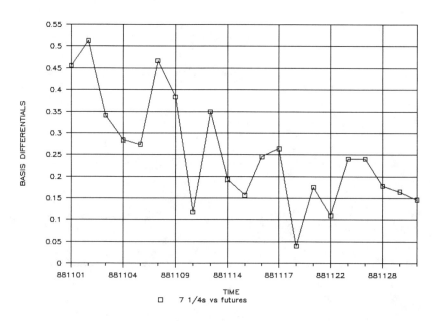

FIGURE 2.2a Adjusted basis: decimal equivalents; conversion factor adjusted simple differences.

Table 2.3 Beta Adjusted Portfolio Relative to Overnight Value Changes

Time	Index	Value Adjusted Index	Beta $ Change	Index Value Change	Portfolio Value
1	269.05	$2,690,500			$2,690,500
2	264.65	2,646,500	($66,000)	($44,000)	2,624,500
3	265.80	2,658,000	17,250	11,500	2,641,750
4	266.90	2,669,000	16,500	11,000	2,658,250
5	268.35	2,683,500	21,750	14,500	2,680,000
6	269.25	2,692,500	13,500	9,000	2,693,500
7	267.35	2,673,500	(28,500)	(19,000)	2,665,000
8	268.90	2,689,000	23,250	15,500	2,688,250
9	271.15	2,711,500	33,750	22,500	2,722,000
10	273.05	2,730,500	28,500	19,000	2,750,500

Beta = 1.50 for value changes

SOURCE: Barkley International Inc.

NOTE: Table implies 30 contracts (1.50 beta) and not 20 contracts.

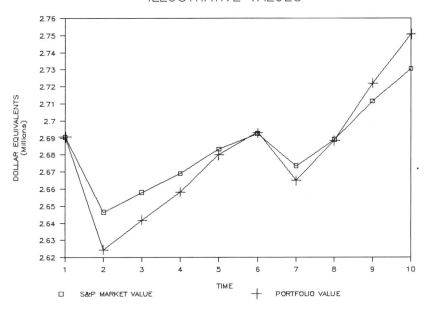

ILLUSTRATIVE VALUES

□ S&P MARKET VALUE   TIME   + PORTFOLIO VALUE

FIGURE 2.3   Illustrative values: index versus portfolio values. Note:

Table 2.4   Premium/Discount to Account for Different Locations

		Illustrative Grain Example (Cents per Bushel)			
Date	Futures	Cash Loc A	Cash Loc B	Loc A Cash Premium Futures	Loc B Cash Discount Futures
1	390.00	395.00	387.25	5.00	− 2.75
2	392.25	397.25	389.50	5.00	− 2.75
3	392.25	397.25	389.50	5.00	− 2.75
4	387.75	392.75	385.00	5.00	− 2.75
5	395.00	400.00	392.25	5.00	− 2.75
6	401.00	406.00	398.25	5.00	− 2.75
7	397.25	402.25	394.50	5.00	− 2.75
8	390.00	395.00	387.25	5.00	− 2.75
9	392.50	397.50	389.75	5.00	− 2.75
10	395.00	400.00	392.25	5.00	− 2.75

where Loc = location
SOURCE: Barkley International Inc.

45

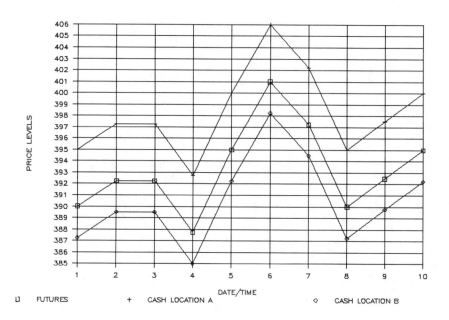

FIGURE 2.4 Stipulated relationships: cash over and under futures; illustrative grain example portraying cash at a discount basis and a premium basis to futures for given locations.

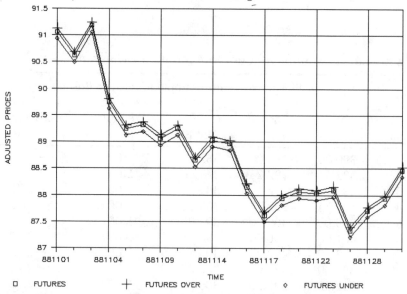

FIGURE 2.5 Plus and minus basis adjustment: decimal equivalents; Treasury futures equivalents at a premium and a discount given stipulated differences.

46

Table 2.5   Treasury Bond Futures Equivalent for Specified or Stipulated Adjustment

Date	T-Bond Futures	Futures Plus 1/16	Futures Less 1/8	Decimal Equivalents		
				Futures	Futures plus	Futures minus
881101	91.02	91.04	90.30	91.06	91.13	90.94
881102	90.20	90.22	90.16	90.63	90.69	90.50
881103	91.06	91.08	91.02	91.19	91.25	91.06
881104	89.24	89.26	89.20	89.75	89.81	89.63
881107	89.08	89.10	89.04	89.25	89.31	89.13
881108	89.10	89.12	89.06	89.31	89.38	89.19
881109	89.02	89.04	88.30	89.06	89.13	88.94
881110	89.08	89.10	89.04	89.25	89.31	89.13
881111	88.21	88.23	88.17	88.66	88.72	88.53
881114	89.01	89.03	88.29	89.03	89.09	88.91
881115	88.31	89.01	88.27	88.97	89.03	88.84
881116	88.05	88.07	88.01	88.16	88.22	88.03
881117	87.20	87.22	87.16	87.63	87.69	87.50
881118	87.30	88.00	87.26	87.94	88.00	87.81
881121	88.02	88.04	87.30	88.06	88.13	87.94
881122	88.01	88.03	87.29	88.03	88.09	87.91
881123	88.03	88.05	87.31	88.09	88.16	87.97
881125	87.11	87.13	87.07	87.34	87.41	87.22
881128	87.23	87.25	87.19	87.72	87.78	87.59
881129	87.30	88.00	87.26	87.94	88.00	87.81
881130	88.15	88.17	88.11	88.47	88.53	88.34

SOURCE: Barkley International Inc.

of exchange-for-physical transactions and the pricing of contractual arrangements. In stipulation, the basis is fixed (constant), although the eventual transactional prices may be open to fluctuation, unlike in the subtraction and ratio techniques. If the hedger places a protective futures position, then both price- and basis-level risks have been hedged, and the price risk is dispensed with as well. All operational risks have not been eliminated, however, because the final performance has not occurred yet. The two commercial parties are jointly responsible for completing their agreed upon transactions, although the clearinghouse bears the ultimate risk for the futures and options positions. Table 2.4 and Figure 2.4 represent a grain situation, and Table 2.5 and Figure 2.5 represent a

Treasury bond situation. Notice that the grain exchange has different stipulated basis relationships to account for different *locations*, a situation readily applied to other markets.

Stipulation is common in traditional commodity markets, and is also gaining greater acceptance in the financial markets. It can be applied successfully to mortgage financing arrangements and hedging programs, which, in recent years, have been plagued by a lack of viable futures delivery contract candidates. The straightforward establishment of a basis would preempt dealing with indices, duration variables, prepayments, and other destabilizing elements. For example, the stipulated basis of two points over the three-month T-bill future for a specified time period (or an exact business day for a designated delivery month) could improve the position management for both issuer and mortgagee and enable both to initiate protective actions, if warranted. Treasury bond, Treasury note, and

Table 2.6   Gold: Cash and Futures Prices in Dollars per Ounce

Date	Cash	November Futures	November–Cash Basis
1101	410.90	411.60	0.70
1102	414.75	421.80	7.05
1103	423.40	421.50	−1.90
1104	421.00	421.50	0.50
1107	420.60	422.80	2.20
1108	419.70	419.10	−0.60
1109	420.80	423.10	2.30
1110	419.10	419.00	−0.10
1111	420.30	421.60	1.30
1114	419.30	423.90	4.60
1115	424.00	424.40	0.40
1116	423.85	424.50	0.65
1117	422.00	420.10	−1.90
1118	417.75	417.40	−0.35
1121	415.95	415.80	−0.15
1122	418.40	417.70	−0.70
1123	419.25	420.00	0.75
1128	424.25	423.30	−0.95

SOURCE: Barkley International Inc.

Eurodollar futures can work equally well: The hedger needs to choose the appropriate instrument and, of course, an acceptable basis.

IDENTIFICATION AND SELECTION

After management chooses a program, the hedging committee must identify and select satisfactory basis relationships. The hedgers will apply different opportunity costs and constraints to each of the hedging program candidates to get many basis relationships, each with its own characteristics. We will now establish one basis relationship and progressively build on that presentation.

We can consider gold for the first basis relationship. Table 2.6 and Figure 2.6 present data on gold. The contract specifications are written in a way to simplify the arithmetic: There are 100 ounces for the popular COMEX contract. First, we will examine only one futures delivery month and one cash price, hence one basis.

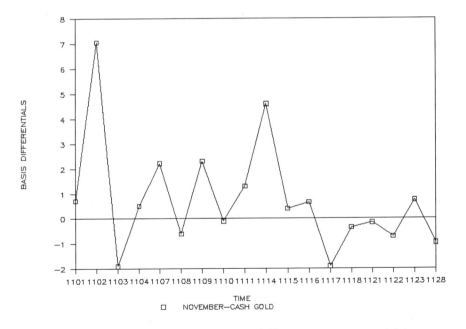

FIGURE 2.6   Futures-cash prices: in dollars per ounce; gold futures versus cash.

Table 2.7   Illustrative Gold Example Highlights Comparatively
Narrow Swing between the Basis versus Cash or Futures
Changes

	Illustrative Gold (Dollars per Ounce)					
Time	Cash price	Cash change	Futures price	Futures change	Basis	Basis change
1	500.00		525.00		25.00	
2	505.00	5.00	531.00	6.00	26.00	1.00
3	505.00	0.00	530.00	−1.00	25.00	−1.00
4	502.00	−3.00	525.50	−4.50	23.50	−1.50
5	500.00	−2.00	524.00	−1.50	24.00	0.50
6	490.00	−10.00	515.00	−9.00	25.00	1.00
7	502.00	12.00	525.50	10.50	23.50	−1.50
8	495.00	−7.00	518.00	−7.50	23.00	−0.50
9	498.00	3.00	522.00	4.00	24.00	1.00
10	500.00	2.00	524.00	2.00	24.00	0.00

SOURCE: Barkley International Inc.

The basis time series is determined by subtracting the cash from the futures price. Because the basis quantifies the physical position and the hedge instrument relationship, these differences are relevant in establishing theoretical values for futures and forward contracts.

RISK TRANSFORMATIONS

The primary importance of a hedge is its capacity to transform price-(interest rate) level risk into the more manageable basis-level risk, as illustrated in Table 2.7. The transformation establishes a criterion for the hedge/not-to-hedge decision: When the dollar risk for the basis is less than the dollar risk for a no-hedge, the hedge should be established. Table 2.7a shows that similar percentage swings for the price and the basis mean smaller dollar value swings for the basis.

HEDGING PARADOX

Favorable basis behavior does not guarantee success for the hedging program, nor does unfavorable basis action invalidate a hedge. Under certain marketplace conditions, these paradoxical statements are true.

Table 2.7a Comparing Percentage Changes in Prices and Basis

Time	Cash price	Cash change	Futures price	Futures change	Basis level	Basis change
	Illustrative Gold (Dollars per Ounce)					
1	500.90		525.00		25.00	
2	510.00	10.00	535.50	10.50	25.50	0.50
3	499.80	−10.20	524.80	−10.70	25.00	−0.50
4	489.80	−10.00	514.30	−10.50	24.50	−0.50
5	480.00	−9.80	504.00	−10.30	24.00	−0.50
6	489.60	9.60	514.10	10.10	24.50	0.50
7	479.80	−9.80	503.80	−10.30	24.00	−0.50
8	489.40	−9.60	513.90	10.10	24.50	0.50
9	499.20	9.80	524.20	10.30	25.00	0.50
10	509.20	10.00	534.70	10.50	25.50	0.50

SOURCE: Barkley International Inc.
NOTE: Here, the basis was quoted in dollars per ounce futures over cash.

The percent changes were generated by .98 and 1.02 relatives with prices rounded to ".10".

Consider the case of a held commodity or security, against which a short hedge was appropriately established. There is a rapid rise in the spot market price of the item. The basis narrows, and the market inverts, most likely because the cash market goes to a premium over the futures. The increase in cash inventory value outruns the rise of the futures prices. The preservation of the short futures position, however, would demand the ability to finance a series of variation margin calls continuously. The rise in the spot price does not immediately generate cash, although it is worth more, because the underlying physical position remains intact.

One way out would be to liquidate the physical position partially, through a series of cash market transactions, in order to acquire funds to maintain the integrity of the futures hedge. An alternative would be to borrow against the physical value and pay interest. The charges would have to be factored against the overall performance of the hedge.

Another approach entails the sale of additional futures contracts against the rise in value of the physical position. This action maintains a fully offsetting basis-point value response for the hedge. Such an alternative, however, does not generate funding for the prevailing hedge and, in fact, requires more.

TWO FUTURES PRICING MODELS

Futures pricing models quantitatively analyze the relationships between commodities or securities and the related futures markets. The hedger can determine the probable response of his intended actions for given sets of market data and conditions.

One futures pricing model is similar to the future value of a Dollar n periods forward model. The time value of money becomes part of the analysis when the underlying cash market is tied to a specified futures delivery. This prepares the foundations for other cash–futures–options modeling efforts.

We have:

Futures price $=$ Commodity price now $\times$ $(1 +$ Rate of interest$)^n$

When we substitute $500 for the spot gold price, 5 percent for the interest rate, and 1 for n, we arrive at:

$$\begin{aligned} \text{Futures price} &= \$500 \times (1.05)^1 \\ &= \$525. \end{aligned}$$

For the $n = 1$ time frame, futures would have a theoretical price of $550 for a 10 percent interest rate, and $575 for a 15 percent interest rate.

The time frame factor is often expressed decimally. When $n = 0.25$ and 0.50, then n respectively refers to the three-month and six-month intervals. Table 2.8 illustrates how time and interest rates influence futures prices on the basic level.

This first pricing model is frequently used for markets in storable commodities, such as gold, silver, and stocks, because it initially attributes a carrying charge structure to the futures markets.

Table 2.8 Time and Interest Rate Variables Which Impact Implied Financial Carrying Charges and Futures Prices

| Interest rates | Implied Gold Futures Prices ($500 Cash Price) | | | |
| | Yearly intervals decimally expressed | | | |
	0.25	0.50	0.75	1.00
5.00	506.14	512.35	518.64	525.00
6.00	507.34	514.78	522.34	530.00
7.00	508.53	517.20	526.03	535.00
8.00	509.71	519.62	529.71	540.00
9.00	510.89	522.02	533.38	545.00
10.00	512.06	524.40	537.05	550.00
11.00	513.22	526.78	540.71	555.00
12.00	514.37	529.15	544.36	560.00
13.00	515.51	531.51	548.00	565.00
14.00	516.65	533.85	551.63	570.00
15.00	517.78	536.19	555.26	575.00

NOTE: Simple compounding model used here.

The second futures pricing model views the situation in discounting terms instead of compounding terms. The model becomes:

Futures price $=$ Commodity price now $\times$ $[1/(1 + \text{rate of interest})^n]$

This model is the starting point for Treasury bills, Eurodollars, and other discounted financial market structures. Table 2.9 and Figure 2.7 show the discounted viewpoint.

When it is a summation for streams of income and terminal payment, the model is an evaluation standard for bonds and notes. When it is applied to physical commodities, it helps in the analysis of inverted markets by showing the extent of the financial aspects of the nearby premiums, relative to deferred discounts. Refinements of the model can include adjustments for seasonality, storage, and multiple interest rates, among other factors.

These futures pricing models do not predict underlying prices: They describe time value attributes of the underlying prices and futures or futures-to-futures relationships.

There are also explanatory models that use supply, demand, inventories,

Table 2.9 Treasury Bill Futures Illustrating Discounting of Price
Process over Time

	Treasury Bill Futures		
1988 Date	September	December	September–December Spread
801	92.87	92.63	0.24
802	92.93	92.68	0.25
803	92.92	92.69	0.23
804	92.96	92.72	0.24
805	92.80	92.51	0.29
808	92.79	92.51	0.28
809	92.73	92.43	0.30
810	92.71	92.41	0.30
811	92.69	92.34	0.35
812	92.69	92.33	0.36
815	92.71	92.30	0.41
816	92.70	92.31	0.39
817	92.70	92.32	0.38
818	92.69	92.32	0.37
819	92.68	92.28	0.40
822	92.68	92.25	0.43
823	92.72	92.28	0.44
824	92.73	92.27	0.46
825	92.67	92.24	0.43
826	92.65	92.21	0.44
829	92.65	92.23	0.42
830	92.68	92.30	0.38
831	92.69	92.35	0.34
901	92.71	92.37	0.34
902	92.77	92.67	0.10
906	92.76	92.68	0.08
907	92.71	92.64	0.07
908	92.72	92.64	0.08
909	92.75	92.71	0.04
912	92.75	92.71	0.04
913	92.77	92.72	0.05
914	92.76	92.80	−0.04
915	92.79	92.80	−0.01
916	92.79	92.77	0.02
919	92.81	92.73	0.08
920	92.82	92.73	0.09
921	92.82	92.77	0.05
922		92.77	

SOURCE: Barkley International Inc.

Table 2.9a Multiple Futures or Spread Basis Relationships for Treasury Bills

| | | | | Treasury Bills Futures Differences | | |
Date	Sep	Dec	March	Sep–Dec	Sep–Mar	Dec–Mar
801	92.87	92.63	92.57	0.24	0.30	0.06
802	92.93	92.68	92.65	0.25	0.28	0.03
803	92.92	92.69	92.64	0.23	0.28	0.05
804	92.96	92.72	92.67	0.24	0.29	0.05
805	92.80	92.51	92.47	0.29	0.33	0.04
808	92.79	92.51	92.48	0.28	0.31	0.03
809	92.73	92.43	92.40	0.30	0.33	0.03
810	92.71	92.41	92.37	0.30	0.34	0.04
811	92.69	92.34	92.31	0.35	0.38	0.03
812	92.69	92.33	92.29	0.36	0.40	0.04
815	92.71	92.30	92.26	0.41	0.45	0.04
816	92.70	92.31	92.25	0.39	0.45	0.06
817	92.70	92.32	92.25	0.38	0.45	0.07
818	92.69	92.32	92.25	0.37	0.44	0.07
819	92.68	92.28	92.20	0.40	0.48	0.08
822	92.68	92.25	92.16	0.43	0.52	0.09
823	92.72	92.28	92.20	0.44	0.52	0.08
824	92.73	92.27	92.20	0.46	0.53	0.07
825	92.67	92.24	92.19	0.43	0.48	0.05
826	92.65	92.21	92.16	0.44	0.49	0.05
829	92.65	92.23	92.17	0.42	0.48	0.06
830	92.68	92.30	92.26	0.38	0.42	0.04
831	92.69	92.35	92.31	0.34	0.38	0.04
901	92.71	92.37	92.34	0.34	0.37	0.03
902	92.77	92.67	92.64	0.10	0.13	0.03
906	92.76	92.68	92.66	0.08	0.10	0.02
907	92.71	92.64	92.64	0.07	0.07	0.00
908	92.72	92.64	92.64	0.08	0.08	0.00
909	92.75	92.71	92.73	0.04	0.02	−0.02
912	92.75	92.71	92.75	0.04	0.00	−0.04
913	92.77	92.72	92.75	0.05	0.02	−0.03
914	92.76	92.80	92.82	−0.04	−0.06	−0.02
915	92.79	92.80	92.82	−0.01	−0.03	−0.02
916	92.79	92.77	92.78	0.02	0.01	−0.01
919	92.81	92.73	92.74	0.08	0.07	−0.01
920	92.82	92.73	92.73	0.09	0.09	0.00
921	92.82	92.77	92.75	0.05	0.07	0.02
922		92.77	92.74			0.03

SOURCE: Barkley International Inc.

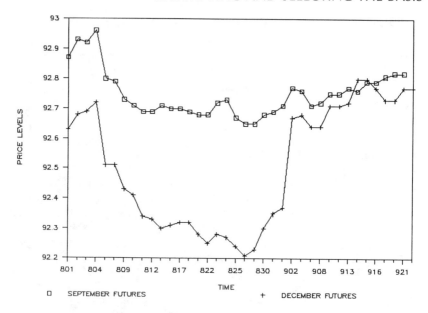

FIGURE 2.7   Discounting scenario: futures in positive yield forma-
tion; nearby futures over next month's futures.

weather, and numerous other variables to predict underlying prices. These
specialized forecasting models are treated in many forecasting textbooks.

EXPECTATIONS

The futures pricing models just described indicate a marketplace consensus
or *fair value*. The hedger determines whether this fair value is reasonable.
Differences between fair values and expected values are positive or negative. Expectations are the dominant pricing factor. Discernment and
assignment of appropriate probability weights is at the heart of the hedging/
trading solution.

For individual hedgers, the costs of storage, handling, and insurance
should be factored in. These relatively fixed ancillary costs tend to be
negligible for the larger and more efficient carriers and spreaders, such as
the commercial banks and brokerage trading operations that own or maintain storage facilities. For banks that are exchange-approved depositories,

their competitive edge is enhanced. (See *A Handbook for Professional Futures and Options Traders*, by Joseph D. Koziol, published by John Wiley, 1987 for a presentation of this topic.)

MULTIPLE BASIS RELATIONSHIPS

Multiple basis alternatives are generated when the hedger adds futures months to the single basis. The resultant relationships are listed in Table 2.9a and depicted by Figure 2.8.

Such a simple extension of the basis demonstrates several points:

1. The existence of multiple solutions
2. The role of the time value of money
3. The importance of spreads, their impact on basis relationships, and their cash-and-carry or reverse transactions implications

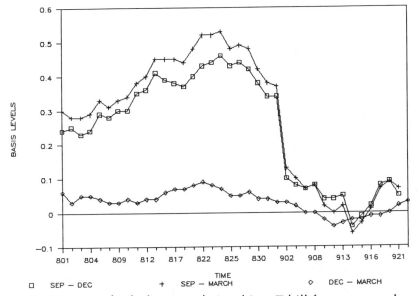

FIGURE 2.8 Multiple futures relationships: T-bill futures spreads or basis; multiple futures spread or basis relationship.

INTERACTIONS BETWEEN SPREAD AND BASIS RELATIONSHIPS

Table 2.10 and Figure 2.9 illustrate the interactions that occur in spread and basis relationships. Table 2.10 lists spreads between two futures months. These relationships are also called the basis between two cash Treasury bills and futures contracts. Notice that the futures-to-futures relationship depicts a positive yield curve because the nearby futures prices are at a premium to the futures prices for the subsequent month. The cash-to-cash relationship, however, is just the opposite. The December 22 Treasury bill was at a price discount to the December 29 Treasury bill, which is a condition that describes a negative carry situation. Thirdly, the December 22 Treasury bill went from a positive basis (cash price over futures) to a negative one (cash price under futures) in early September. This twisting in the yield curve is symptomatic of a potential inversion, in which the nearby instruments are discounted in comparison to more deferred matu-

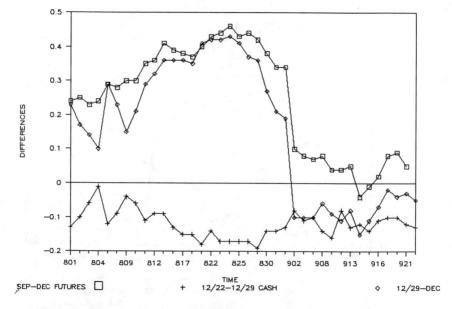

FIGURE 2.9   Cash versus futures Treasury bills: spreads and basis relationships; interactions between cash and futures spreads and basis relations.

Table 2.10 Interactions between Basis and Spread Relationships

1988 Treasury Bills Cash and Futures

Date	Futures Sep	Futures Dec	Cash 12/22	Cash 12/29	Futures Sep–Dec	Cash 12/22–12/29	Cash 12/22–Sep	Cash 12/29–Sep	Cash 12/29–Dec
801	92.87	92.63	92.73	92.86	0.24	−0.13	−0.14	−0.01	0.23
802	92.93	92.68	92.75	92.85	0.25	−0.10	−0.18	−0.08	0.17
803	92.92	92.69	92.77	92.83	0.23	−0.06	−0.15	−0.09	0.14
804	92.96	92.72	92.81	92.82	0.24	−0.01	−0.15	−0.14	0.10
805	92.80	92.51	92.68	92.80	0.29	−0.12	−0.12	0.00	0.29
808	92.79	92.51	92.65	92.74	0.28	−0.09	−0.14	−0.05	0.23
809	92.73	92.43	92.54	92.58	0.30	−0.04	−0.19	−0.15	0.15
810	92.71	92.41	92.56	92.62	0.30	−0.06	−0.15	−0.09	0.21
811	92.69	92.34	92.52	92.63	0.35	−0.11	−0.17	−0.06	0.29
812	92.69	92.33	92.56	92.65	0.36	−0.09	−0.13	−0.04	0.32
815	92.71	92.30	92.57	92.66	0.41	−0.09	−0.14	−0.05	0.36
816	92.70	92.31	92.54	92.67	0.39	−0.13	−0.16	−0.03	0.36
817	92.70	92.32	92.53	92.68	0.38	−0.15	−0.17	−0.02	0.36
818	92.69	92.32	92.52	92.67	0.37	−0.15	−0.17	−0.02	0.35
819	92.68	92.28	92.51	92.69	0.40	−0.18	−0.17	0.01	0.41
822	92.68	92.25	92.53	92.67	0.43	−0.14	−0.15	−0.01	0.42
823	92.72	92.28	92.53	92.70	0.44	−0.17	−0.19	−0.02	0.42
824	92.73	92.27	92.53	92.70	0.46	−0.17	−0.20	−0.03	0.43
825	92.67	92.24	92.48	92.65	0.43	−0.17	−0.19	−0.02	0.41
826	92.65	92.21	92.41	92.58	0.44	−0.17	−0.24	−0.07	0.37
829	92.65	92.23	92.40	92.59	0.42	−0.19	−0.25	−0.06	0.36
830	92.68	92.30	92.43	92.57	0.38	−0.14	−0.25	−0.11	0.27
831	92.69	92.35	92.42	92.56	0.34	−0.14	−0.27	−0.13	0.21
901	92.71	92.37	92.43	92.56	0.34	−0.13	−0.28	−0.15	0.19
902	92.77	92.67	92.49	92.57	0.10	−0.08	−0.28	−0.20	−0.10
906	92.76	92.68	92.47	92.58	0.08	−0.11	−0.29	−0.18	−0.10
907	92.71	92.64	92.44	92.54	0.07	−0.10	−0.27	−0.17	−0.10
908	92.72	92.64	92.44	92.58	0.08	−0.14	−0.28	−0.14	−0.06
909	92.75	92.71	92.46	92.62	0.04	−0.16	−0.29	−0.13	−0.09
912	92.75	92.71	92.52	92.60	0.04	−0.08	−0.23	−0.15	−0.11
913	92.77	92.72	92.51	92.64	0.05	−0.13	−0.26	−0.13	−0.08
914	92.76	92.80	92.53	92.65	−0.04	−0.12	−0.23	−0.11	−0.15
915	92.79	92.80	92.55	92.69	−0.01	−0.14	−0.24	−0.10	−0.11
916	92.79	92.77	92.59	92.70	0.02	−0.11	−0.20	−0.09	−0.07
919	92.81	92.73	92.61	92.71	0.08	−0.10	−0.20	−0.10	−0.02
920	92.82	92.73	92.59	92.69	0.09	−0.10	−0.23	−0.13	−0.04
921	92.82	92.77	92.62	92.74	0.05	−0.12	−0.20	−0.08	−0.03
922		92.77	92.59	92.72		−0.13			−0.05

SOURCE: Barkley International Inc.

rities. On the other hand, the nearby issues offer higher interest rates than the more deferred issues do.

EMERGENCE OF ARBITRAGE

Arbitrage opportunities occur when there are large enough financial departures among prevailing levels (differences). The differentials should be at a particular level.

Look again at the gold case example which has 5, 10, and 15 percent interest rates. The theoretical levels for gold futures one year out for $500 spot gold are $525, $550, and $575. Table 2.11 shows that parities do not exist between actual and theoretical levels.

Figures 2.10, 2.11, and 2.12 display the variations in potential basis relationships that come from changes in interest rates and maturities. Figure 2.10 contrasts market-price levels with implied price levels. Figure 2.11 illustrates cash-and-carry and reverse cash-and-carry opportunities. Figure

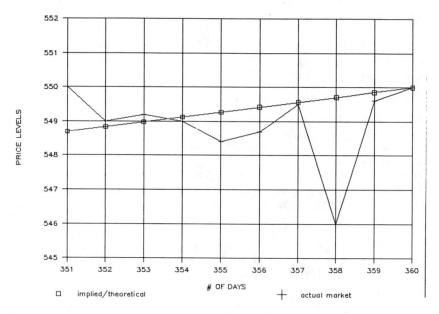

FIGURE 2.10 Comparing market versus implied levels: gold example in dollars/ounces; illustrative gold example highlighting market versus implied levels.

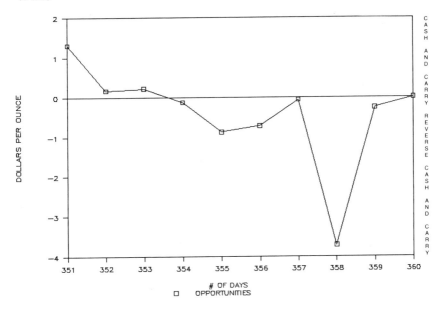

FIGURE 2.11   Evaluating implied versus prevailing: over/under analysis; illustrative gold example highlighting cash and carry and reverse cash and carry opportunities.

2.12 illustrates implied opportunities in the case of convergence. A closer examination of these figures reveals the relationships among market prices, implied prices, and basis levels. Such situations generate opportunities.

TAILS

Interest rates influence the basis and spread differentials profoundly. In an inventory model, the rise in interest rates will indicate a divesture of inventory. This implies that there is selling pressure on the spot market in an effort to reduce financing costs. At the least, it stresses the minimization of holdings, particularly reorders, because the carrying charges have become onerous. For the firm to optimize its resources, it must reduce the inventory commitment.

A simple carrying charge perspective calls for wider intramonth differentials. Such an expectation assumes a stable spot price and the marketplace's capacity to absorb completely the higher costs of carry.

Table 2.11 Comparing Market Levels and Implied Levels

Illustrating Theoretical versus Actual Price Levels: Potential Opportunities

No. of days	Theoretical simple	Actual market	Dollar difference per ounce	Opportunity (gain/loss) partial hedge	Implied difference
351	548.69	550.00	1.31	$13,089.55	1.31
352	548.84	549.00	0.16	1,636.69	1.16
353	548.98	549.20	0.22	2,183.46	1.02
354	549.13	549.00	−0.13	(1,270.17)	0.87
355	549.27	548.40	−0.87	(8,724.18)	0.73
356	549.42	548.70	−0.72	(7,178.57)	0.58
357	549.56	549.50	−0.06	(633.35)	0.44
358	549.71	546.00	−3.71	(37,088.52)	0.29
359	549.85	549.60	−0.25	(2,544.06)	0.15
360	550.00	550.00	0.00	0.00	0.00

SOURCE: Barkley International Inc.
NOTE: Positive dollars favor cash and carry while negative dollars favor reverse cash and carry.
10% interest rate assumed
360 day year assumed

Tails can refer to changes in the hedge position coverage (over/under), as generated by changes in the principal carrying costs, particularly interest rates.

Now look at the gold example to see the effect of a change in interest rates from 5 percent to 10 percent on the $500 spot gold. There is a jump in the one-year spread from $25 to $50 per ounce, or $2,500 per 100-ounce contract. A further rise in rates from 10 percent to 15 percent causes an additional financial burden of $25 per ounce, or another $2,500, bringing the cumulative increase in financing charges per 100-ounce futures contract to $5,000.

Tails can also occur when prices fluctuate. If prices fall by 50 percent from $500 to $250 per ounce, then the one-year spread is $12.50 for a 5 percent interest rate, $25.00 for a 10 percent interest rate, and $37.50 for a 15 percent interest rate. The financial impact from a short hedge is substantially different from that for a long hedge. The short hedger benefits from earlier access to the carrying charges that come from the decline in the spot market. The short hedger can enhance returns by investing the

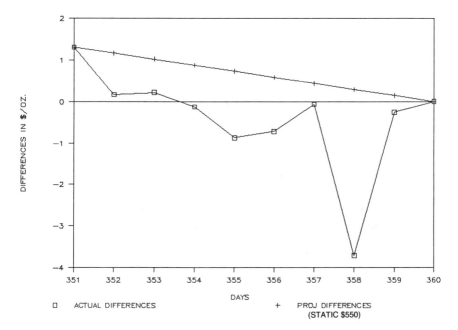

FIGURE 2.12 Relating projected/actual differences: implied carry versus convergence; illustrating implied opportunities against one convergence scenario.

positive variation in equity. The long hedger, on the other hand, would have to satisfy a stream of variation margin calls, thereby reducing the efficiency of the strategy.

The mathematical expression used to determine the necessary adjustments, or tails, is:

$$TA = C \times [(P_f - P_n) / P_n]$$

where TA = number of contracts for the tail adjustment
C = number of contracts for either leg of the position
P_f = price of the forward position
P_n = price of the nearby position*

This expression highlights the ratio relationship between different deliveries and is related to the ratio method of basis determination.

* SOURCE: Chicago Mercantile Exchange, *Market Perspectives,* "Midas Refined: Turning Gold into Interest Rates," August 1987.

The importance of the tail is shown in an example: Between December 1979 and January 1980, precious metals prices doubled, and interest rates rose substantially. Because of market conditions, many banks curtailed further credit advances for the financing of metals positions, whether they were hedged or not. Thus, one may have been precluded from borrowing against a rapidly increasing inventory value to satisfy variation margin calls imposed against the futures positions.

GRADES

Grades or fineness of a product are important variables for evaluating the hedge. The purity of the held or desired gold inventory can reduce or increase the responsiveness of the hedge and, thus, can require the use of a relative value approach (a/b) and not that of a subtractive one ($a - b$).

In Table 2.12, which illustrates the relative value approach, the criterion was weight adjusted by fineness. (The use of gross weight would be progressively misrepresentative.) The relative value approach is applicable to other markets as well. All major exchanges have invoicing rules that take into account grading differences for physical commodity deliverables.

CREDIT RATINGS, COUPONS, AND MATURITIES

The better the credit rating is, the higher the price will be, all other things being equal. For financial futures, the grades refer to the credit ratings.

Table 2.12 Relative Value Approach for Gold

Relative Value Approach: 10,000 Ounces			
	18K	24K	12K
Number of Contracts	75	100	50

where 12K = 50% pure gold
      18K = 75% pure gold
      24K = 100% pure gold

The test here is for relative fineness or weight adjusted by fineness.

The vast number of outstanding maturities and coupons do not readily conform to the 8 percent coupon, 20-year maturity standards for the T-note, T-bond, and municipal bond futures and options contracts. The determination of a basis can be difficult, even when a conversion factor, which is primarily an invoicing factor, is taken into account. Credit risk, call or put features, questionable tax status, and subordination of debt complicate the construction of representative basis models.

CONTINUOUS COMPOUNDING

Earlier in this chapter, we examined a linearly weighted arrangement for the time value of money and the implied differentials. Now we will look at nonlinear weights, or what is better known as *continuous compounding*. This subtle change in the theoretical benchmark affects the selection process and the eventual results significantly. Table 2.13 and Figures 2.13 and 2.13a illustrate various theoretical models.

For the specified time series:

Table 2.13 Comparative Analysis of Straightforward Models

Comparative Compounding Models 100,000 Ounces			
Interest rates	Simple 1 year	Continuous 1 year	Annual differences
5.00	525.00	525.56	$55,535.90
6.00	530.00	530.82	82,108.06
7.00	535.00	536.14	113,956.14
8.00	540.00	541.51	151,132.98
9.00	545.00	546.94	193,691.98
10.00	550.00	552.42	241,687.08
11.00	555.00	557.95	295,172.72
12.00	560.00	563.54	354,203.93
13.00	565.00	569.19	418,836.27
14.00	570.00	574.89	489,125.85
15.00	575.00	580.65	565,129.37

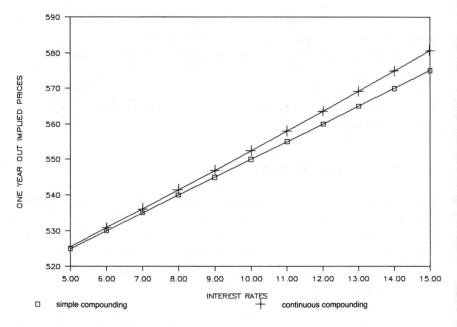

FIGURE 2.13 Differences due to specifications: simple versus continuous compounding; comparative implied price for given models.

$$F = SPe^{rt}$$

where   F   = futures price
       SP = spot price or specified time series level
       e = 2.71
       r = rate of return
       t = time

These concepts are important to arbitrage efforts and trading the basis programs, particularly for financials.

TIME DEPENDENCY

The construction of the basis is time dependent: A 2:30 P.M. New York time cash gold price is computed against the 2:30 P.M. New York time futures prices. Any deviation from this arrangement can taint the analysis. Sometimes, the basis may seem to be acting peculiarly, but it is not: Distortions

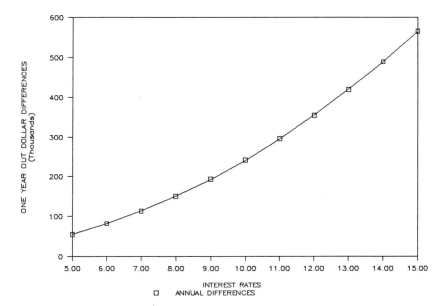

FIGURE 2.13a Differences due to specifications: simple versus continuous compounding; dollar differences between implied prices adjusted by weight for given models.

result from the basis being calculated by mixing dynamic and static price series. In an analysis, the sources used for prices and quotes should be the same as those used for the construction of the basis time series in order to maintain the series' consistency. Consistency is important because many traders and organizations have different latitudes and techniques for extending and accepting bids and offers.

The examination of various quotes, on machines or from the floor, does not ensure that trades are executable at desirable levels or for desirable differences. This condition is magnified when trading actual securities, especially for settlement dates other than those ordinarily assumed. The pulling of bids and offers exacerbates the problem of executing basis trades, particularly for arbitrage programs. Unless the hedger/arbitrageur has a predetermined plan of action, based on knowledge of the many boundaries for an expected successful execution of the trades, he or she is at a disadvantage, because the market appears to be perpetually moving away from the orders.

FOUR TEMPORAL BASIS PERSPECTIVES

There are four primary temporal basis perspectives: *historic, current, theoretical,* and *expected,* which the hedger needs to understand. The hedger's response to the information gleaned from each perspective has a major effect on the success or failure of a hedge.

Hedgers use the *past* as a guide for making ongoing and forthcoming trade decisions. The evaluation of the present against the past is one method used to conduct volatility hedge trades, isolate arbitrage candidates, and trade the basis. One aspect which is used, though seldom described, is the expected basis response. Sometimes, the expected and the theoretical coincide. This occurrence refers not only to the precise mathematical point, or observation, but to its expected time path as well.

Strategies function differently under various conditions. The placement of hedges requires a strategic overview in order to capture the greater benefits from prevailing, as well as expected, conditions. Even hedge-neutral or delta-neutral strategies require what-if scenarios, since the marketplace experiences trends and unexpected price changes. One example of market change is the progressive increase in trading ranges for one day, one week, one month, one year, and one decade. This increase comes from nonstationary time series characteristics, which exhibit shifting mean values and dispersion statistics, such as variance. Many times, the shifts in these two popular statistics are so dramatic and unstable that evaluative techniques built upon them are seriously weakened. Variance becomes infinite, since it does not converge or approach a true underlying estimate. Although these models generate a specific number for this statistic, it can be grossly misleading.

By recognizing the analytical limitations of the data, the hedger can be in a better position to implement trades and take advantage of what is known, though by no means certain.

Historic Basis

The construction of a *historic* basis series is usually a good way to start. The historic basis series lists where the basis has been for many time frames: It can reflect crop years, options cycles, or calendar years. At the outset, the manager is aware of past relationships and behavior. It is important to know the minimums, maximums, and average basis relationships and how the basis behaved from a trading perspective. The application of the 20-year Treasury bond futures contract to hedge 20-year mortgage securities appears a simple and adequate process on face value. In reality, it is an intricately complex process because of the underlying characteristics of both instruments, compounded by movements within the yield curve. The hedge manager must know whether the mortgage securities are *interest only, principal only,* or *interest and principal.* Some mortgage securities may approximate the behavior of zero coupon securities while others may approximate Treasury bond futures, which respond to an optimal blend of the cheapest to deliver.

At any time, the basis can strongly suggest that it is responding to the cheapest to deliver. Trends in interest rates and yield curve movements, however, can cause issues to show heightened response from other anticipations.

Current Basis

The *current basis* is the numerical representation of where the basis is now, or, specifically, the prevailing basis levels which are executable. Prices have bids, offers, and last-traded prices: Many basis relationships have analogous parts—bids, offers, and last-traded levels. There are times when the basis relationship appears to be out of line, and indeed it is: it may be the 10:32 A.M. June gold futures against a 10:34 A.M. quote from a major metals dealer in a fast moving market. Prices or quotes listed on the screen are not equally valid and representative at a later moment, no matter how close in time they occur. Things change, prices change, and the basis changes.

Theoretical Basis

The *theoretical basis* perspective indicates where the basis should be given specific data for the specified explanatory model. The theoretical dimension can be intertwined with the expected approach, although there are important differences. A hedger may suspect that a primary theoretical basis model may not be accurate over the near term because of unusual events or pronounced pricing disturbances. In such cases, the basis may not only depart from its theoretical levels but it may do so in a persistent, substantial manner. The transition from the theoretical to the expected perspective brings us to the expected basis.

Expected Basis

The *expected basis* is a discriminating perspective that can separate superior hedge program performances from average or inferior ones. The theoretical basis is applied because it behaves when events are going according to schedule; the expected basis is applied for a broader or more forward-looking perspective. The expected basis tries to anticipate from a what-if perspective, and often (but not always) the expected determination is synonymous with the theoretical determination.

The ability to interpret basis behavior is more subjective than it is objective. One can characterize the theoretical basis as the scientific aspect and the expected basis as the artistic aspect of determination. One can calculate what the theoretical basis should be at the same time that one assesses that the expected basis behavior may wander (or trend) away from the theoretical level before converging upon it. The expected time path of the basis is frequently overlooked, yet its importance cannot be overemphasized.

GOING FULL CIRCLE

The hedging process starts with a simple analysis of the basis and its behavior and becomes more sophisticated when multiple factors are introduced into the evaluation process. For a discussion of various basis relationships, we will use the following notations:

1. Historic = H(b)
2. Current = C(b)
3. Theoretical = T(b)
4. Expected = E(b)

A first elementary look at basis relationships shows that inequalities between the T(b) and C(b) basis levels give rise to simple arbitrage programs. For example, if C(b) < T(b), then the trader would buy the futures and sell the cash. The trader/hedger may defer the placement of trades pending the emergence of more favorable basis relationships. With this action, he or she is potentially forgoing the beneficial financial offsets of a hedging program during dramatically moving markets.

The next move (bringing greater sophistication to the process) would be to impute a time value for these basis relationships. When this is done, the predictive model is modified into a time-oriented theoretical one. The decision-making criteria for this step are also the evaluation of the $C(b)$ versus the $T(b)$. For example, if municipal bond futures seem to be trading below their theoretical levels, it is inferred that the basis discount is too deep and futures should be bought and cash sold. Some hedgers may postpone the sale of futures in such circumstances, feeling that the relatively deep discount is too unfavorable, and they would rather sell the futures at an opportune time when the basis is not so deep.

Expected basis levels and behavior inject the progressive element into the hedging process, which takes potential departures from the norms into account. Although these various basis determinations are equal upon final settlement, deviations introduce arbitrage or strategic hedge decisions. The best reason for equality is seen in cash settled futures: There is a specific benchmark, index, or other standard which relates the futures to its settlement device exactly. At that time, all four basis perspectives (historic, current, theoretical, and expected) must be equal; otherwise, their evaluative powers are suspect and do not empirically uphold the important property of convergence.

Consider the case in which stock futures go to a discount to the cash market index. Program trading approaches would act to capture these misaligned variables. However, portfolio insurance programs may become activated simultaneously, thereby placing additional selling pressure on the futures. The decision made here is to forgo the basis trade and protect the overall level of portfolio values, thus reflecting concern that the basis may further deteriorate before getting better or recovering. Different values would be calculated progressively on subsequent days, and the initial advantage may not be achieved. In fact, the result may be less.

Expected basis behavior recognizes the propensity of basis disturbances to continue until they abruptly change direction. The process is easy to discover through statistical tests, which show that there are interdependent movements in price and basis series. The movements described by these statistical conditions are also known as cycles and trends.

TIME PATHS

The route that prices take is the key to trading. The route that the basis takes is the key to hedging. Arbitrage and trading-the-basis programs examine and act upon departures and discrepancies. Figures 2.14 and 2.15 illustrate these uptrends and downtrends in the marketplace. It is often assumed that the departures will correct immediately, an assumption that can be costly and erroneous. Corrections may not be immediate: While the trends or cycles are temporarily dominant, their behavior is causing more departures in the differences, and is not causing rapid closure. Departures are the result of an extraordinary event sometimes, or of the confluence of several factors, none particularly potent in and of itself but when joined together, they become powerful pricing forces. The anticipated closures or adjustments do occur, but one may have to be there until the end, the last trade, which is usually the case for cash settlement futures predicated upon indices.

Business decision making should be an "elegant," and not cumbersome, process. A program is less likely to break down if it has "fewer moving parts." Another benefit of structuring and following an ordinary business flow is the ease with which positions can be monitored and mechanisms adjusted. (An excellent example of this will be demonstrated in Chapter 11, Options.) The best advantage that accrues from a well-maintained program, however, is in the application of the hedge program: Although the program criteria are grounded in sophisticated reasoning and empirical efforts, the actual hedging/trading structure should be functionally simple.

MERCHANDISING FEATURE

A primary purpose of the futures and forwards markets is to provide a risk management technique, not a delivery mechanism. *Merchandising* is when a hedger intends to market commodities or securities through the delivery process.

A government securities dealer may seek to sell particular issues which are not readily marketable (because he is not satisfied with the available bids). The dealer who knows the delivery and invoicing provisions can determine whether it is profitable to unload those securities by selling or

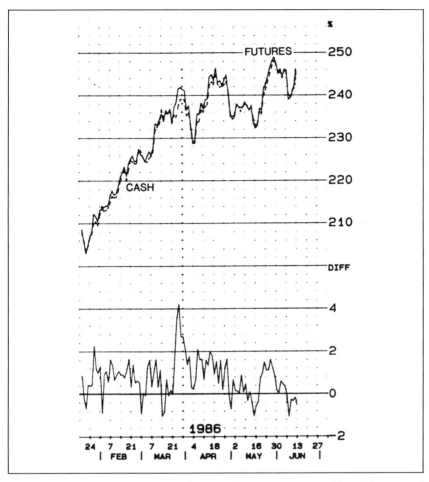

SOURCE: Reprinted from CRB Futures Chart Service, a weekly publication of Commodity Research Bureau, a Knight-Ridder Business Information Service, 100 Church Street, Suite 1850, New York, New York 10007

FIGURE 2.14. Stock market uptrends: differences between S&P 500 cash index and nearby futures.

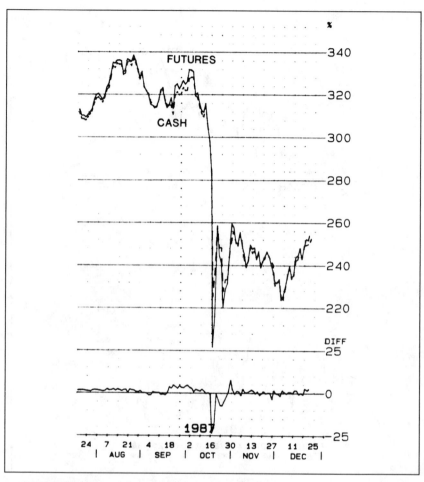

SOURCE: Reprinted from CRB Futures Chart Service, a weekly publication of Commodity Research Bureau, a Knight-Ridder Business Information Service, 100 Church Street, Suite 1850, New York, New York 10007

FIGURE 2.15 Stock market downtrend: differences between S&P 500 cash index and nearby futures.

merchandising them. A grain firm may prefer delivering wheat, corn, or beans rather than directly selling those products, thus maintaining a degree of anonymity without shopping the deal. The degree of anonymity is greater when the trades go through other clearing members.

The connection between futures and cash markets stresses the economic justification, correlation, and convergence principles and, thus, binds the two marketplaces together.

WILDCARDS

The wildcard feature is the ability of the short seller to issue delivery notices at his or her discretion. The associated long position must be prepared to accept delivery of commodities or securities, which may not satisfy individual requirements exactly (though they satisfy exchange) and which may entail funding greater than or less than that desired. For example, big coupons and long maturity bonds have sharply higher conversion factors than small coupon and short maturity issues do. Because of this, the big coupons and long maturity bonds will also have substantially greater financial requirements to satisfy the taking of delivery than short or small issues will. The potential for huge variations in funding requirements for cash-and-carry operations injects an important element of uncertainty into modeling efforts, market pricing, and applications, even if it all works out in the long run. The lingering effects of inferior decisions influence current actions and future plans. One trading action may be strongly influenced by previous success or failure outcomes, and funding capacities can be seriously affected.

Abrupt adjustments in the hedge positions may be necessary. The hedge may have been constructed to account for basis-point risk, but with the intention of making deliveries of other than 8 percent coupon, 20-year Treasury securities.

Risks

Besides basis-level risk, there are other risks associated with hedging. Essentially, the risks should be less than those that existed prior to the placement of a hedge, but a lack of planning, extraordinary conditions, or sudden changes in corporate policies do cause problems.

The merger and/or acquisition of a company that hedges by an organization that does not hedge can be a major problem. The new organization can mandate that hedge positions be lifted immediately, thereby jeopardizing the firm as a whole. Cross-hedge programs can be dramatically affected by unusual developments in one or both parts of the hedge position. While there may be hedge adjustment procedures, they may not rapidly correct the situation and they tend to be reactive and not anticipatory.

Employee dishonesty, lack of other party performance, failure of the clearing organization or the insurer, legal proceedings against the futures commission merchants (FCMs), and so on, can impact the overall effectiveness of the hedge.

ADVANTAGES

The most commonly acknowledged advantages of hedging include:

1. flexibility
2. financial benefits
3. income enhancement
4. risk transformation
5. marketing alternative
6. procurement alternative
7. funding candidacy
8. versatile instruments: forwards, futures, options
9. early, premature, or deferred offsets
10. market efficiency, low costs
11. coverage and deductibles
12. amenability to strategic planning and program implementation

When the hedger introduces a basis relationship he or she has simplified transactional and observational variables into one factor.

Pricing now does not have to be solely conducted through spot transactions, inventories do not have to remain vulnerable to the marketplace, and early or premature offsets need no longer be problematical.

DISADVANTAGES

There are other trading or financial techniques that can achieve degrees of price or yield protection. These are not viewed as hedging positions usually, but they do accomplish risk reduction and have other favorable attributes. Among these techniques are: leasing, consignments, and swaps.

While marketplace liquidity may be comparatively deep, the ability to lift hedges sometimes can be limited. Market circumstances may be such that to prematurely close futures–forwards–options positions would mean an unfavorable basis trade and the opening of exposure once again for the firm.

INTEREST RATES

Interest rates infuse the discounting/compounding mechanism into the model. The choice of an appropriate interest rate is crucial, because a hedger should determine his or her correct borrowing/lending rate, and that of the competition as well. Rate determination is required on a prevailing rate basis and on an expected basis too.

The insertion of implied rates rather than actual rates, actual and expected rates, and historical and actual rates in the theoretical model, changes the solution from each of the different focal points.

Yield-Curve Analysis

The myriad relationships within the interest rate structure are described by yield-curve analysis. This subject examines the linkages among the short–intermediate–long term segments of the yield curve. The theory of interest rate expectations states that the differences between maturities or securities of different grades should not be so large as to allow a continuing situation of exploitable differences. When exploitable differences do occur, they will quickly be pounced upon. To determine exploitable differences, the hedger applies repo–reverse repo analysis. One would expect comparatively low rates for short-term instruments with a geometrically weighted progression of higher rates for longer maturities. This progressive increase in yields is referred to as an ordinary, normal, or positive yield curve. When yields progressively diminish over time, that structure is known as an inverted or negative yield curve. Figures 2.16 and 2.17 illustrate these concepts, which categorize the two principal yield-curve formations. Figure 2.18 portrays one variation of this concept by showing a "hump" within a yield curve.

These curves are constructed for governments, tax-exempts, and corporates. Finer detailed analyses are performed by specifying whether the issues are general obligations or revenue issues, high, medium, or low grade corporates, and whether they are agencies or the federal government itself. Each of these groups has its own creditworthiness, idiosyncrasies, and supply/demand characteristics due to institutional constraints.

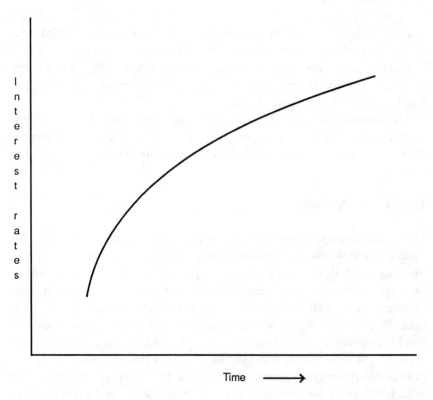

FIGURE 2.16 Normal yield curve (positive carry).

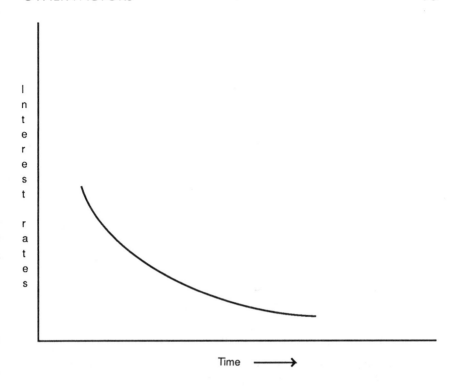

FIGURE 2.17   Inverted yield curve (negative carry).

OTHER FACTORS

The cheapest to deliver may not be what it seems. Implied over actual repo rate models against deliverable maturities and coupons result in easily defined prima facie choices for financial futures. The issues themselves, however, have their own supply/demand considerations. The seemingly cheapest to deliver issues may not be readily available. They may have proven so popular for stripping that the coupons and the principal (corpus) are widely scattered. To reconstitute the issue can cost much more than the implied arbitrageable differentials, thus precluding those issues from truly being cheapest to deliver.

Inventory composition may be such at commercial or investment banks that they use the delivery mechanism to market securities and rearrange portfolios by masking their ownership up until the time of the notice to

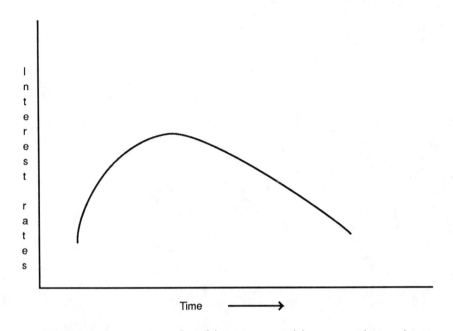

FIGURE 2.18   Humped yield curve (variable carry relationships).

deliver and the subsequent delivery of securities. Securities can be sold in a manner similar to the merchandising for commodities. This "selling," in part, accounts for the discrepancies that can occur during the delivery period, during which issues other than the so-called cheapest to deliver are tendered.

Sometimes, there may be adequate or equal quantities of particular commodities, yet short squeezes can develop due to inclement weather conditions, lack of acceptable storage, insufficient certified amounts in approved storage facilities, strikes, transportation problems, and other factors. There are also situations of plenty, but with the product in the wrong places or so influenced that good deliveries will be few or none. This can give rise to erratic basis behavior. At times like these, convergence may not occur for noncash settled futures, since the offsetting trades can not be executed at reliable differences.

Cheapest to Deliver

Futures contracts are oriented from a seller's perspective as far as deliveries are concerned. The seller can be expected to deliver commodities or securities by means which reflect the cheapest, yet deliverable, specifications. To deliver anything more than the specifications would be a financial mistake (aside from answering other intentions), particularly if there was no consideration or assignment of premiums/discounts, fineness, or conversion factors plus accrued interest. The cheapest to deliver for the overall marketplace, and not the actual delivering party, is a benchmark and not an absolute standard. There are many things that make one issue cheaper to deliver than another, or one commodity grade or weight more desirable than others are at a moment in time.

Contract, Delivery, and Settlement Specifications

The contract, delivery, or settlement specifications narrow the range of problems to the potential delivery candidates or settlement regulations. Is the contract governed by weight, grades, delivery points? Is it influenced by coupons, maturities, types of issues, or cash indices? Or, is it the settlement price of the last trading day, an opening range, or whatever else is stipulated in the contract's specifications to determine what constitutes good delivery or final settlement? The hedger who is familiar with the contract specifications and regulations is in a strong position for identifying potential hazards and is better able to capitalize on potential opportunities than one who is unfamiliar with them.

FUTURES CONTRACT EQUIVALENTS

Futures contract equivalents place the physicals, forwards, options, and futures positions on comparable footing. They quantify how many or how much of a commodity or security is necessary to imply comparable basis-point responses for the standard futures contract. If $100,000 par value of 20-year bonds is *equivalent* to the T-bond futures contract, then $1,000,000 par value of such bonds would reflect the futures contract equivalent position of ten T-bond contracts. An example of a futures contract equivalent for physical commodities: it may require 50,000 pounds of scrap copper at a certain recovery rate to reflect one lot of the futures contract, which specifies a standardized quantity of 25,000 pounds of deliverable copper.

CASH-FLOW CONSIDERATIONS

There are funding variables besides tails and hedging paradoxes that impact a program.

Municipal bond hedging programs have three main futures alternatives:

1. municipal bond index futures
2. Treasury bond futures
3. Treasury note futures

Each of these three alternatives has its own characteristics. The hedge via municipal bond futures may seem like the best alternative; however, price compression within the index and duration analysis considerations can alter its attractiveness. Treasury bond futures have the greatest liquidity, yet they are prone to the widest variations in basis amplitude, indicating the need for substantially higher funding capacity.

The Treasury note futures are not comprised of municipal issues, yet their duration characteristics and comparatively tighter basis fluctuations can make them leading candidates for hedging programs under certain conditions. This can be more apparent when considering liquidity features relative to the municipal bond futures contract.

Options programs that are permitted by corporate charter to include sales or writes are subject to marked-to-market margining as well as to involuntary exercise. Involuntary exercise can be quite destructive to a hedging strategy because it produces significant changes in the positional mix. Often these changes produce overhedged positions that oppose the underlying market trends.

Forward contracts may require little or no initial and variation margins, although they can require letters of credit, compensatory balances, or commitments to conduct specified levels of business (subject to penalty in the case of default). Unlike futures hedging programs, forwards do not generate cash flow, even though the forward positions provide protection. The effect is similar to option-purchase programs.

3
Analyzing the Basis

INTERPRETING THE FACTS

An identified basis requires careful analysis of its behavior and time paths. Attention should be focused both on its ordinary movements and statistical values and on its departures from the norm. Empirical facts must be interpreted. Understanding the process and carefully implementing it are what make the program work—not blindly applying mean average and standard deviation statistics.

TIME PATHS

The evolution of the price and basis series is critical to a hedging program. How the basis attained its current levels is as important as what those levels are. An explosive widening in the basis may present an arbitrage-oriented hedge opportunity, but it may not be an optimal choice at that moment. The abrupt change in the basis could have coincided with a contractual revision, policy announcement, or other important event. At times such as these, there are often strong prevailing forces that can prolong the departures. Hedgers must be aware that disturbances can and do happen.

Hedgers can learn what to expect under various conditions, study alternative actions, and establish guidelines on how to cope. This is very important from a funding perspective and from an implementation and adjustment viewpoint as well.

Basis behavior is more than the analysis of the middle ground. The favorable and unfavorable boundaries are examined as well. Figure 3.1 presents the clustering effect of a stock market up-move.

COMPONENTS OF BASIS SERIES

Basis series fluctuate over time, with the exception of the stipulated basis. Basis series exhibit seasonal, cyclic, trend, and random movements (as do

SOURCE: Reprinted from: CRB Futures Chart Service, a weekly publication of Commodity Research Bureau, a Knight-Ridder Business Information Service, 100 Church Street, Suite 1850, New York, NY 10007.

FIGURE 3.1   Clustering effect for stock market up move.

other economic time series); therefore, each tendency must be analyzed separately and compositely. This chapter introduces several statistical techniques to quantify these components.

Aberrant Behavior

A common mistake in the construction of a hedging program is a myopic search for typical or common behavior. Analysis often centers on averages, not departures, because most research and analysis efforts rely on ordinary regression analysis routines. The search for the mean average and its predictive mechanism places inordinate emphasis on solitary lines, be they linear or nonlinear, and then entails constructing confidence intervals about the mean estimates, using questionable variance-oriented statistics. Consider that outliers in many financial time series occur much more frequently than can be explained by using a normally based distribution. Moreover, there is a growing body of empirical evidence that these outliers tend to cluster within economic series and not to occur independently of one another. For example, sharp swings in stock, bond, and other market prices do not occur independently of one another; rather, the generating mechanism "bunches" these large changes together. The bunching of outliers has substantial bearing on trading and hedging programs, and has been recognized by members of the risk management community, such as insurers, who have been fairly successful in partitioning major risk groups. Phenomena such as earthquakes, freezes, heavy rains, droughts, and so on tend to happen in a cyclical fashion and not in a randomly independent manner.

Assume that the occurrence of a limit-type move in bonds or equally substantial move in stocks is a three-standard deviation occurrence. Empirically, these events, however, are more frequent than 1 out of 10,000 or approximately once every thirty years. If they were independent, the associated expected value would then view these major changes, regardless of whether they are up, down, or both, in the order of 1 out of 100,000,000 (1/10,000 × 1/10,000) for two such back-to-back occurrences, and 1 out of 1,000,000,000,000 (1 × 1/10,000 × 1/10,000 × 1/10,000) for three such occurrences. Yet they are more common than that, and the likelihood of a cluster of major changes is substantially high, given one such occurrence. (The situation is referred to as conditional states in this book.)

Figures 3.1, 3.2, 3.3, and 3.4 illustrate up and down movements of the market and the clustering that occurs.

It is also obvious that the basis relationships were temporarily distorted from average expectations. These distortions did not immediately correct, although that did happen within short order. This can pose a formidable funding problem, depending on which way the hedge was placed—buy or sell—rather than on the accuracy of the hedge itself.

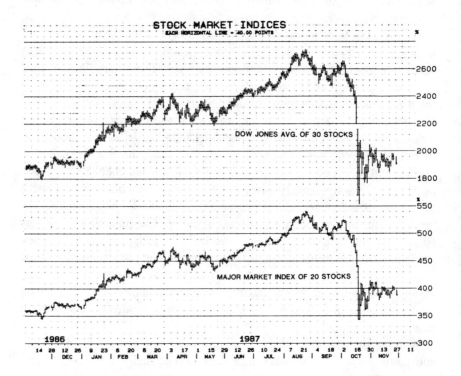

SOURCE: Reprinted from CRB Futures Chart Service, a weekly publication of Commodity Research Bureau, a Knight-Ridder Business Information Service, 100 Church Street, Suite 1850, New York, NY 10007.

FIGURE 3.2 Clustering effect for stock market down move.

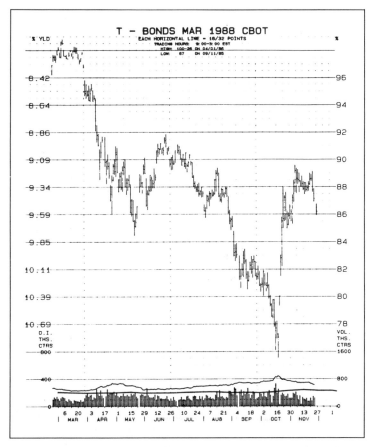

SOURCE: Reprinted from CRB Futures Chart Service, a weekly publication of Commodity Research Bureau, a Knight-Ridder Business Information Service, 100 Church Street, Suite 1850, New York, NY 10007.

FIGURE 3.3   Clustering effect for bond market up move.

Aberrant behavior is the high-risk element for a hedging program. Alternative courses of action should be prepared and then executed if circumstances become extraordinary. Studying atypical basis behavior can be a rewarding enterprise: Sometimes the analyst is faced with market

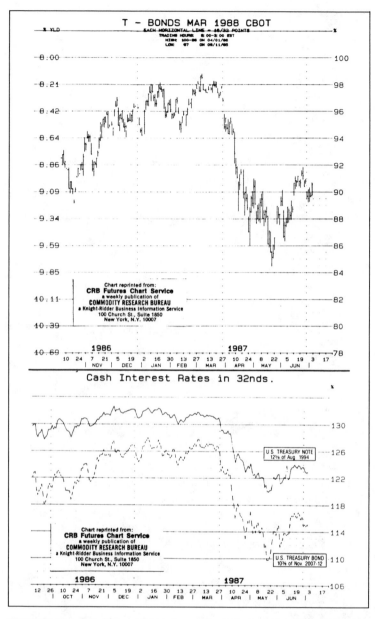

SOURCE: Reprinted from: CRB Futures Chart Service, a weekly publication of Commodity Research Bureau, a Knight-Ridder Business Information Service, 100 Church Street, Suite 1850, New York, NY 10007.

FIGURE 3.4   Clustering effect for bond market down move.

action directly related to the hedge program. At other times, the hedger must use similar markets for comparative study, or diverse markets for a historical perspective. These exercises lend breadth and depth to the process. A hedger can appreciate how things went awry for others, even if they were in different industries.

Unprecedented Moves

Consider the October 1987 crash in stock prices. The meltdown in equity values was not limited to the United States, but was worldwide. Many commentators stated that the drop was unprecedented for a market. This is not true: Markets such as coffee, sugar, silver, platinum, and others have experienced as great if not greater declines. What has this to do with IBM, an S&P basket portfolio, or oil inventories? The answer is simple: A lot! These markets are major economic ones, and when they decline, the devastation is wrought on many organizations by the extraordinary price movements. Curiously, many arbitrage or basis trading organizations appear to bear the brunt of a decline following what seemed to be very favorable circumstances for their operations. Those organizations, however, were eventually gutted because of an over-emphasis on normalcy or for taking quick returns to mean expected values.

Stages of Hedge Program Analysis

Hedging programs are built in stages. Choosing the hedge instruments, defining hedging relationships, settling on an operable basis, and securing financial arrangements can lead to an effective hedge program. To hedge a position without understanding the relationships involved would introduce risk into the operation. Hedge analysis and basis analysis are separate but intertwined stages of a program. The analysis starts with individual basis relationships, then multiple basis relationships, and then progresses with other variables and constraints. Although a few basis relationships may seem very stable and tight, funding requirements can be prohibitive, and dramatic markets have an effect. Sometimes secondary basis relationships may have to be utilized because of a lack of funding or other internal or external constraints.

QUANTITATIVE APPROACHES

This section describes statistical terms and highlights several powerful nonparametric tests. The tests identify statistical properties that describe basis behavior and characteristics. The presentation of quantitative approaches is not exhaustive: there are numerous techniques available, each with its own operating properties, which intermediate and advanced statistics textbooks cover in more detail.

Minimums, Maximums, and Ranges

Minimum, maximum, and range statistics place initial quantitative boundaries on program behavior. These three parameters are focal points for trading and hedging programs, and an early analysis of their behavior can indicate how well or how poorly a program may act.

The *minimum* is the lowest or most negative number in the specified time series, whereas the *maximum* is the highest or least negative number. The *range* is the difference between the two; or maximum − minimum = range. Minimum, maximum, and range statistics for municipal bonds are given in Table 3.1.

Minimum, maximum, and range statistics are used in cyclical analysis to find the turning points, or *peaks* and *troughs*. The length between turning points is a phase and the length between two consecutive peaks or troughs is a cycle.

Means, Medians, and Dispersions

Generally, the *mean* refers to the arithmetic averaging of a time series. This can be expressed as:

$$\frac{\Sigma p_i}{n_i} = \text{arithmetic mean}$$

The mean need not be limited to the averaging of just one aspect of a price or a basis, such as the closing level, but can refer to its daily (or weekly, monthly, and so on) highs, lows, or ranges. Determination of a mean lays the groundwork for *dispersion* statistics, or *variance* and *standard*

Table 3.1   Municipal Bond Index, Futures, and Basis Relationships

| 1988 date | Municipal Bonds Decimal Equivalents Futures | | | Basis | | |
	Index adjusted	Sep adjusted	Dec adjusted	March adjusted	Index-Sep adjusted	Index-Dec adjusted	Index-Mar adjusted
801	89.28	88.03	85.75	83.69	1.25	3.53	5.59
802	89.56	88.50	86.28	84.25	1.06	3.28	5.31
803	89.59	88.44	86.19	84.16	1.16	3.41	5.44
804	89.81	88.78	86.59	84.59	1.03	3.22	5.22
805	89.63	88.41	86.25	84.31	1.22	3.38	5.31
808	89.66	88.47	86.31	84.44	1.19	3.34	5.22
809	89.53	88.28	86.25	84.44	1.25	3.28	5.09
810	89.31	87.69	85.66	83.84	1.62	3.66	5.47
811	88.56	86.94	84.69	82.84	1.63	3.88	5.72
812	88.38	87.00	84.94	83.09	1.38	3.44	5.28
815	88.31	86.91	84.78	82.94	1.41	3.53	5.38
816	88.31	87.22	85.06	83.19	1.09	3.25	5.12
817	88.31	87.16	84.97	83.09	1.16	3.34	5.22
818	88.44	87.53	85.34	83.47	0.91	3.09	4.97
819	88.50	87.50	85.31	83.44	1.00	3.19	5.06
822	88.47	87.47	85.31	83.44	1.00	3.16	5.03
823	88.56	87.75	85.56	83.78	0.81	3.00	4.78
824	88.72	88.03	85.97	84.19	0.69	2.75	4.53
825	88.50	87.88	85.88	84.16	0.62	2.62	4.34
826	88.63	88.09	86.03	84.28	0.53	2.59	4.34
829	88.81	88.50	86.41	84.69	0.31	2.41	4.13
830	88.88	88.44	86.34	84.66	0.44	2.53	4.22
831	88.97	88.56	86.44	84.69	0.41	2.53	4.28
901	89.00	88.56	86.31	84.56	0.44	2.69	4.44
902	89.69	89.69	87.69	85.94	0.00	2.00	3.75
906	89.69	89.75	87.84	86.03	−0.06	1.84	3.66
907	90.00	89.78	87.88	86.06	0.22	2.13	3.94
908	89.97	89.78	87.84	85.94	0.19	2.13	4.03
909	90.00	90.16	88.22	86.44	−0.16	1.78	3.56
912	90.22	89.97	87.91	86.13	0.25	2.31	4.09
913	90.22	90.03	87.91	86.13	0.19	2.31	4.09
914	90.59	90.44	88.34	86.53	0.16	2.25	4.06
915	90.63	90.41	88.31	86.50	0.22	2.31	4.13
916	90.50	90.38	88.25	86.44	0.12	2.25	4.06
919	90.31	90.25	88.06	86.22	0.06	2.25	4.09
920	90.22	90.13	87.84	86.00	0.09	2.38	4.22
921	90.22	90.22	88.19	86.28	0.00	2.03	3.94
922	90.25		88.03	86.19		2.22	4.06
Max	90.63	90.44	88.34	86.53	1.63	3.88	5.72
Min	88.31	86.91	84.69	82.84	−0.16	1.78	3.56
Range	2.31	3.53	3.66	3.69	1.78	2.09	2.16

SOURCE: Barkley International Inc.

deviation. Often these parameters are used for the appraisal of market volatility and for volatility measurements for the pricing of options. This approach provides a starting point for subsequent evaluations, although it may not reflect the marketplace precisely. Averages, standard deviations, and variances are shown in Table 3.1.

The *median* is the midpoint or middle value in a series of observations— half the observations are of greater value than it is and half the observations are of less value than it is. In odd numbered series, the median value is whatever the midway point is; in even numbered series (where there is no obvious median), its value is estimated by computing the arithmetic average of the two center observations.

When these distributions are symmetrical, the mean and the median coincide because there is no loss in accuracy or difference in parameter estimate for the average value. If there are substantial differences, then this is an important alternative central tendency statistic.

Medians are important because they can display greater stability than arithmetic means and are variables which assist in the definition of skewness. Because of their relative stability and ease of calculation, they are preferable to mean statistics (regardless of type) for numerous applications, including: arithmetic, geometric, harmonic, or exponential.

Seasonalities and Delivery Cycles

The seasonal cycles refer to recurring economic behavior which, though not necessarily precise, happens on a reasonably repetitive basis. Tradi-

Table 3.2 Averages, Standard Deviations, and Variances of Prior Data

	Municipal Bonds Decimal Equivalents						
	Futures				Basis		
1988 date	Index adj	Sep adj	Dec adj	March adj	Ind-Sep adj	Ind-Dec adj	Ind-Mar adj
Average	89.37	88.68	86.60	84.76	0.67	2.77	4.61
Std Dev	0.75	1.14	1.18	1.20	0.52	0.57	0.62
Variance	0.56	1.30	1.40	1.44	0.27	0.33	0.38

Adj = adjusted
NOTE: See Table 3.1 for data

tionally, this concept pertained to crop-year or calendar-year movements. Now the definition has been broadened to include fiscal, corporate, and contract (security) cycles for expirations of futures and options.

Indices or weights identify and quantify these movements. An abbreviated version would be pre-expiration basis behavior, which analyzes only the brief 10-, 20-, or 30-day time and basis segments prior to futures contract expirations. This behavior is twofold: the relationship between the underlying index, security, or commodity and the nearby futures, and the nearby futures versus forward delivery months. It is not uncommon to experience convergence between the nearby futures and the underlying index, security, or commodity; however, the spread differentials may actually seem to be acting in an aberrant manner, although they are not. For example, as expiration approaches, the nearby financial futures contract and the index move toward convergence, and the more deferred months may actually widen their discount relationships. This may be partially attributable to a considerable pickup in rollovers, which are now being done late in the maturity. On close examination, one can isolate these expiration departures and behavioral characteristics and discover other reasons for departures.

Figure 3.5 illustrates a straight line theoretical basis delay versus an actual basis behavior line. Figure 3.6 illustrates the actual index and nearby (spot) futures versus the theoretical futures. Figure 3.7 illustrates the nearby futures progressively gaining relative to the next delivery month— they did not move toward convergence here.

Cyclical Test

As we discussed earlier in this chapter, the distance between two consecutive turning points, a peak and a trough, is a phase. The distance between two consecutive peaks or two consecutive troughs is a cycle, which reflects the two phases, upward and downward. These phases need not be of identical length. Table 3.3 contains data on Fed funds and T-bills and their expected and actual runs. When we look at the data, we can see that the basis behavior indicates movements are occurring in an ordered or grouped fashion, not in a random fashion. An important test for cycles in economic data, developed by Wallis and Moore, is comparable to other hypothesis techniques because it tests for goodness of fit. (See ''A Significance Test

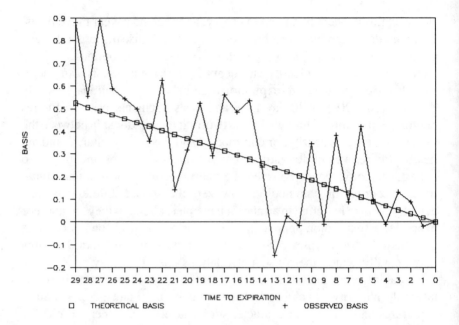

FIGURE 3.5 Straight line theoretical basis delay versus actual basis behavior line.

for Time Series and Other Ordered Observations,'' by Allen Wallis and Geoffrey H. Moore. Technical Paper 1: September 1941, National Bureau of Economic Research.) Here, there are two hypotheses: (1) the series acts as an independently random one; (2) the series displays cyclical characteristics. The solution compares the number of theoretically expected phase-run lengths versus the observed phase-run lengths. The formulas are:

$$EL_1 = \frac{5(n-3)}{12}$$

$$EL_2 = \frac{11(n-4)}{60}$$

and

$$EL_3 = \frac{4n-21}{60}$$

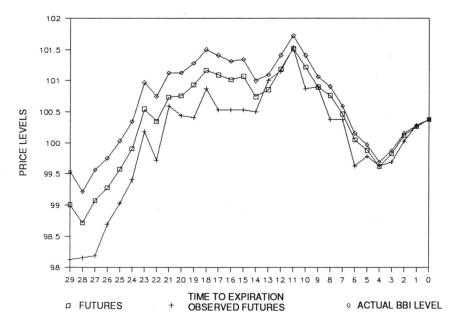

FIGURE 3.6 Actual index and nearby (spot) futures versus theoretical futures.

where: EL_1 = all expected phase runs of length 1
EL_2 = all expected phase runs of length 2
EL_3 = all expected phase runs >2

The goodness of fit is evaluated by:

$$\chi^2_p = \frac{(A_1 - EL_1)^2}{EL_1} + \frac{(A_2 - EL_2)^2}{EL_2} + \frac{(A_3 - EL_3)^2}{EL_3}$$

where χ^2_p is the chi-square phase run statistic. A_1, A_2, and A_3 are the actual observations for the phase runs of lengths 1, 2, and 3 or more.

Here, the swings in Treasury bill rates did not fluctuate as rapidly as the federal funds did. This behavior has important ramifications. Many banks employ a matrix of federal funds and Eurodollar rates as criteria for cost of capital, and also focus on Treasury rates as indices for lending practices. Together they reflect asset and liability management analysis; therefore it

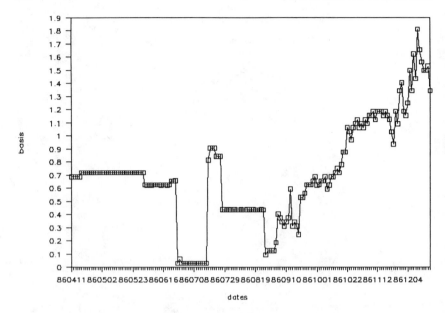

FIGURE 3.7   Futures versus futures when differences or basis widens
as expiration approaches.

is critical to understand how these two important rates fluctuate. If a bank
decides to hedge its requirements via the Treasury bill and Eurodollar
futures and options markets, then it may experience intolerable swings.
Also, Fed funds are overnight and T-Bills and Eurodollars 90 days (they
can be more or less). Pursuit of complex application of basis-point response
or duration-oriented approaches can produce solutions that require an
inordinate amount of hedging adjustments (realignments) with a comparatively high cumulative cost. Improperly conceived hedges can be very
expensive and potentially dangerous.

Trend Test

One trend test has been suggested by Maurice Kendall.* By ranking
observations, an analyst can determine whether the occurrences behaved

* See M. G. Kendall, *Rank Correlation Methods* (London: Charles Griffin & Co.
1969), and *Time Series* (New York: Hafner Press, 1976).

Table 3.3a Fed Funds and T-Bill Data

Selected Interest Rates

Date	Federal funds	3-Month T-bill	Date	Federal funds	3-Month T-bill
1	N9.73	N9.10	36	+8.06	−6.90
2	+9.87	−8.65	37	+8.07	+6.99
3	−9.55	+8.68	38	−7.77	+7.07
4	−9.47	−8.55	39	+7.88	+7.25
5	−9.00	−8.41	40	−7.64	+7.28
6	−8.83	+8.44	41	+7.92	−7.21
7	−8.70	−8.27	42	−7.88	−7.13
8	−7.99	−7.81	43	+8.06	−7.07
9	−7.95	−7.67	44	−7.78	N7.07
10	+8.75	+7.83	45	+7.88	+7.08
11	−8.27	−7.75	46	−7.80	+7.23
12	−8.23	−7.72	47	+7.85	−7.16
13	−8.19	−7.65	48	+7.96	−6.89
14	+8.45	+7.92	49	+8.12	+7.01
15	+8.59	+8.15	50	−7.84	+7.17
16	−8.44	+8.21	51	+8.03	+7.20
17	+8.57	+8.31	52	+8.14	+7.22
18	−8.40	+8.47	53	−7.89	−7.20
19	+8.63	+8.69	54	+8.30	+7.25
20	−8.52	−8.54	55	−7.95	+7.29
21	+8.75	−8.51	56	+8.13	−7.23
22	−8.38	−8.29	57	−7.71	−7.18
23	+8.18	−8.17	58	+8.49	+7.24
24	−8.45	−8.08	59	−8.03	−7.14
25	+8.46	−7.86	60	+8.05	−7.06
26	−7.69	−7.73	61	−8.02	−7.02
27	+8.35	+7.78	62	+9.55	+7.04
28	−8.19	−7.76	63	−8.20	+7.13
29	−8.14	−7.58	64	−7.94	+7.17
30	−7.91	−7.25	65	−7.87	−6.99
31	−7.60	−7.19	66	−7.83	−6.97
32	+7.75	−7.01	67	+7.97	+7.06
33	−7.62	+7.03	68	−7.85	+7.11
34	−7.13	−6.81	69	−7.84	−7.05
35	+7.46	+7.05	70	−7.82	N7.05

N represents no change sign for data as given.

SOURCE: U.S. Financial Data, Federal Reserve of St. Louis and *A Handbook for Professional Futures and Options Traders,* Joseph D. Koziol, copyright ©, 1987. Reprinted by permission of John Wiley & Sons, Inc.

Table 3.3b   Runs for Selected Interest Rates

	Expected Versus Actual Runs			
	Federal Funds		Treasury Bills	
Length	Expected	Actual	Expected	Actual
L1	11.25	18.00	11.25	3.00
L2	4.77	1.00	4.77	5.00
L3	1.65	3.00	1.65	5.00

SOURCE: U.S. Financial Data, Federal Reserve Bank of St. Louis and *A Handbook for Professional Futures and Options Traders,* by Joseph D. Koziol, copyright ©, 1987. Reprinted by permission of John Wiley & Sons, Inc.

in a statistically ordered or random manner. Table 3.4 applies this test to the basis (difference) between spot gold and futures prices, and Figure 3.8 illustrates it.

Table 3.4   Data for Trend or Correlation Test

	Gold Futures Prices				
Date	November	December	Nov–Dec	Nov–Dec rank	Positive score
1101	411.60	414.00	−2.40	1.5	16.00
1102	421.80	424.20	−2.40	1.5	16.00
1103	421.50	423.70	−2.20	3.0	15.00
1104	421.50	423.50	−2.00	5.0	13.00
1107	422.80	424.70	−1.90	6.0	12.00
1108	419.10	421.20	−2.10	4.0	12.00
1109	423.10	424.70	−1.60	7.0	11.00
1110	419.00	420.50	−1.50	8.5	9.00
1111	421.60	423.10	−1.50	8.5	9.00
1114	423.90	425.20	−1.30	10.0	8.00
1115	424.40	425.60	−1.20	11.0	7.00
1116	424.50	425.60	−1.10	12.0	6.00
1117	420.10	421.10	−1.00	13.0	5.00
1118	417.40	418.10	−0.70	14.5	3.00
1121	415.80	416.50	−0.70	14.5	3.00
1122	417.70	418.10	−0.40	16.0	2.00
1123	420.00	420.10	−0.10	17.0	1.00
1128	423.30	423.30	0.00	18.0	0.00
				Sum	148.00

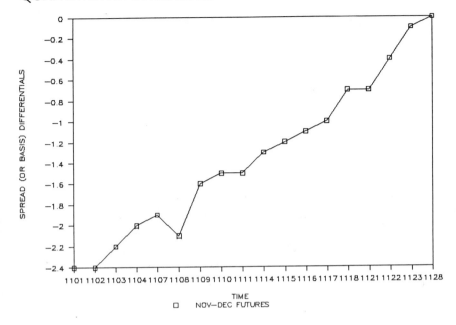

FIGURE 3.8 Graph depicting Table 3.4 data and highlighting convergence properties for selective market.

Notice how the two series approach one another. The strong affinitive property reflects convergence. This test measures the degree to which a series seems to be acting in a directional manner, a trend, over time.

This varies from other correlation tests which examine behavior between component parts. Here, the components would be the cash and the hedge instrument.

This statistical test (S) attempts to determine whether observations within a time series are behaving as though they are ordered.

The formulas for this test are:

$$S = 2P - (1/2)(N)(N-1)$$

$$S = 2(148) - (1/2)(18)(17)$$

$$S = 296 - 153$$

$$S = +143$$

The calculation of Kendall's tau(τ) is performed now:

$$\tau = \frac{2(+143)}{(18)(17)}$$

$$= \frac{286}{306}$$

$$= +.93$$

The tau value of $+.93$ suggests a positive relationship of the basis over time; a minus sign before the tau value would indicate a negative trend, thus suggesting a decline in basis premium value over time. Examples of this would be spot versus futures for precious metals and the generalized behavior for various stock index futures, relative to their underlying indices. The test statistic (S) is used to determine the degree of statistical significance.

Chi-Square Test

The chi-square test is useful for determining if there are statistically significant differences between theoretically postulated and observed series, as discussed earlier in this chapter.

The generalized formula for this test is:

$$\chi^2 = \frac{(o_i - e_i)^2}{e_i}$$

where o $= $ observed value
    e $= $ expected value
    χ^2 $= $ evaluative statistic

The chi-square statistic is available in tables in many statistics texts.

Defining Boundaries

The trend and chi-square tests statistically analyze basis and its behavior. These numerical guidelines (degree of convergence, cyclical and seasonal properties, means, ranges, and other statistical aspects) establish boundaries or decision making thresholds. All statistical distributions have means, but not all of them have variance statistics, a condition which can affect testing, analysis, and implementation. For example, the normal distribution has a mean and variance. If one knows the values of these two parameters, one can define the entire distribution.

Such is not the case for the Cauchy distribution, which has a mean but no variance statistic (unless you consider infinitive variance a parameter). This bell shaped curve distribution has some remarkable properties. Outliers or observations in the tail regions can occur twice as frequently in Cauchy distributions as in normal distributions. Also, the premise that approximately 68 percent of the observations fall within one standard deviation of the mean and 32 percent beyond it (for a normal distribution) is not accurate here. Approximately 45 percent of these observations can fall about the mean and the other 55 percent are likely to occur beyond the inflection points. This difference in boundaries has ramifications for many hedge applications: It implies a greater-than-normal propensity for large changes in price or basis. In a situation where large changes occur, a hedger's hesitancy to place hedges can result in an even more unfavorable posture. Thus, there can be comparatively high success or failure rates for individual operations.

In addition, the practical and financial outcomes of hedging–trading programs based upon models that require normality and independence are jeopardized. Point estimates can be very unstable (regression analysis). Even the placement of confidence intervals about the mean can be rendered questionable. The probability of a number hitting the mean regression line (or even near it), given confidence-level bounded statistics, is uncertain, because the boundaries may be substantially broader.

DEFINING EXPECTATIONS

The construction of a framework of expectations adds vitality to the hedging process. Perhaps it is most critical for options-hedging strategies. How the process starts, continues, and finishes does affect it; and how the hedge was placed, adjusted, and lifted (removed) affects it too.

Floors

A *floor* protects price or yield by limiting downside exposure. It preserves a particular level of price, portfolio valuation, yield, and so on. Placing a forward or futures position, and then implementing an options position is the most rigorous case using a floor. Buy-oriented options strategies have readily discernible strike or floor prices. Table 3.5 illustrates a crude oil situation which has floor prices.

Compare the sale of a futures contract with the purchase of the two different strike price puts. For puts, the strike price offers price protection; whereas the sale price of the futures sets the hedge price. Notice that the lower strike price indicates a lower degree of protection or a lower floor. The market can sell off sharply before there is any offsetting price relief from the hedge, but getting the higher strike price put provided more and earlier coverage. The futures price was the most responsive, for it underlies the options. The goal, then, is to match the appropriate futures (options) market contracts to the crude oil at hand.

Caps

The strategy that limits price (or yield) effects is a *cap*. The purchase of a futures contract establishes price protection; the sale of a financial futures

Table 3.5 Comparing Futures and Options Floors

	Comparative Floors Crude Oil Example			
	Long cash	Sold futures	Put strike no. 1	Put strike no. 2
Prices	16.75	16.75	16.00	15.00
Protection	—	Immediate	At strike	At strike
Deductible	—	0	.75	1.75
Premium	—	0	.95	.55
Effective level	—	16.75	15.05	14.45

Here: Deductibles assume contract grades and no disparities.
One futures contract equivalent

SOURCE: Barkley International Inc.

contract generates yield protection. Yield protection sees that subsequent rises in interest rates do not impair the organization's position. In the event of lower interest rates, there would be variation margin calls to finance the short financial futures hedge.

For options-related strategies, protection occurs at the strike price; further movements from that level generate asymmetrical protection. For example, with the purchase of a British pound futures contract, protection is created at the level of the purchase price, while with the options purchase, protection is created at the strike price. Table 3.6 shows three different scenarios.

The table lists the outcomes of two different strikes and the futures contract. Notice how tight the futures behaves compared to the purchase of either of the two calls. Also, the call with the lower strike more nearly approximates the behavior of the futures and the desired underlying actual position.

Collars

A *collar* is the implementation of both a floor and a cap: It places a dual boundary about the basis (or desired protection level benchmark). Such a

Table 3.6 Comparing Futures and Options Caps

	Comparative Caps British Pound Example			
	Short cash	Long futures	Call strike no. 1	Call strike no. 2
Prices	1.7800	1.7800	1.8000	1.8250
Protection	—	Immediate	At strike	At strike
Deductible	—	0	.0200	.0450
Premium paid	—	0	.0290	.0195
Effective level	—	1.7800	1.8290	1.8445

Here: No basis or interest rate differentials assumed between forward cash requirement and futures.
One futures contract equivalent

SOURCE: Barkley International Inc.

technique can immunize a portfolio from a drop below the specified strike point, while also limiting gains beyond the specified level. The approach often generates a synthetic position, which can have desirable features. A primary benefit is the generation of potential income through writing options. However, this benefit forges potential upside gains. Table 3.7 shows the use of a collar with S&P futures, options, and cash.

Again, compare the effects of the options to that of the futures. Here, the sale of the calls capped the upside while the purchase of the puts floored the portfolio. Together, the purchase of a put and the sale of a call created a synthetic short-futures position of some unspecified degree. The hedger can synthesize degrees of futures replication by applying options pricing models.

CONDITIONAL STATES

What happens to the basis as the contract moves toward delivery or maturity? Does it remain flat (constant)? Does it converge because futures

Table 3.7   Comparing Futures and Options Collars

| | Comparative Collars Standard & Poors Example | | | |
	Long S&P cash	Short futures	Long Put 275 strike	Short Call 280 strike
Levels	276.80	280.00	275.00	280.00
Protection	—	Immediate	At strike	Limited
Deductible	—	*	−1.80	+3.20
Premium (±)	—	*	−6.10	+8.20
Effective level	—	280.00	268.90	288.20

* Secured a 3.20 or $1,600 implied carry or basis since sold futures at premium relative to cash position given contract grade equivalency.

SOURCE: Barkley International Inc.

NOTE: Futures limited gain to basis or carrying charge differentials. Futures capped position as well as floored position at trade price. Long put and short call approximate synthetic short futures position. Partial offset between options premium paid and received.

are losing their premium? Or, does it converge with futures gaining on cash?

Conditional states refers to the methodology the trader/hedger uses to recognize particular attributes of the marketplace. In the simplest form, it is a binomial arrangement: Market states are only up or down. The next step is to allow for a neutral, trading affair, or consolidation phase. This arrangement imparts three states to the market's condition: up, neutral, and down.

The neutrality state has dramatic ramifications for hedge programs which entail basis point-loss, or convergence value-loss, due to the movement of the futures, relative to the cash or underlying index. The effect is especially dramatic for evaluating and implementing options-trading strategies because it stresses the importance of time value decay, underlying to strike, and even the probability generating functions that account for the expected value outcomes.

The conditional states viewpoint recognizes that basis and underlying markets respond differently in various market situations and, therefore, the hedger may be required to implement alternative strategies. The trading/hedging environment, while random, is not strictly independent and unconditional. Success and failure influence subsequent actions. The larger the successes, the closer the firm is to achieving its targets; the greater the failures, the sooner the firm is to be constrained by regulations, resources, and competitive pressures.

For the organization, success or failure outcomes do not set the environment back to pre-action conditions (unconditional game) but, rather, they modify subsequent abilities to perform (conditional game). Many approaches, nevertheless, assume a resetting takes place because it is fairly representative of the marketplace on the whole. It is not, however, representative of its individual participants.

Suppose an organization is hedged and seeks to generate $1,000,000 of coverage per each 1 percent change in yield for its portfolio. Here, the model will assume an equal chance of favorable/unfavorable behavior and equal size changes. If the behavior starts out unfavorably and does not return to normal on the next outcome, it would require two consecutive favorable events to return to the initial state of normalcy. Thus, the chances become one out of four (.25) and not one out of two (.50). Pressing the logic a little further, if the basis moved unfavorably five sessions in a row, the return may not be immediate (the next outcome) but would entail the propitious market action of $(1/2)^5$ or $1/32$ $(.5 \times .5 \times .5 \times .5 \times .5)$, or approximately 3 percent likelihood, and not the 50 percent initially suggested by the model.

The trend test described above is one method for numerical assignment for the conditional states. As mentioned earlier, $+1.00$ is the maximum value for an uptrend, a -1.00 is the extreme value for a downtrend, and values about 0.00 (zero) indicate the lack of a statistical trend or interdependence between ordered observations. By employing this easy to use weighting scheme, the hedger can assign conditional states values and compute the impact of the erosion of time value on premiums or basis relationships.

Another technique is discriminant analysis, a statistical tool that searches for distinguishing characteristics which can classify data, such as market conditions, into bullish, bearish, or neutral categories. The technique looks for ways to categorize market states, unlike regression analysis, which specifies point estimates for price and basis movement. There are nonparametric variations to this discriminatory approach.

QUESTIONS TO ASK

It is valuable to ask why the basis performed the way it did, particularly in situations where there were major departures from central tendency values. Was it a policy change on the part of the Federal Reserve, Department of Agriculture, OPEC, a central bank, a government marketing board, or other organization which can influence prices, production, consumption, interest rate yields, or currency relationships?

By asking questions before and during a hedge program (which may continue to be quite viable), one can avoid, or at least be prepared to minimize, the impact of adverse events. A firm is better able to face the challenges of the marketplace and its risk management/hedging program if it anticipates outcomes and makes forward-looking adjustments, rather than if it is exclusively reactionary and acts only on yesterday's action or basis. It is analogous to a chess match, in which the better players anticipate and respond to the moves and the expected moves of their opponents, and other players only make moves based on previous action, not planning for future events.

4

Adaptive Processes

STATIC OR DYNAMIC

Changes in supply and demand continually alter price and basis relationships. *Dynamics* refers to this process of movement over time. *Static* analysis represents a snapshot view of a market: There is no time variable, so it does not change over time. This static analytical approach is useful because it examines the interrelationships among important variables in the absence of time. It simplifies the construction of what-if scenarios. For the moment, the hedging analyst does not have to contend with unexpected changes and developments with the passage of time. He only has to evaluate what happens to outcomes, given specified values for variables.

Static procedures are often identified as passive hedge management, whereas dynamic procedures are identified as active hedge management. Essentially, the dynamic or adaptive processes require adjustments which are more frequent than those required by passive risk management strategies.

STATISTICAL FRAMEWORKS

In Chapter 2, we defined historic basis, current basis, theoretical basis, and expected basis, written as H(b), C(b), T(b), and E(b), respectively. In this chapter we will define the hedge program (account).

The *historic hedge*, H(H), is the previous valuation of the economic benefit of the cumulative hedge account; it indicates what the particular value has been in the past. The *current hedge*, C(H), indicates the value of the hedge program now. The *theoretical hedge*, T(H), is the predicted or model-generated estimate of what the hedge account value should be. Finally, the *expected hedge*, E(H), is what the hedger anticipates as a probable value for the established hedge program or the one to be implemented. This value gives the program a sensitivity to expectations, particularly when values are moving away from the theoretical estimates. E(H) is very sensitive to reasoning under adverse states because it evaluates how much further the unfavorable basis, or hedge, action may go before the series, or account, adjusts to its central tendency.

In each case, the parenthesized variable is capitalized to emphasize that it refers to the entire hedge program, as opposed to its constituent basis hedge positions. Hedge programs entail many different instruments, which are both being hedged and being used as hedges, not just one all-encompassing hedge trade. For example, a government securities dealer can be hedging new issues, inventories, sales requirements, and so on. Each group can place its own hedges, and each trader can place his own hedges within the group. This aggregation is sometimes referred to as *pooling*; its purpose is portfolio risk reduction and some degree of natural hedging. Treasury departments call this procedure asset and liability management from a gap analysis perspective.

To start the analysis, assume that the sum of H(b) cases equals H(H), the sum of C(b) equals C(H), the sum of T(b) equals T(H), and the sum of E(b) equals E(H):

$$H(b) = H(H), C(b) = C(H), T(b) = T(H), \text{ and } E(b) = E(H)$$

A more detailed version is:

$$H(b_{ij}) = H(H), C(b_{ij}) = C(H), T(b_{ij}) = T(H), \text{ and } E(b_{ij}) = E(H)$$

where i = time period
j = j^{th} basis hedge position

Organizations can have many basis trade positions within the structure of the corporate hedge program.

CONDITIONAL ENVIRONMENT

Many textbooks implicitly present hedging as the special case of an assumed set of market conditions. Proponents of this viewpoint go on to conclude that all hedges should produce identical returns over the long run. Any other conclusion would imply arbitrageable situations or relative dominance of one method of hedging over another. And this conclusion is unavoidable if one subscribes to the underlying assumptions, particularly, the independence between returns (actions), unconditional payoffs as opposed to conditional ones, and a resetting of the game to initial conditions and resources. A simplistic adoption of this belief propagates the popular misconception that successful traders and hedgers have essentially—not effectively—enjoyed the luck of the draw. It is analogous to saying that two bridge champions were "lucky" to defeat two novices. It is obvious that this is not the case. Intellectual capacity, experience, knowledge, and basic gaming temperament and ability influence the outcomes. There is a positive, although not a guaranteed, expected value to the champion or grandmaster which is not attributed to the inexperienced player. The randomness continues to exist from game to game and situation to situation, and the prospect of higher payoffs is not a 100% certainty; but in multiple trials, or even a one-shot situation, there is a participant who is expected to win.

A weighting arrangement based on expected value and the implied distributive characteristics for many options pricing models can generate widely variant and different signed ($\pm$) outcomes, depending on the applied probability functions.

For the whole trading population, the central average rate of return overwhelms the participants, yet some hedgers do better than others. The effects of changes in the firms, especially if the decision makers leave or die, are often neglected when the hedging-trading scenario is considered. Such changes, in part, explain why some hedgers and corporations experience a higher market rate of returns than is typically expected. Essentially, because the game (business) does not continue indefinitely, but changes over time, extraordinarily high performance is not sustainable over time. Also, inept players (hedgers) are likely to be heading toward a rapid end.

Statistically, there is often participant replacement; however, that replacement will most likely not be identical to the replaced hedger, but better or worse. When replacements occur, strategic adjustments might have to be made quickly, which is not always simple, and early decisions and actions modify subsequent choices and hedging paths.

Futures is a zero-sum game. The net results for all participants can be negatively biased when commissions, fees, and other trading costs are introduced. Consider two firms that trade the same market, and both start with $1,000,000. The next trade will generate a ± $200,000 outcome; then, after just one turn, the competitive advantage has swung to the firm with the initial win it now has a $1,200,000 as opposed to its competitor's $800,000. A firm may find itself limited to buying only options-hedging strategies, when it has a funding setback, because the organization can no longer maintain suitable futures-only strategies.

Figure 4.1 illustrates how inferior decisions with their attendant undesirable outcomes are not readily overcome, particularly as the game (business) progresses. Failures (on a trial-by-trial basis) impact the ability of brokers/dealers, insurers, and other organizations to recover quickly, especially because the New York Stock Exchange, NASD, and other reg-

Market Conditions

	Difficult	Typical	Easy
Superior	C_1	C_2	C_3
Average	C_4	C_5	C_6
Inferior	C_7	C_8	C_9

Decisions

FIGURE 4.1 Highlighting nine potential outcomes for individual hedge trading actions, where C_5 is the average.

ulatory bodies proscribe the firms' ability to carry securities, transact business, and underwrite insurance policies, among other things. A rapid write-down of capital can impair an organization's ability to get even, because a higher positive return is needed for subsequent events and payoffs, given the smaller capital base and transactions capacity that replaced earlier and healthier financial conditions.

Figure 4.2 highlights nine potential outcomes for individual hedge trading actions. Figure 4.3 highlights twenty-five potential outcomes for the composite hedge account. Only the central one, cell C5 (Figure 4.3) and cell C13 (Figure 4.4) gives ordinary market rate of returns or successes. These central cells are the exceptional situations: When returns are generalized, all hedgers or all hedges produce identical results or averages. The marketplace, however, can and does produce dissimilar results for the participants, each of whom has his or her own objectives, constraints, talents, and luck. In academic circles, an elusive performance factor is called the stochastic factor, which governs the generation of ''better than,''

Individual Hedging Conditions

		Favorable	Typical	Chaotic
H e d g i n g R e s u l t s	Superior	C_1	C_2	C_3
	Average	C_4	C_5 Average	C_6
	Inferior	C_7	C_8	C_9

Note: Probabilities or percentages are not necessarily equal for all cells.

FIGURE 4.2   Nine potential outcomes for three conditional states and three potential results.

Composite Hedge Account Conditions

Composite Hedging Results	Very favorable	Good	Typical	Poor	Very unfavorable
Superior	C_1	C_2	C_3	C_4	C_5
Better-than-average	C_6	C_7	C_8	C_9	C_{10}
Average	C_{11}	C_{12}	Special C_{13} Case	C_{14}	C_{15}
Less-than-average	C_{16}	C_{17}	C_{18}	C_{19}	C_{20}
Inferior	C_{21}	C_{22}	C_{23}	C_{24}	C_{25}

Note: Cells are not necessarily equal. One division's (subsidiary's) activities can dominate overall results.

FIGURE 4.3 Twenty-five potential outcomes for composite hedge account given cumulative impact of individual hedging activities.

"equal to," or "less than" for expected outcomes, and which impacts traders, hedgers, and insurers. In the insurance industry, some firms perform better than others or have wider variations in their returns, even for something as basic as the underwriting of life policies, which have accurate actuarial tables.

DYNAMIC MONITORING

By adding subscripts to the statistical notations for hedge programs, we can arrive at a dynamic series. The following four columns represent the historic, current, theoretical, and expected hedge account valuations. (This approach can be applied to the basis presentations as well.)

Market Conditions

		Crisis	Difficult	Typical	Favorable	Easy
	Superior	C_1	C_2	C_3	C_4	C_5
D e c i s i o n s	Moderately good	C_6	C_7	C_8	C_9	C_{10}
	Average	C_{11}	C_{12}	C_{13}	C_{14}	C_{15}
	Moderately poor	C_{16}	C_{17}	C_{18}	C_{19}	C_{20}
	Inferior	C_{21}	C_{22}	C_{23}	C_{24}	C_{25}

FIGURE 4.4 Highlighting 25 potential outcomes for individual hedge trading actions where C_{13} is the average.

$H(H_n)$ . . . $C(H_n)$ . . . $T(H_n)$ . . . $E(H_n)$

$H(H_{n-1})$ . . . $C(H_{n-1})$ . . . $T(H_{n-1})$ . . . $E(H_{n-1})$

$H(H_{n-i})$ . . . $C(H_{n-i})$ . . . $T(H_{n-i})$ . . . $E(H_{n-i})$

$H(H_1)$ . . . $C(H_1)$ . . . $T(H_1)$ . . . $E(H_1)$

$H(H_0)$ . . . $C(H_0)$ . . . $T(H_0)$ . . . $E(H_0)$

The n subscript can refer to 5th, 6th, 50th, 100th week, day, hour or whatever time interval. It is a reference point that anchors the time series. The o subscript refers to the last day, especially as an expiration point. This time flow state is diagrammed in Figure 4.5.

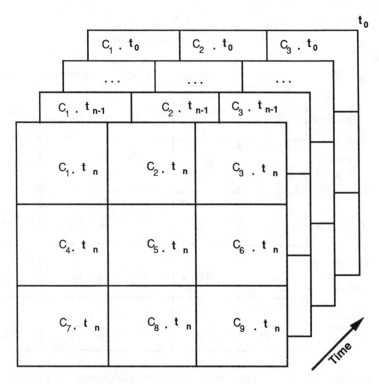

FIGURE 4.5   Time-adjusted matrix.

Thus far, we have made no claims about the equalities or inequalities of
these series. For cash-settlement futures, the last day o observations between the underlying index and the expiring futures contract are equal.
Mandated by exchange regulations, this condition produces complete
convergence. The basis behavior for deliverable futures can be less than
perfect, even when there are rigorous delivery specifications. Any number
of things can countribute to this: short squeezes, seemingly inefficient
deliveries that may not be popularly perceived as cheapest to deliver, or a
glut of deliveries that can find no home (storage) or that are no longer
tenderable because of crop-year considerations, such as August instead of
the following calendar-year February bellies. For financials, the less-
than-perfect situations arise when the maturity is too short, and thus, does
not comply with the deliverable provisions for Treasury note or bond
contracts.

If we look at Figure 4.5, it is easy to visualize the basis-hedge account values snaking their way through the maze of cells from one period to the next. The equality conditions probably become impaired until the last day. Until then, these disturbances give rise to adjustment tactics and trading-the-basis opportunities.

UPDATING AND TRADING

Once a course of action has been established, the hedge is implemented. If it is observed performing as well as was to be expected, there is little or no need for adjustment. Updating and trading a hedge program is brought to the forefront when programs go astray, rollovers are warranted, or when changes in position size are required to reflect increases or decreases in overall exposure. The purpose is to take advantage of a preferable premium/discount structure, and the related repo-reverse repo variables (among other factors).

From an individual basis hedge perspective:

$$C(b) \neq T(b) \neq E(b)$$

and the inequalities for the program are

$$C(H) \neq T(H) \neq E(H).$$

Adjustments, therefore, are to be considered. First, it must be determined whether an alignment is required immediately; if the extent of departure from equality is slight (or uneconomic) to close, at the moment. A slight dollar, ounce, or poundage differential does not demand immediate action. Each adjustment costs commissions, fees (exchange members are exempt from their own fees), and slippage from transactions. Transactional slippage accounts for the unlikelihood that all sales will be conducted at the offers and all purchases at the going bids even in a fluid market. The quote-spread differential between bids and offers holds the market together. The tighter the spread, the more liquid and efficient the market. Because an organization would be "going to market," implying the payment of the spread differential (here, slippage), or scaling its orders, then these orders are not necessarily filled immediately. Scaling is a variation of series of limit orders.

For the case of precious metals, when the current basis is less than the theoretical or the expected basis (C(b) < T(b) or E(b)), the hedger can consider a reverse cash-and-carry-operation, select a more opportune delivery month, or evaluate the feasibility of using options. For financials, the hedger would consider a reverse repo operation.

THRESHOLDS

If the current basis and the expected (theoretical) basis are equal, basis adjustment is not required to realign the hedge for that singular trade, although there may be extenuating circumstances. Likewise, if the current hedge and the expected (theoretical) hedge account are equal adjustments are not required. Adjustments and thresholds for a hedge account can be determined by the following formulas. To apply the formulas to singular basis situations substitute the parenthetical b.

$$C(H) \quad = \quad E(H) \qquad\qquad \text{generalized case}$$

$$C(H_n) \quad = \quad E(H_n) \qquad\qquad \text{dynamic case}$$

$$C(H_{n-i}) \quad = \quad E(H_{n-i}) \pm a(H_{n-i}) \quad \text{threshold/adjustment}$$

The generalized case lists an equality between the current hedge account and the expected hedge account. This means that the financial offsetting mechanism (hedge) is producing returns inverse to those experienced in the actuals or portfolio accounts perfectly. It must be realized that the production of perfect financial offsets is not the only rationale for a hedge; in fact, strict allegiance to this notion, particularly when hedging with options, can be quite costly and can place an organization at a competitive disadvantage within short order.

When the current hedge is less than the expected hedge, then the implemented hedge is not producing sufficient coverage, and the hedge must be adjusted by $+a(H_{(\ )})$. When the implemented hedge is producing too much coverage, then the adjustment is $-a(H_{(\ )})$. (For both of these examples, the subscript is omitted because the time frame for adjustment becomes a troublesome issue, and it will be addressed in the next section.) Theoretically, the adjustment process is considered instantaneous, continuous, and costless. All three assumptions are incorrect and must not be neglected or dispensed with for simplicity's sake; moreover, their residual errors are cumulative. One does not and can not continually or instantly update a hedge, although it may seem that it is under constant surveillance. Instead, an organization must determine and establish criteria (thresholds) to account for the disturbances and the adjustment processes. A threshold expression is established by rearranging the elements of the formula. The ends of the expression are the threshold points where point realignments are enacted.

$$C(H_{( )}) - a(H_{( )})<C(H_{( )}) <C(H_{( )}) +a(H_{( )})$$

As long as the hedge remains within its predetermined boundaries, no adjustment is implemented. When an adjustment is activated, it is of a magnitude that restores the hedge to the initial state. (Again, we have omitted the subscript denoting the dynamic element specification.)

RANDOM WALKS AND OTHER BEHAVIOR

The connection between the basis series and the price series is frequently the difference between the two, otherwise it tends to be a relative weighting arrangement. The n subscript used in the threshold expression notation is usually referred to as t, which increases over time and does not collapse to zero (time) as the basis-time factor (subscript) would, if a hedge were carried until expected delivery (out) or until it reaches terminal value for cash settlement.

Expressions for random price series are:

$$P_t = P_{(t-1)} + e_t$$

where P_t = current or t point price
$P_{(t-1)}$ = previous point price
e_t = random, error, or noise variable

In other words, today's price is yesterday's price plus the error term (or, the net change between yesterday's price level and the current price level).

If we use this method for the basis and the hedge account behavior, the result is: Today's basis is equal to yesterday's basis plus any net change. The revised notation is:

$$C(b_t) = C(b_{t-1}) + e_t$$

The concept of random error is critical to trading and hedging. In a stipulated hedge or exchange-for-physical transaction, the basis is predetermined and it is constant at the initiation point, over time, and at the termination point. For such hedges, only the prices (yields) change, not the basis. In the event that the hedger locks in a price (yield) through another hedging action (in addition to the stipulation of the basis) then both the basis risk and the price (yield) risks have been dispensed with, leaving only financing and second- or third-party performance risks. The second- and third-party risks that can arise include: the default on the stipulated basis by the side opposite the valid hedge, the collapse of the clearing member, or the financial impairment of the clearing house. Acts of nature, drastic exchange, or governmental actions can also influence the overall success of the hedge, but then the problem would not be in the hedging mechanism itself.

At this point, the adjustment mechanism must be responsive to other variables, such as financing or revisions in the expected hedge mixture, not to the basis variations, because the hedging basis never left the stipulated level. For other hedging transactions, however, the basis can be fluid, since its determination changes over time. Because most hedgers track some sort of basis activity, introducing basis-only oriented adjustments here could be detrimental to the hedge program; it also introduces unnecessary costs and potential slippage expenses, which are not trivial.

Frequent reactions to fluctuations in the hedge account can be very costly (this will be demonstrated in Chapter 11, Options). Two of the key issues are: What type of protection is sought? And, at what price? All other things being equal, the hedgers who have adjustment programs with a high cost structure will quickly be at a competitive disadvantage to hedgers who have programs that are ''equal'' but less costly to adjust.

Although the basis can usually exhibit some sort of deterministic mechanism, especially when evaluated for cash settled futures, forwards, and options markets, these other basis-hedging situations do not necessarily get implemented and lifted at one specific basis level, but rather at *expected* on-off basis levels. The principles of correlation, economic justification, and convergence, however, lend important empirical support and financial verification to these programs. Hedgers can expect the basis to behave in certain ways or to be consistent—not necessarily perfect—in order to be viable.

ADJUSTMENTS AND REALIGNMENTS

In the discussion thus far, a specific time subscript has been assigned to a pricing series and not to the basis (and hedging) series. This was done to stress that, although change occurs, how the response to it is constructed can have a significant bearing on the outcome of a hedge. Does the hedger seek to gain immediate and continual parity between the hedge account and the commodities or instruments being hedged? Does the hedger seek to preserve assets (reduce risk) within a bounded framework, while recognizing that numerous adjustments to disturbance terms can be expensive, counterproductive, and reactionary? Here, reactionary is defined as bringing a basis relationship or hedge account to parity with its desired theoretical (expected) level even though adjustments are being done over time. In effect, the hedge program has been thrown from an initiation-through-termination perspective to a perspective in which the hedger tries to balance values or relationships with a shifting past level, instead of toward the expected terminal value point.

The $\pm a(\mathrm{H}_{(\mathrm{c})})$ subscript can refer to:

1. Hourly adjustments
2. Daily adjustments
3. Opening/closing adjustments
4. Weekly adjustments
5. Any defined time frame

These adjustments can be between the previous night's equity and the prevailing market value or between previous equity and the prevailing equity, but with the intention of making the adjustments against the expected terminal value. The issue becomes, then, whether to adjust to balance prevailing equities to past values, no matter how current, or to adjust toward the objectives. The hedger may not always have to act to adjust the current against the past basis (hedge) values, but should do so only when specified thresholds are violated or when a structural event, which can force values away from initial estimates, has occurred. This shifts the focus away from the past-to-present perspective toward the present-to-future terminal value point of view, thus ensuring that adjustments become less frequent. Generally, ordinary influences and even extraordinary events should allow the basis to return to its convergence paths eventually, in which case, the subscript can actually take on a futuristic value that calculates the time frame from the present to the expected terminal date. To do so otherwise, or to do so on a reactionary approach exclusively, imposes adjustments when there are actually random disturbances, such as noise, and not structural developments. The overall adjustment can refer to an absolute dollar or other measure within the specified time frame, whichever comes first.

This demonstrates that familiarity with the adjustment process is as necessary to the hedger as understanding the hedge process itself is. Many approaches take the mean value viewpoint as the only solution which contains the assumption that the next change or realignment will be in the correct direction and will not wander from the mean value (which is often defined as zero, implying a random though stationary or trendless state). Often, at the most dangerous or volatile times, this assumption is temporarily invalid because a further distortion of certain benchmarks occurs and the marketplace and its basis do not behave as is expected. Although market participants attempt to act rationally, they are faced with different objectives, constraints, and problems.

SEQUENTIAL ANALYSIS

An effective way of determining and monitoring a singular hedge or a hedge program is with sequential analysis. Abraham Wald was the originator of this ingenious theory of statistical inference. The following material highlights this powerful approach. (For additional details see Abraham Wald, *Sequential Analysis*, 1973, Dover. The text was originally printed in 1947 by John Wiley & Sons.)

Sequential analysis does not presuppose a fixed sample or a trial size, which is usually referred to as *n*. Rather, the process determines the sample, so the number of observations necessary to terminate the testing process is open (variable) and is referred to as *m*. The acceptable size of Type I and II errors must be established beforehand. Type I refers to a likelihood of rejecting a statistically true hypothesis. For example, if one assigned a level of 95 percent confidence to a hypothesis or proposed program, an event which occurs only three out of one hundred times, and it happened, then one would erroneously reject the hypothesis if that event was the trial test. Type II refers to incorrectly accepting the wrong conclusion, or a false hypothesis. The probability of a Type I error is often denoted as alpha (*a*) and the probability of a Type II error is denoted as beta (*b*).

The time path and hedging process are bounded and actions are taken only when one of the predetermined criteria is violated. These criteria can be arbitrary, although they are better served by having an empirical underpinning.

A hedger wants to establish boundaries about the behavior of an often useful, but occasionally erratic, basis series. She thinks that the behavior is expected to be .60 favorable and .40 unfavorable.

The test is conducted by assigning values for *a* (alpha) and *b* (beta). Here, we will substitute .10 and .30 for alpha and beta. The likelihood ratio expression is:

$$LR = \frac{LF_2}{LF_1}$$

where LF_1 = first likelihood function
LF_2 = second likelihood function

Upper and lower decision boundaries are established by applying:

$$UB = \frac{1 - b}{a} \quad \frac{\text{(beta)}}{\text{(alpha)}}$$

$$\text{and } LB = \frac{b}{1 - a} \quad \frac{\text{(beta)}}{\text{(alpha)}}$$

where UB = upper-boundary
LB = lower-boundary

After substituting .10 and .30 for a and b, we determine that the upper boundary is 7 and the lower boundary is .33.

This binomial arrangement represents success or failure. A "1" will mark a favorable outcome and a "0" will mark an unfavorable outcome. For example, if the first movement is favorable it is listed as:

$$\frac{(.60)^1 \, (.40)^0}{(.40)^1 \, (.60)^0} = 1.5$$

If the next outcome is favorable, then the likelihood ratio will advance to 2.25; otherwise it will drop to 1. The drop is represented by 1.5 × .6666. This is the reciprocal case of the 1.5 occurrence. The procedure continues until either of the boundaries is violated, at which point the process is terminated. Of course other criteria can be superimposed on the overall decision-making process.

Sequential analysis is particularly well-suited for situations in which the costs of observations (and actions) are relatively high—trading and hedging—and when the manager or monitor may not have the opportunity for numerous trials such as for testing light bulbs, pens, or marketing surveys.

A PREVIEW OF DELTA NEUTRALITY

Option-evaluation models that are predicated on (log) normal distributions function well under the following conditions:

1. Small price changes
2. Independence between price changes
3. No costs
4. Instantaneous adjustment capability

Such assumptions, in part, account for disparities between expected as opposed to observed outcomes for deep-in-the-money and deep-out-of-the-money options, because the probabilities assigned to those potential occurrences are significantly less than what they should be.

Reinforcing these distortions between projected fair value and actual market observations is the shifting mean statistic that indicates (at the least) statistical dependence between observations, and (perhaps much more) the existence of trends.

Trends or conditional states tend to reflect a high frequency of relatively large price or basis swings. The clustering of large changes is easily tested for and validated, particularly given stratified data. The ability to stratify data is important because, sometimes, major moves up and down are highlighted by strings or runs of changes in one direction which can continue until an abrupt change in the conditional state occurs and generates another prolonged series of changes in the other direction (a sign change). For example, a market may catapult upward for 10 or more days in a row, only to reverse and then plummet for 10 or more days in a row. This behavior can be described by stating that the market and its changes were up 10 times and down 10 times; however, much useful information has been lost or neglected in such a simple description. The highest risk phases have not been distinguished, an insight that is beneficial to developing correct research analysis designs and helps the analyst break away from often used, but misleading, research designs and findings.

PART II
PRACTICES

5
Physical Hedging

TRADITION AND TRANSITION

Institutions such as the Chicago Board of Trade, the New York Cotton Exchange, and COMEX have a common purpose: They were established to help producers, merchants, and users manage risks. The emergence of financial futures and options instruments has benefited these exchanges and trading parties as well. Although many of the new underlying commodities are sec rities, their principles are the same as those for other commodities. Many delivery and basis problems experienced in the financial markets can be eliminated if a hedger has a full understanding of how to apply contract regulations, especially the exchange-for-physical provision.

ACTUAL DELIVERIES VERSUS CASH SETTLEMENTS

The trend of new futures and their related options contracts toward using cash settlements on the last trading day recognizes hedging's insurability over its merchandising capability. This practice sees insurability as an important quality and it defuses problems that can arise, such as depository problems, weather, short squeezes, the inability to move grain because of transportation strikes, decertification of commodity lots and so on. Unusual conditions no longer have the destabilizing capacity they had before.

SAMPLE HEDGING PROGRAMS

Chapter 5 begins with neatly defined hedging circumstances and examples and then shows how complications arise with each progressive relaxing of the hedging standard. Prices, interest rates, basis behavior, and external factors all influence the hedge program and its success.

Metals

Metals are an excellent model commodity group for the analysis of key hedging concepts and practices. Financials, grains, and currencies all have distinctive qualities, yet the underlying principles are the same for each group: convergence, correlation, economic justification, and consistency. The hedges are implemented to reduce risks or to enable firms to secure financing on more favorable terms than would have been available without the hedges.

By examining metals, we do not have to be concerned with waste, quality deterioration, moisture, infestation, temperature-induced volume expansion or contraction, and a host of potentially upsetting variables which eventually influence the hedging success.

There are behavior distinctions within the metals complex. Precious metals tend to exhibit widening or narrowing between the intramonth differentials (spreads), depending on whether the market is bullish or bearish or whether interest rates are going up or down. Markets such as aluminum, copper, and platinum tend to invert backwardation when the sentiment is bullish and to assume a carrying charge structure (contango) when supplies are adequate to satisfy near-term demand.

Cash and Carry

When the hedger maintains the commodity (cash) and carries it against a short-futures (or other offsetting) position it is called *cash and carry*. The procedure is frequently implemented to secure higher rates of return than those provided by short-term investments, and it highlights the impact of interest rates, price levels, expectations, and other important decision-making criteria. To see a cash-and-carry operation in its simplest form, we will examine the placement of a spread position that will stay for delivery and that will eventually deliver out the commodity that was initially acquired and hedged. This one-to-one operation demonstrates how destabilizing influences enter into the equation.

Gold. Gold, the primary metal for important coinage, serves as bullion (store of wealth) and is an industrial metal. Its financial connection is noticeable in the cash and carry: The effects of interest rates and price levels on gold (and other commodities) and the opportunity to secure financing charges or interest rates from its position are clearly shown. The fineness criteria is comparable to the many financial futures contracts' conversion factor invoicing feature, which allows different coupons and maturities for good delivery.

COMEX gold futures are based on a standardized contract of 100 ounces, with the implied fineness of 1.000, or perfectly refined gold. The precise fineness, such as .999, is established upon delivery. The trader/hedger initiates her position in the gold market by the placement of a spread, through which she purchases the nearby contract month and sells a deferred month. Upon taking delivery of the nearby month and paying for it in full, she is now long one warrant representing one lot of acceptable-for-delivery gold at a specified depository. If we assume that the warrant represents 100 ounces, the fineness will be less than perfect. The hedge has been slightly altered because its instrument is based on a standardized 100-ounce position that implies perfectly refined gold when, in actuality, there is no such physical. If the gold were only .995 fine, then there would be a fineness discrepancy of .005 between the actual (cash) position and the futures position, despite the fact that the entire operation has its foundations in the futures markets. If the received warrant represented 98 or 103 ounces, then the sold hedge instrument would provide somewhat too little or too much coverage, respectively. Because futures are predicated on the standardization of contractual specifications, there would be few alternatives to adjust for this simple one-to-one case. When positions become larger, there are more adjustment alternatives. The hedger must be aware of potential problems from delivered physicals (securities) that are other than the standard grade.

Table 5.1 highlights the value of conducting cash and carrys and their focal importance for other transactions and evaluations. Interest rates are assumed to be 6 percent for case one and 6, 6½, and 7 percent for case two, which would reflect the three-, six-, and 12-month interest rates. The cash price is $450 per ounce, and time periods are represented decimally. For

Table 5.1　Cash and Carry Differences over Time and Interest Rates

	Different Interest Rate		
	Time		
	0.25	0.50	1.00
Case 1	456.75	463.50	477.00
Case 2	456.75	464.63	481.50
Differences	0.00	1.13	4.50

The $4.50 difference here means a $450 difference over one year. Analysis assumed 6, 6½, and 7 percent for CASE 2 and 6 percent for CASE 1.

example, .25 reflects a quarter of a year and .50 reflects a half-year. If we use the futures pricing model, whereby

$$\text{futures price (FP)} = \text{Cash price } (1 + i)^t;$$

the 6 percent, three-month situation would be

$$\$450 \times (1.06)^{.25} = \$456.75$$

or a differential (basis) of $6.75 for the three-month difference. The financial impact of these small amounts is magnified with the passage of time. The simple difference, whether interest rates are 6 or 7 percent over the course of a year, means the difference in performance of $4.50 per ounce of $450 per futures contract. We can see that these differences add up quickly, particularly if a program is fairly active, thereby opening the way for considerable slippage as well as for trading the basis opportunities. Look at the $6.75 basis again; even this number is not absolutely correct because COMEX futures trade in tenths (.10, .20, not .05, .10, .15, etc.), which introduces the need to round the basis differential up or down to $6.80 or $6.70. The example is computed by:

$$\frac{\text{Futures price } - \text{ Cash price}}{\text{Cash price}} = \text{Interest rate}$$

$$\text{or, } \frac{(456.75 - 450.00)}{450.00} = .015$$

Because the time frame was three months or .25, then the annualized rate would be:

$$.015 \times \frac{1.00 \text{ year}}{.25 \text{ year}} = .06$$

or, 6 percent for the year. Time adjustments are conventionally computed on a 360-day year, which would mean the substitution of 360/90 or .25, as we indicated previously. To achieve accurate comparisons, it is very important to match the financing and alternative investment year's durations (360, 365, 366 days) exactly. Notice the slight improvement in locking in higher implied financing (repo rates) by selecting the deferred futures month here. These slight improvements enhance the competitive posture of a firm by producing higher internal rates of return, providing an evaluative framework for deciding whether to engage in specific rollover policies, and providing a framework for matching inventories/productions against various months' trading on the board. It can help to ascertain whether deliveries should be made now or later, or even to consider doing the opposite transaction, which is known as the reverse cash and carry or reverse repo.

Reverse Cash and Carry

The reverse cash and carry, or reverse repo, evaluates prevailing differences and then indicates, against the predetermined criteria, that the sale of the physical (security) and the purchase of the futures contract is the transaction of choice. Suppose that a firm can obtain 6 percent on its funds invested in Eurodollars, and that the prevailing differences between the cash gold market and a futures contract three months away is $5.70, which implies a carrying charge of slightly more than 5 percent. In this case, the firm fares better if it sells the gold on the cash market and reestablishes its physical claim by purchasing the futures three months forward. Because it receives funds now and reinvests those proceeds at 6 percent, the organization betters its returns from 5 percent to 6 percent, or 20 percent more with the base rate of 5 percent as the implied carry. Table 5.2 shows a sample of a reverse cash-and-carry outcome.

The firm can improve its posture by speeding up deliveries to take advantage of what is, essentially, interest rate differentials reflected by the intramonth differentials. Why reestablish the physical position? Assume

Table 5.2   Reverse Cash and Carry Outcome

Reverse Cash and Carry (10 Contracts)			
	3 months	Ounces	Value
Case 1	456.75	1000	$456,750.00	Implied value
Case 2	455.70	1000	455,700.00	Prevailing value
			1,050.00	Opportunity

for the moment that all the firm's gold is delivered out (to take advantage of the interest rate differentials); however, it has sales commitments that must be honored three months hence. By selling the gold at today's rates and pocketing the arbitrageable interest rate differential (which requires the reinvestment of proceeds at the prevailing higher interest rates), the organization is financially stronger and is capable of satisfying its sales commitments.

Comparative Perspectives

The organization will do better when interest rates, and/or gold prices, drop after the placement of a cash-and-carry-operation because it can gain the cash flow benefits of an improved short-futures position. A further incremental advantage is gained by reinvesting those variation sums. Rising interest rates, and/or gold prices, is not desirable. The firm is obligated to post additional variation margin funds. Under certain conditions, the firm can find itself in a funding bind, despite favorable basis action, if the demand for funds is increasing in a sharply advancing commodity market. One classic case of funding problems under these conditions occurred during the end of 1979 and the first quarter of 1980. At that time cash gold prices doubled, and what appeared to be favorable cash-and-carry opportunities turned into sour arbitrage operations. Although the position was hedged on an ounce-for-ounce basis (eventually the hedger would redeliver out the warrant against the short-futures position), the demand for cash to sustain the futures short was in excess of the actual paid-in-full price for the underlying gold itself. These unusual circumstances do not exist every day, yet they must be considered in position placements: The hedger must access the firm's ability to pursue such operations and must be aware that the operations will work if carried to the end, in order to capitalize on the apparent advantages. Premature exits can cause financial losses even if the position seemed like a lock. Even one-to-one futures operations or receipts versus futures possess characteristics that can distort the overall performance and behavior of a position. In such a situation the hedger would adjust for tails by positioning the trade to reflect the impact of unfavorable widening or contraction in the spreads and in the requirements for additional funding.

Tails

Tails are computed as spread yields: (1) the difference between the deferred and the nearby months' prices is divided by the nearby month's price and (2) this yield is multiplied by the size of the position. For example, 10 percent interest for one year and a $400 spot price indicate a $440 futures price one year out. When the position consists of one lot (100 ounces), the dollar differential between the nearby and the deferred is $4,000 ($44,000 − $40,000). This discrepancy is the equivalent of 10 ounces priced at the nearby level. The question for the hedger is whether to hedge the ounces or the dollars. To hedge on an ounce basis, the one nearby versus the one deferred contract is adequate. To approach the situation from a tail-adjusted perspective, the hedger would hedge 110 ounces of nearby gold (110 × $400 = $44,000) against one deferred futures contract ($440 × 100 = $44,000) to protect the dollars. Table 5.3 highlights the tails for several alternative positions.

Table 5.3   Accounting for Tails for Gold

	Tails for Gold (Contracts or Ounces)				
FCE	Value now	Value 1 year out	Dollar differ- ence	Spot ounces	Futures contracts
1 contract	$40,000	$44,000	$4,000	+10	*
10 contracts	400,000	440,000	40,000	+100	−1
100 contracts	4,000,000	4,400,000	400,000	+1,000	−10

FCE = Futures Contract Equivalent
NOTES: Spot price here is $400 per ounce.
    * To account for tails must hedge additional 10 ounces. Can not adjust with futures due to quantity involved.

The hedger who adjusts for tails has shifted the emphasis from ounces to dollars. The tail-adjustment technique removes the advantage of capturing the implied repo or reverse repo rate in exchange for protection against basis swings and wide price moves. In the situation where gold doubles to $800 per ounce, with a 10 percent implied carrying rate, the deferred month is priced at $880. Essentially, the basis (spread) doubled, as did the prices; however, the short hedger is obligated to finance the rise in gold prices and basis. A comparable situation occurs when a one-to-one ounce hedge has the nearby 100 ounces valued at $80,000 and the deferred futures valued at $88,000, or a larger discrepancy of $8,000. If the hedge is placed as 110 ounces nearby and 100 ounces deferred, then both positions are valued at $88,000, and there is no dollar widening in the spread (basis).

Silver. An example from the silver market will help in the analysis of a problem that arises when the hedged commodity has a grade less than the deliverable specification. A manufacturer produces silver artifacts that have a fineness of .900, or 90 percent silver. The silver is not exchange deliverable, so the hedge must take a broader perspective. The weight of the artifacts is 50,000 ounces or the equivalent of 45,000 refined troy ounces. At the outset, the hedger is faced with protecting the value of his inventory. Yet he is unsure whether to use nine or ten futures contracts because each futures contract represents 5,000 ounces. By focusing on the refined troy ounces of his product, he determines that nine futures contracts is the appropriate hedge position. This was computed by ascertaining the refined weight of the inventory 50,000 ounces × .90 = 45,000 ounces, or nine futures contracts. The formula for refined content or recovery rate is:

Total weight × Fineness factor (recovery rate) = Hedgeable weight

The hedging problem and its solution set have expanded with the introduction of cash and carrys, tails, and recovery rates to the process. The hedger must evaluate which of these parts has precedence and to what extent. By using deferred futures months for the silver case, the hedger may require fewer than nine contracts to hedge on an adjusted dollar-basis perspective (consideration of tails).

Copper. Copper and aluminum experience normal carrying charge, flat, and inverted market structures. We will consider the ramifications of inversion, or backwardation, on copper hedging operations. During inverted markets there are diametrical forces which strain to hold values in check; however, the intramonth differentials can often swing more than the underlying components prices themselves. Table 5.4 lists five futures contract prices and the dollar differences per contract equivalents from a seller-hedger's perspective.

In this inverted market example, there is a financial advantage for a producer who delivers copper immediately. The premium he captures for the spot month delivery will be larger than that for the distant months or even for the next delivery month. There are often hefty premiums for actual cash supplies relative to the board on a spot delivery as well. Sometimes these can be 10 cents per pound or an additional $2,500 per futures contract equivalent. A word of caution is necessary: Substantial penalties are imposed on the short hedger who cannot deliver copper (or any other commodity or security). Also, the penalties can accrue while the short hedger is scurrying to cover the short-futures position or while the hedge months are being moved forward to better approximate revised delivery capabilities.

Platinum. Platinum and palladium, like aluminum and copper, can trade in market structures that have normal carrying charge, flat, or inverted configurations.

Table 5.4   Copper Futures Market in Inverted Form

Copper Dollar Differences per Contract Equivalent (Price in Cents per Pound)				
Futures months				
December	January	March	July	December
Months 157.25	149.80	137.30	124.80	118.00
December $ 0.00	$1,862.50	$4,987.50	$8,112.50	$9,812.50
January	0.00	3,125.00	6,250.00	7,950.00
March		0.00	3,125.00	4,825.00
July			0.00	1,700.00
December				0.00

NOTE: The December contracts are one year apart.

Consider a hedger who needs to approach the platinum market from a long-hedge perspective in order to fix the price of this critical input. Once again, the market structure is inverted: The nearby months have premiums relative to the deferred delivery months.

The manufacturer has a steady production schedule and, therefore, does not require immediate possession of the platinum. According to his expectations, he will use 2,400 ounces over the next eight months. He decides to hedge 600 ounces per the four delivery months listed in Table 5.5. Rather than buying all 2,400 ounces now at premium prices and financing it, he can structure a hedge that will give him price protection and a supply of platinum when he needs it. This hedge has also improved his working capital position: He saved $25 an ounce, for a total of $15,000, by deferring some of the hedge from April to January. Additional savings were realized from other long hedges.

This example shows that hedges need not be limited to one month. The hedging framework is developed to determine what is at risk, and to evaluate the implied repo rates, the effects of interest rates and prices, the impact of nondelivery grades, and the market structure. A hedger who carefully chooses delivery months can establish price protection and improve the efficiency of the operation.

Consignments

Consignments and borrowing metal will be discussed together because the net effect is similar, although industries and financial groups may use

Table 5.5 Utilizing Multiple Months during Inverted Market

Platinum
Illustrative Inverted Market
Delivery to Delivery Savings
Buyer's Perspective

	April	July	October	January	
Months	611.40	608.90	602.50	586.40	Total savings
April	$0.00	$1,500.00	$5,340.00	$15,000.00	$21,840.00
July		0.00	3,840.00	13,500.00	
October			0.00	9,660.00	
January				0.00	

Requirements: 2,400 ounces
Hedged: 600 ounces per delivery month
Quoted in dollars per ounce

different terms to refer to these transactions. Essentially, banks, depositories, and major precious metals firms lend gold and silver to obtain interest on what would be sterile inventory holdings. Table 5.6 highlights a borrowing from the borrower's perspective, while Table 5.7 highlights a consignment from the lender's perspective.

The borrower in Table 5.6 has access to funding or metal to produce jewelry. The flexibility of this arrangement allows borrowing against work in progress as well as against refined bars. The user minimizes the cost of borrowing by returning the metal plus a fee (interest charge). The metal changes ownership as it is identified and used; until then, the jeweler does not have to finance the gold. A bank is the owner of the gold until the dealer takes it. During the time it owns the gold, the bank usually hedges its value, and in doing so, captures the implied repo rate afforded by the futures market to the cash market. This operation can enhance the spread yields between cash and futures and intramonth deliveries. Should the bank fail to hedge its holdings earmarked for consignment, then either the jeweler's failure to take the gold or if he takes it in a declining market, leads to a reduction in inventory values (unless there is a provision to account for this).

During January 1988, it was reported that the Newmont Mining Company arranged to borrow 1,000,000 ounces of gold for the preferential rate of approximately 1½ percent per annum for five years. These terms were considerably more favorable than those available in the fed funds, Eurodollar, secured and, especially, unsecured loan markets. The operation enabled Newmont to attempt to achieve its production potential by having gold available for sale that would be replaced by new production that was expected to come on line.

A similar operation in the jewelry business is a consignment, in which the jeweler borrows against work in progress or against inventories at

Table 5.6   Illustrative Gold Borrowing Given One-Year Interval

	Simplified Gold Borrowing (Borrower's Perspective)				
Ounces	Value	Implied value	Implied interest charges	Value plus fee 1½%	Net savings
1000	$450,000	$486,000	$36,000	$456,750	$29,250

One-Year Implication

Table 5.7   Illustrative Consignment Example from Lender's View

	Simplified Gold Consignment Lender's Perspective ($450 Spot Price)		
Ounces	Implied futures carry	Consignment fee secured	Total return
10,000	$315,000	$90,000	$405,000

NOTE: Assumes 7 percent implied rate, 2 percent fee, 1 year interval. In actuality, the transfers would be occurring through the interval.

preferential rates. The loan is secured by the precious metal content of the goods. The lack of initial and variation margins is an additional advantage of consignments. Disadvantages are the need to replace the gold or repay the loan in a specified timely fashion within guidelines, the need to borrow so much every quarter or designated period, and the need to sustain potential losses after sharp borrowing and gold market rallies. A firm can institute hedges to protect itself from catastrophic losses that can arise in such circumstances by purchasing options at acceptable strike prices to initiate coverage.

Energy Complex

The energy complex is principally composed of crude oil, heating oil, and gasoline futures contracts. The interrelationships among the three markets gives rise to processing spreads (hedges) known as crack and reverse-crack strategies. The crack spreads assume the purchase of crude oil and its production into refined products, heating oil and gasoline, given a positive processing margin. If this refining operation can not be conducted at favorable processing margins, then the reverse transaction would be implemented or, at least, evaluated in regard to prevailing market conditions.

Crude Oil. A short crude oil hedge needs to be established by a firm that produces 10,000 barrels of crude per month, or the equivalent of 10 futures contracts. The grade is below the contract standard and, as such, sells at a 70 cent discount to the board. The firm sold production at the market previously and did not manage the marketing of its oil strategically. Realizing that a hedge would stabilize returns by locking in favorable margins, the producer sold 10 contracts of February futures. The prices were five contracts at $17.40 and five at $17.20 for an average price of $17.30 per barrel. This range of prices and the average hedged price reflects that not all hedging is accomplished at one price level or basis level. While the first sale was 20 cents a barrel higher than the second, the overall strategy secured a favorable price. Subsequently, the crude oil market fell, with the futures trading at $15.90 and the hedger's production grade at $15.20. Although the market fell, in this particular case, the differential for grades remained intact. The producer priced his production at $16.60 per barrel, given the average futures price of $17.30 and the expected discount for grade of 70 cents per barrel. When the producer markets the crude on the open market and receives the $15.20 per barrel, he benefits from the financial offset generated by the hedge of $1.40 per barrel or $14,000. Table 5.8 illustrates this short hedge.

Gasoline and Heating Oil. We will now examine a heating oil firm buying fuel and locking in a price. Typically, its supplier charges a three-cent premium; therefore, when the hedge is established the heating oil company recognizes that it will gain comprehensive, but not total, coverage because the premium can increase or the basis can widen. With heating oil trading at $.5410 per gallon, the firm purchases five contracts of March futures. Table 5.9 illustrates this example.

Table 5.8 Illustrative Short Hedge (Futures Sold Initially)

	Short Crude Oil Hedge				
	Hedged/Sold		Covered/Buy		
	Contract grade	Production grade	Futures back	Production marketed	Financial offsets
Price 1	$17.40	$16.70	$15.90	$15.20	$7,500.00
Price 2	17.20	16.50	15.90	15.20	6,500.00
Average	17.30	16.60	15.90	15.20	Total $14,000.00

Table 5.9 Illustrative Long (Initially Buy-Futures) Hedge

	Heating Oil Example (Dollars per Gallon)				
	Heating oil price	Typical premium	Premium adjusted price	2½ cent adjusted price	3½ cent adjusted price
Before	$ 0.5410	$0.0300	$ 0.5710	$0.5660	$0.5760
After	0.4610	0.0300	0.4910	0.4860	0.4960
Change	0.0800	0.0000	0.0800	0.0800	0.0800
$ before	$113,610		$119,910	In @3	In @3
$ after	96,810		103,110	Out @2½	Out @3½
$ change	16,800		16,800	$1,050S	$1,050C

Key: S = savings, C = cost
NOTE: Five lot example, 42,000 gallons per lot

After the buy hedge was established, heating oil futures fell eight cents per gallon. On a futures-contract basis, this drop equalled $3,360 or $16,860 for the five lots. However, the firm was now able to acquire actual fuel at $.4910 ($.5410 − .0800 + .0300) per gallon, with the premium it must pay. Had the basis narrowed when the fuel market sold off, then the firm would have benefited by that amount. For example, if the premium came in to 2.5 cents per gallon because of depressed market conditions, then the company would profit by one-half cent per gallon or $1,050 (210,000 gallons × .005).

Crack Spreads. A crack spread reflects the relationship that exists in and the profitability of refining crude into two principal products: heating oil and gasoline. It views a long crude oil position against a short products position; the reverse crack poses a short crude position against a long products one. A positive value for the crack implies that operations can be conducted at a profit: A refiner could process crude into petroleum products at a gross profit margin. If the margin (crack relationship) is negative, it suggests that, for the market as a whole, the process is no longer profitable and should cease. Theoretically, a negative value implies the sale of crude and the purchase of the products. While this may seem an awkward practice, it is useful because oil trading operations swap oil and products and their different grades and locations. The situation effectively reflects an optimization problem that can be solved, in part, by product allocation through a transportation network approach.

The mechanics are similar, but not identical, to cash and carry and reverse cash and carry. The twelve-month futures contract delivery calendar for crude and its products enables the hedger to fit the hedge more closely to his production schedule. It can take two to four weeks to process crude into the specified products. To get an accurate representation of a crack spread operation for this time entails the use of the nearby crude futures contract and the products from the next subsequent month.

Agricultural Markets

The United States marketplace is a feed and livestock economy, because most of the grain produced is earmarked for feeding cattle, hogs, and poultry. The corn and soy (meal) crops are of particular importance because they are the underpinnings of the carbohydrate and protein components of a balanced feed mix. Agricultural modeling efforts are often boundary ones, with one boundary very strong (reliable) and the other less so. These boundaries have maximum and minimum values and are defined by the dominant marginal economics involved. Meal-price to corn-price ratios tend to reflect a strong boundary at the indifference point between meal and corn on a pound-for-pound feeding basis in surplus years. (Meal prices tend to hold price ratios that reflect their underlying nutritional ratios relative to corn.) Essentially, it becomes a large scale optimization problem: Input the comparatively cheapest to feed grains and proteins within life-cycle optimization criteria. In other words, feed grain mixes are not going to change radically for the animals on feed mixture one but they can change between feeding crops. Feed mixture two will better reflect the prevailing or locked-in relative prices since there will be less of a drop in feeding efficiencies by changing mixtures in midstream. Of course, changing feed can be impractical in specific locations. From the overall market perspective, in general, feed relationships are motivated by relative protein values for specified nutritional guidelines.

Grains. Corn, wheat, and oats are the principal grains that have active futures markets. We will look at corn and wheat from buy- and sell-hedge perspectives, respectively. One hedge has a fixed basis and fixed price, whereas the other has a fixed basis and price protection, but no fixed price. The use of options here provides a floor price, but also the opportunity to reap better prices should the market rally.

A poultry operation estimates it needs 10,000 bushels of corn per month. It is located in an area where the basis is fixed (the premium predetermined): It must pay a nine-cent premium for the corn relative to the board. By pricing the corn via the futures, the poultry operation can now have an established basis as well as an established price, once the buy hedge is placed. This hedging transaction has eliminated the price and basis risk, unlike the previous transactions we have studied.

At this juncture, the firm can offset the position by exchanging the two long-corn futures contracts against the physical purchase of corn or it can liquidate the futures position against the actual possession of the grain. Either way it protected both the price and the basis. Table 5.10 lists alternatives for this transaction.

A wheat farmer sets the basis for his crop at four cents under the board, yet he perceives the market environment as steady to bullish. He is determined to be protected, but does not want to forgo price appreciation. He buys two at-the-money puts against his expected crop of 10,000 bushels, thus gaining immediate price protection should the market sell off. The value protection is adjusted by the amount of premium paid (less any recovery value). The puts purchase establishes a floor price for his crop at the strike-price level. This hedge position has asymmetric traits: The farmer can participate in an underlying market advance and still be protected against any weakness in the wheat market. The farmer has already agreed to a predetermined basis, so without the put hedge or a short-futures

Table 5.10 Hedge with Futures Where Basis Predetermined

Poultry and Corn Operation		
	Cash position	Futures position
Initial	Needs 10,000 bushels $2.50/bushel	Opens long 2 futures $2.41/bushel
Terminal	Receives 10,000 bushels priced @ $3.55/bushel	Closes 2 futures $3.46/bushel
Net effect	Costs increase by $10,500	Offset defers cost by $10,500

position, he is protected on the basis, but not on the price. The at-the-money (330 strike-price) puts are trading at 12½ cents (per bushel) and the underlying futures at $3.30 per bushel. The total value of the put premium purchase is $1,250 (2 × 5,000 × .125). If the market remains flat, the farmer will have effectively forfeited the put premium and will receive $3.30 − .04 − .125, or $3.135 per bushel. Table 5.11 lists alternative outcomes for this hedge.

Soybean Complex. The soybean complex consists of three interrelated parts: soybeans, meal, and oil. It is analogous to the crack in the energy group. Both rely on one input (soybeans or crude oil) and both have two products (meal and oil or gasoline and heating oil). When margins are profitable in soybeans it is called the *crush,* and when they are not, the *reverse crush.* Each bushel of beans weighs 60 pounds and produces approximately 11 pounds of oil and 48 pounds of meal. The crush can be calculated by multiplying the price of bean oil by 11 and the price of meal by 2.4 (conversion factor), and then by subtracting the price of the beans. For example, July oil is 21.91, meal is 179.50, and the beans are 627 ($6.27 per bushel). This works out to 241.01 for the oil and 430.8 for the meal. Because the value of the products is 671.81 and the beans are 627, then the gross processing margin is +44.81 cents per bushel.

Table 5.12 lists several days of fluctuating margins. By instituting a

Table 5.11   Basis Established but Price Conditionally Subject

	Wheat Crop (10,000 Bushels)	
	Cash position	Options position
Market Behavior	Sold crop at 4 cents under board market @3.30/bu	Buys 2 at-the-money puts @12½ ¢/bushel $1,250 cost
Flat	Board remains at $3.30/bushel	Nets $3.135/bushel ($3.30 − .04 − .125)
Up	Board advances to $3.95/bushel	Nets $3.785/bushel ($3.95 − .04 − .125)
Down	Board declines to $2.95/bushel	Nets $2.785/bushel ($2.95 − .04 − .125)

Table 5.12   Illustrative Processing Spread Reflecting Gross Margins

	Soybean Complex Example		
Day	Input beans	Output oil	Output meal	Gross margins
1	627.00	21.91	179.50	44.81
2	627.00	22.00	179.50	45.80
3	621.50	21.91	179.50	50.31
4	619.75	21.75	173.20	35.18
5	615.25	21.65	173.00	38.10
6	635.00	22.15	177.90	35.61
7	649.50	22.72	181.80	36.74
8	649.50	22.91	183.00	41.71
9	627.00	21.91	180.00	46.01
10	657.00	22.91	190.00	51.01

crush hedge, a processor locked in the cost of his input and priced the finished products at acceptable levels, securing the positive crushing margin. The operation is now a success both financially and in terms of efficiency. (Similar transactions could be implemented with the energy group in order to obtain profitable crack margins.)

In the event that the finished products were to sell at substantial discounts, the opposite hedging action would be considered. Because the value of the products is less than the input, processors could curtail high utilization rates or look for opportunities to adjust production and input purchases. These transactions serve as checks and balances on the processing mechanism.

Cotton. A dependent application of ratio hedging techniques is dramatized by the situation of July and December 1986 cotton futures. During the spring and summer of 1986, the July 1986 contract attained a substantial premium over the December contract; in fact, the premium was more than the December futures price. Figure 5.1 shows the divergence in the cotton price series and the repercussions for a hedge program.

Consider a merchant who takes delivery of May cotton and sells a July to hedge the May inventory. Then as July is going off the board, the months of October, December, March and so on are at substantial discounts to the

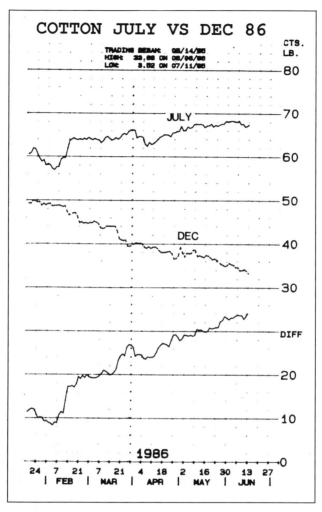

COTTON JULY VS DEC 86

SOURCE: Reprinted from CRB Futures Chart Service, a weekly publication of Commodity Research Bureau, a Knight-Ridder Business Information Service, 100 Church Street, Suite 1850, New York, NY 10007.

FIGURE 5.1. July versus December 1986 cotton

145

July and to the present value of the inventory. The merchant is now faced
with the problem of how to maintain a hedge. The solution is straightforward from a ratio perspective: Sell approximately two contracts of the
forward months so that the dollar values are equal to the July cash situation.
By doing this, however, the merchant will have sold twice the poundage.
Unlike earlier cases that entailed recovery rates, fineness, or other processing considerations and used ratios (less than one), here, the cotton is
the same but the timing of the crops and the underlying fundamentals are
different. If the merchant had implemented a rollover based solely on ratio
or dollar value considerations, then the initial hedge coverage would have
been twice as much as required (which was subsequently discovered).

Now consider a mill that takes delivery of July cotton at 65 cents a pound
and seeks to establish a long hedge to protect the input cost for December
material. On an outright dollar-hedge basis, it seems to require the purchase
of two December futures contracts against the acceptance of one contract
of July cotton, but to do so would increase the hedge coverage by a factor
of two. Besides, the mill is interested in pounds (bales) and could lock in
a much lower price by choosing a satisfactory month. This potential
overhedge condition, predicated on dollar valuation and not on units,
occurs in other markets as well, usually for rolling over hedges between old
and new crop months, even if the product is potentially redeliverable.

Table 5.13 illustrates the serious problems that can occur when there is
a required rollover for price protection. If the hedge months reverse their
unfavorable paths in an abrupt fashion, the merchant has essentially hedged
twice as much cotton on a poundage basis.

Looking at it another way, the December cotton could be purchased for
half the value of July. If purchases could be deferred and the inventories
on hand used (until the new crop came in), then there is a savings of 50
percent for waiting a few months. A similar situation occurred in the
July/October cotton delivery months. The hedger, therefore, must be
keenly aware of the risks involved in attempting ratio hedges because the
conditions that are considered stable can turn into something unusual.
Divergence may last longer than desirable, so the hedges and the adjustments must be strategically planned. Figure 5.2 illustrates an implied
contract hedge ratio.

Table 5.13 Variations on Ratio Hedge

Illustrative Ratio Approaches
(Prices in Cents per Pound)

1986 date	May futures	July futures	December futures	Ratio May/July	Ratio July/Dec	Spread July-Dec
307	62.21	63.05	43.45	0.99	1.45	19.60
318	63.42	64.23	43.82	0.99	1.47	20.41
404	63.45	64.25	39.81	0.99	1.61	24.44
418	64.13	64.94	37.80	0.99	1.72	27.14
502	66.28	65.92	36.86	1.01	1.79	29.06
516		67.00	37.25		1.80	29.75
606		68.18	34.50		1.98	33.68
620		68.30	34.25		1.99	34.05
709		68.45	31.89		2.15	36.56

NOTE: The July-December spread widens to premium, whereby December price is less than the premium difference.

Meats

Hogs, pork bellies, live cattle, and feeder cattle constitute the meat complex for futures. When corn and feeder cattle are purchased and live cattle are sold, the hedge position is known as a *feed spread*. It is undertaken when there is a positive feeding margin; otherwise, it is sold and is known as a *reverse feed spread*. The economics are similar to those for the crush and crack spreads—all of them look for favorable margins; but unlike the other two strategies, the feed spread is the purchase of two inputs and the sale of one finished product.

Pork. A packing house that purchases hogs for its packing operations implements a hedge. While most of the hedge is accomplished through the purchase of hog futures contracts, the purchase of calls complements the hedging process and allows the packer to take advantage of any decline in hog prices for that portion of the hedge.

Table 5.14 shows that the futures provide the tightest fit, or basis, while the options entail the purchase of a wasting asset. If price should remain flat, the option loses its time value, which may be the entire premium value.

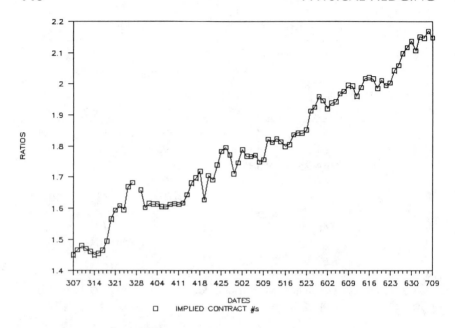

FIGURE 5.2 Implied contract hedge ratio.

Table 5.14 Futures and Options Complementing the Hedge

Effective Cost per Pound Analysis					
	Cash market	Futures	Terminal value @1.50 54 strike call	Effective net cost 2 futures	Effective net cost futures and call	Effective net cost 2 calls
Start	54.00	54.00	0.00			
Alternative 1	64.00	62.00	8.00	56.00	56.75	57.50
Alternative 2	64.00	64.00	10.00	54.00	54.75	55.50
Alternative 3	54.00	54.00	0.00	54.00	54.75	55.50
Alternative 4	44.00	46.00	0.00	52.00	48.75	45.50
Alternative 5	44.00	44.00	0.00	54.00	49.75	45.50

Beef. A major restaurant chain is determined to protect itself from fluctuating beef prices. It has several outlets that cater to the fast food sector as well as to the upscale dining crowd. Analysis has revealed that ordinary correlative measures show weak correlative properties between the necessary cuts of beef and the futures markets. However, the firm statistically determined that its average pricing relationship between beef and cattle prices is 3.75, or it has paid 3.75 times the value of the live cattle futures. Empirically, the firm has discovered that this ratio has averaged 3.75 with a range of 3.25 to 4.25. (Note: The ratio was more stable than that in the cotton example, and a finished product was linked to its raw beginnings, while the cotton was not processed.)

To protect itself against value rises in the beef market the chain purchases 3.75 times as many futures per pound of trimmed beef. Table 5.15 demonstrates different outcomes using the logic of the 3.75 ratio factor. Outcomes vary, dependent on the application of a delta-neutral initial condition, futures, or the matching of pounds.

The application of a delta-neutral ratio involved the purchase of 7.5 at-the-money options, and the application of a ratio required the purchase of 3.75 options per pound requirement.

Tropical Products

Cocoa, coffee, orange juice, and sugar are considered tropical products. The dangerous element to hedging this group of commodities from a production viewpoint is weather damage. Coffee and oranges are partic-

Table 5.15   Interaction between Ratios and Deltas

		(in Cents per Pound)		
	Live Cattle Futures	3.75 Adjusted Beef Price	Call @3.20 3.75 Ratio One Call/lb	Initial Delta Neutral 3.75 Ratio Two Calls/lb
Start	70.00	262.50		
Alternative 1	80.00	300.00	274.50	286.50
Alternative 2	75.00	281.25	274.50	286.50
Alternative 3	70.00	262.50	274.50	286.50
Alternative 4	65.00	243.75	255.75	267.75
Alternative 5	60.00	225.00	237.00	249.00

NOTE: Cannot buy a fractional option. Example stresses poundage analysis.

ularly vulnerable to subfreezing temperatures. All are influenced by the lack of water.

A sudden freeze can ruin crops And, thus, ruin "perfect" hedge positions. Organizations may have to exit from hedge positions at unfavorable prices and basis relationships, because the expected hedge was larger than the eventual harvest. This poses special problems because growing areas with weather-vulnerable crops have to rely on a weighted arrangement to calculate expected values. Coffee has a typical seasonal price pattern that peaks near the end of May to the beginning of June. Prices will discount rapidly and fall with the passing of problem-free time, such as no frost occurences. If no problems occur, the prices will be at their seasonal lows near the end of the southern hemisphere's winter because the crops have been made, in terms of both old and new prospects. Prices for many agricultural products, especially the tropical ones, are at their seasonal peaks when the crops are most susceptible to weather damage. (Energy prices peak prior to their demand periods because heating oil inventories are at their maximums heading into the winter heating season, and gasoline stocks are at maximums heading into the summer driving season.) Typically, prices will have absorbed the worst expectations by this time and, therefore, the highest prices will exist going into these sensitive time frames. If no damage, bottlenecks, or unusual factors prevail, then prices sell off, instead of rising, because each passing day removes some risk.

Tropical commodities experience their seasonal highs just before the new crop-year harvest begins, at which time the crops are most prone to cold weather damage. With each passing day of harvest, the failure of a freeze to materialize reduces the overall crop exposure. As the weeks roll by without major weather problems, a higher percent of the crop will be harvested. The plants or trees can often survive cold weather later in the season, and the young plants will have had time to become acclimated or a bit hardier.

The hedger should be aware of the unique growing-hedging-marketing process for tropical commodities. Expected values are particularly appropriate to hedging because they inject the insurability feature into the hedging process. Using options can moderate the impact of adverse events.

Coffee. Coffee is traded both in London and New York, however the contract specifications vary. Figures 5.3, 5.4, and 5.5 examine the situ-

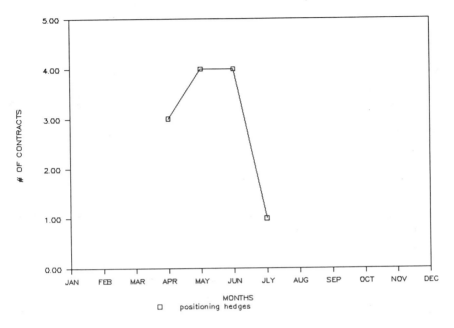

FIGURE 5.3   Staggered seasonally oriented hedging.

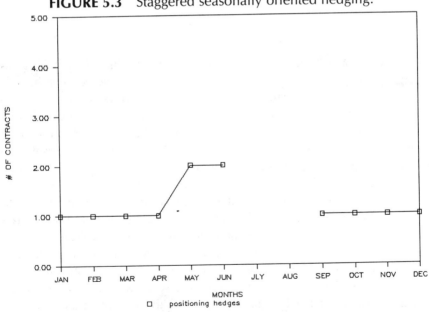

FIGURE 5.4   Moderate profile-flexible hedge program.

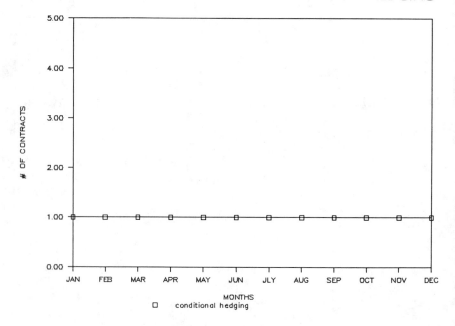

FIGURE 5.5 Low profile-conditional hedge program: contracts sold as crop progresses.

ations of three coffee growers. Each one is capable of delivering the equivalent of 12 contracts of New York futures, or one per month.

Figure 5.3 illustrates that the low-risk producer can concentrate his sales in order to exploit seasonal price behavior. Figure 5.4 shows that there is a gap during the height of the frost season for themoderate risk producer. Figure 5.5 portrays the situation for the high-risk producer: Her sales are intended for even distribution. Note that all three of these producers have not sold their production in one hedging action. Also, as time passes, they can elect to continue with the hedge actions relative to the condition of the crop. Additional hedges can be placed to reflect bumper crops as the risk dissipates. Conversely, poor conditions can warrant fewer hedges or even a reduction in the number of hedges outstanding. This production/ marketing flow analysis focuses on the dynamic nature of hedging.

Tables 5.16, 5.17, and 5.18 represent these same three growers who are capable of producing 12 futures contract equivalents of coffee. Weather-wise, grower 1 has low risk, grower 2, a moderate risk, and grower 3, a

Table 5.16 Dollar and Production Adjusted Hedge Results

Low-Risk Producer
Zero Percent Production Loss

Average Prices No Freeze cash/ futures	Freezes cash/ futures	No Freeze cash receipts	Freeze cash receipts	Freeze futures offset	Net adjusted receipts
1.35	2.05	$607,500	$922,500	$315,000	$607,500

Table 5.17 Dollar and Production Adjusted Hedge Results

Moderate-Risk Producer
(25 Percent Production Loss)

Average Prices No Freeze cash/ futures	Freeze cash/ futures	No Freeze cash receipts	Freeze cash receipts	Freeze futures offset	Net adjusted receipts
1.35	2.05	$607,500	$691,875	$315,000	$376,875

Table 5.18 Dollar and Production Adjusted Hedge Results

Low-Risk Producer
(50 Percent Production Loss)

Average Prices No Freeze cash/ futures	Freeze cash/ futures	No Freeze cash receipts	Freeze cash receipts	Freeze futures offset	Net adjusted receipts
1.35	2.05	$607,500	$461,250	$315,000	$146,250

Table 5.19a No Freeze versus Freeze Futures and Options Programs

Frozen Concentrated Orange Juice Example
(Premiums, Strikes, Effective Prices)

	Cash and futures	@7.00 in 145 put 1	@9.00 at 150 put 2	@12.00 Out 155 put 3
Start	$1.50	$1.38	$1.41	$1.43
No Freeze 1	1.40	1.38	1.41	1.43
No Freeze 2	1.30	1.38	1.41	1.43
Freeze 1	1.70	1.63	1.61	1.58
Freeze 2	2.00	1.93	1.91	1.88

NOTE: Cash and futures here are assumed equal to highlight options.
1 and 2 refer to alternative states.
Freeze conditions imply that the next trade would be x.
Analysis simplified to start and end points.

Table 5.19b No Freeze versus Freeze Futures and Options Programs

Net Dollar Receipts
10 Futures Contract Equivalent Crop
(Freeze—80 Percent Loss)
No Recovery Value

	Futures	Put 1	Put 2	Put 3
Freeze 1	$21,000.00	$40,500.00	$37,500.00	$33,000.00
Freeze 2	−15,000.00	49,500.00	46,500.00	42,000.00

NOTE: Cash and futures here are assumed equal to highlight options.
1 and 2 refer to alternative states.
Freeze conditions imply that the next trade would be x.
Analysis simplified to start and end points.

high risk. Grower 1 is expected to lose no production, grower 2 is expected to lose 25 percent of his production, and grower 3 would lose 50 percent of her production. While all three are located in the same country, regional growing differences influence the probabilities of serious damage if there is frost.

The no-risk grower locked in a higher effective price and priced all the coffee at its typical seasonal high. Grower 2 could not do so because there was a 25-percent chance of production risk and, therefore, established a lower effective price to lessen the impact of an adverse event. Grower 3 had to be the most cautious because a frost could claim half the production. Attempts to close out the hedge would be done at a moment when grower 3 was effectively overhedged by 100 percent, because she was no longer capable of satisfying deliveries against the outstanding 12 contracts.

Frozen Concentrated Orange Juice. The background analysis for a freeze-no freeze situation is similar to that for coffee's vulnerability to cold temperatures. High risk growing areas can be isolated by analyzing maps that identify them for crop insurance purchases. High risk areas are more sensitive to adverse events, so their hedges must be modified accordingly. The single application of futures could lead to undesirable results if there is a frost because the product is unavailable for delivery and the grower is temporarily obligated for much more production than she can deliver (until the lifting of the overhedge positions). The use of options or futures and options is more appropriate because the hedger can blend the two instruments to minimize time-value payments and possibly to capture implied carrying charges by a careful selection of futures contract delivery months. Table 5.19 lists outcomes for the freeze–no freeze scenario. If there is a freeze, consider the loss of 80 percent of the production as the outcome.

Notice that the selection of different strike prices for the puts changed the net time-value payment for the hedge program. In the event of a freeze, the value of the puts diminishes rapidly. Greater market volatility still reduces the rate of loss from a time-value perspective, although the in-the-money options then suffer a loss of intrinsic value.

SUMMARY

A variety of commodities has been examined in Chapter 5. Each example developed a different aspect of the hedging problem and its solution set.

There was a gradual progression in hedge instruments from futures to options. A hedger can acquire insight for making choices by being aware of techniques used by other firms and industries. Many exchanges and their regulations allow hedgers to use similar tactics for physical or intangible products. The hedger can identify and prepare for potential high risk and opportunities prior to the hedge.

6
Debt Hedging

IDENTIFYING THE INSTRUMENT

During recent years, the *fixed income* market has undergone so many substantive changes that this topic is better addressed as debt hedging. More and new instruments are issued with variable maturities, payment rates, options, and other conditions. Corporations continue to offer debentures that are convertible into stock although the conversion can be to securities other than ordinary common shares.

Twenty-year maturities are not all the same: They can vary in features such as the industry they are from, their credit rating, a call or put, their insurance, or the letter-of-credit backing. The interest rates may fluctuate according to stipulated benchmarks, making such instruments variable and not fixed in rate or maturity.

The stripping of securities has produced exotic instruments that represent *interest only, principal only,* and *interest and principal.*

IDENTIFYING THE RISKS

The main risks associated with debt instruments are: price risk (protection of principal value), reinvestment risk (protection of income stream), basis-level risk, and credit (default) risk.

The most important of these, price risk, calls for protecting the principal amount or the portfolio value of the instrument held by a buyer. The borrower focuses on securing protection through payments, or by renegotiating the instrument to take advantage of the lower interest rates that accompany the higher prices of an improved market. Reinvestment risk focuses on a firm's ability to reinvest income stream flows at rates comparable to what the bond is generating. For example, in a steep positive yield-curve environment, the near-term rates can be at 5.5 percent and the long-term rates at 9.25 percent. There is a substantial risk in reinvesting the stream of periodic coupons, whether they are fixed or floating, because the cash flow could be locked in at substantially lower rates, thereby dragging down the overall rate of return for the investment. While the value of the security can rise somewhat in this scenario, it is possible that the long end of the market will remain static and only the nearby end will be in the midst of a price rally. In general, the latter situation tends to occur for limited intervals because short-term interest rates are more volatile than long-term rates. Also, the short end of the market is a focal point for monetary policy—it is the engine that drives the market. Much written and empirical research substantiates this view of short end behavior, which is characteristic of other markets as well. Physical commodities, such as the energy complex, grains, or copper, experience wider variations in nearby prices than in deferred prices. These markets can invert because of either administered prices or marginal economic forces, which suggest relatively high spot demand compared to spot availability.

IDENTIFYING THE COSTS

The costs of hedging can be substantial, for they are not confined exclusively to transactional fees and commissions in the futures or options markets. Rather, they often refer to the spreads between bids and offers for cash securities, as well as the futures/options markets. A hidden cost is convergence value loss, which occurs when a hedger is long debt securities and sells a futures-contract equivalent position at a discount to spot. This is typical for a positive yield-curve environment. The loss occurs when the forces of correlation and convergence cause the differential between the cash instrument and the futures contract to dissipate.

Consider municipal bonds as an example in which the futures contract is predicated on the Bond Buyers Municipal Bond Index. In a positive yield-curve situation, the deferred futures months trade at progressively lower prices. The index would be above all the futures months because it is considered spot. A hedger of long actual municipal bonds sells futures and maintains the hedge until expiration. Then the forfeiture of the basis, which was established at the time of the hedge initiation would be complete and absolute. Futures may be trading at a premium to the index within a positive yield-curve environment sometimes because of erratic and volatile market conditions. These cases usually occur in negative yield-curve environments. Table 6.1 lists some of the convergence loss outcomes for different months. Figures 6.1, 6.2, and 6.3 illustrate the effect of the convergence impact as a considerable cost for the nearby, intermediate futures, and long-term futures. There are expected-value techniques which are geared to minimize the convergent loss.

In each case, there was *slippage* or a cost for implementing a hedge. Selling futures against the cash position alters durational characteristics. What had been long-term maturities now approximate short-term instruments; however, the net cost impact can be relatively high. Figuratively,

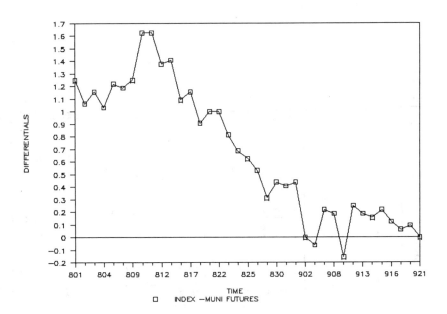

FIGURE 6.1 Municipal bond index—nearby futures contract convergence loss (1.0 equals $1000.00).

Table 6.1. Muncipal Bond Convergence Losses Date and Basis Dependent

1988		Municipal Bonds				Dollar Convergence Losses			
Date	Index	Sep	Dec	Mar	June	Index-Sep Loss	Index-Dec Loss	Index-March Loss	Index-June Loss
801	89.09	88.01	85.24	83.22	81.24	−1250.00	−3531.25	−5593.75	−7531.25
802	89.18	88.16	86.09	84.08	82.11	−1062.50	−3281.25	−5312.50	−7218.75
803	89.19	88.14	86.06	84.05	82.09	−1156.25	−3406.25	−5437.50	−7312.50
804	89.26	88.25	86.19	84.19	82.23	−1031.25	−3218.75	−5218.75	−7093.75
805	89.20	88.13	86.08	84.10	82.15	−1218.75	−3375.00	−5312.50	−7156.25
808	89.21	88.15	86.10	84.14	82.21	−1187.50	−3343.75	−5218.75	−7000.00
809	89.17	88.09	86.08	84.14	82.21	−1250.00	−3281.25	−5093.75	−6875.00
810	89.10	87.22	85.21	83.27	82.03	−1625.00	−3656.25	−5468.75	−7218.75
811	88.18	86.30	84.22	82.27	81.02	−1625.00	−3875.00	−5718.75	−7500.00
812	88.12	87.00	84.30	83.03	81.10	−1375.00	−3437.50	−5281.25	−7062.50
815	88.10	86.29	84.25	82.30	81.05	−1406.25	−3531.25	−5375.00	−7156.25
816	88.10	87.07	85.02	83.06	81.14	−1093.75	−3250.00	−5125.00	−6875.00
817	88.10	87.05	84.31	83.03	81.11	−1156.25	−3343.75	−5218.75	−6968.75
818	88.14	87.17	85.11	83.15	81.23	−906.25	−3093.75	−4968.75	−6718.75
819	88.16	87.16	85.10	83.14	81.22	−1000.00	−3187.50	−5062.50	−6812.50
822	88.15	87.15	85.10	83.14	81.22	−1000.00	−3156.25	−5031.25	−6781.25
823	88.18	87.24	85.18	83.25	82.01	−812.50	−3000.00	−4781.25	−6531.25
824	88.23	88.01	85.31	84.06	82.17	−687.50	−2750.00	−4531.25	−6187.50
825	88.16	87.28	85.28	84.05	82.17	−625.00	−2625.00	−4343.75	−5968.75
826	88.20	88.03	86.01	84.09	82.21	−531.25	−2593.75	−4343.75	−5968.75

829	88.26	88.16	86.13	84.22	83.03	−312.50	−2406.25	−4125.00	−5718.75
830	88.28	88.14	86.11	84.21	83.02	−437.50	−2531.25	−4218.75	−5812.50
831	88.31	88.18	86.14	84.22	83.02	−406.25	−2531.25	−4281.25	−5906.25
901	89.00	88.18	86.10	84.18	82.30	−437.50	−2687.50	−4437.50	−6062.50
902	89.22	89.22	87.22	85.30	84.10	0.00	−2000.00	−3750.00	−5375.00
906	89.22	89.24	87.27	86.01	84.12	62.50	−1843.75	−3656.25	−5312.50
907	90.00	89.25	87.28	86.02	84.13	−218.75	−2125.00	−3937.50	−5593.75
908	89.31	89.25	87.27	85.30	84.08	−187.50	−2125.00	−4031.25	−5718.75
909	90.00	90.05	88.07	86.14	84.26	156.25	−1781.25	−3562.50	−5187.50
912	90.07	89.31	87.29	86.04	84.16	−250.00	−2312.50	−4093.75	−5718.75
913	90.07	90.01	87.29	86.04	84.16	−187.50	−2312.50	−4093.75	−5718.75
914	90.19	90.14	88.11	86.17	84.28	−156.25	−2250.00	−4062.50	−5718.75
915	90.20	90.13	88.10	86.16	84.27	−218.75	−2312.50	−4125.00	−5781.25
916	90.16	90.12	88.08	86.14	84.25	−125.00	−2250.00	−4062.50	−5718.75
919	90.10	90.08	88.02	86.07	84.17	−62.50	−2250.00	−4093.75	−5781.25
920	90.07	90.04	87.27	86.00	84.10	−93.75	−2375.00	−4218.75	−5906.25
921	90.07	90.07	88.06	86.09	84.19	0.00	−2031.25	−3937.50	−5625.00

SOURCE: © Barkley International Inc ., 1989
NOTE: Losses are dependent on date and basis, initiated and terminated. The assumption here is long cash municipal securities and short the futures.

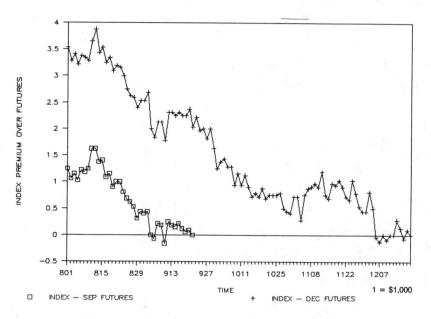

FIGURE 6.2 Nearby and next month convergence losses.

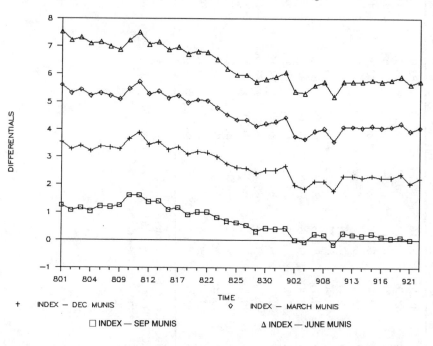

FIGURE 6.3 Municipal bond convergence loss for multiple futures contracts.

it can cost a hedger the coupons in order to protect the principal. The shortening of outstanding durations may not be the preferred strategy for the hedger, although it depends on his or her circumstances and objectives.

PREPARING BASIS TABLES AND CHARTS

The preparation of basis tables and charts begins the quantitative and visual frameworks and is similar to constructing basis statistics for physical commodities. The financial hedger can either subtract or divide the futures and cash price series, and in a further refinement, can apply a conversion factor to the selected series. Table 6.2 lists data for the 7¼s of 2016 and 12⅜s of 2004 and indicates the basis construction for both unadjusted and conversion adjusted series. Figures 6.4, 6.5, 6.6, and 6.7 are the unadjusted and conversion adjusted pictures.

BASIC APPROACHES

The basic approaches, beginning with the simplest, are: par value, market value, conversion factor, duration, and basis-point response. Other approaches, such as modified duration, are modifications of these five. A hedge program can secure the benefits of several approaches by blending the techniques to meet the requirements of a good hedge.

Par Value

The application of par value is naively intuitive. Match the outstanding par value of the specified issue with the standardized par value of the futures (option). For example, whether $10 million par value of 7¼s of 2016 or $10 million par value of 12⅜s of 2004 were to be hedged, both actual issues would indicate the placement of 100 futures contracts (10,000,000/ 100,000 = 100) as the appropriate hedge. The criterion is:

$$\frac{\text{Par value}}{\text{Standardized contract par value}} = \text{Number of futures contract}$$

Table 6.2 Treasury Bond Cash Futures and Basis Series

Date	7¼s	12⅜s	T-bond Futures	7¼s Decimal Equivalent	12⅜s Decimal Equivalent	Futures Decimal Equivalent	Futures CF Adjusted Decimal Equivalent 7¼s	Futures CF Adjusted Decimal Equivalent 12⅜s	7¼s Raw Basis Decimal Equivalent	7¼s CF Adjusted Basis Decimal Equivalent	12⅜s Raw Basis Decimal Equivalent	12⅜s CF Adjusted Basis Decimal Equivalent
881101	83.31	129.16	91.02	83.97	129.50	91.06	83.51	125.78	−7.09	0.46	38.44	3.72
881102	83.20	129.07	90.20	83.63	129.22	90.63	83.11	125.17	−7.00	0.51	38.59	4.05
881103	83.31	129.20	91.06	83.97	129.62	91.19	83.63	125.95	−7.22	0.34	38.44	3.68
881104	82.19	128.02	89.24	82.59	128.06	89.75	82.31	123.96	−7.16	0.28	38.31	4.10
881107	82.04	127.17	89.08	82.13	127.53	89.25	81.85	123.27	−7.12	0.27	38.28	4.26
881108	82.12	127.22	89.10	82.38	127.69	89.31	81.91	123.36	−6.94	0.47	38.38	4.33
881109	82.02	127.09	89.02	82.06	127.28	89.06	81.68	123.01	−7.00	0.38	38.22	4.27
881110	81.31	127.04	89.08	81.97	127.13	89.25	81.85	123.27	−7.28	0.12	37.88	3.85
881111	81.21	126.25	88.21	81.66	126.78	88.66	81.31	122.45	−7.00	0.35	38.13	4.33
881114	81.27	127.00	89.01	81.84	127.00	89.03	81.65	122.97	−7.19	0.19	37.97	4.03
881115	81.24	126.27	88.31	81.75	126.84	88.97	81.59	122.88	−7.22	0.16	37.87	3.96
881116	81.03	126.04	88.05	81.09	126.13	88.16	80.85	121.76	−7.06	0.25	37.97	4.36
881117	80.20	125.10	87.20	80.63	125.31	87.63	80.36	121.03	−7.00	0.26	37.69	4.28
881118	80.22	125.18	87.30	80.69	125.56	87.94	80.65	121.46	−7.25	0.04	37.63	4.10
881121	80.30	125.23	88.02	80.94	125.72	88.06	80.76	121.63	−7.13	0.18	37.66	4.09
881122	80.27	125.21	88.01	80.84	125.66	88.03	80.73	121.59	−7.19	0.11	37.62	4.07

881123	81.01	125.28	88.03	81.03	125.88	88.09	80.79	121.68	−7.06	0.24	37.78	4.20
881125	80.11	125.01	87.11	80.34	125.03	87.34	80.10	120.64	−7.00	0.24	37.69	4.39
881128	80.20	125.13	87.23	80.63	125.41	87.72	80.45	121.16	−7.09	0.18	37.69	4.25
881129	80.26	125.20	87.30	80.81	125.63	87.94	80.65	121.46	−7.12	0.17	37.69	4.17
881130	81.09	126.06	88.15	81.28	126.19	88.47	81.13	122.19	−7.19	0.15	37.72	3.99

Key CF = Conversion factor where

CF = .9171 for 7¼s

CF = 1.3812 for 12⅜s

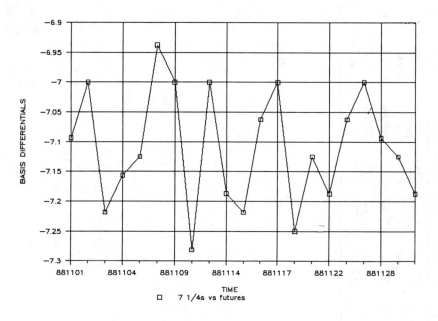

FIGURE 6.4 Raw basis chart.

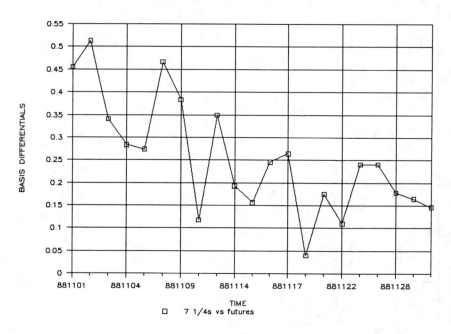

FIGURE 6.5 Conversion factor adjusted basis chart.

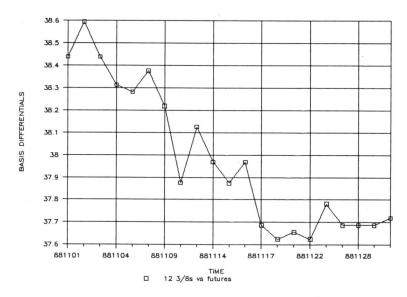

FIGURE 6.6 Raw basis chart.

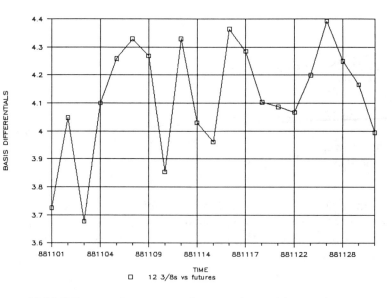

FIGURE 6.7 Conversion factor adjusted basis chart.

In an 8-percent environment, this 100-lot position would generate too much coverage for the 7¼s and too little coverage for the 12⅜s. It is a good first step, however, because it provides algorithmic guidance to the hedge transaction at hand.

Market Value

The market value perspective recognizes that the two debt issues discussed previously have widely different market values attached: The first bond is trading at a discount and the latter at a premium in an 8-percent market. We will consider the 7¼s trading at 88.10 (88¹⁰⁄₃₂, with a market value of $8,831,250 and the 12⅜s trading at 134.12, with a market value of $13,437,500. The criterion here is:

$$\frac{\text{Market value}}{\text{Standardized contract value}} = \text{Number of futures contracts}$$

or, for the 7¼s the criterion is:

$$\frac{8,831,250}{100,000} = 88.31 \text{ contracts}$$

and for the 12⅜s the criterion is:

$$\frac{13,437,500}{100,000} = 134.37 \text{ contracts}$$

When rounded, the number of required futures contracts is 88 for the 7¼s and 134 for the 12⅜s. This is an improvement over the first approach, which considered only par value and indicated 100 lots for either bond. The hedge has become tighter.

Conversion Factor

The conversion factor is a specific invoicing statistic and an approximate hedging ratio used to estimate the market value of deliverable securities relative to the futures standardized value. The higher the conversion factor value is, the more futures contracts are required; the lower the conversion factor value, the fewer the number of futures contracts required. Table 6.3 lists conversion factors in tabular form for the Treasury bond futures contract. Note that conversion factors less than 1.00 increase with the passage of time, while those greater than 1.00 decrease with the passage of time. The conversion factor is 1.00 for 8 percent issues of any maturity.

The conversion factor effectively incorporates maturity and coupon into one statistic, which is a critical reference point for the invoice process, although there are some deficiencies associated with it. The conversion factor also improves the accuracy of the hedge process.

The conversion factors for the 7¼s and 12⅜s issues are .9167 and 1.3876, respectively. See the June 1988 delivery column in Table 6.3. The new decision rule is:

$$\frac{\text{Specified cash bond par value}}{\text{Standardized contract value}} \times \text{Conversion factor} = \frac{\text{Number of}}{\text{contracts}}$$

or for the 7¼s, the result is:

$$\frac{10,000,000}{100,000} \times .9167 = 91.67 \text{ contracts}$$

and for the 12⅜s the result is:

$$\frac{10,000,000}{100,000} \times 1.3876 = 138.76 \text{ contracts}$$

The conversion approach is also called a weighted hedge. Over time, the number of contracts will increase slightly for the 7¼s and decrease for the 12⅜s because of convergence forces. This subtle change can influence cash-and-carry operations because the position was entered into at one ratio and exited at another.

Conversion Factor Formula. The conversion factor formula standardizes maturities and coupons into one numerical benchmark. The statistic is a key

Table 6.3 Conversion Factor Table

Deliverable T-Bond Conversion Factors

Listed below are all U.S. Treasury Bonds eligible for delivery into the CBOT's Treasury Bond futures contract (as of November 18, 1986) along with their conversion factors.

Coupon (Percent)	Maturity	Dec 86	Mar 87	June 87	Sept 87	Dec 87	Mar 88	June 88	Sept 88
7-1/4	May 15, 2016	.9155	.9159	.9159	.9163	.9163	.9167	.9167	.9171
7-1/2	Nov 15, 2016	.9434	.9437	.9436	.9439	.9439	.9442	.9441	.9445
7-5/8	Feb 15, 2002–07	.9676	—	—	—	—	—	—	—
7-7/8	Nov 15, 2002–07	.9887	.9890	.9889	.9892	—	—	—	—
8-3/8	Aug 15, 2003–08	1.0340	1.0336	1.0335	1.0330	1.0330	1.0325	1.0324	—
8-3/4	Nov 15, 2003–08	1.0683	1.0681	1.0673	1.0670	1.0663	1.0660	1.0652	1.0648
9-1/8	May 15, 2004–09	1.1041	1.1036	1.1026	1.1021	1.1011	1.1005	1.0995	1.0989
9-1/4	Feb 15, 2016	1.1402	1.1396	1.1395	1.1390	1.1389	1.1383	1.1382	1.1376
9-3/8	Feb 15, 2006	1.1332	1.1322	1.1316	1.1306	1.1300	1.1289	1.1283	1.1272
9-7/8	Nov 15, 2015	1.2096	1.2093	1.2086	1.2083	1.2076	1.2073	1.2065	1.2062
10	May 15, 2005–10	1.1900	1.1891	1.1876	1.1866	1.1851	1.1841	1.1826	1.1815
10-3/8	Nov 15, 2004–09	1.2228	1.2216	1.2199	1.2186	1.2168	1.2155	1.2136	1.2122
10-3/8	Nov 15, 2007–12	1.2383	1.2374	1.2360	1.2350	1.2336	1.2326	1.2310	1.2300
10-5/8	Aug 15, 2015	1.2930	1.2921	1.2916	1.2907	1.2902	1.2892	1.2887	1.2876
10-3/4	Feb 15, 2003	1.2458	1.2436	1.2418	1.2396	1.2378	—	—	—
10-3/4	May 15, 2003	1.2474	1.2458	1.2436	1.2418	1.2396	1.2378	—	—
10-3/4	Aug 15, 2005	1.2632	1.2614	1.2600	1.2581	1.2566	1.2546	1.2532	1.2511
11-1/8	Aug 15, 2003	1.2836	1.2812	1.2793	1.2768	1.2748	1.2723	1.2702	—
11-1/4	Feb 15, 2015	1.3611	1.3599	1.3593	1.3581	1.3574	1.3561	1.3554	1.3541
11-5/8	Nov 15, 2002	1.3211	1.3188	1.3158	1.3134	—	—	—	—
11-5/8	Nov 15, 2004	1.3402	1.3383	1.3357	1.3337	1.3311	1.3289	1.3262	1.3240

		1.3545	1.3520	1.3500	1.3473	1.3452	1.3425	1.3403	1.3374
11-3/4	Feb 15, 2005–10	1.3545	1.3520	1.3500	1.3473	1.3452	1.3425	1.3403	1.3374
11-3/4	Nov 15, 2009–14	1.3898	1.3885	1.3866	1.3853	1.3833	1.3820	1.3799	1.3785
11-7/8	Nov 15, 2003	1.3539	1.3516	1.3487	1.3463	1.3433	1.3408	1.3376	1.3350
12	May 15, 2005	1.3802	1.3782	1.3755	1.3733	1.3705	1.3682	1.3653	1.3630
12	Aug 15, 2008–13	1.4074	1.4053	1.4037	1.4015	1.3999	1.3976	1.3959	1.3935
12-3/8	May 15, 2004	1.4052	1.4027	1.3996	1.3970	1.3937	1.3910	1.3876	1.3847
12-1/2	Aug 15, 2009–14	1.4662	1.4640	1.4623	1.4601	1.4583	1.4560	1.4542	1.4517
12-3/4	Nov 15, 2005–10	1.4570	1.4546	1.4516	1.4491	1.4459	1.4433	1.4400	1.4373
13-1/4	May 15, 2009–14	1.5414	1.5394	1.5368	1.5347	1.5320	1.5299	1.5270	1.5248
13-3/4	Aug 15, 2004	1.5366	1.5327	1.5293	1.5252	1.5217	1.5175	1.5139	1.5095
13-7/8	May 15, 2006–11	1.5718	1.5689	1.5653	1.5623	1.5586	1.5554	1.5515	1.5483
14	Nov 15, 2006–11	1.5903	1.5875	1.5840	1.5810	1.5773	1.5743	1.5705	1.5672
14-1/4	Feb 15, 2002	1.5404	1.5875	—	—	—	—	—	—

SOURCE: Chicago Board of Trade, deliverable T-bond conversion factors, © Board of Trade of the City of Chicago, 1986.

invoicing factor and presents opportunities for cheapest to deliver and arbitrage-related activities. The formula is used by the Chicago Board of Trade as a standard for the Treasury bond, Treasury note, and the municipal bond contracts. The formula is:

$$CV = \frac{1}{(1 + Y/2)^{x/6}} \left[\frac{C}{2} + \left[\frac{C}{Y} \left[1 - \frac{1}{(1 + Y/2)^{2N}} \right] + \frac{1}{(1 + Y/2)^{2N}} \right] \right] - \frac{C}{2} \frac{(6 - X)}{6}$$

where: CV = conversion factor
       C = coupon rate of bond
       Y = 0.08
      N = whole number of years to call if callable;
             number of years to maturity if not callable;
             number of years to first call at par for municipal bonds
      X = number of months maturity exceeds N, rounded down
             to the nearest quarter (e.g. X = 0, 3, 6, 9).

Note: If $X = 0$, 3, or 6, the formula is used as shown above. If $X = 9$, set $2N = (2N) + 1$, and set $X = 3$, and calculate as above.

(This formula was reproduced from The Chicago Board of Trade's Municipal Bond Futures Contract, 1985.)

The conversion formula assists in calculating conversion factors for securities that are not deliverable yet are suitable for cross hedging. For example, they can be from different issuers such as government agencies, foreign governments, and corporations.

Duration

Duration refers to the expected life of a security. Discounted issues with no special features have a duration that is equal to the time left to maturity. For other issues, the duration is less than the stipulated term. Duration for these securities is affected by changes in interest rates and attached special features. If a hedger knows a security's duration, he or she can approximate the expected change in price, given a change in yield. For example, a 1 percent change in yield for a note with 3.5 years of expected life (duration) indicates a price response of 3.5 percent. Similarly, a 2.5 percent change in yield for a security with a 10-year duration indicates a price change of 25 percent (duration × yield change = expected price response).

Duration analysis extends the asset and liability management methodology further by classifying assets and liabilities into expected life categories and into unadjusted term categories. The classification of assets and liabilities into durational groups isolates particular risk groups. The different futures and delivery months, as well as the underlying securities, have specific durations that change.

Futures markets are extremely helpful in modifying durations of assets and liabilities. A manager can stretch or shorten the prevailing durations of the underlying instruments by including futures (the purchase or sale) in the portfolio. For example, a money manager has the bulk of the funds in discounted paper averaging less than six weeks. The manager stretches the maturity by purchasing T-bill futures, because the duration of the security underlying the T-bill futures contract has a maturity of three months. Such a transaction is not always appropriate; in fact, regulatory rules prohibit it for some transactions. In this example, the purchase of futures highlights the power to alter the expected life of a portfolio. Hedging is transformed from a simple sale of futures against assets into a process that may entail the purchase of futures to achieve organizational objectives.

One weakness of this approach in its basic form is that it assumes a flat yield curve, an interest rate situation where all interest rates are equal, regardless of term. It assumes that any changes in interest rates subsequently produce a parallel shift in the yield-curve line and not the usual response of hills and valleys. This assumption is not particularly problematic, however, and alternative hedges can be worked around this point.

The results attained by the conversion factor technique and the duration technique are close. Duration, however, lists indicated expected lives, while the conversion factor technique incorporates maturity and interest rate into one number that does not reflect the expected life of the outstanding issue.

Basis-Point Response

The basis-point response relates the dollar changes in the specified security to the standard contract change through the cheapest-to-deliver security. It is a popular method for hedging nondeliverable securities because it shifts the emphasis from a conversion factor and invoicing perspective to one in which basis-point value changes in the specified cash security are expected to be offset by basis-point value changes in the hedge. Looked at from this viewpoint, it has qualities that align it with the durational hedging methodology, which is predicated on price responses, given yield changes.

DISCOUNTED OR STIPULATED

The hedger needs a mechanism to relate common instruments, depending on whether an issue is discounted (such as a Treasury bill) or has a stipulated coupon (such as a Treasury bond). Discounting formulas and bond-yield equivalents are used for the discounted paper, whereas conversion formulas are the starting point for the coupon securities. The bond-yield equivalent formula places the issues on an arbitrarily equal footing: It does not necessarily make them identical. For notes and bonds, the futures approach is to standardize the securities to reflect a twenty-year maturity and an 8-percent coupon.

IMPLIED REPO RATE

The implied repo rate is a benchmark for evaluating which specific issues provide the best returns on investment. It considers interest income, the principal amount or market value, and the length of the holding period. By computing the implied repo rate, a firm can evaluate the locked-in implied repo rate versus the yield of the instrument.

This operation's physical commodity counterpart is the cash and carry. The approach is the same: The actual security is bought and financed and the futures contract is sold. When an implied repo rate is used, the futures contract invoice plus any received coupon proceeds, minus the cost, divided by the cost, and adjusted by the length of the holding period.

Alternatively, if a security will pay 7¼ percent and it costs 6.5 percent to carry, the firm should consider purchasing the 7¼-percent security and financing it with 6.5-percent funds, which, in effect, is a repo transaction. If conditions are the opposite, then the firm should contemplate doing a reverse repo (similar to the reverse cash and carry).

WILDCARD ATTRIBUTE

The choice of securities and of the delivery date is known as the wildcard. It is the seller's option to determine the exact securities and the delivery date (this does not apply for cash settlement futures).

The seller's option places an advantage in the hands of the short, since he can select what is to be delivered. Under unusual circumstances, the action of the short may be substantially different from the expectations of the long. Consider the short who delivers out relatively high coupons and long maturities in an environment in which the cheapest to deliver suggests low coupons and long maturities. The long will have to arrange for greater financing than initially anticipated, because of the weight given the conversion factor for invoicing purposes.

The potential problems most readily discerned are those that occur between delivery months for implied repo transactions. Had a hedger engaged in a reverse repo, then the cash securities sold short may not correspond to what is received in the delivery process. This situation occurs with physical commodities as well.

TAILS

Tails for financial futures refers to the difference between the contract standard and the actual securities delivered and pertains to the difference between the two conversion factors. In financial futures, even given deliverable securities, the variations for tails can be substantially wider than those for gold, in which slight differences occurred for the tails for deliverables. For example, the delivery of 12⅜s against the board during June 1988 leaves a considerable tail of .3876, which translates into a 38-percent tail.

Assume a hedger sold 139 futures contracts against his holdings of $10 million par value of the 12⅜s from the previous example. The hedger is faced with a dilemma because the futures contract mandates the delivery of $100,000 par value of deliverable securities against each contract. Does he cover 39 contracts and deliver out the $10 million par value of 12⅜s? Or, should he acquire an additional $3.9 million par value of the 12⅜s to deliver against the 139 contracts? It depends: The implied put feature of the financial futures contract can work to the advantage of the short here, particularly if, after the close, the market sold off abruptly. Also, the invoicing and delivery process is geared to the settlement price of that afternoon, so subsequent trading that day (up until notice time) can work to the benefit of the short. Assume that the market did sell off—the short could secure the additional monetary advantage of the tail multiplied by the subsequent downward price change.

CHEAPEST TO DELIVER

The cheapest to deliver is a reference point for the more likely "security to be delivered" against a financial futures contract. The cheapest-to-deliver security changes over time and through prevailing interest rates. In general, when the market interest rate is greater than the 8-percent standard, shorts will favor the delivery of low-coupon and long-maturity issues; when the market rate is less than 8 percent, they favor the delivery of high-coupon issues.

Discrepancies among the cheapest to deliver are due to the construction of the conversion factor and its role in invoicing. By carefully evaluating the prevailing prices of cash securities against their delivered-in value, a firm can identify those issues that are cheaper to deliver, though not necessarily the cheapest to deliver.

Sometimes, the cheapest-to-deliver security does not exist in sufficient quantities. This can occur despite a large outstanding amount because the security may have been stripped, and locating all the parts in the correct arrangement can be a costly and time-consuming task. Additionally, the marketplace's perception of a cheapest-to-deliver issue does not guarantee that only that issue will be tendered. Individual circumstances can prompt a futures short to deliver other securities. Large inventories or rapid disposition of "unwanted" securities can enter into the delivery equation and hold more sway than the strictly defined cheapest-to-deliver issues. While some deliveries can appear less attractive than others, there can still be economic justification for these seemingly maverick transactions. (Recall the implications of the tails.)

SHORT-TERM SECURITIES

Unlike intermediate or long-term obligations, short-term issues tend to be discounted and not to be coupon securities. Discount securities of this type are classified as zero-coupon securities. This condition precludes certain durational adjustments that may be warranted for other debt hedges because the duration of these issues is not sensitive to changes in interest rates.

Consider the case of a Treasury bill. The active futures contract calls for the delivery of a 90-day bill with a face value of $1,000,000. To hedge a $55,000 three-month issue is strained, at best, even if the hedger applies delta-oriented hedging techniques, because there is a gross mismatching in values. The situation is much clearer with a $2,000,000 three-month T-bill position. The hedge is the placement of two futures contracts because this provides the closest integer fit for the hedge.

The duration hedge of a zero coupon of a six-month or one-year bill is readily accomplished by placing multiple positions of the Treasury bill futures contract. For example, to hedge a $2,000,000 six-month T-bill, the hedger positions four contracts of three-month T-bills and not two, since the appropriate criteria is two contracts to account for the face (par) value and to multiply that component by two to account for the longer duration (twice) of the six-month T-bill, relative to the three-month standardized futures contract.

INTERMEDIATE AND LONG-TERM SECURITIES

Distinctions between intermediate and long-term securities have become hazy. Durational contexts have proven more important than the stated terms to maturity, in many cases. Option features can drastically modify the expected life of these securities. Bonds or mortgages with listed lives of 25 years can actually be better described and hedged as five-, seven-, or twelve-year securities. The several futures and options contracts for bonds and notes are of different durational periods and are useful for many applications. One Treasury-bond futures contract, carefully used, can weigh a hedge so that adjustment and maintenance costs are lessened (there is a potential for less margining and smaller transactional costs). Other short-term instruments, however, have the added appeal of flexibility. All of these points are important, particularly for cross hedging corporate bonds, revenue bonds, convertible bonds, or other debentures. Even the shift from Treasury offerings to agency offerings can spark substantive changes in the hedging mix.

FIXED OR VARIABLE RATE

It is equally important to determine the payment terms of debt issues. While the maturities may be fixed and not subject to call, put, or prepayment provisions, the coupon may vary widely over time. Consider some adjustable rate mortgages—they may be limited to interest rate changes not to exceed a specified percent on each renewal date. Some instruments may have upside caps not only per period but for the life of the mortgage as well. The mechanism for the instrument's coupons can be a short-term index or a three-, a six-, or twelve-month Treasury rate. A basket of intermediate-term Treasury security rates, Federal Home Loan Board rates, or other designated benchmark can serve this purpose too. These rates may react differently to money and credit market conditions, so to protect the position of the institution, as well as that of the borrower, more sophisticated techniques and analyses need to be performed.

MUNICIPAL BOND FUTURES AND OPTIONS

We will examine municipal bond futures and options to illustrate the influence of various hedging techniques and how they strategically alter a hedge position. Both instruments share a common expiration and have settlement in cash based upon an index, which precludes convergence problems common for Treasury notes and bonds.

A portfolio manager has $10 million par value of diversified holdings. He decides to hedge the portfolio and commences the process with the sale of futures to protect 50 percent of the holdings. The delivery month breakdown for this operation is 30 percent in the nearby and 20 percent in the next delivery month. The yield curve is sloping positively, so the hedger must sell the futures at progressive discounts to the cash market. This basis relationship will result in convergence loss for the hedger. Table 6.4 indicates the amount of the convergence loss.

It is important to note that intramonth spreads can behave differently from the theoretical models on a daily basis going into the final month of the nearby delivery. There are times when the discount between the nearby month and the next delivery month widens. This can indicate that rollovers of positions into the next available delivery month would be conducted at disadvantageous price and basis levels.

Table 6.4 Convergence Loss Expressed in Dollars for Partial Hedge

		Illustrative $10,000,000 Portfolio Fifty Percent Hedge		
"Cash" bond buyer index	"20%" December futures	"30%" March futures	December convergence loss	March convergence loss
90.00	89.75	88.50	$5,000.00	$45,000.00

NOTE: Bond index and futures are expressed as decimals here.
Cash holdings correspond to index composition.
There were approximately two weeks to expiration for the Decembers.

Subsequently, the portfolio manager decides to increase coverage by purchasing at-the-money puts to protect an additional 25 percent of the portfolio. The manager's concern is the establishment of a floor and not delta-neutrality. Table 6.5 illustrates the impact of the purchase of the 25 at-the-money puts. These purchased options incur implied convergence losses that are attributable to time-value decay if there are flat or rising market prices for municipals. Only if there are declining market prices will time value be transformed into intrinsic value.

Table 6.5 Impact of 25 At-the-money Puts

	Effective Price after Put Purchase	
"Cash" Bond Index	@32/64 Purchase of Puts	Premium Cost or Loss
90.00	89.50	$12,500

Prices are in decimal equivalents.
NOTE: There is a similarity between convergence loss and premium.
In the event of a flat market, both techniques lose value over time.
The purchase of 25 at-the-money puts synthesized 25 percent of the position into a synthetic call.
The purchase of 50 at-the-money puts would have doubled the cost for initial delta-neutral state.

The put purchase alters the hedge mix: It allows the portfolio manager to capture subsequent value increases in the underlying securities that were paired against the purchased at-the-money puts. The inclusion of the purchased puts has modified this portion of the portfolio to reflect a *synthetic call.*

The manager decides to recapture some of the time value that was paid out for the purchase of the puts by selling 25 or 50 at-the-money calls. If the portfolio manager sells 25 at-the-money calls, he has effectively changed the total option configuration into a synthetic short-futures position (long 25 at-the-money puts and short 25 at-the-money calls); and thus, has 75 percent of the portfolio covered by short futures or short-futures contract equivalents. If the underlying market remains flat, the hedger forfeits the put premium and the calls move into the money as futures progressively close in on the cash index.

Alternatively, the coverage could be viewed as complete: Fifty percent of the portfolio is covered from the sale of futures, 25 percent is protected by a floor from the purchase of the puts and 25 percent is a covered call sale (the sale of one at-the-money call per futures contract equivalent).

The covered call sale is the weakest link in this hedge because it provides downside coverage only to the extent of the premium received; beyond that point, the portfolio manager is on his own. The sale of calls

Table 6.6   Sale of At-the-money Calls

Effective Price after Call Write		
"Cash" Bond Index	@32/64 Sale of Calls	Premium Received or Gain
90.00	90.50	$12,500

Prices are in decimal equivalents.

NOTE: There is a similarity between time values for at-the-money options.

Here, in the event of a flat market, the hedger secures the time value for the written calls.

Sale of 25 at-the-money calls synthesized 25 percent of position into a synthetic put.

Sale of 50 at-the-money calls would have doubled coverage for initial delta-neutral state.

predicated on delta neutrality addresses the problem of limited coverage. The transaction requires the sale of two at-the-money calls, which doubles the downside protection (the manager receives twice the premium). There are, however, several unfavorable factors associated with this process. The first concerns a substantial jump in the underlying market which pushes the call options into the money and requires the financing of intrinsic value. It is conceivable that the volatility has increased as well, which subjects these call premiums to greater upside pressure. Finally, the margining for this transaction would be greater now, and these additional trades would be considered uncovered writes.

These conditions highlight the need for a strategic orientation. A hedger can try to minimize convergence and time-value decay losses by implementing a program aimed at particular interest-rate environments. Volatile conditions can adversely influence the adjustment process and incur higher-than-expected costs for the program.

LETTING THE STRING OUT

This topic dramatizes the mathematical progression from a simple hedge to a delta-hedge ratio-conversion factor adjusted hedge. We will study the impact of using options, and for our purposes, at-the-money ones with a delta of .50. The par amount is $10 million of the 12⅜s.

The options contract is predicated on the futures contract, which seems to indicate a one-to-one correspondence between the futures and the options. This is not strictly so, however. If the hedger purchases 100 at-the-money puts to protect the inventory value of his holdings, this position is partially correct. To compensate for the greater market value of the 12⅜s relative to the nominal 8-percent coupon of the futures/options contracts, the conversion factor approach dictates the purchase of 139 options (CF = 1.3876). However, to delta neutralize the position, the hedger has to purchase 278 put options. This is shown by:

$$\frac{\text{Cash par value}}{\text{Contract par value}} \times \text{CF} \times \text{Delta hedge ratio} = \text{Number of options}$$

or,

$$\frac{10,000,000}{100,000} \times 1.3876 \times \left(\frac{1}{.5}\right) = 278 \text{ (rounded) contracts}$$

Such a progression of the hedge can be quite dangerous. Assume the hedge was implemented with sold calls of the same delta value. If the market experiences a sharp rally, especially after hours, then the portfolio manager will find the position substantially overhedged.

HYBRIDIZATION

Securities have become increasingly complex. Sweeteners, option features, and other appendages alter the essential characteristics of these securities. For example, a twenty-eight-year bond issued with a call date of after five years is quoted as priced to the first call date and not necessarily to the twenty-eighth-year. Thus, seemingly long-term securities may actually behave as intermediate or short-term instruments. Moreover, the optional features can cause countervailing pricing influences—the underlying debenture versus the option—and not necessarily reinforce each other. This hybridization requires the evaluation of the components in order to arrive at a value for the opposite instrument.

Implicit Features

The two major implied characteristics are: implied puts and implied calls. Unless a trader, hedger, or portfolio manager is aware of the actual issuance terms for a specific issue, proposed or implemented hedges may be inappropriate or weaker in fact than actually intended. These features are more difficult to comprehend because they are less obvious than those explicitly stated.

Implied Put Option. The implied put characteristic pertains to potential delivery mechanics that allow a futures short to exploit cash flow situations that come from coupon mismatchings. It arises when the cash market declines after the futures close. At that time, the futures short can determine if, when, and what to deliver. (The actual delivery configuration can be different from the ideal hedge configuration.) Recall the conversion factor adjustment: More or less contracts, relative to par value, need to be hedged to achieve better market value and basis-point response fits. The short, under certain conditions, can arbitrage the hedge position to exploit a basis swing. First, the hedger can purchase additional cash securities at lower prices, relative to the futures close and then, he can deliver the total package against the outstanding futures-short position in a matching against par values.

Implied Call Option. Implied calls are typically associated with mortgages, particularly those granted for the residential market. If rates move lower, the borrower (mortgagee) may prepay or refinance the outstanding mortgage balance. Prepayments need not be complete; they can be partial, which accounts for some of the complexity facing owners (mortgagors) of such debt instruments. Essentially, the lender has granted or written an implied call to the borrower, who can readjust the payment stream of high coupons for lower ones. The main problem is that when rates drop, the expectation is for debt instruments to increase in value; but these increases may become restrained, particularly as the downward move in rates becomes greater. The advantage to the borrower is a wider choice: to reconsider his or her outstanding obligation and refinance or repay. This scenario constrains the upside potential for the value of such issues.

Conversely, if there is a substantial advance in interest rates, the borrower will be content with the comparatively low rates relative to new issuances in the mortgage market. The owner of such instruments is faced with a sharp decline in market value.

Explicit Features

Explicit features are readily recognized as the stated call provisions, put provisions, and the occurrence of anniversary dates or windows that allow the party holding the option the right to exercise it. These features must be evaluated individually and then compositely to arrive at a better approximation of the value of the chosen security. The improved approximation of total value enhances the hedge identification as well.

Table 6.7   The Effect of Combining Strategies

| | Two Alternative Strategies | | | | | | | |
| | Alternative 1 | | | | Alternative 2 | | | |
	Sold 50 futures	Buy 25 puts	Sold 25 calls	Combined coverage	Sold 50 futures	Buy 50 puts	Sold 50 calls	Combined coverage
FCE	50	12.5	12.5	75	50	25	25	100

Key: FCE = Futures Contract Equivalent
NOTE: Options here are at-the-money.
Depending on floor, cap, or futures contract-equivalent perspective, different strategies can be initiated.

Putable Bonds

Putable bonds allow the purchaser of the bond to present it to the issuer on a specified date for redemption at the stipulated exercise price, which we will view as the par value. A bear market is the incentive for doing this: The market value of the issue is diminished, and the owner has the opportunity to recoup, in part or in full, the price paid for it.

Callable Bonds

The issuing body retains the right to call in such securities for early redemption, according to the terms of the instrument. In the event of lower capital costs, an organization is expected to reissue its debt at more favorable rates and terms. These features can dramatically alter the duration of a security.

SUMMARY

The correct identification of the debt instrument is vital. It must be determined whether the issue is floating-rate or fixed-rate oriented, is comparatively long or short in duration, has attached option characteristics, implied or explicit, and has other value-added or diminishing features attached. To arrive at an accurate market value, the hedger must calculate the theoretical values and hedgeable characteristics of all of these factors. The implied repo and reverse repo rates act as the equilibrium forces on the yield curve and as evaluative focal points for the carrying or shorting of securities. (These processes are the cash and carry and the reverse cash and carry for physical commodities.)

7
Asset and Liability Management

COMPARISONS

Hedging and asset liability management have much in common: Both are structured to control risks and capitalize on opportunities and both seek to generate offsetting positions. Traditionally, firms tried to protect against inventory, production, or anticipated input requirements. Asset and liability management focuses on restructuring maturities and changing the composition of balance-sheet items through hedging techniques. These techniques include, but are not limited to, transactions in futures, options, forwards, or swaps. Some techniques are off-balance sheet tools; nevertheless, they alter reportable balance sheet items.

ASSETS AND LIABILITIES

Common assets are: fed funds sold, commercial loans, instalment loans, fixed-rate mortgages, adjustable rate mortgages (ARMS), municipal securities, and U.S. government securities. Common liabilities are: fed funds bought, demand deposits, savings accounts, and certificates of deposit (CDs). For many financial institutions, the asset and liability management problem focuses on funding long-term commitments with short-term sources. This chronic mismatching of maturities between assets and liabilities is a central issue for risk management for treasurers and asset and liability management committees (ALCOs).

MATCHED FUNDING

The basic approach to asset and liability management is to match the maturities of fund sources to fund uses. A natural hedge or intrinsic offset occurs when an 18-month certificate of deposit finances an 18-month commercial loan. The depository strives to stabilize the maturity or duration of the funding liability by attaching substantial penalties for early withdrawal or liquidation of the CD.

There are multiple funding maturities and multiple uses: The more important funding maturities can be categorized into distinct periods or *buckets* for both assets and liabilities. Simple, duration, and modified-duration weighted maturities are variations on the matching principle.

INSTRUMENTS

Asset and liability managers have access to many risk management instruments. Among these are: forwards, forward rate agreements, swaps, futures, and options. The first three instruments are nonstandardized and are considered bilateral agreements. These transactions are not guaranteed or processed by a central clearing house. Rather, the faith and credit of the trading partners binds the transaction. These transactions can be more flexible in timing, amounts, and special provisions.

Futures and options on futures are standardized contracts that are cleared through a central clearing organization that backs the performance or the trade. Because of the clearing house mechanism, hedgers can remain anonymous and do not have to show themselves (as they would with other techniques).

There are different provisions governing the financial initiation and maintenance of positions for all of these instruments. Some require credit lines, letters of credit, or the deposit of earnest money; others require the deposit of initial margin and variation funds.

An important benefit of all these instruments is that asset and liability management can be pursued in a cost-effective manner. Treasurers can alter their debt structure without recalling outstanding securities and reissuing new ones. Underwriting, registration, and legal fees can be very expensive or prohibitive. By engaging in suitable hedging transactions, the hedger can accomplish the same end by synthetic means.

Forwards

Forwards or forward contracts originally were used for foreign exchange purposes and have extended their usefulness into the interest-rate sphere. They are bilateral agreements in which two known parties agree to negotiated terms of interest rates, timing, amounts, and other features. These negotiated agreements permit a tailor-made treatment for hedging purposes. A major disadvantage is that the transaction is dependent on the credit worthiness and performance capabilities of the two parties.

Forward contracts are constructed from spot rates and are similar to futures. By progressing from the spot rate to the forward market, a hedger must be aware of the interrelationships between the spot rate, the implied forward rates, and the forward rates. The implied forward rate is the statistical framework against which forwards and futures are evaluated.

One expression for relating forwards and implied forwards is:

(term forward)   (term forward)   (implied forward)

$$(1 + fr_t)^t = (1 + fr_{t-n})^{t-n} \ (1 + ifr_{n,t-n})^n$$

where fr_t = forward rate for term t
       fr_{t-n} = forward rate for term $t - n$
       $ifr_{n,\,t-n}$ = implied forward rate at time n and extends for the remainder of the term

Forward rates are constructed from spot rates; by knowing two interest rate points, the hedging analyst can theoretically slide along the implied curve.

A formulation for term structure is made with a few changes. Term structure views rates as multiplicatively related. To arrive at a value for a rate at time n, one only needs to extend the left side of the above equation to represent the nth root of the multiplicative series. That is:

$$(1 + fr_n) = (1 + fr_1) (1 + fr_2) \dots (1 + fr_n)$$

Essentially, the rate for term n is the geometric mean of the intervening 1 period rates.

Forward rate agreements (FRAs) are primarily used by European-based organizations and are usually based on the LIBOR (London Interbank Offer Rate) market.

Forwards are the dominant factor for foreign exchange trading and secondary factors to the interest-rate arena.

Swaps

Swaps are conducted for assets as well as for liabilities. Some of the appeal of these transactions for hedgers is that they require a minimum of reporting. Many financial institutions and other corporations do not have to place these items on their balance sheets; instead they may only have to mention swaps in footnotes, if at all, depending on their relevance. Some regulatory agencies accept swaps more readily than futures and options hedging techniques, which can be precluded or severely restricted.

A typical transaction can be the swapping or exchange of a series of floating interest-rate payments for a series of fixed interest-rate payments. The underlying securities (assets or liabilities) are not exchanged; only their associated income streams are. These require a different place in financial reports than do the futures options positions, which are specifically highlighted. Swaps can modify the durational characteristics of the asset and liability items, or they can expedite the transfer of currencies.

Futures and options hedging techniques are dependent on standardized contracts, swapping is not. Other important distinctions between swaps and futures and options are the credit risks attached to the swapping parties and the potential jeopardy of the streams of interest and underlying securities. The credit risks for the futures and options trading parties are eventually carried by the clearing house and not by the parties to the trade. Futures and options markets can be more liquid and provide a broader vehicle for risk transference—swaps can be flexible in terms of size, timing, accounting, and financial requirements. Swaps do not entail margins as do the futures and options markets.

Benchmark rates for swaps include: Treasury bills, Eurodollars, prime lending, certificates of deposit, or LIBOR. The following example is of a swap of a fixed cash flow for a floating cash flow. The principal does not change ownership and is referred to as notional in character.

Hedger 1 seeks to swap $20 million fixed-rate debt with a 10 percent coupon. The interest is payable semiannually. Hedger 2 agreed to swap a principal amount of a $20 million floating debt. The terms were: 150 basis points over the six-month Treasury bill rate and net interest differences to be paid semiannually. At the time of the swap agreement, the Treasury bill rate was 8.5 percent.

After six months, the Treasury bill rate rose to 10 percent; therefore, Hedger 1 owed Hedger 2 (.10 × .5 × $20,000,000) $1 million. Hedger 2 owed Hedger 1 (.115 × .5 × $20,000,000) $1.15 million. This difference in interest owed was to be reconciled on a net basis, which means that Hedger 2 would pay Hedger 1 the net interest of $150,000 after six months. If rates fell to 8 percent on the next adjustment date, Hedger 1 would owe Hedger 2 (.10 × .5 × $20,000,000) $1,000,000; however, Hedger 2 would now owe Hedger 1 (.095 × .5 × $20,000,000) $950,000. Therefore, Hedger 1 would pay to Hedger 2 the net interest differential of $50,000 for this period.

Futures

Futures are standardized contracts that are traded on regulated exchanges and guaranteed in terms of transactional performance by the clearinghouse. Futures allow for transactional anonymity that forwards and swaps do not. When futures and options transactions are material in nature, they may have to be reported separately on financial reports. Currently, off-balance sheet items such as swaps and swaptions do not have to be reported in the same way as the futures and options.

Options

Options, when purchased, are wasting assets. Purchased options provide the right and not the obligation to exercise that instrument into the underlying instrument. The underlying instrument can be a futures contract or an actual security or physical commodity. Exchange-traded options are standardized relative to the underlying instruments and enjoy the same guarantee extended by the clearinghouse for transactional performance as the underlying instrument does.

For off-exchange traded or generated options, performance is tied to the transactional parties. Off-exchange traded options require the disclosure of the two trading parties, whereas exchange-traded options do not require this disclosure and can be readily offset by entering the marketplace (like securities or futures) to initiate or close out positions.

Swaptions

Swaptions are hybrid or composite instruments that combine a swap with one or more options. A floor-ceiling swap combines a swap (floating-to-fixed or fixed-to-floating) with two options: a call and a put. Depending on how the options are configured, the swapper can limit the upside payment risk, limit the downside, forgo some of the potential payment relief, and so on. These arrangements are only limited to whatever is agreeable between the two swapping parties.

Building Blocks and Synthetics

Financial instruments, derivative products, and exotic securities are often constructed by adding one or two features to a simple instrument. These additions can increase the flexibility and the complexity of the securities. By understanding the role of each building block (underlying component) the hedger can assess the prices of these securities against the theoretical values of the parts. If there are discrepancies, these differences would then be subject to arbitrage forces.

Synthetics replicate an actual instrument. For example, by adding a day, a hedger moves from the spot to the forward market. A series of forwards properly constructed is equal to a swap. A long position in Treasury-bond futures coupled with an appropriate long position in Treasury-bond put options is equal to a long-synthetic-call option in Treasury bonds.

This chapter and Chapter 11, Options, demonstrate the concept of synthesizing instruments from basic, underlying building blocks. You will recognize that many instruments draw upon the same body of principles.

NET INTEREST MARGINS

Net interest margins (NIMs) are methods of calculating profitability for financial institutions. The margin is the difference between the interest income and the interest expense, divided by the assets, and it can be computed for all assets, earning assets, and other classifications. It can be fine tuned to reflect the contribution of questionable assets that can soon become nonperforming.

Consider a $100 million financial institution. It has $100 million in assets broken down to $90 million in earning assets and $10 million in nonearning assets.

$$\frac{\text{Interest income } - \text{ interest expense}}{\text{asset classification}} = \text{net interest margin}$$

Substitute an average rate of 8.5 percent for the earning assets and 7 percent for the liabilities:

$$\frac{\$7,650,000 - \$6,300,000}{\$90,000,000} =$$

$$\frac{\$1,350,000}{\$90,000,000} =$$

.015, or 1½ percent.

The net interest margin is used for sensitivity analysis as well. It can imply what the change in interest income, interest expense, and net interest will be, given changes for the underlying assets and liabilities. If liabilities are of such duration that they quickly reflect changes in borrowing rates, a financial institution may have to pay more to maintain its assets. For example, suppose the borrowing rate jumped to 8 percent overnight and stayed there, and the financial institution was unable to improve the earnings rate for its assets immediately. This means that the firm will pay an additional $900,000 ($90 million $\times$ .01) over the near-term with no increase in interest income. Under such conditions, the company can expect a reduction in net interest margins because net income will fall from $1,350,000 to $450,000.

Interest Rate Sensitivity

Interest rate sensitivity influences assets, liabilities, and the value of the firm. Rate sensitive assets (RSAs) and rate sensitive liabilities (RSLs) can swiftly alter their characteristics. Rate sensitive assets can be called away or refinanced depending on fluctuations in the market rate structure and economic climate. Rate sensitive liabilities can migrate from one institution to another or from one instrument to another.

Financial institutions such as banks, savings and loans, brokerage firms, and other depositories typically are highly leveraged enterprises. Slight shifts between interest between interest rate income (revenues) and interest rate expenses (cost) can generate a dramatic swing in the value of the firm, its net profitability, and even its survival.

TED SPREAD

One gauge of pessimism-to-optimism is the TED (Treasury bill-Eurodollar) spread. By evaluating the yield differences between these two instruments, one has a quantitative yardstick that focuses on yield differences due to quality. Generally, pessimism generates buying interest for Treasury bills and selling interest in the Eurodollars because the Treasury bills are considered the surrogate instruments for the risk-free rate.

FUNDING MIXES

Abrupt shifts in earnings stress the important role the composition of funding plays for asset and liability management. Each group has its own characteristics and elasticities. Liabilities such as fed funds, certificates of deposit (CDs), and Eurodollars are the primary sources for funding loan and investment portfolios, mortgages, and other assets.

A firm that looks at the funding and investment climates strategically can position itself without engaging in a series of frequent and dubious adjustments. A financial institution can concentrate its efforts on securing more stable deposits and liability sources in order to fund long-term commitments when it is prepared. Although duration analysis can assist in coping with these flighty liabilities, it is not the complete answer. Some funding or sourcing mixes exhibit better stability than others and should be pursued more aggressively.

DISCOUNTING AND COMPOUNDING

The two primary mechanisms for interest rate analysis are compounding and discounting. Generally, a 360-day year is used for money market instruments (of less than one-year maturity) and a 365-day year for credit market instruments (of more than one-year maturity). These two concepts cover zero-coupon securities, net present values, present values, annuities, bond pricing, instalment loans, mortgages, lump-sum payments, and balloon loans.

Discounting can be expressed as:

$$\frac{CF}{(1 + i/n)^{nt}} = DCF$$

where CF = cash flow
$\quad\quad\; DCF$ = discounted cash flow
$\quad\quad\; i$ = decimalized interest rate
$\quad\quad\; n$ = number of periods in a year
$\quad\quad\; t$ = number of years

The discounted cash flow of a receipt of \$100, one year hence, given a 10-percent discount interest rate, is \$90.91. The straightforward discounting application for Treasury bills, Eurodollars, and zero-coupon securities. When this technique is progressively applied, one can generate net present values and annuity values.

An expression for compounding is:

$$CF(1 + i/n)^{nt} = CCF$$

where CF = cash flow
$\quad\quad\; CCF$ = discounted cash flow
$\quad\quad\; i$ = decimalized interest rate
$\quad\quad\; n$ = number of periods in a year
$\quad\quad\; t$ = number of years

The compounded cash flow of a deposit of $100, now given a 10 percent (.10) compound interest rate for one year, will be worth $110. Compounding is used for determining future values, implied futures prices, and the term structure of interest rates.

NET PRESENT VALUE

Net present value is the result of discounted cash-flow stream. Generally, this stream is computed over subsequent intervals. Cash flow can be revenues (interest income), costs (interest expense), or net profits and losses.

Net present value is computed by:

$$NPV = \sum \frac{NCF^t}{(1 + i)^t}$$

where NPV = net present value
     NCF = net cash flow
     i = interest or discount rate
     t = time interval

The net present value is the cumulative valuation of a series of zero-coupon bonds. This valuation model can be extended to take into account different is (interest rates) for different periods to reflect yield-curve expectations as well as to distinguish between the cost of capital (funding) and the use of capital (investments).

ANNUITIES

Annuities are, effectively, a cumulative series of zero-coupon securities. An example of an annuity is the coupon stream attached to a bond. For government securities, these coupons are fixed in rate and are payable semiannually. For corporations, these securities can be either fixed or variable (floating). When they are floating, they must be approached as variable annuities. The concept of annuities and the mathematics of annuity pricing also have significance for swaps.

CREDIT INSTRUMENT PRICING

Bonds and other credit market instruments can be computed by adding the annuity value (net present value of the coupon stream), the net present value of the principal (corpus), and any implied or explicit option feature.

One expression for computing the market value of a bond is:

$$BMV = \sum \frac{CP_t}{(1 + i)^t} + \frac{PRIN}{(1 + i)^t}$$

where BMV = bond market value
CP$_t$ = coupon payment at time t
PRIN = principal or par amount
i = interest rate
t = time period

The first part of the expression represents the net present value of the income or coupon cash flow. The second part is the discounted (zero-coupon equivalent) for the principal payment, typically viewed as occurring at maturity, although it can be *priced* relative to first call date.

CASH FLOW ANALYSIS

The accurate determination of the cash flows, both in and out, is crucial to the asset and liability management plan. By carefully matching asset and liability flows, the organization can reduce its financial operating risks and avoid costly readjustments or imbalances that arise from swings in the interest rate markets, forces of intermediation and distintermediation, and vulnerability to adverse yield-curve movements.

The basic analytical approaches are macro and micro gap analyses, which refer to the broad-stroke view, and the narrowly construed framework, respectively. Each has its place in the construction and the implementation of a hedge program.

GAP ANALYSIS

A gap is the imbalance between the dollar amount for an asset (use) and liability (source) for a specified maturity period or maturity interval. Gap analysis systematically examines these imbalances. When the target is a specific maturity, it is a periodic gap; when the targets are sequential, they form an interval and are considered a cumulative gap.

Gaps can be absolute dollar amounts, net present-value dollar amounts, or market-value amounts. Gap time periods can be listed maturities or durationally weighted maturities. Depending on the degree of maturity categorization, gap analysis can be macro (bucket) or micro oriented.

Static gap analysis views current or historical balance sheet situations. Dynamic gap analysis relies on simulation techniques to evaluate what-if balance sheet compositions and potential net present values of the firm. The usual dynamic approach incorporates yield-curve analysis.

Macro Gap Analysis

Macro gap analysis can be as simple as short- versus long-term assets and liabilities, or, it can involve many classifications that are representative of key maturities. Partitioning does not have to follow identical increments such as one month, two months, three months, and so on. It can be irregular but more statistically indicative of actual positions and requirements, such as one day, two and a half weeks, three months, eleven months, and so forth. An $110 million example of a macro gap situation would be the composition of a new $110 million firm. It consists of $110 million in assets, $100 million in liabilities, and $10 million in equity. Per accounting principles, the assets are balanced against the liabilities and equity. In the following example, items less than 10 years are short term, 10 years and over are long term, and only earning assets against funding liabilities are viewed. The difference of a week or a day can shift the weight of the arrangement from long term to short term because such a subtle change may be enough to cause an item to be classified in the next group. For short versus long maturities the arrangement is:

	Short-Term Maturity	Long-Term Maturity	Total
Assets	$25,000,000	$75,000,000	$100,000,000
Liabilities	$75,000,000	$25,000,000	$100,000,000
Gaps	$50,000,000	$50,000,000	$0

There is an imbalance (gap) of $50 million per maturity period. For the short term, the assets are overwhelmingly funded by short-term liabilities, which are also a major portion of the long-term assets. The asset and liability manager does not yet know what the underlying maturities are. He knows only that they are greater than or less than ten years. Additional information is necessary. Finer breakdowns and durational techniques are used to get closer approximations.

Micro Gap Analysis

Micro gap analysis provides additional detail and refines the process by partitioning the assets and liabilities into more maturity groups. It is helpful because it highlights not only disparities between the classes and the attendant maturities, but it also stresses that there may be distinctive maturity classifications for asset and others for the liabilities. For example, the short-term liabilities may be better represented by 1-, 2-, and 30-day maturities while the assets may be 3-, 90-, and 120-day maturities.

Table 7.1a Illustrative Asset and Liability Breakdowns

Illustrative Micro Gap Analysis
(in Millions of Dollars)

	Asset and Liability Breakdowns										
	Days						Years				
	1 day	2 days	3 days	30 days	90 days	120 days	10 years	15 years	20 years	25 years	Total
Assets	0.5	1.5	5.0	2.3	12.1	3.6	10.3	9.2	5.7	49.8	100.0
L&E	11.4	10.7	0.8	24.3	26.1	1.7	3.2	4.5	5.7	11.6	100.0
Gaps	−10.9	−9.2	4.2	−22.0	−14.0	1.9	7.1	4.7	0.0	38.2	0.0

NOTE: The asset and liability percents are the same as the dollar breakdown amounts because of the $100 million example used.
Only the 20-year period is balanced here. The totals must balance by definition.
L & E = Liabilities and Equity.

Table 7.1b　Illustrative Net Interest Rate Differentials by Period

| | Interest Rate In-and-Out Analysis | | | | | | | | | |
| | Days | | | | | | Years | | | |
	1 day	2 days	3 days	30 days	90 days	120 days	10 years	15 years	20 years	25 years	Total
In	6.7	8.4	8.4	8.5	11.7	13.3	10.8	10.9	11.0	11.2	10.1
Out	8.9	8.5	8.3	7.8	7.2	7.1	8.4	8.4	8.5	8.3	8.1
Net Interest Rate Differentials by Period	−2.2	−0.1	0.1	0.7	4.5	6.2	2.4	2.5	2.5	2.9	1.9

NOTE: The first two periods show a negative carry. Other periods and totals show a positive carry.

Table 7.1c　Illustrative Weighting of Interest Cash Flows

| | Weighted Interest Cash Flows (in Millions of Dollars) | | | | | | | | | |
| | Days | | | | | | Years | | | |
	1 day	2 days	3 days	30 days	90 days	120 days	10 years	15 years	20 years	25 years	Total
WIN	0.03	0.13	0.42	0.20	1.42	0.48	1.11	1.00	0.63	5.58	10.99
WOUT	1.01	0.91	0.07	1.90	1.88	0.12	0.27	0.38	0.48	0.96	7.98
	−0.98	−0.78	0.35	−1.70	−0.46	0.36	0.84	0.62	0.14	4.61	3.01

Key: WIN = weighted interest in
　　WOUT = weighted interest out
NOTE: For this table it is assumed that these rates (both in and out) hold over the year; and, thus, these weighted numbers represented the net cash flows.

The NIM or net interest margin here is 3.01. It is the weighted difference between the cash flows.

The assets in the previous example are primarily zero-coupon bonds of 25-year maturity and 30-year mortgages with approximate durations of 14 years. The main components of the liabilities are 30-day certificates of deposit (CDs) and 90-day time deposits. Table 7.1a, b, and c illustrates this more comprehensive listing.

The table shows greater detail, but on an unadjusted basis. Further refinements would involve the durational breakdowns of the components. The micro analysis could also portray the groups with optional features (such as implied or explicit put and call items) that seriously alter the composition of the financial (corporate) institution and hedge under certain market conditions. During these times, when items can be put or called away, the organization can face substantial losses if it does not adjust or anticipate probable adjustment.

CURRENT YIELD

Current yield relates the coupon or return to the market price of the security. The current yield is different from the yield to maturity or yield to first call. The current yield is calculated by:

$$CY = \frac{\text{coupon}}{\text{market price}}$$

where CY = current yield.

For bonds trading at a discount to par, the current yield is less than the yield to maturity; and for bonds trading at a premium to par, the current yield is more than the yield to maturity.

YIELDS TO MATURITY AND FIRST CALL

Yields to maturity and first call take into account the discount or premium between the current price and the par value or redemption price. The yield to maturity views the maturity date and its terms as the terminal point, however, while the yield to first call views the first call date and its terms as the termination point.

Discounts are adjusted by an accrual method and premiums are adjusted by an amortization method. Accruals enhance the yields to maturity or first call as they upwardly adjust the current yields, while amortizations trim yields to maturity or first call as they reduce the current yields.

Evolution in Yield to Maturity

Yield to maturity is slowly giving way to other concepts, including: yield to first call, yield to put date, and yield to an important redemption date (other than the stipulated term of the security). The emergence of these explicit and implicit options alters the potential and expected yield for the security. Issues are not necessarily held to maturity, and transactions prior to the maturity date can entail price risk and reinvestment risk, or both.

BOND-EQUIVALENT YIELD

The bond-equivalent yield relates discounted rates, such as Treasury bills and Eurodollars, to a bond standard for more accurate comparisons, which is an important adjustment mechanism for asset and liability management. Typically, discounted interest rates are calculated for a 360-day year; bonds are premised on a 365-day year. For the simple financial institution presented in the previous example, yields associated with different maturities and instruments have to be placed on equal footing. Otherwise, the quoted short-term rates for discounted instruments are understated.

Consider a $1,000,000 face (par) value Treasury bill that underlies the Treasury-bill futures contract. If the discount rate is 8 percent, and the maturity is 90 days, then the market price is:

$$\text{Face (par) value} - \frac{\text{days to maturity} \times \text{discount rate} \times \text{face value}}{360 \text{ days (year)}}$$

Substitute 8 percent and 90 days to arrive at:

$$\$1,000,000 - \frac{90 \times .08 \times 1,000,000}{360} =$$

$980,000 for the three-month 8-percent bill

Look at it from another perspective: The same bill could be traded at a $20,000 discount-to-face value. To compare this 8-percent return to its bond equivalent, one has to extend the year. For example, the bond-equivalent yield (BEY) is:

$$\text{BEY} = \frac{\text{face value} - \text{market price}}{\text{market price}} \times \frac{365 \text{ days (bond year)}}{\text{(number of days to maturity for the bill)}}$$

$$= \frac{20,000}{\$980,000} \times \frac{365}{90}$$

$$= .08276 \text{ or } 8.276 \text{ percent.}$$

Note that the duration for this instrument is exactly equal to its time to maturity: The 90-day bill has a duration of 90 days. A 180-day bill has a duration of 180 days, and a bill with 342 days to maturity has a duration of 342 days.

BASIS-POINT RESPONSE

The basis-point response relates the expected price change in a security for a .01 percent (1 basis point) change in yield—it measures elasticity between price and yield. For the Treasury bill in the previous example, the basis-point response for an 8.00 to 8.01 percent rise in the discount rate is calculated in the following way.

The market price for the three-month bill discounted at 8 percent is $980,000, the price for a three-month bill with an 8.01-percent rate is calculated in a similar way. The discount is now $20,025, or a difference of $25 between the two $1,000,000 face value bills. The $25 price difference is the basis-point response for the three-month $1,000,000 Treasury bill.

Other maturities have different basis-point responses, but, given the futures contract standardization and the nature of discounted instruments, one can readily arrive at a suitable hedge.

Consider a one-year $1,000,000 Treasury bill: How many three-month futures contracts would be necessary to hedge this cash position? Since the basis-point response of a one-year bill is $100, the hedge requires four contracts of three-month maturity futures to equate the basis point response. This hedge also matches the duration of the cash position to the duration of the hedge vehicle.

ZERO-COUPON ISSUES AND EQUIVALENCY

Zero-coupon issues are the initiation factors for the construction of durational approaches. The simplest security to consider is one represented by only one cash flow with no optional features attached: a zero-coupon issue. Treasury bills are zero-coupon issues because they have no coupon and a fixed maturity date. The concepts of maturity, coupons, and optional features undergo intensive analysis for the many kinds of hybrid securities.

The determination of the zero-coupon issue is the straightforward application of expected cash flow (in or out, asset or liability) discounted by time and applicable interest rate. For example, a 20-year zero that pays off in a single $1,000 payment twenty years later at the given rate of 8 percent has a present value of $214.50, which is computed as:

$$ZC = \frac{\text{expected payment at end of term}}{(1.00 + i)^t}$$

where ZC = zero coupon value
$\quad\quad\quad i$ = interest rate
$\quad\quad\quad t$ = time to maturity.

It is obvious that higher is and longer ts discount the issue more deeply. The extended application of a series of zero-coupon issues gives rise to duration analysis.

DURATION ANALYSIS

Duration analysis evaluates cash flows by replicating the zero-coupon equivalency discussion. By imputing interest rates to cash flows, the analyst can determine the expected lives for different securities. There are no coupons or explicit interest payment streams for instruments such as Treasury bills; instead, there is one payment, that represents both principal and interest, at the end of the process. This is the case for zero-coupon bonds as well. For other securities, such as debentures and mortgages, there are coupons (fixed or variable) and a final principal payment.

Duration analysis breaks the security down into its components, calculates the present value and weight for each, sums the weighted parts, and divides by the market value (or present value of the instrument). Mathematically, this is represented by:

$$\frac{\Sigma\, w \times PV(i)}{\Sigma\, PV(i)} = D$$

where D   =   duration (expected life)
       PV(i) =   present value of each cash payment
       w   =   weighting factor

The weighting factor is computed by dividing the present value contribution of each cash flow by the instrument's total present value, where the sum of the weights equals 1.00.

A helpful property of duration is that it provides an indication of elasticity. For example, given a 1 percent change in yield, a bond with a 5.3-year duration is expected to move by 5.3 percent. This statistic can help answer: Which issues are expected to fall faster in dollars in a rising interest rate environment? and: Which issues are expected to move faster in a declining interest rate environment? The answers are dependent on coupons, maturities, and expected maturities.

Macaulay's postulation of duration (presented in numerous sources, including Robert Platt's *Controlling Interest Rate Risk,* published and reprinted by permission of John Wiley & Sons, Inc., copyright © 1986) is:

$$D = w_1 \times t_1 + w_2 \times t_2 + w_3 \times t_3 + \ldots + w_n \times t_n$$

where D =   duration
       w =   weighted cash flow
       t =   time period

Because M (maturity) is equal to D (duration) for the zero-coupon issue, it can be found that D is less than or equal to M; therefore, the duration can be expected to be less than the stated maturity, except for zero coupons.

Duration for an Instrument

The duration for a noncallable five-year maturity, 8-percent coupon paying instrument is calculated in Table 7.2. Coupons are payable at the end of each semiannual period, and the principal is to be paid at the end of the fifth year. This bond consists of an annuity stream of ten coupon payments and one principal payment, which is essentially a five-year, zero-coupon bond.

Table 7.2 shows that the duration is 4.217 years, when maturity was five years. The table discounted the entire cash flow, coupons and principal, and combined those streams into one statistic. Note that the sum of the discounted cash-flow stream (coupons and principal) equalled the $1,000

Table 7.2 Duration Example for Five-Year Maturity, 8 Percent Bond

Period	Discounted Semiannual $40 Coupons (1)	Period Discount Factors (2)	Period Weighted Cash Flow (col 1 × col 2)
1	38.46	0.9615	38.46
2	36.98	0.9246	73.96
3	35.56	0.8890	106.68
4	34.19	0.8548	136.77
5	32.88	0.8219	164.39
6	31.61	0.7903	189.68
7	30.40	0.7599	212.78
8	29.23	0.7307	233.82
9	28.10	0.7026	252.93
10	27.02	0.6756	270.23
Coupon Sums	324.44		1679.69
Discounted Zero	675.56		6755.64
Total Flow	1000.00		8435.33

Key: 8435.33/1000 = 8.435 duration, based on half year
8.435/2 = 4.217 duration in years adjusted for semiannual coupon payments

NOTE: The discount rate is 8 percent. The semiannual coupon payment is $40.00 for an 8-percent bond. The principal is $1,000, and the market value $1,000.

market value. The discount factor is the yield-to-maturity number. Here, the yield to maturity was equal to the coupon rate.

Modified Duration

Modified duration is considered a more accurate representation of a bond's weighted cash flows. Modified duration is computed by the following expression:

$$MODD = \frac{DUR}{(1 + ym/fc)}$$

where MODD = modified duration
      DUR = duration
      ym = yield in market
      fc = frequency of coupon payments in a year

Applying this expression to the previously obtained duration of 4.217 years, the modified duration is 4.05 years.

This statistic alters simple duration by reducing the expected weighted average time of all cash flows.

Additivity for Duration

Duration is additive, which means that assets, liabilities, equities, and swaps can be added relative to their weighted durations to determine a portfolio or book duration. For example, if an institution had $1,000,000 in a one-year duration asset and $1,000,000 in a nine-year duration asset, the combined $2,000,000 portfolio would have an average duration of five years. Similarly, if another institution had $1,000,000 in a four-year duration asset and $1,000,000 in a six-year duration asset, its $2,000,000 portfolio would have an average duration of five years. Although the average durations for the two institutions are identical, the variance is potentially greater for the first institution relative to the second: The first institution's duration observations are more dispersed from the mean average than are those for the second institution. This suggests that the first institution's risk may be greater, particularly because in a year, its one-year asset will mature and, depending how it was rolled over, its duration could be subject to a major shift. This simple example emphasizes the need to more nearly match the probabilistic characteristics (means and dispersions) of assets and liabilities and not the averages alone.

Guidelines for Duration

Several guidelines for duration analysis are:

1. The duration of a zero-coupon bond is equal to its maturity.
2. The duration of a coupon bond is less than its maturity.
3. The longer the maturity is, the higher the duration will be.
4. The higher the coupon rate is, the lower the duration will be.
5. Market rates and duration are inversely related (declines in market yields increase duration).
6. Deep discount bonds, under certain circumstances, trace a concave curve. These bonds may show an increase in duration with an increase in maturity up to a point, after which the duration tails off.

Duration is time and interest rate sensitive and thus, it can shift subtly or jump dramatically. Although duration statistics can behave in a linear manner under conditions of stability and with all other things being equal, under market conditions they can readily depart from the initial straight line. Macaulay's duration model was dependent on flat yield curves and parallel moves for it. While this assumption may not be overly dangerous many times, it can be devastating for the few times that the yield curve seesaws between positive (normal) and negative (inverted) structures.

Convexity

Convexity measures the implied *instantaneous* price response of a credit market instrument to a change in yield. This statistic recognizes that for a specified change in yield (in basis points) the price response is greater on the upside for lower interest rates that it is on the downside for higher interest rates. (There is an inverse relationship between prices and interest rates.)

Figure 7.1 depicts the convexity concept as the distance between the straight line and the curved line. This distance can translate into a substantial financial difference between intended and observed occurrences when changes in market behavior are not smooth, slight, and instantaneous.

Convexity is used in conjunction with a duration-oriented analysis to better determine price sensitivity. The hedger optimally narrows the estimate for expected price response by adding the individually calculated terms for duration and convexity induced changes.

Dynamic Characteristics

Duration statistics are prone to drift or to movements even in the absence of market behavior, given the simple passage of time. The drift is similar

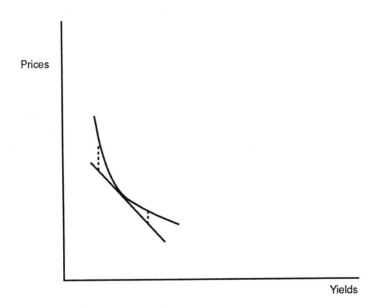

FIGURE 7.1 Convexity depicted by curved line to straight line. (Potential errors measured by dotted lines.)

to that experienced by delta when the prices remain the same, the interest rate remains the same, and the volatility remains the same. Only for a strict at-the-money option does the delta remain stable up to its expiration. An analogous durational stability exists for the zero-coupon issue. Although the passage of time defines precisely how many more days, months, or years are left to maturity for the zero-coupon issues, this precision is not subject to variation over time. For other issues, the duration statistic changes over time in ways not exclusively dependent on time.

Such a condition poses adjustment concerns and problems similar to those for delta-oriented hedging approaches. The absence of market action will prompt realignments in the hedge, and abrupt, unexpected changes will generate the need for major revisions. For example, a sudden and large gyration occurs in the interest rates and the market suddenly inverts. The assets were funded primarily by short-term liabilities. Does the hedger then adjust the duration-based hedge to this anomaly, partially adjust it, or not adjust it at all? There are conditions that suggest that it is too late to adjust: The coverage may appear theoretically correct by day's end, but the potential financial offsetting may not be there anymore. In fact, this late adjustment can restrain an organization from equilibrating behavior in the marketplace that can actually raise the risk level of the firm.

STRETCHING AND SHORTENING

Stretching and shortening refer to the impacts on maturities for assets and liabilities. Stretching lengthens durations; and shortening reduces durations. Usually the sale of a Treasury-bond future against the holding of an actual Treasury bond reduces the maturity or duration of the asset to that approximated by a short-term instrument. The purchase of a Treasury-bond future in this case would increase the maturity. Note that this technique can be prohibited by law for certain institutions.

STACKS AND STRIPS

Stacks and strips attack the hedging problem differently. A stack is the vertical compilation of the futures (or instruments) in one delivery month. A strip is the horizontal arrangement of the hedge across delivery months.

Both techniques access what is at risk, the timing of the risks, and then attempt to match the risks with an acceptable hedge. Typically, the hedge focuses on generating sufficient basis-point response to coincide with the item to be hedged.

Strips tend to be self-liquidating over the passage of time: As each reset date is passed, then a portion of the hedge is liquidated. Also, periodic liquidations can occur with amortizing or installment loans.

Stacks are frequently seen as hedgers bunch up their positions in a comparatively few nearby months. They perceive nearby contract liquidity as having additional management value despite the additional costs of rolling over the hedge. A thorough analysis is required, however, to determine whether a simple stack is truly the best way to proceed. Stacks are configured when the horizon of available futures or options months is limited and coverage is required beyond the currently available delivery months.

For the hedger to apply strips and stacks, a perspective on implied forward rates presented by the prevailing yield curve and on the reasonable construction of a hedge to minimize the associated basis-point risk is required.

YIELD-CURVE CONSIDERATIONS

Many models and approaches assume that the yield curve is stable, flat, and should move in a parallel manner; it is a main assumption of the Macaulay duration approach. These assumptions are not accurate representations of yield-curve movements and, depending on their application, can be dangerous because suitable adjustment and monitoring processes may not be implemented. Violent shifts and diverging twists must be factored in. For example, the short rates can head in one direction and the long rates in another, and the intermediate rates can behave erratically.

Three Basic Approaches or Models

The three basic approaches for yield-curve analysis are: term structure or expectations theory, market segmentation or preferred habitat theory, and liquidity preference hypothesis. These approaches can be blended because there is partial economic and regulatory justification for each.

Term Structure or Rational Expectations Theory. Term structure is also known as the rational or pure expectations theory. It is related to the implied carry and forward rate models because it approaches the yield curve and each individual rate as determinable by a geometric average. The expectations theory assumes that market participants act in a spontaneous, costless, and unhampered manner.

Market Segmentation. The market segmentation theory recognizes regulatory constraints placed on financial organizations such as banks, savings and loans, broker/dealers, insurance companies, and pension funds. The regulations categorize these institutions into those who must favor short-term instruments and those who must favor longer term instruments. The emergence of money market funds, unit trusts, and other investment vehicles also demonstrates the emphasis on one part of the yield curve versus another.

Typically, depositories and money market funds must maintain specified, though variable, percentages of assets in short-term instruments. Insurance companies and pension funds are directed towards longer term projects and investments. The organizations are not completely free to pursue financial opportunities across the yield curve because of regulatory requirements, and therefore, the smoothing process can be delayed and can result in discernible segments.

Liquidity Preference Hypothesis. The liquidity preference hypothesis is intertwined with the segmentation theory. The liquidity hypothesis assumes that investors will prefer to stay in the more near-term security, if interest rates and all other considerations (creditworthiness, taxes, implied and explicit options, costs) are equal. Moreover, the liquidity hypothesis is best illustrated by a normal or positive (upward sloping) yield-curve shape, in which the longer term rates are progressively higher than the short-term rates (to compensate for higher risk that comes from longer maturities, as well as to attract investors to instruments that do not resemble money-market paper).

INSOLVENCY AND BANKRUPTCY

Asset and liability management and cash management techniques must be in tune with insolvency and bankruptcy models and the regulatory requirements for staying afloat and fully operational must be complied with.

Derivative forms of inventory and portfolio management models apply equally to funds management—financial institutions function under severe limitations when the capital position is impaired. This impairment may unduly precipitate or delay corrective measures and not foster smooth realignments.

SIMULATIONS

Asset and liability management as well as other hedging analysis is becoming increasingly dependent on what-if or simulative processes. Simple to complex models that can be geared to an individual firm or an industry are built. These models are very valuable when properly understood and used: They can spotlight potential problems and opportunities in advance, given the application of sound model construction, reliable data, and reasonable hypotheses.

Simulations provide early warnings for highly leveraged, interest-rate sensitive firms that are vulnerable to vagaries in the financial markets. Depending on how the assumptions are laid out, they can help an organization cope with stochastic interest-rate risk, which emphasizes the aberrant or more dramatic random elements of change.

Simulation models make the transition from static asset and liability management (gaps, duration, interest rate sensitivity) to a dynamic managment. This transition gives the management committee the statistical framework to dynamically match cash flows and alter specified balance-sheet line items over time.

Simulative approaches will become more critical as banks and savings and loans must conform to more stringent reporting standards in the early 1990s.

MORTGAGES AND MORTGAGE-BACKED SECURITIES

Mortgages and mortgage-backed securities face special problems such as: prepayments, refinancings, and defaults. The ability of the borrower to refinance or partially prepay a mortgage dramatically affects the expected cash flow, income stream, and price of the mortgage. Drops in market rates of interest can cause price compression for many outstanding mortgages because they are callable by the borrower, who would seek to refinance the balance at more favorable interest rates. Price compression arises when potential traders and buyers of mortgage-backed securities expect those who are vulnerable to refinancing mortgages as on the verge of being called. The potential traders and buyers would not be likely to pay substantial price premiums despite sharp declines in interest rates because the instruments could be imminently exercised (called).

Embedded Options

A provision for refinancing viewed as an embedded option (here a call) can be very interest-rate sensitive and complicated to analyze. One way to partially identify the current value of an embedded option is to relate the embedded mortgage instrument to an unembedded instrument. The hedger would then subtract the current embedded mortgage price from the assumed (unembedded) price. The difference is an estimate of the value of the option. (Other considerations are liquidity, resets, and special features.) Like options, embedded options have high value when they are at-the-money and progressively higher values as they move deeper in-the-money. These in-the-money movements increase the likelihood of potential exercises, especially for mortgages.

Reinvestment Risk

Typically, mortgages are refinanced when interest rates drop, thereby exposing the lender to a reinvestment risk. The lender can no longer profit from a comparatively high interest rate, but faces the prospects of reinvesting the prepayment funds at considerably lower rates.

Pipeline Risk

Another risk associated with mortgage financing is "pipeline" risk, which occurs from the time an application is accepted to the sale of the asset. Some analysts divide pipeline risk into two parts: production and inventory. Production risk starts at the time of application and continues until the closing of the mortgage. Inventory risk commences at the time of the closing and continues until the sale or hedge of the mortgage. Because mortgages in application may not be closed, put and call option strategies may be more suitable for coping with the first half of pipeline risk and futures and forwards for the second half of pipeline risk.

SECURITIZATION

Securitization is the homogenizing and packaging of financial instruments into new fungible securities. Acquisition, composition, classification, and distribution are functions within this process. Securitization occurs when there are financial needs that are not being satisfied by prevailing instruments. The zero-coupon bond is one success story because it provided an instrument that allowed investors to avoid reinvestment risk for the term of the security, required only small payments for a substantial final payoff, and deferred immediate cash-flow interest payments from the issuer of the underlying security.

The following example describes how an equity-related security can evolve from necessity and focuses on multiple features that suit different requirements. This securitization process outlines HOMERS™ or Home Owners Marketable Rights Securities. The concept is applicable to land, buildings, commercial structures and other real estate properties. As an asset and liability management tool, it could benefit owners, banks, savings and loans, FDIC, FSLIC, traders, hedgers, and investors.

A serious problem for the mortgage market is default and subsequent foreclosure. A default would destroy a cross hedge because the usual instrument used is the Treasury-bond futures contract, predicated on Treasury bonds that are viewed as risk-free. Although many mortgages may be insured, the underlying collateral is still vulnerable to market fluctuations that can seriously impair the owner or insurer of the property, given a default/foreclosure situation.

At that time, property ownership reverts to the lender, who then possesses the beneficial equity ownership in the property. Prior to the reversion, the impaired (defaulted) security would effectively trade as equity since it is conceivable and probable that the market value of the property is below the initial and subsequent loan balance. For example, at period one a property was funded by $25 down in equity and financed by a $175 mortgage, for a total market price (the initial trade) of $200. Subsequently, the market collapses and the appraised value for the property is $100. This indicates that the initial (beneficial) owner lost his or her $25 equity stake, the lender experienced a $75 write down in the value of the mortgage (all other things being equal), and the lender witnessed a $100 markdown of the collateral value of the property. Thus, the impaired mortgage is worth $100 because that is all the underlying property is worth. If the lender were able to sell the property at the new appraised market value of $100, the lender would recover only $100 of an initial loan of $175.

In the event that the lender, who now owns the beneficial interest in the property, is unable to sell the property immediately, he has only a limited number of choices. He can further "distress price" the property, although such an action may further reduce the value of other similar properties in the loan or REO (Real Estate Owned) portfolios. The lender can decide to stick it out, thereby financing the property implicitly by forgoing the opportunity returns on the nonperforming asset. This decision would adversely impact the overall returns for the institution because it would damage the net interest margins or widen the operating loss.

To generate funds for operation purposes, the typical depository sells certificates of deposit and may have to be very aggressive in offering above average rates of interest to attract depositors. These rates place an immediate drain on the institution because, even if it is insured, the institution must pay the interest payable and return the deposited funds at maturity unless there is a rollover, at which time the financial drain in terms of interest payable is similar, but the return of funds has been deferred.

Another alternative would be to sell a partial equity participation interest, but not the beneficial ownership in the property. This sale would generate immediate cash inflow at no immediate cost (cash outflow) to the institution. (This is because the HOMER™ distribution is on the qualified sale of the property, and no additional payments need to be generated to the HOMER™ buyer until that liquidation time.)

One material difference between the HOMER™ here and a zero-coupon bond is that the zero has a specified holding period—its maturity—whereas the equity certificate has a qualified random or unknown holding period or life expectancy. Another distinction is that the zero bond has a specified yield to maturity if held until maturity, whereas the HOMER™ does not have a specified return until it is determined on the liquidation day.

The HOMER™ is not an option, such as a call to buy a portion of the property, since options grant the purchaser the right and not the obligation to exercise. Rather, the HOMER™ is an in-the-money preemptive right, encumbering the property, which participates in the proceeds of the property upon disposition.

This security works by granting the HOMER™ owner the preemptive claim on the initial amount of the in-the-money funding. For example, an institution sold a 10 percent HOMER™ for eight dollars against the now revalued property worth $100. This means that if the property subsequently sold for $100, the security owner would receive the first eight dollars, plus 10 percent beyond the eight dollars or $17.20 ($8 + (.1 × (100 − 8)) = $17.20). If all other things hold constant, the longer the term of retention before the final disposition, the lower the effective rate of return will be. The earlier the liquidation is, the potentially higher the rate of return will be. Also, the security owner is immunized down to the level of eight dollars after costs and, thereafter, shares in the losses. If the market advanced back to the $200 level, then the security owner would receive $27.20 ($8 − (.1 × (200 − 8)) = $27.20). The formulation and construction of this security can be multiple classes to allow for various participation rates and other stipulations. Figure 7.2 presents various class numbers and participation rates.

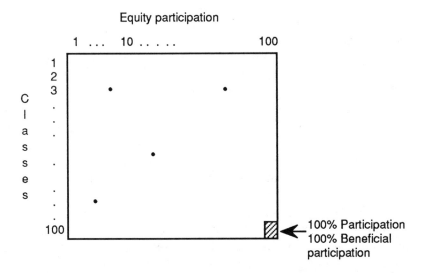

FIGURE 7.2   Depiction of HOMER™ classifications and participations. (Source: Barkley International, Inc., Bedford, N.Y., © copyright 1989.)

The 100-100 extreme in Figure 7.2 reflects 100-percent beneficial ownership and 100-percent equity participation. This corner sets the upper price limit because at that point it is the entire value of the property. Equity rights will trade at lower prices, aside from complete ownership. To keep the example simple, it can be assumed that these rights do not participate in any interim cash flows (rentals and so on), only in the final distribution, and therefore, the rights behave in a nonlinear manner.

One approach to analyzing the funding properties of the security is to relate it to a zero-coupon bond which, it can be assumed, represents the maintenance or opportunity costs. By determining the indifference points for expected holding periods and variable market rates, an analyst can isolate the indifference region for financing with either the zero coupon or the equity security.

The application of portfolio theory enhances the value of this instrument. By collectivizing numerous properties, the entire security is not one event dependent but, rather, is predicated on diverse properties and events. (The sale of each property within a portfolio that is the security class generates an immediate cash flow similar to an extraordinary dividend declaration.) The construction of these portfolios can be configured with land-only properties, condos, houses, commercial buildings, and so on. These portfolios can then be partitioned into trading units or equity rights participation securities. The collection and distribution procedures created homogenized security units. A powerful hedging tool emerges because the market can essentially sell-hedge ''pure'' real estate equities, not the underlying singular properties.

The attractiveness of the source of this security is that it would reduce the funding commitments for the depository or other beneficial owner and allow for the creation of a homogenized security that could be shorted (unlike real estate, which is prohibited from being sold short). The attractiveness of using this security is that it would enable an investor to participate in equity real estate values without any further obligation such as maintenance, taxes, rentals, and other operational concerns. These underlying securities could form the basis for forwards, futures, and options markets that could be short-salable for hedging purposes. The securities would directly refer to the equity collateral value for a mortgaged property. The mechanics would approximate the cash settlement and indexation of the municipal bond futures contract or similar instruments.

FOREIGN EXCHANGE

The foreign exchange markets are amenable to asset and liability management and other hedging techniques for several reasons. Profitable operations are often damaged by unfavorable changes in currency rates. Importers may find themselves at severe disadvantages despite the establishment of fixed prices for the import of raw commodities, finished goods, or services. Similarly, exporters may find themselves accumulating balances of rapidly depreciating currencies that are substantially less valuable upon conversion than at the time of the commitment or shipment. Global securities markets demand the tracking and hedging of currency movements because advances in securities (stocks or bonds) will actually be losing ventures if the currency dimension is neglected.

The possibilities of intervention activities, devaluations, reevaluations, and currency controls inject risk elements into the hedging process.

Unlike most physical commodities, the relatively weaker currency reflects a discount for the forward rate basis the spot. It reflects interest rate differentials, inflationary expectations, yield-curve views for both currencies, and other pricing influences.

There are active forward, or bank, markets for a variety of currencies. The foremost futures markets are the Australian dollar, British pound, Canadian dollar, Deutsche mark, Japanese yen, Swiss franc (traded on the CME), and the United States Dollar Index traded on the FINEX.

The combination of futures, options, and forwards makes currency trading a comparatively efficient marketplace. Forward markets generally do not require any margining (banking relationships, however, are important); futures transactions require marked-to-market margining.

Options

Consider a United States corporation that imports West German office equipment for sale in Britain. The merchant must convert dollars into Deutsche marks and pounds into dollars.

Assume that the equipment costs DM 1,724,138 and sells for £750,000. The exchange rates are 1.724 DM/$ and $1.70/£. The dollar value, therefore, is $1,000,000 for the importation of the presses and $1,275,000 for their sale in Britain, leaving a profit of $275,000, provided the exchange rates do not change adversely.

Table 7.3 lists profit and loss outcomes for different pound and mark rates. Table 7.4 lists the results of a hedge accomplished with the purchase of at-the-money puts and calls. These positions have modified the merchant's exposure, and the purchase of options has taken on the characteristic of insurance. If the mark rallies, the merchant has locked in a rate which is the strike. If the mark falls, then the merchant can buy the mark at a cheaper rate. His total cost is then the lower rate plus the forfeited premium. The purchase of the puts protected the merchant against a drop in sterling. In the event that the pound rallies, then the importer-exporter can benefit (less the cost of the put premium). See Tables 7.5a and 7.5b for examples of rate changes, costs, and benefits.

Futures

A corporate takeover specialist decides to buy an Australian film company for 15,000,000 Australian dollars. The Australian dollar is quoted at $.7120 (U.S.) for a month forward and $.7050 for four months forward, and the corporate buyer decides to hedge his currency commitment. According to the terms of the deal, he is to pay $5 million Australian one month from now and $10 million four months from now. The hedger bases his purchases on these rates of exchange and buys 50 futures contracts at $.7120 (or $3,560,000 U.S.) and 100 futures of the next delivery month at $.7050 (or $7,050,000 U.S.). Notice that if the takeover company hedged the currency commitment in the spot market or entirely in the

Table 7.3 Profit/Loss Outcomes for Different Exchange Rates

	Profitability Matrix for Different Rates				
	Dollars per pound				
$/DM	1.6500	1.6750	1.7000	1.7250	1.7500
.56	271983	290733	309483	328233	346983
.57	254741	273491	292241	310991	329741
.58	237500	256250	275000	293750	312500
.59	220259	239009	257759	276509	295259
.60	203017	221767	240517	259267	278017

NOTE: Merchandise purchased for 1,724,138 DM.
Merchandise sold for 750,000 pounds.

Table 7.4 Hedge Strategy Using Puts and Calls

Comparative Costs and Effective Prices

Units	@.47 Cost $/DM .5800 strike	Call effective price	@.70 Cost $/£ 1.7000 strike	Put effective price
1:1	$7,637.50	0.5847	$5,250.00	1.6930
2:1	$15,862.50	0.5894	$10,500.00	1.6860

NOTE: In both unit 1:1 and unit 2:1, the coverage started at the same price (the strike), but the effective prices and costs were different.
The application of an initial delta state doubled costs. It is important to ascertain the quality of coverage beforehand.
1.724 million/125,000 = 13.79
750,000/62,500 = 12

Table 7.5a Cost and Benefit Analysis for Purchased Options

Various Conditions and Alternative Outcomes
(No Adjustments)

$/DM	Net cost outcome 1:1 strategy	Net cost outcome 2:1 strategy	Dollar value 1,724,138 DMs	1:1 Terminal value calls	2:1 Terminal value calls
Start	+13 Calls	+27 Calls	$1,000,000	$7,638	$15,863
0.5200	$904,189	$912,414	$896,552	$0	$0
0.5500	955,913	964,138	948,276	0	0
0.5800	1,007,638	1,015,863	1,000,000	0	0
0.6100	1,010,612	966,337	1,051,724	48,750	101,250
0.6400	1,013,586	916,811	1,103,448	97,500	202,500

NOTE: For the 1:1 strategy, financial outcomes for the purchased calls would be the same, starting at the .5800 level and going higher, if options quantities exactly matched the requirements.
For the 2:1 strategy, financial outcomes for the purchased calls display lower costs as the market moves from its initial at-the-money level.

nearby market, it would have lost an edge from the rate structure. In this example, it was important to match funding dates with the hedge contract delivery months.

Table 7.5b   Cost and Benefit Analysis for Purchased Options

Various Conditions and Alternative Outcomes
(No Adjustments)

$/£	Net revenue outcome 1:1 strategy	Net revenue outcome 2:1 strategy	Dollar value 750,000 pounds	1:1 Terminal value puts	2:1 Terminal value puts
Start	+12 Puts	+24 Puts	$1,275,000	$5,250	$10,500
1.6000	$1,269,750	$1,339,500	$1,200,000	$75,000	$150,000
1.6500	1,269,750	1,302,000	1,237,500	37,500	75,000
1.7000	1,269,750	1,264,500	1,275,000	0	0
1.7500	1,307,250	1,302,000	1,312,500	0	0
1.8000	1,344,750	1,339,500	1,350,000	0	0

NOTE: For outcome 1:1 strategy, the financial outcomes for the purchased puts are the same, starting at the 1.7000 level and lower. This highlights the asymmetric characteristic of options.

For outcome 2:1 strategy, net revenues are enhanced as the market moves away from its initial at-the-money level.

Futures and Options

This example describes the impact of hedging partially with futures and the remainder with the sale of calls. A financial software company is in the midst of a $4,000,000 (560 million yen) transaction with a Japanese conglomerate. The current rate is 140 yen per dollar. The firm decides to hedge 80 percent of the revenue with futures and the rest with the sale of at-the-money calls. Table 7.6 shows the results if the rates move by ± 10 yen to the dollar.

The sale of futures provided the tightest fit because the options were not adjusted or implemented as a delta hedge. The options, however, provided an enhanced return within the confines of a stable exchange environment.

SUMMARY

Asset and liability managers can alter the composition of their balance sheet items through the futures and options markets or through swapping. These

Table 7.6   Blending the Sale of Futures with the Sale of Calls

	Corporation to Be Paid with Yen				
Offsetting $ Swing Sold 36 Futures	@1.40 Sold 9 SP 71 Calls	@.85 Sold 9 SP 72 Calls	Impact with SP 71 Calls	Impact with SP 72 Calls	$ Swing No Hedge Action Taken
130 Yen/$	−247253	−50885	−45822	−298137	−293075	307692
140 Yen/$	0	10935	9563	10935	9563	0
150 Yen/$	214286	15750	9563	230036	223848	−266667

SP = Strike Price
NOTE: 540 million yen approximate 44.8 futures contract equivalents.
80% rounds up to 36 futures.
Integer for the calls is nine without applying delta neutrality.
140 yen/$ equals .0071428 dollars per yen.
If the dollar rallies (140 to 150 yen/$), then there is a loss of $266,667; otherwise the futures hedge generated a financial offset of $214,286.

techniques do not necessarily cause the removal or the addition of cash market components; rather, the processes can be complementary. Moreover, the manager can employ a wide array of hedging techniques used by both physical and financial hedgers.

Foreign exchange is amenable to many hedging and asset and liability approaches. Financial instruments and currencies are influenced by time, interest rates, and yield-curve considerations. The foreign currency markets complicate situations further by including different sets of fundamentals and technicals. A hedger who has a broad overview of the market is in a better position to respond strategically when implementing the hedge program.

8

Equity Hedging

VARIETIES

Equity hedging has many forms: It can pertain to the hedging of actual or anticipated portfolios, common or preferred stocks, specific issues, or sub-indices or broadly based market indices. Other definitions refer to program trading, portfolio insurance arrangements, dividend capture programs, and stock market-linked certificates of deposit accounts. Futures, options, and other instruments can be used whole or in part, yet the intention is the same—protection.

FUTURES-PRICING MODEL FOR SECURITIES

The futures-pricing model for securities is similar to that for physical commodities because both consider the time value of money. More sophisticated versions of securities-pricing models account for dividends and the present value of dividends. For example, the following represents the ordinary futures-pricing model:

$$FP = CI (1 + i)^t - D$$

where FP = futures price
     CI = cash index
     i = interest rate
     t = time (or holding period)
     D = sum of dividends for holding period

The futures price is inversely influenced by dividends: The larger the dividend sum is, the larger the negative impact on the futures prices will be, because the holder of a futures contract is not entitled to the dividends. Conversely, the smaller the dividend sum is, the higher the futures prices will be, because a holder of such futures contracts is no longer forgoing substantial income through dividends. These points do not directly take into account differential taxation policies for capital gains (long term or short term; corporate or individual tax rates; and other investment variables).

Futures are evaluated against a framework of time value for money through the underlying cash index as is the associated dividend stream. Therefore the present value of such dividends is used during the holding period because dividends captured today are worth more than those captured tomorrow. The present value is used for dividend capture programs because those investment and hedging approaches seek stocks that pay comparatively high dividends, such as utility or mature manufacturing issues. The timing of these payments show pronounced clustering effects. For example, securities that satisfy the clustering and comparatively high payout rates have occurred in the past during February, May, August, and November. The quarterly dividend dates are particular important to the Major Market Index (MMI) futures contract because the index is comprised of these issues. In addition, the index is comparatively narrow, only 20 issues, versus the broader S&P 100, S&P 500, and NYSE indices. MMI's narrow focus can also facilitate dividend capture and program trades from lower transactional costs and simplification of the basket of securities (which are among the more active issues traded). A limited aspect is particularly useful at times of great market turbulence, such as that which prevailed around October 19, 1987. It is useful in making a quick estimate of where those values should be trading if there are issue trading halts or untimely openings for a limited number of issues.

The model with a present value aspect now becomes:

$$FP = CI (1 + i)^t - D_{pv}$$

where D_{pv} = present value of the dividend stream over the holding period. Higher dividend payouts have a negative impact on futures prices because the holders of futures (relative to the holders of the actual securities) would not be entitled to dividend payments and the potential to reinvest that income stream.

LINKED INSTRUMENTS

The emergence of instruments linked to the performance of equity indices has become more common. Typically, a bank will offer variable payouts tied to the performance of a stock market index. These payoffs can be call or put oriented. Essentially, the account will participate to a stipulated extent in subsequent market movements whether they are up (call oriented) or down (put oriented). In addition, the accounts will return, at least, the initial deposit upon expiration or at the end of the required holding period. An analysis of the parts shows that the accounts are time deposit accounts coupled with implied calls or puts.

The financial institution secures the benefits of the initial deposit's time value of money to fund other projects. A simple example of this is the purchase of a one-year Treasury bill, which hedges the obligation to return or payoff the initial deposit. There is no durational shift risk because there is a mandated holding period, and the set terms can subject the account to heavy penalties that can compensate the institution's durational risk. The residual funds from the purchase of the asset that funds the deposit can be utilized to fund the purchase of the call or put with the appropriate strike price. If the exchange or off-exchange options are too richly priced, the institution can create a synthesized position to hedge the performance of the implied option.

Remember that at the outset, the institution is, in effect, granting an option (call or put). To hedge that exposure it must buy or create a synthetic position.

The problem and the solutions fall within the province of asset and liability management when the possibilities for funding are extended. The institution can then evaluate the relative merits of funding other loan projects, fed funds, Eurodollars, or other alternatives.

This situation is represented by:

$$DA - DA_{pv} = RF$$

where DA   = deposit amount (initial account size)
       DA_{pv} = present value of DA
       RF   = residual funds, which can be additional income
              for the financial institution or funds available for the
              financing of the hedge.

It is imperative that the RF cover the financial commitment to satisfy the outstanding option feature for the accounts. This can be achieved by buying an option or creating a synthetic position with the RF availability. If this is not done, the institution is bearing the risk that the options will not be exercised (cashed in). By offering both types of accounts, the institution is effectively selling straddles. In all cases, the key issue is to efficiently cover the option obligations.

RISKS

The primary risks are systematic and nonsystematic, and the latter can be subdivided into issue and credit risks. Issue risks are germane to an individual security, and credit risks reflect distinguishing characteristics for issues within the same classification such as: high-, medium-, or low-grade utility stocks. These credit risks can pertain to different securities (ratings) issued by the same corporation, though usually these risks relate to preferred or subordinated issues.

Systematic Risks

Systematic risks are those that are inherent to the marketplace and are viewed as nondiversifiable risks. For example, if an investor owns the stocks that comprise the marketplace in the amounts that reflect their weighted capitalization, then he or she has widely held (diversified) holdings, but is still subject to market risk and can achieve only the market rate of return. In other words, while owning the marketplace in the correct proportions dispenses with the nonsystematic risks, the underlying market risk remains. This market risk and the associated market rate of return become a building block for beta analysis and individual comparative security rates of return. In these cases, the rate of return for securities is assumed to be linearly related to the market rate of return. Issues that have less risk than the market risk have less return, while issues that offer higher rates of return than those offered by the market have higher attendant risks.

Nonsystematic Risks

Nonsystematic risks are aside from the broad marketplace, and it is in this area that portfolio risk reduction can be effective. A composite portfolio of assets which, for given return levels, exhibit greater stability in variation and composite market value can reduce portfolio risks. The investor must try to structure the portfolio with issues that do not have substantial correlation with one another because systematic risks are nondiversifiable.

Nondiversifiable risk can be addressed by the placement of suitable hedges that generate financial offsets, an action that is often referred to as portfolio insurance.

Risk-Free Rate

Another integral concept of portfolio theory and individual security analysis is the risk-free rate. Generally, this rate is assumed to be the available Treasury-bill security rate. If the market rate of return is less than the Treasury-bill rate, the investor has a strong motive for divesting him- or herself of risky securities and depositing those funds in a risk-free asset. For situations in which this unusual condition does not occur, the risk-free rate relates to the market and individual security returns in a linear fashion and presents the demarcation line for ascertaining whether investments are optimal. Note that unless the risk-free rate instrument is hedged itself, either explicitly or implicitly, the follower of such a strategy is vulnerable to holding-period risk, whereby the price change of such an asset can offset any interest income and, in the event of an unexpected divestiture, generate a financial loss.

Covariation

Covariation is the relationship between two issues. Specifically, it is:

$$V_p = V_1^2 + V_2^2 + 2COV\ (V_1,V_2)$$

$$\frac{V_p - V_1^2 - V_2^2}{2} = COV\ (V_1,V_2)$$

where V_1^2 = variance for asset 1
       V_2^2 = variance for asset 2
       V_p = portfolio's variance
       $COV(V_1,V_2)$ = zero for the case of independent variables

This is important for that special case in which the variation of return for the portfolio is equal to the weighted parts. The covariance is the numerator term for the expression that determines the correlation coefficient.

PORTFOLIO THEORY

Portfolio theory evaluates the reduction of nonsystematic (diversifiable) risks through the careful selection of securities or other assets into efficient portfolios. Theoretically, the portfolio, when appropriately constructed, should offer lower risk (more stable returns) for a given level of expected return. By selecting issues that have independent returns or returns that are inversely related, the portfolio manager can construct a portfolio that exhibits stability. The theory relies on independent observations (returns), homogeneous investor (portfolio manager) expectations, and stable probability functions that contain additive properties, assumptions which may not be accurate or valid.

Departures from these assumptions can result in substantive differences between intended results and actual performance. One simplistic assumption is the application of homogeneous expectations to all the participants, which would mean that traders have the same view of risk and reward for all the assets in the investment universe. This is not true—distinct differ-

ences occur between holding periods because hedgers have day, intermediate, or long-term position perspectives. Intentions vary as well:
Participants are speculators, market makers, arbitragers, hedgers, pension
managers, and so on.

The theory ordinarily assumes that investors have the same constraints,
although they are linearly administered. This indicates that while the
financing levels may be different, the amount or contribution or commitment toward the assets is similar in across-the-board percentage allocation,
but different in dollar amounts. One assumption, for example, is that an
investor with 100 times the financial capacity of another investor would
own 100 times as much stock even though they are similarly allocated.
Once again this is not true. Some investors or investment firms are narrowly
focused on industries, high or low capitalization issues, management
shares (tied to incentive programs, or options on stocks, or profit sharing)
and so on.

As stated previously, the additive properties may not exist because there
can be significant dependence between returns instead of the required
independence. In fact, an analyst may compute a zero covariance term for
dependent variables, but the application of this statistic could then be
misleading.

Benefits

The benefits of an efficiently constructed portfolio are such that, for a given
rate of return, there are no other dominant portfolios that have the same
return for less risk. Alternatively, for a given level of risk, there are no other
portfolios that have higher rates of return. Essentially, an efficient portfolio
reduces the variability of return through the diversification of holdings.
Portfolio techniques allow for the rapid simulative analysis of altered
risk/reward characteristics by including, excluding, or otherwise substituting one asset for another.

Portfolio theory and its standardized applications are premised on independent and normally distributed returns for all assets. This means that
returns for one asset (corporation) occur independently of another. This
would suggest that the returns for stocks, such as Intel, IBM, and Mi-
crosoft, were not dependent upon one another or similar market environments. It does acknowledge that variations in some assets may be closer

to some than to others in the investment population, and because of this risk, an asset can be reduced down to its systematic component by eliminating the nonsystematic component. There is statistical evidence that the occurrence of outlier days, weeks, and months, however, do not happen as remotely randomly as the theories imply. Rather, the major changes, whether they are large positive or negatives ones, are more likely to concur than they are theoretically expected to, according to many of these models. Portfolio diversification can work least well when you need it the most. Although this sounds contradictory, it has been empirically the case.

Major Price Changes

Major price changes occur more frequently than normally expected; moreover, there is a pronounced statistical dependence among issues that have big up days and down days together. (This, too, is contrary to common expectations based on the assumption of statistical independence.) While statistical independence recognizes that major price changes occur for an issue here and an issue there, it implicitly assumes that these big changes are spread out over time. It is evident that this is not so.

Futures and options can provide protection through the establishment of a suitable hedge program. There are other important concerns besides basis-level risk, including financial risks, which are induced by dramatic market behavior that can produce substantial operational problems. Destabilizing events for cash and carry and reverse cash and carry positions and the survival perspective of protecting portfolio values during turbulent times affect physical commodities. Sometimes, the latter view is overwhelming because participants scramble for protection despite unfavorable basis levels. Prices may not stabilize until sharply lower or higher prices are attained, at which point, the basis relationships once again reflect their theoretical or favorable levels.

PORTFOLIO INSURANCE

There are two primary approaches to portfolio insurance: One advocates posturing with a trading emphasis, and the other presents a traditionally oriented hedging—not trading—technique.

In the first approach, the trading emphasis is manifested by the testing of strategies that enable the portfolio insurer to establish positions when the market goes up by a specified percentage and reduce the futures hedge/trade by a predetermined amount for subsequent price moves. In other words, if the market goes up x percent, then increase the short futures hedge position by y percent; or, if the market (portfolio) goes down by x percent, then reduce the sell hedge by y percent. Table 8.1 illustrates trading-oriented strategies.

For certain arrangements, it is conceivable that a hedge could be lifted at a time most needed. For example, if historical studies demonstrate that the market (designated portfolio) typically rallies after an eight, nine, or 10

Table 8.1 Trading-Oriented Portfolio Insurance Strategies

	Illustrative Trading-Oriented Strategy			
Market move	1 Percent portfolio adjustment	2 Percent portfolio adjustment	5 Percent portfolio adjustment	10 Percent portfolio adjustment
−10.00	−10.00	−20.00	−50.00	−100.00
−9.00	−9.00	−18.00	−45.00	−90.00
−8.00	−8.00	−16.00	−40.00	−80.00
−7.00	−7.00	−14.00	−35.00	−70.00
−6.00	−6.00	−12.00	−30.00	−60.00
−5.00	−5.00	−10.00	−25.00	−50.00
−4.00	−4.00	−8.00	−20.00	−40.00
−3.00	−3.00	−6.00	−15.00	−30.00
−2.00	−2.00	−4.00	−10.00	−20.00
−1.00	−1.00	−2.00	−5.00	−10.00
0.00	0.00	0.00	0.00	0.00
1.00	1.00	2.00	5.00	10.00
2.00	2.00	4.00	10.00	20.00
3.00	3.00	6.00	15.00	30.00
4.00	4.00	8.00	20.00	40.00
5.00	5.00	10.00	25.00	50.00
6.00	6.00	12.00	30.00	60.00
7.00	7.00	14.00	35.00	70.00
8.00	8.00	16.00	40.00	80.00
9.00	9.00	18.00	45.00	90.00
10.00	10.00	20.00	50.00	100.00

percent decline, then a portfolio insurer's trading rules could require the purchase back of futures so that for each one percent decline in portfolio (market index) value, the hedge is lifted by 10 percent. Under such circumstances, a 10 percent decline from the decision point indicates the complete removal of the sell hedge. To put this state of affairs into perspective, on October 19, 1987, the equity markets were effectively down 10 percent by the end of the first trading hour and eventually closed down by more than 20 percent that day. If the rule was a singular adjustment on the opening or early part of the day, the subsequent sales would occur on the early morning weakness the following day, which was also an important turnaround day for many indices (excluding the OTC classifications). Here, sales of futures could have been conducted at substantial discounts relative to the actuals (10–15 percent of the value).

Portfolio insurance strategies are also known as dynamic hedging strategies. They are called dynamic because of the potential for frequent adjustments in the hedge mixture in order to adapt to changing emphasis for potential upside gains. Some managers pursue portfolio insurance within the context of a purchased put protection plan: They seek a floor to the downside portfolio valuation while striving to capture upside profit potential, similar to the characteristics of a synthetic call position (long securities and long-put options). For some insurers this approach is referred to as replication of an option through dynamic hedging.

The second type of portfolio insurance requires placing a sell hedge, accomplished via the futures or options markets, against actual portfolios. The hedge placement through the options market would correspond to the degree of sought protection (none, partial, or complete) and the level of deductible (options' strike price).

The placement of a hedge via the futures could entail additional financing, particularly in the event of an advancing market. Variation margin funds would be necessary because the hedger is short the board. In a declining market, the hedger would have access to improved cash flow because of the drop in futures prices and the opportunity to reinvest that accelerated cash inflow.

Coinsurance

Coinsurance is the equity term for a partial hedge. If a hedger places an offsetting futures or options position that produces 75 percent coverage, then that hedger is coinsuring the exposed 25 percent. Similarly, a hedger who maintains a 90 percent hedge is viewed as coinsuring the portfolio for 10 percent. The coinsurance, unless provided for otherwise, is the percentage of potential loss from adverse market conditions; or, it can be the percentage amount that the insuring party (pension, portfolio, funds program) will internally insure or absorb. These programs often tout the opportunity for additional fianancial gains in the event of advancing markets because the uncovered percentage (25 or 10 percent in the preceding example) would be open to further price appreciation. If the market sold off, then only the insured portion of the portfolio would be covered, and the money manager would bear the loss, realized or unrealized, as a cost of doing business. Of course, this would also affect the performance of such portfolios.

Coinsurance has its roots in the insurance industry: The policy holder purchases coverage with no deductible or a stipulated one. In addition, the portion of the potential loss or degree of exposure beyond the deductible is referred to as the amount (degree) of coinsurance or self insurance.

PROGRAM TRADING

The arbitrage aspect of equity hedging is program trading. In its typical form, the program trader purchases a preselected basket of securities and sells a predetermined number of futures contracts whenever it is deemed that the securities were trading at a sufficiently large discount to the futures. The sufficiently large discount is determined by computing the selected futures pricing model. Conversely, if securities are considered comparatively rich relative to futures, then the program trader sells the underlying stock and purchases the appropriate number of futures contracts. This arbitrage behavior is necessary to keep values from straying too far from their fundamental relationships. The arbitrager is indifferent to the location of the prices levels as long as the differences are favorable for exploitation. It is this program trading mechanism that keeps upmoves or downmoves from being over extended and not the other way around. Figure 8.1 illustrates theoretical and actual lines, and Figure 8.2 highlights the implied 7 percent rate difference between actual and theoretical futures. Figure 8.3 plots the index versus the actual futures differences against the actual futures versus theoretical

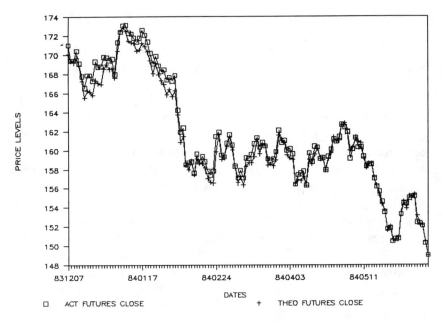

FIGURE 8.1   Actual futures versus theoretical futures values.

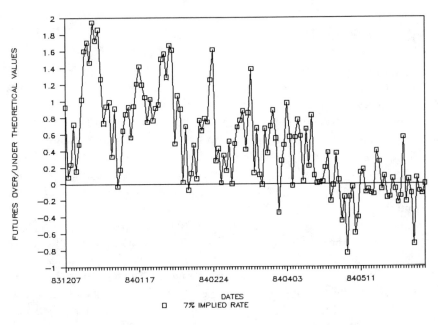

FIGURE 8.2   The implied seven percent rate (7%) for the differences between actual and theoretical futures.

236

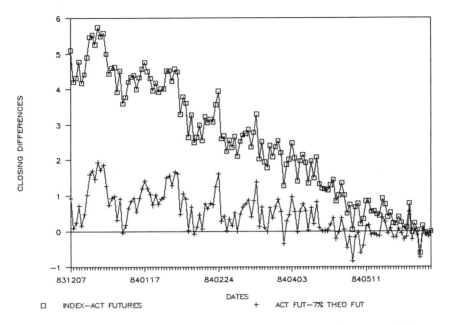

FIGURE 8.3 Illustrative plot at index versus actual futures differences against actual futures versus theoretical futures differences.

futures differences. Figure 8.4 displays fluctuations in the differences series for various imputed interest rates.

When the actual differences are higher than the theoretical indications, then the program trader would purchase futures (options) and sell the underlying securities. Otherwise, the program trade would require the opposite transactions and reflect the cash-and-carry operation.

One important, albeit short-lived, problem is that the correction may not always be immediate. This is attested to by the events of October 19 and 20, 1987, and different expirations; however, program trading did attempt to tie values to one another even then. Other financial shocks rocked the securities and futures markets, including portfolio insurance trading and hedging programs, the lack of timely openings, and the disruptions caused by disarrayed market making in the underlying securities. A severe loss of confidence from dealing with stock specialists whose firms were on the brink of financial ruin also disrupted orderly markets. Unlike futures markets, in which many individuals or locals make up a significant portion of the liquidity of the given marketplace, in organized securities trading,

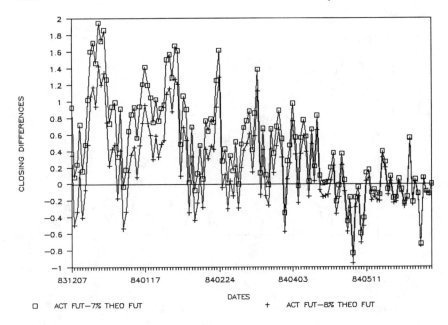

FIGURE 8.4 Fluctuations in differences series for two implied rates.

one specialist firm is essentially franchised to make a market. The futures clearing houses stood as the ultimate parties to those trades, which was not the case for the stock transactions. Program trading is much maligned despite the fact that many of the programs entail only $25 to $50 million in value on both sides (futures values and stock values), while portfolio insurance programs for even one party can entail the transaction of one billion dollars or more. Also, portfolio insurance transactions can be one-sided, unlike the execution of program trading transactions, which include the purchase and the sale of stocks, futures, or options.

It is interesting to note that equity management organizations engage in program trades with the dividend income streams from the held securities and protect the portfolios, at least in part, with a portfolio insurance arrangement.

Sampling

The construction of a representative basket of securities to reflect the financial impact of broad based equity indices is a sampling approach to hedging strategies. Which securities and in what proportion would better approximate the S&P 100 or S&P 500 or the New York Stock Exchange (NYSE) indices? As many participants have discovered, the "best" approximations may not be sufficient for pure arbitrage-related program trades. When program trades based on representative samples and not on the actual configuration of the index are positioned, losses may occur, because the few issues that were not included in the sample eventually accounted for the actual profitable performance of the conceptual trade.

These trades may sometimes have to be maintained until the final settlement and not exited beforehand because the discrepancies have not rapidly adjusted but can, under certain conditions, become further aggravated, and only the final day, last minute rush provides the economic force for complete closure.

The expiration of S&P futures illustrates such a case. Figure 8.5 presents the movements in the cash index and futures contract. Figure 8.6 illustrates the raw differences or basis between the cash index and the actual futures. Figure 8.7 shows the basis action versus a time adjusted differential, which represents a simplified theoretical line for the differences. Note that the closure did not occur until imminent expiration.

ACTUAL VERSUS ANTICIPATORY HEDGING

Actual hedging strategy is one against the actual ownership of stocks or the commitment to deliver securities (short position in actual securities), and is the departure point for portfolio insurance programs. Anticipatory hedging refers to the placement of buy or sell hedges prior to the actual purchase or sale of stocks. For instance, a portfolio manager may reasonably anticipate the inflow of funds (for a pension or management agreement) within a specific time frame and will view the market optimistically. By purchasing futures (or calls), the fund's manager can establish an anticipatory hedge in that he is prudently anticipating the flow of funds into management and has protected his management from intervening market advances. The relationship is tighter through the use of futures. The manager would have to provide variation funds in the event of a decline. An advance would generate a positive flow of funds and provide price (portfolio) protection basis the cash securities–futures relationship.

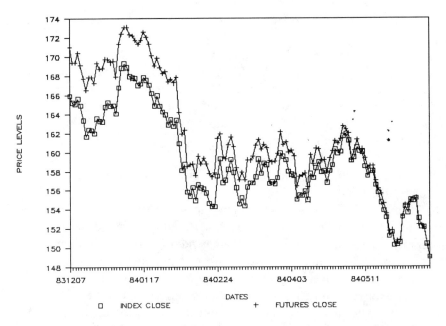

FIGURE 8.5 Plot of cash index against actual futures.

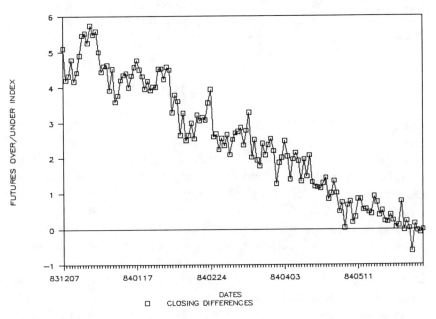

FIGURE 8.6 Basis or raw differences between cash index and futures.

240

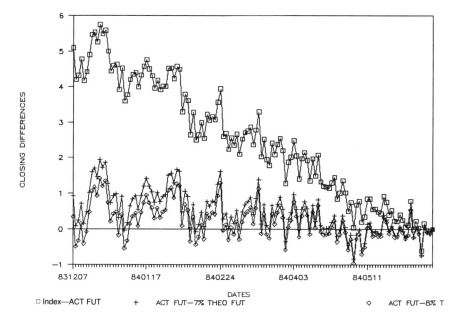

FIGURE 8.7 Plotting two actual futures versus two different implied differences against framework of raw differences (actual futures-cash) or basis.

The purchase of calls establishes a cap for the intended portfolio, and if there is a subsequent decline in equity values, the loss in call premium could effectively be amortized.

The length of the expected holding period is assessed against the length of the expected waiting period. The longer the period, the greater the potential for wider price moves. This magnification of price movement and the attendant risk is the price diffusion condition, in which an annualized 10 percent variation in price suggests a potentially wider range when applied to nine months versus three months. This price diffusion process underlies the option-pricing models as well.

DIVERSIFICATION VERSUS MIRROR IMAGING

There is a need for proper diversification. However, the basic premises of diversification and its inherent statistical inability to modify several important risks, among which is market risk, does not preclude alternative hedging techniques. Consider two identically positioned portfolios that reflect the composition of the S&P 500 index and that were established at identical prices. In the event of a subsequent market decline, each would lose value identically. Now consider that portfolio 2, in addition to being diversified, is appropriately hedged with S&P 500 futures or options.

The hedge offsets the market risk and is the counterpart to the actual underlying securities. By relaxing some of these assumptions we can still observe the beneficial effects of a hedge versus a diversification-only portfolio. The diversification-only portfolio addresses nonsystematic risks although it is incapable of moderating market risks. At the times when protection is needed the most, the simple (or even complete) diversification of nonsystematic risk is partial protection, at best, because major price changes will occur in clusters, given important market events, rather than in isolated instances. Market risk clearly dominates in such circumstances and the protection arrangement must take this into consideration. Theoretically, the occurrence of 5 percent changes in Dow, S&P, NYSE, or AMEX indices components probably should not occur on the same day or within tightly defined time periods; however, that is not the empirical case. Statistical documentation does not support the assumption that a 2 percent change should happen only 1 out of 1,000 times. The joint probability of 2 percent simultaneous changes should be $(.001)^{500}$—and this is not the case. Even the limited example of sector analysis illustrates the principles behind this substantial price-change mechanism. If technology stocks, particularly the larger capitalized issues, are surging or collapsing, the value impact is great enough to influence the entire group. The ramifications for other service-related and hardware-related issues is important as well.

A focus on extreme pricing behavior is central to a discussion of market risk as it addresses worst-case scenarios. The standard methodology for portfolio analysis and security analysis is predicated upon regression analysis. Although some of the statistics, such as standard deviations and variance, are approximations of dispersion, they can be misleading because the actual market mechanisms may show radically different shapes and operating properties. In the long run, while the empirical distributions will show bell-shaped curves, they may not be easily transformed into normally based distributions. They may be generated by *ordered* strings or runs of pluses and minuses and not be independently, randomly distributed changes. By putting all the numbers together, one can easily get the impression that the series are trendless and the fluctuations about the means should be normally explained, which is probably not the case. Beta analysis is dependent on normalization and it linearly relates rates of return and risk to a market standard. Extreme price behavior, however, focuses on greater than midpoint changes or events and considers worst-case scenarios and risks more directly. It is akin to identifying whether property to be under-written for insurance coverage is lying in a tornado or hurricane belt, earthquake sensitive area (fault line), or flood zone. Nationally, these risk areas may cancel out because of locational diversity, but on a local level they do not. The study of the tails of distributions can be more germane to these issues because one departs from singular predictions (linear lines with one mean/mode) and considers the strong possibility of two distributive mechanisms (up and down trends) overlapping. The latter readily leads to the summation of disastrous probabilities, and the areas of concern quickly become the areas between two points or from one point (and summed out for the remainder of the distribution) rather than a grossly misconceived joint probability statistic, which can be substantially off the money.

Figures 8.8–8.10 graphically represent the sequence of returns. Figures 8.11–8.12 highlight the potential for error if one assumes standard deviation-oriented models versus a broader dispersion statistic. In particular, note the larger values that are added for points beyond the inflection ones. On an expected-value basis, this indicates the potential for greater than normally expected extraordinary losses as well as gains.

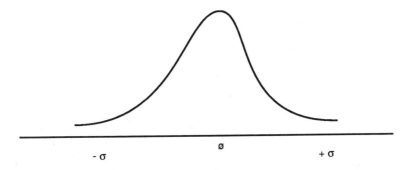

FIGURE 8.8   Bell-shaped curve of singular risk.

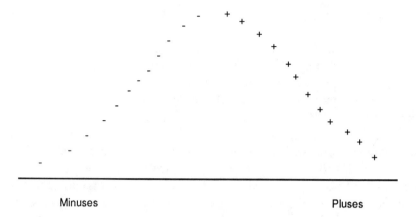

Minuses   Pluses

FIGURE 8.9   Bell-shaped curve constructed with runs.

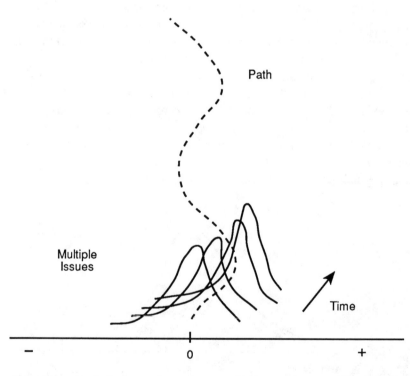

Path

Multiple
Issues

Time

   −   0   +

FIGURE 8.10   Bell-shaped curve summed over issues (time) in the tails or the snake function. (Notice that the path "snakes" over time.)

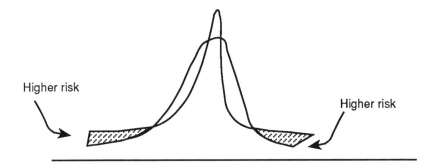

FIGURE 8.11   Highlighting potential for error of standard deviation-based models versus wider dispersion ones.

FIGURE 8.12   Highlighting potential for error of standard deviation-based models versus skewed or truncated.

SUMMARY

Equity hedging programs have the breadth of other hedging programs. They can be formulated to take advantage of pricing discrepancies, as in program trading, or they can establish price-level protection for either the buy or sell sides via portfolio insurance arrangements. Whatever the type of equity hedging used, the principles of the time value of money and the options-pricing concepts interact with the underlying securities and hedging matrix.

PART III
STRATEGIES

9
Trading the Basis

AN ARTFUL SCIENCE

Basis trading evaluates and executes positions based on the assessment of richness or cheapness. Richness occurs when the actual basis is more expensive than the theoretical or implied value. Cheapness occurs when the basis is less expensive or at a discount to the implied or theoretical basis value. Trading the basis is the culmination of the hedge process. Entering a basis trade early can be uncomfortable sometimes. Wider than normal basis variations may occur and rapid closure is not the order of the day. One can quantify and computerize the parameters, models, and rules; however, the decision to go ahead is just as critical. Previously, we examined applications that transform substantial price-yield-level risks into more manageable basis-level risks. Now we will explore approaches that try to minimize these lesser risks. Cash and carry, reverse cash and carry, repo, and reverse repo are inherent to trading the basis. Although they are conceptually the same, the first two terms tend to be used in physical situations and the last two in financial situations.

These sophisticated programs are exacting mathematically and in their operational mechanics. Although slight advantages (discrepancies) are pursued, the total dollar size of gross positions can be quite large. Net exposure generally is small; however, the path is important—further departures can be destabilizing because additional funds may be necessary. When to strike is as important as what to strike and how.

PURPOSES

While ordinary hedging techniques remove important risks, trading the basis takes the program to the "razor's edge." Successful applications result in higher-than-average performances, while unsuccessful applications cause less-than-average performances. Favorable basis conditions generally provide protection and satisfactory operating margins, but if one of two hedgers conducting the same trade receives a better price, that hedger is in an advantageous position. Even when both traders have similar orders, particularly limit orders, the inability to receive a complete fill can make a difference. For example, one hedger in a jumpy bond market filled at 89-11, and another at 89-15. Both had market orders, but the fills produced a $125 difference between the two, per $100,000 par value (one futures contract) position. The ability to obtain efficient executions is vital to such operations. Slight pricing discrepancies ($\frac{1}{32}$ for the bonds or $\frac{1}{64}$ for the options), knowledge, experience, or other advantages can benefit the hedger.

Analogous situations in the equity markets occur with both portfolio insurance and program trading. Portfolio insurance provides comprehensive coverage, while program trading seeks to exploit discrepancies between current basis levels and theoretically computed ones. Rapid price swings during the fourth quarter of 1987 placed a special emphasis on expected valuations beside theoretical valuations. Many important stocks that comprise key equity indices failed to have timely openings or were disrupted by trading halts. Program traders had to rely on "best estimates" of where the components might be trading in addition to where they should be trading.

MARKET EFFICIENCY

Market efficiency is relative—if everything were absolutely fair valued then the marketplace would stagnate. This is not the case because opportunities and risks change their shapes and sizes throughout time. Because

participants aim for ideals (theoretical points) but are satisfied with suffi-
ciency (economic feasibility), there are multiple basis relationships. Multiple basis relationships derive from the individual circumstances
surrounding each organization, such as cost of capital, opportunity costs,
and position limits. Accordingly, slight variations in interest rates and price
levels magnify variations in performance.

EQUALITIES AND DISPARITIES

Equality among the historic, current, theoretical, and expected bases
suggests that there are no trading-the-basis opportunities, although hedging
opportunities may be present. This is symbolically represented as:

$$H(b) = C(b) = T(b) = E(b)$$

where H(b) = historic basis
      C(b) = current basis
      T(b) = theoretical basis
      E(b) = expected basis.

Unlike speculative trading, trading-the-basis programs focus on basis
levels instead of price or yield levels: It is a special case of spread trading.
Economic discrepancies or inequalities may be due to wide price swings;
however, it is the prevailing basis and its expected terminal value that is
important: Differences among these concepts indicate that there are trading
opportunities. When the current basis is greater than the historic or theoretical basis (C(b) > T(b)) there may be opportunities that warrant the
selling of futures against the purchase of the underlying instrument (commodity) in order to gain the differences.

Physical: Gold

Two firms are evaluating the basis relationships and intramonth differentials for gold. Their costs of capital are slightly different; therefore, their
outlooks are also different. Firm 2 finds it in its interest to deliver gold into
the market now, given a 6 percent implied repo rate (cash and carry), while

Firm 1 finds the implied rate attractive for conducting a cash and carry. Firm 1 conducts the cash and carry (holding the physical against a short futures position) for the advantage of comparatively more favorable financing and because it can reap the slight differential. Firm 2 finds that its financing costs are slightly higher than the implied rate between the cash and the futures and elects to deliver now. This action precludes receiving a slightly impaired financial return because the financial cost is slightly larger than the implied interest return.

This one situation demonstrates that firms can have different motivations, outlooks, and outcomes. In the trading environment, a broad spectrum of outcomes and motivations prevails.

Additional slight advantages may accrue to approved depositories for metals deliveries—the cost of the transaction is smaller because a firm is able to satisfy deliveries from its own storage space. Table 9.1 lists the data for this multiple trading-the-basis situation.

The slight basis-point difference in carrying costs was sufficient to cause Firm 2 to be a deliverer of gold on the spot market. It could save $40 (or $200) in financing, depending on the case. Firm 1 preferred to take the metal, given its appraisal of comparatively attractive rates (implied and

Table 9.1 Multiple Basis Listing for Gold—Two Firm Evaluations

	Illustrative Gold Example $400 Spot/6% Implied Rate/$424 One Year Futures			
	Corporate rates			
	5.9/6.1	5.5/6.5	Case 1	Case 2
Firm 1	423.60	422.00	40.00	200.00
Firm 2	424.40	426.00	−40.00	−200.00
Market	424.00	424.00		

NOTE: This table shows that for a slight difference in the cost of capital there are different outcomes for firms. For example, in Case 1 Firm 1 can borrow at 5.9% while Firm 2 can borrow at 6.1%. The implied market rate is 6 percent. Therefore Firm 1 can lock in an extra $40.00 per contract difference by doing a cash and carry. Firm 2 in effect is penalized by $40.00 for its cash and carry though the overall hedge can still be worthwhile.

The results are more dramatic when the market rate remains at 6% but the borrowing rates are now 5.5 and 6.5 percent for the two firms.

The table illustrates that the implied differences can also vary according to fill prices for the hedges. Better prices mean better implied rates.

actual), and would benefit by similar amounts. These financing differences can arise within the same industry, whether it is banking or smelting, due to the underlying funding mixes as well as credit ratings and so forth.

Financial: Securities

One criterion for evaluating the attractiveness of carrying or shorting securities is the implied repo rate. When the actual interest costs of carrying securities is less than the implied rate, a firm would consider holding securities, an operation also recognized as a repurchase agreement. The firm would then trade the basis by borrowing at a comparatively cheaper rate and delivering out securities at a better rate. The opposite transaction is a reverse repo or reverse repurchase agreement. Again, slight discrepancies in financing capability influence the delivery process as well as the trading-the-basis evaluation.

The reverse repo is more difficult to pursue because the cheapest to deliver or the invoiced securities can be different from those that were shorted to initiate this transaction.

The implied repo rate is determined by computing the total cost and receipt for carrying a specified security. The process uses the mechanics that would be activated when a security is presented for delivery. This methodology is used to establish the hierarchy of cheapest-to-deliver securities.

The total cost is the market price plus accrued interest for a security. The total receipt is the market price of the futures contract adjusted by the conversion factor for the ''deliverable'' security, plus any coupon interest received, plus any accrued interest. These two factors are then evaluated in Table 9.2. The net return is then adjusted by the number of days for which the position is to be carried. The implied repo rate was .0339 or 3.39 percent. This compares unfavorably with the 9.01 percent yield for the 12⅜s of 2004.

Reverse repo transactions are more difficult to pursue. The securities that were shorted may not be the ones that are tendered against the open long-futures position. Even though the trade may have considered possible cheapest-to-deliver candidates, these securities experience shifts over time and interest rates. Similar reverse carry problems can occur for physical commodities. The fineness, weights, grades, or locations delivered may be

Table 9.2 Implied Repo Rate

Total Cost			Total Receipts	
Market price of 12⅜s	127-16	March futures		90-26
	($127,500)			($90,812.50)
Accrued interest	3,244.16	Conversion adjusted futures price		125,430.22
		Interest received		6,193.75
		Interest accrued		292.48
Total	$130,596.87	Total		$131,916.45

$$\frac{\$131,916.45 - \$130,596.87}{\$130,596.87} \times \frac{360}{17} = .0339$$

Implied rate of 3.39%

different from those expected when the reverse was initiated. One must remember that the futures short has the control over the delivery process. It is the short-futures party who decides what will be delivered within exchange guidelines.

ARBITRAGE SITUATIONS

Trading the basis and arbitrage programs are often synonymous. Physical and financial examples discussed previously focused on differentials between cash and futures. This discussion is expanded in the following example by incorporating options into the analysis, an action which suggests that futures versus cash differences alone may not be sufficient. Opportunities may be greater elsewhere.

Table 9.3 illustrates a hypothetical arbitrage situation. Each COMEX silver futures contract represents 5,000 ounces of .999 fineness. There is no fineness valuation adjustment like there is for gold. Notice that futures remained flat but the expected volatility for the options increased, which raised option premiums. An arbitrage situation developed in which the long silver position was better hedged by the sale of a synthetic short. Similar

Table 9.3   Illustrative Silver Arbitrage—Hedge Opportunities

Silver Example—in Cents per Ounce

	Cash price	Futures price	Call SP 600	Put SP 600
Earlier	599.00	605.00	23.00	*24.00
Later	600.00	606.00	**31.00	31.00

* Initial transaction
** Subsequent transaction

opportunities can arise from changes in expectations about the implied interest rate as well as from choppy market-price conditions.

The arbitrageable situations can be more than one, which is highlighted by the multitude of cash-futures-options relationships. The hedger initiated the hedge by purchasing a put with a $6.00 strike price, which effectively converted the overall position into a synthetic long call. Subsequently, the options markets experienced an increase in expected volatility, which pushed premiums higher. The hedger now was faced with a choice: Should she liquidate the put and sell the futures? Or, was there a more attractive alternative? The call premium rallied by eight cents, the put by seven cents, and the futures contract by only one cent. By selling the futures she would lock in a six-cent cost of carry. This sale of futures versus cash did not change the implied carry reflected by cents per ounce. The sale of the put would realize a seven-cent gain; however, there was still another alternative. By selling the 600 strike price call, the hedger transformed the position into an effective conversion. The sale of a call and the purchase of a put with identical strike prices and expiration months produces a synthetic short position. This position coupled with the long-cash leg generated a hedge that would behave as though it were covered by the sale of a futures contract. Interestingly, this transaction netted the hedger an additional one cent per ounce in terms of carry because the course of events shifted the relative time value components of the option legs. (Note: In the event that the market did not subsequently move, the hedger would lose 24 cents on the put and gain 31 cents on the call for a net gain of seven cents. This compares favorably with the six-cent implied carry offered by a futures-only hedge against cash.)

BASIS ANALYSIS

The following sections analyze the basis analysis from trading perspectives. The topics examined include costs of capital, taxation, and available issues. Similar situations can be developed for grains, meats, stocks, currencies, and bonds and each group can include numerous subsets. For example, bonds can include: Treasuries, corporates, municipals, mortgage backed securities, Eurodollar and forex denominated issues.

One Starting Point

One excellent example for this analysis is the municipal bond market, which has cash, futures, and options. The futures and options expire on the same day on a cash settlement procedure, and the cash market has many issues that offer a complexity of returns.

Figure 9.1 illustrates the relationship between the Bond Buyer Index versus the March 1989 futures contract. It shows that for the last thirty days, the widest basis relationship was 76/32nds, the narrowest 12/32nds and the average 35/32nds. The standard deviation was 15, there was a correlation of 71.5, and a beta of 0.39 between the index and the futures.

Figure 9.1 indicates the last observation for the basis was 33/32nds and shows that the basis narrowed near the end of October, widened during early through mid-November, and then displayed fairly consistent narrowing through the middle of December. Figure 9.1 accurately describes

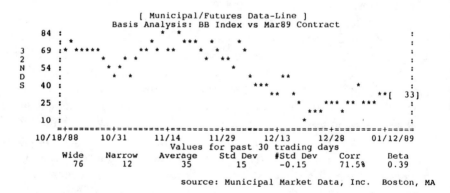

FIGURE 9.1   Bond Buyer Index versus March futures basis plot.

the abbreviated data listed with it. It shows how the futures behaved relative to the underlying cash index, a linked behavior that was assimilated into a basis statistic and plotted over time. The comparatively low beta value of .39 reflects the strong convergence that is underway. The relatively high correlation statistic attested to the degree of association between the cash index and futures.

The next step is to evaluate the basis relationship from an actual versus theoretical viewpoint. Figure 9.2 illustrates this from one set of underlying assumptions, which include the rate of convergence between the futures and actuals and the implied costs of carry and taxation rates. Figure 9.2 is a graph that demonstrates that the actual March 1989 futures contract was trading at a ²⁰/₃₂ discount relative to its imputed theoretical value. The plotted timeframe shows that the March contract had frequently traded at a sizable discount relative to cash for most of the time. Only during mid-December did the contract overrun its theoretical value and establish a premium to its theoretical value.

One explanation for this frequent pattern of relative underpricing is that it can be quite difficult (but not impossible) to short the actual municipal market. While at times there are major deals that enjoy popular demand (broad participation) there are many other times when these bonds get locked away. The tight free-floating supply of many issues makes it difficult to short the actual issues and buy the futures (reverse-repo-oriented transaction). This difficulty causes a chronic bias. Such an asymmetrical condition does not destroy the hedging applications of the futures and options,

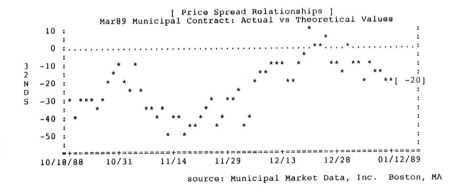

FIGURE 9.2   Actual versus theoretical price spread relationships.

but alerts the prudent hedger to potential pitfalls while highlighting more favorable opportunities. The hedger's objective is to achieve a consistent approach and program, which can be accomplished by a rigorous basis analysis.

Basis and Implied Repo Analysis

The cost of funds, applicable taxation rates, and the deductibility of carry charges, yields, and the time to expiration all interact to determine an implied rate of return, or the implied repo rate. Multiple examples reinforce the idea that there is no one implied rate because many organizations are subject to different tax rates (federal, state, and local) and costs of financing and transactions.

Table 9.4 provides examples for implied repo and basis analysis. The "8:30 to close" timeframes provide momentary views of the basis. Transactions are potentially fluid: The market flows over time and does not change at half-hour intervals only. It should be recognized that participant ability to conduct many of these trades can be limited by conditions such

Table 9.4   Basis and Implied Repo Rates

```
                         [ Municipal/Futures Data-Line ]
Basis and Implied Repo Rates (Cash Mkt: Funds@ 9.12%  T/E Yld@ 7.56%  Tax: 34%)
           (EST) :     69 Days  0.18%   :    160 Days  0.08%   :   251 Days  0.05%   :
           BB Index:Mar89  Basis   IRR    :Jun89  Basis  IRR     :Sep89  Basis   IRR      :
  8:30   91-24 : 91-01    23   7.37%: na                   :  na                  :
  9:30   91-25 : 90-25    32   5.77%: 89-26    63   6.63%:  na                  :
 10:00   91-27 : 91-03    24   7.19%: 90-06    53   7.40%: 89-12    79   7.60%:
 10:30   91-28 : 91-07    21   7.73%: 90-10    50   7.63%: 89-16    76   7.75%:
 11:00   91-28 : 91-07    21   7.73%: 90-09    51   7.55%: 89-14    78   7.65%:
 11:30   91-29 : 91-08    21   7.73%: 90-12    49   7.71%: 89-20    73   7.89%:
 12:00   91-30 : 91-07    23   7.38%: 90-11    51   7.55%: 89-20    74   7.85%:
 12:30   91-31 : 91-07    24   7.20%: 90-12    51   7.56%: 89-20    75   7.80%:
  1:00   91-31 : 91-08    23   7.38%: 90-13    50   7.63%: 89-20    75   7.80%:
  1:30   91-31 : 91-09    22   7.55%: 90-13    50   7.63%: 89-20    75   7.80%:
  2:00   92-00 : 91-12    20   7.91%: 90-16    48   7.79%: 89-22    74   7.85%:
  2:30   92-01 : 91-13    20   7.91%: 90-17    48   7.79%: 89-26    71   8.00%:
 Close   92-03 : 91-12    23   7.38%: 90-16    51   7.56%: 89-24    75   7.80%:
```

SOURCE: Municipal Market Data, Inc. Boston, MA

as size of offerings (availabilities) and settlement procedures for the actual bonds.

Table 9.4 indicates that there are 69 days to expiration for the March 1989 contract. There are 160 and 251 days left for the June and September 1989 contracts, respectively. It is assumed that the cost of finance is a fed funds rate of 9.12 percent and that the tax rate is 34 percent. The tax exempt average yield is 7.56 for the selected securities. These securities do not necessarily have to be index components.

Table 9.4 lists the basis between the cash index and the three futures months in terms of 32nds. In all the listed cases, the index was at a simple arithmetical premium relative to the futures contracts.

The IRR, or implied repo rate, was 7.30 percent on the close between the index and the March 1989 contract. Assuming that a trade could be made at prevailing levels, the rate suggests that the futures contract was at a slight discount relative to its theoretical value. How do we determine this? First, the implied rate shows that it is less than the actual prevailing cost of carry (the 9.12 percent funds rate). The implied rate defines an equivalency condition which compares the cost of carrying the actual securities with a position in the futures contract by evaluating the attendant rates of return. The IRR looked at from another perspective implies that the cost of carrying the actual securities would be 7.30 percent. This is significantly different from the current 9.12-percent cost of carry.

For the given day, all the listed IRRs in Table 9.4 suggest the futures to be a better alternative to owning the cash. Institutional regulations and requirements may prevent the marketplace from ironing out these discrepancies completely. Yet this analysis serves a useful purpose because it effectively relates the cost of carrying actual securities to futures.

Concept of Cheapness

One definition of cheapness is the comparative value of a bond to an index or a futures contract. If the issue is comparatively cheap, then you buy the issue and sell the futures. Alternatively, you can use this process to select comparatively cheap issues to construct a portfolio, while avoiding more costly (comparatively rich) issues. Table 9.5 lists several municipal secu-

Table 9.5   Hierarchical Listing of Cheapest Relationships to Cash
Index

```
                              [ Municipal/Futures Data-Line ]
         Cheapest relationships to Bond Buyer's Municipal Bond Index @ 01/12/89
         Issue                        #obs   Corr   Beta    Avg    Last  #Std Devs
Salt River Project AZ       7.875%  '28   30     76%   0.93   9.99   9.56   -2.07
Missouri Hlth & Ed Fac Au   7.750%  '16   30     84%   1.02   9.87   9.69   -1.97
Orange Co FL HFA(MBIA)B     7.875%  '25   29     86%   0.93   9.81   9.19   -1.61
Virginia Trans Bd           7.800%  '16   30     84%   0.98  10.52  10.31   -1.53
NY Metro Trans Auth         8.000%  '18   18     83%   0.98   9.54   9.19   -1.48
Oklahoma Hsg Fin Agcy       8.250%  '20   29     85%   1.01   9.39   8.94   -1.29
Illinois Hsg Dev Auth(AMT   8.100%  '22   30     86%   1.09   8.24   8.06   -0.97

Chicago O'Hare Airport      8.200%  '18   30     81%   0.99   9.42   9.19   -0.90
Baltimore Co MD GO          7.750%  '16   30     84%   1.02  10.32  10.19   -0.87
Maryland Health & Ed        7.500%  '20   30     91%   1.20   8.15   8.06   -0.86
Ohio HFA (AMT)              8.125%  '20   30     86%   1.01   8.87   8.81   -0.49
Philadelphia Muni Auth      7.800%  '18   30     81%   1.13  10.23  10.19   -0.39
Georgia Muni Elec Auth      8.125%  '17   30     81%   1.09  10.59  10.56   -0.31
Brazos River TX/ Houston    7.750%  '15   30     72%   1.16   5.73   5.69   -0.28
```

SOURCE: Municipal Market Data, Inc., Boston, MA

rities that exhibit different degrees of cheapness relative to the Municipal
Bond Index.

For example, the Missouri Health and Education Facilities Authority 7¾s
of 2016 shows a correlation of 84 percent to the index. This describes its
price behavior to the index. The 30 in the number of observations column
indicates the number of days as observations. The beta relates the prices
between the specified security and the index level. The basis statistics in
this table are the "Avg." (average) and "Last" (last basis differences)
between the price of the security and the index. Since all the differences in
the average and last columns are positive, they indicate that the specified
security is trading above the index level. The securities, however, are
comparatively cheap by definition. The last basis differential of 9.69 for the
Missouri bonds is .18 under the 30-day average spread or basis relationship. The number of standard deviations column lists the number of

standard deviations that this most recent basis relationship is under the average basis. The comparatively large −1.97 value indicates that the bond is trading 1.97 standard deviations under its 30-day average. (The minus sign accounts for the negative or cheapness implication of the standard deviation statistic.) The Brazos River issue was trading at a comparatively small .04 basis "discount" to its 30-day average basis (spread). It is of equal importance that this difference was a modest −.28 standard deviation away from its 30-day average basis relationship. Although these numbers are simple, they impart a formidable amount of information about the relationships and departures.

Concept of Richness

Richness defines the value of a specified issue to the index. By evaluating richness, a trader, portfolio manager, or hedger can better determine whether to include or remove an issue from his or her holdings. Table 9.6 provides indications of the comparatively rich securities.

Table 9.6 lists the Mercer County bonds as the richest, with a last basis of 9.17 versus an average of 9.44. The additional premium of .27 is +2.47 standard deviations above the 30-day average. At the other end of the richness scale are the Lower Colorado River Authority bonds that list a last basis of 8.56. This is only +.94 standard deviations above their 29-day average. The other columns are the same as those defined earlier in the cheapness section.

Basis Points, Futures Values, and Durations

Three other analytical tools are the value of a basis point, or the ".01," duration, and the imputed futures value. The basis point response, or the ".01," is a measure of the expected price response of a security given a .01 change in the basis yield. For example, Table 9.7 shows the basis point response of the index to be 0.079. This means that if the yield were to change by one basis point then the price of the index would be expected to

Table 9.6   Hierarchical Listing of Richest Relationships to Cash
Index

```
                        [ Municipal/Futures Data-Line ]
     Richest relationships to Bond Buyer's Municipal Bond Index @ 01/12/89
     Issue                            #obs   Corr   Beta   Avg    Last   #Std Devs
Mercer Co Imp Auth NJ      7.875% '13   30    75%   0.85   9.17   9.44    2.47
N Carolina Pwr #1 Catawba  7.875% '19   30    84%   1.01   9.05   9.44    2.26
Salt River Project AZ      7.500% '29   30    75%   1.49   6.57   7.31    1.61
N Carolina Power (East)    8.000% '21   30    73%   0.99   9.32   9.56    1.58
Intermountain Power Agcy   7.750% '20   30    79%   1.14   8.02   8.69    1.56
Municipal Assist Corp NY   7.625% '08   30    79%   1.35   8.71   9.06    1.55
New York State Med Care    7.700% '22   30    78%   1.17   7.34   7.94    1.41

NY Metro Trans Auth        7.500% '17   30    67%   1.19   7.15   7.94    1.29
Pennsylvania Turnpike(FGI  7.625% '17   30    85%   1.24   9.04   9.31    1.28
Piedmont Muni Power Ins    7.400% '18   30    77%   1.33   6.18   7.06    1.20
Hudson Co NJ               7.600% '21   30    80%   0.84   8.55   8.81    1.18
Municipal Assist Corp NY   7.300% '08   30    89%   1.47   5.91   6.31    1.18
Orlando-Orange Xway Fla/A  7.625% '18   30    77%   1.13   8.59   9.06    1.17
Lower Colo River Auth TX   7.625% '16   29    74%   1.04   8.38   8.56    0.94
```

SOURCE: Municipal Market Data, Inc., Boston, MA

change by $7.90. The duration for the index is listed as 7.88. Durations are frequently calculated to the first par call date, according to convention. Variations are durations calculated to the first call or the stipulated maturity; however, there is always the risk that the issue will be called.

Similarly, yields are frequently quoted in terms of the first call date and not the yield to maturity. The cost of carry or financing the holdings of the index or the securities is 9.12 percent. Consider the New Jersey Turnpike 7.20s which mature in 2018 and are callable at par in 1999. They have an implied conversion factor of .95. Note that the municipal bond contract is predicated on the Municipal Bond Index and has a cash settlement—there is no physical delivery of actual securities. The application of technologies developed for the treasury market are applicable here as well. One of these devices is the conversion factor, which assimilates coupon and maturity information and provides a singular statistic. The conversion factor statistic is used for invoicing, for determining convergence and for calculating the cheapest-to-deliver securities.

Table 9.7   Specific Municipal Issues Basis Point Analysis

```
                       [ Municipal/Futures Data-Line ]
              [ Municipal Cash/Futures Analysis as of 01/13/89 ]
Muni Future: Mar89 @  90-25,  69 days to expiration            Fed Funds  9.12%
Bond Buyer's Index:  Value of ".01":  0.079  Duration:   7.88
    Issue            Mat  Par Factor  Dur     $Pr     Val.01    Fval    Implied
NJ TPK           7.200 '18  '99  0.95   7.25   95.750   0.113   101-06   -41.61%
IPA              7.200 '19  '99  0.94   7.49   95.250   0.113   100-27   -40.04%
Puerto Rico      7.125 '02  '01  0.93   8.42   98.000   0.083   105-04   -59.28%
Pied Pwr         7.400 '18  '00  0.96   7.70   99.250   0.117   103-22   -52.66%

NY Port Auth     8.000 '23  '02  1.00   8.35  101.250   0.082   101-08   -40.61%
NC Catawba       7.875 '19  '00  0.99   7.57  101.250   0.074   102-06   -45.07%
SC PSA           7.875 '21  '00  0.99   7.57  101.500   0.074   102-14   -46.22%
Brazos River     7.750 '15  '00  0.98   7.91   98.500   0.110   100-12   -36.90%
Salt River       7.875 '28  '00  0.99   7.57  101.500   0.074   102-14   -46.22%
```

SOURCE: Municipal Market Data, Inc., Boston, MA

The conversion factor is less than 1.00 since the coupon is less than 8 percent, according to the standards promulgated by the Chicago Board of Trade. The New York Port Authority 8s of 2023 have a conversion factor of 1.00 because the coupon is exactly 8 percent. If the coupon were greater than 8 percent, the conversion factor would be greater than 1.00.

Each security has the potential for a different duration. Some of the listed securities have durations in excess of the 7.88 for the index while others are less. The dollar price column represents the dollar price of each specified bond. The value of one basis point column lists the basis-point response value for each bond in the listing. The imputed or implied futures value (Fval) indicates the bond's implied future value. The Puerto Rico 7.125s of 2002 have an implied futures value of 105-04 and the bonds have an implied rate of return that is -59.28 percent. This is an expensive premium to deliver into the marketplace without receiving appropriate compensation. The implied rate from the perspective of an imputed futures value for the issue suggests that the issue is not cheap to deliver. In Table 9.7 we see that the March futures had a price of 90-25 while the Puerto Rico 7⅛s had an imputed futures value of 105-04 which is 14¹¹⁄₃₂ more than the actual futures price (standard). Because of governmental guarantees and benefits the quality of those bonds is considered extremely high. Some traders evaluate them relative to treasuries in credit terms, although they offer tax advantages as well.

CROSS-HEDGING PURPOSES AND TACTICS

The popularity of the MOB, NOB, and MUT spreads has fostered an important cross-hedging mechanism. The MOB is the level of the municipal futures over the Treasury bonds. The NOB is the level of the Treasury notes over the bonds. The MUT is the level of the municipals under the Treasury notes. Occasionally these over/under relationships invert. For example, muni futures have traded under Treasury bond futures. This happened when market perceptions changed about the tax consequences of owning these distinctive government securities.

These transactions are basically spreading techniques that define comparative prices and, eventually, comparative yields. Their merits are apparent when one needs to execute complex or large positions in the municipal market. They keep intermarket differentials from wandering too far; however, there are more exogenous variables. Perceptions can include expectations about tax-law changes for both treasury and municipal issues. During the mid-1980s there were expectations that the interest on municipal securities would eventually be subject to federal taxation. This brought forth a rush to issue securities that would lose their exempt status if issued after the law. The increase in municipal financings was compounded by a wave of refinancings. The tax code changes became more stringent for various municipal offerings, which has fractured the municipal market into heterogeneous sectors.

Table 9.8 lists basis relationships or spreads between several municipal futures months as well as the MOB and MUT spreads. The MOB lists the prevailing differences as well as the implied MOB. According to Municipal Market Data, Inc. (Boston, MA), the implied MOB compares percentage price relationships between the municipal and Treasury futures to their converted yield ratios. These values are predicated on the cash market. The hedger/trader with knowledge of the actual and the implied MOB relationships can evaluate both futures and cash market movements.

Table 9.8 Municipal versus Treasury Issues, Futures and Cash

```
                      [ Municipal/Futures Data-Line ]
      Muni & Muni/Treasury Contract Spreads        (Muni:  7.56%   Treas:   8.89%)
         (EST) : Muni Calendar :      MOB (Implied)        : MUT (Note-Mun)  :
         BB Index:Mar-Jun Jun-Sep:  Mar89      Jun89      Sep89  :Mar89 Jun89 Sep89:
 8:30   91-24:   na      na   :  37( 77)  na( 77)   na( 77):  61    na    na  :
 9:30   91-25:   31      na   :  32( 77)   8( 77)   na( 77):  67    93    na  :
10:00   91-27:   29      26   :  30( 67)   8( 66)  -14( 66):  67    92   114 :
10:30   91-28:   29      26   :  29( 64)   8( 64)  -12( 64):  66    91   113 :
11:00   91-28:   30      27   :  30( 67)   7( 66)  -13( 66):  66    91   114 :
11:30   91-29:   28      24   :  26( 64)   7( 64)  -11( 64):  67    90   109 :
12:00   91-30:   28      23   :  30( 64)   8( 64)  -10( 64):  65    89   109 :
12:30   91-31:   27      24   :  28( 64)   9( 64)  -10( 64):  67    91   110 :
 1:00   91-31:   27      25   :  27( 61)   7( 61)  -12( 61):  66    91   112 :
 1:30   91-31:   28      25   :  28( 64)   8( 64)  -11( 64):  67    90   111 :
 2:00   92-00:   28      26   :  25( 58)   3( 58)  -17( 58):  68    92   114 :
 2:30   92-01:   28      23   :  25( 56)   4( 56)  -12( 55):  67    92   111 :
Close   92-03:   28      24   :  31( 61)  11( 61)   -8( 61):  64    89   110 :
```

SOURCE: Municipal Market Data, Inc., Boston, MA

OTHER FACTORS

Some issues may be scarce because of delays in new bond offerings, which can temporarily dry up availabilities for a given municipality. Taxes on both the state and local levels can also alter the analysis. The formulas in the previous example consider only a 34 percent (federal) rate. There is a tendency for high income tax states to show a bias toward richness issues. The rationale is that the higher cumulative marginal tax rate would allow lower gross yields to compete.

The change in expectations and dramatic swings in yield curves can influence actual versus theoretical basis levels. Figure 9.3 provides a historical overview of basis analysis. Market perceptions shifted rapidly and widely during the mid to late 1980s. Pending tax code revisions, as well as monetary policies, generated substantial premium and discount situations. During early 1986, the municipal bond futures experienced sizable premiums relative to the cash index, conditions favorable for convergence as far as holders of actual bonds were concerned. The predatory basis

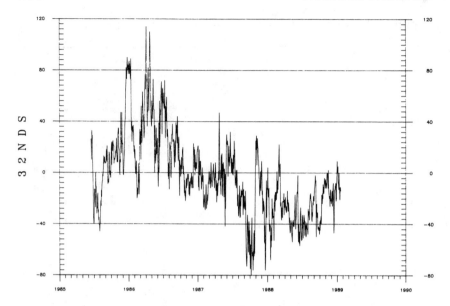

FIGURE 9.3 Historical overview of municipal futures versus theoretical value: July 1, 1985–January 10, 1989. (Source: Municipal Market Data, Inc., Boston, MA.)

convergence loss was now a very positive benefit. Once the new tax code provisions were enacted and the money and credit markets extended their substantial rallies, however, the market reverted to its typical carrying charge structure. Once again, convergence losses were important considerations. The spring 1987 bond market underwent vicious price adjustments and the swings in the basis were turbulent. Municipal futures went from a comparative premium to a discount relationship in short order. It is important to note that the sharp spikes in this basis series coincided with important turning points or accelerations of major price movements. Finally, substantial overruns induced market forces to correct value imbalances between the cash and futures (and options) series.

Some institutions can have an advantage in holding and financing portfolios of municipals. While the revised tax laws of the 1980s altered the tax deductibility of interest to carry municipals, under certain conditions the interest can be allowed. This stratified the marketplace—some organizations can possess an effective edge in maintaining and transacting positions in municipal securities. Because of the specialized nature of taxation, the hedger can seek essential information from additional study and analysis.

CONTRACT-MONTH SELECTION

Hedgers and traders alike attempt to make the most of an efficient situation: The flexibility to use different months for futures or options can open up opportunities for the hedger to engage in trading-the-basis programs. Sometimes, slight basis disparities exist because of market conditions or individual circumstances. A large market participant may be limited to one month because of contractual considerations. At other times, strictly buy options programs limit the hedger's flexibility, since writes specifically are prohibited by corporate charter. In either case, other hedgers may be unwilling to take advantage of the situation because they are sufficiently covered for the moment. Another large market participant may be limited to another delivery month because of pricing commitments. Arbitrage firms, however, would be waiting for such inequalities to arise since they present basis trading opportunities. If the basis moves wider in terms of opportunities, then there can be a restructuring of open hedges in order to capitalize on these differences, which would tend to equilibrate the market once again.

Often a simple rolling forward or backward is adequate to capture a few basis points. Not much dollarwise for a few lots, but when positions require hundreds or even thousands of futures contract equivalents, even $20 per futures contract equivalent means $20,000 per 1,000 lots of gold. Similarly, two ticks in the bond market add up to $62,500 per $100,000,000 par value.

Depending on how the basis trade is configured, there may be substantial margining required. The time value of these funds then enters into the determination of the efficient use of capital.

ENHANCING PERFORMANCE

There can also be large discrepancies among basis relationships that tend to occur at dramatic turning points in the market, under the influence of strong seasonal factors, or major structural changes. When grains fall to substantial discounts relative to the board during their harvest periods, it would seem easy to buy cash grain and deliver it against a short futures contract. The snag is that there may not be sufficient storage to hold the newly purchased grain—a necessity so that it is positioned for good delivery. Organizations with acceptable delivery capacity would utilize that space to reap the arbitrage or trading-the-basis profits. One may be able to procure the space but only upon paying a substantial premium for it, which would render the operation profitless.

Flight to quality runs in the capital markets may open up repo situations—short-term rates could be falling and long-term rates could be rising. Resource allocation is critical because early opportunities may not be as attractive as subsequent ones. At such times, the market environment tends to generate progressive basis relationships that are attractive. Eventually they achieve their turning points and revert to normally expected values. Chaotic market conditions or wider quotes differentials between bids and offers contribute to such environments.

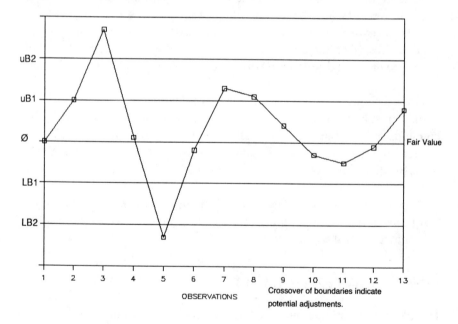

FIGURE 9.4   Two sets of coverage boundaries.

LOWERING RISKS

The firm's competitive posture will improve when better basis levels are secured to increase performance and lower risks. Consider an options writes program: The ability to implement trades that take into account distortions between current and expected (fair) values adds additional premium income, which effectively widens the coverage boundaries. The underlying market can move in broader ranges without triggering additional adjustments to maintain the level of coverage. Figure 9.4 illustrates two sets of coverage boundaries—successful basis trading broadened the coverage of the hedge program.

APPLYING CONDITIONAL INFORMATION

Recurring events, such as auctions, refinancings, triple expirations, dividend payment dates, plantings, harvests, seasonal weather patterns and the like, can be introduced into the analysis. They alter the configuration of theoretical basis levels as variables assume greater or lesser weights at

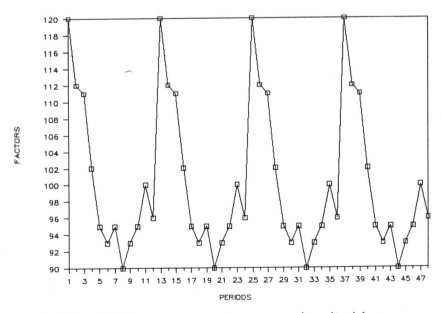

FIGURE 9.5   Illustrative recurring seasonal/cyclical factors.

different points in time. Figure 9.5 highlights recurring critical event phases.

The hedging operation can be sensitive to potential developments if contingency hedging plans are ready when identifiable events occur. Crisis planning and alternative hedging arrangements should be considered before dangerous market conditions (such as freezes, embargoes, or currency interventions) exist—not afterwards as a stopgap to panic. The hedger may not know the specifics or all of the facts of given conditions; but he or she can establish a matrix of expected values for given occurrences/nonoccurrences of important events. Figures 9.6 and 9.7 reflect the prior-event percentage of occurrences and post-event evaluations.

Awareness of these types of dramatic triggering events enables the hedger to have trading-the-basis techniques at the ready. The organization can then rapidly implement positions at times of potentially great profitability, to its benefit.

| | Behavior | | |
	Narrowing	Neutral	Widening
Up	3	15	3
Conditions Neutral	19	20	19
Down	3	15	3

FIGURE 9.6   Prior event expected occurrences (pre-crisis matrix).

		Behavior	
	Narrowing	Neutral	Widening
Up	10	7	20
Neutral	15	5	15
Down	10	3	15

(Conditions)

FIGURE 9.7 Post-event evaluations (post-crisis matrix).

PAPER, CASH, OR ACTUALS

This chapter examined analytical techniques that are germane to the trading, delivery, and settlement decision-making processes. While it is but one of many factors, the status of the basis can dictate whether hedgers are inclined to make or receive deliveries. The hedger can encounter aberrant basis conditions that strongly indicate that a firm make deliveries, yet the underlying market conditions may be such that there is very little available for immediate and good delivery under contractual stipulations. Although such a situation can eventually work itself out, for that one moment in time it may not be possible. These situations have led to an increase in cash-settled futures for both new and revised contracts.

BASIS SWINGS

Although models predict smooth paths, either linear or nonlinear, for basis relationships, the actual behavior can be quite different. The strongest

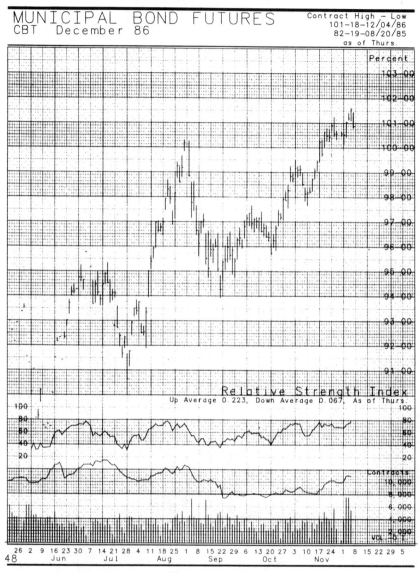

SOURCE: © Financial Futures, Data Lab Corporation, 7333 N. Oak Park, Niles, IL 60648.

FIGURE 9.8 December 1986 municipal bond futures contract.

MUNICIPAL BOND
Spreads

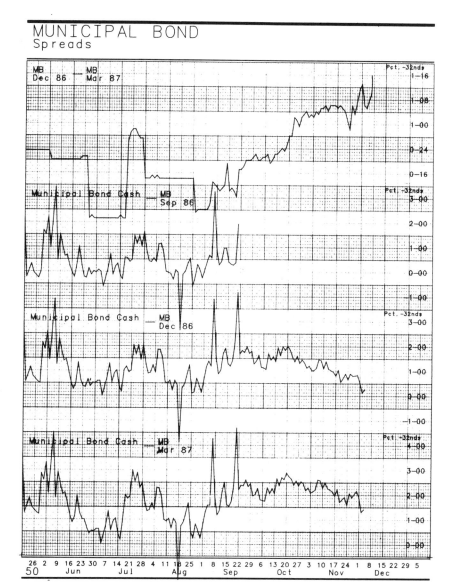

FIGURE 9.9　Various basis and spread relationships.

elements are correlation and convergence. Yet, these statistical measures may not appear to be properly functioning for each moment over the designated time frame.

Usually aberrant basis behavior indicates that a key fundamental variable has not been factored into the equation. There is an overriding market influence at work. Or, the market may be setting the stage for a reactionary move either in price or in the basis itself.

Basis relationships can reveal much about the underlying character of the marketplace. Sudden swings between high quality and low quality financials (physicals) often precede important price moves. Extreme basis behavior can act as a market trigger. At such times it either reinforces an acceleration of a trend or reverses it.

Figures 9.8 and 9.9 illustrate the cases in which the basis overran its theoretical levels on the upside and downside. Figure 9.8 depicts the futures and Figure 9.9 depicts the basis. In particular, note the sharp spike appearance of the basis overruns. Note that the markets soon posted sharp turnarounds.

The highest grades often lead the way or are suggestive of important turning points for major trends. Shifts in the intermarket basis differentials can be precursors of substantial market moves. Each basis relationship imparts a clue to the puzzle and can assist in optimizing rather than neutralizing results. Similar relationships can be found for other financial and physical market groups.

SUMMARY

Trading-the-basis programs rely on savvy as well as statistics. The simple application of theoretical values may not be sufficient to lock in favorable differentials. There are times when overwhelming fundamental events take precedence over ordinary trading techniques. The imposition of temporary emergency powers or any rules changes can adversely influence these trades during extraordinary market conditions. Basis behavior, like price behavior, conveys information about the market processes.

10

Deliveries, Settlements, and Other Offsets

IMPORTANCE

Deliveries, settlements, and other offset procedures terminate the hedging processes and underlie the futures-options markets. When futures transactions are concluded by the simultaneous making and taking of delivery by two parties, the paper aspect of the futures market is completed by an actual physical transfer. This transfer, when conducted according to the *delivery* rules of the exchange, constitutes good delivery.

A delivery transforms a futures position from a standardized contract into one with tolerable allowances. The various exchanges stipulate which commodities, grades, locations, premiums/discounts, payment, and procedural steps are necessary to satisfy the delivery process. In a strict sense, the delivery mechanism is the most limited of the physical transfer processes.

Only a small percentage of trades are concluded by actual deliveries of securities or physical commodities; however, it is important to recognize the steps entailed in and the possible alternatives to deliveries. Every alternative has ramifications on the eventual outcome and degree of success/failure for each hedging program, even if the hedger does not intend to complete any hedge transaction by a delivery.

When the definition of hedging is broadened, cross hedging and exchange-for-physicals (EFPs) are permitted. These techniques allow for wider variations in grades, delivery points, effective quantities, and considerations other than those allowed by ordinary delivery specifications.

The hedger should be thoroughly familiar with prevailing exchange regulations and delivery specifications, which change over time, before any of these techniques are attempted. This is as true for cotton as it is for Treasury bonds—questions, such as if an accepted delivery is valid for redelivery or what additional steps are required to obtain approval for redelivery, are decided by the subtleties of specifications or regulations, which can influence the same contract month as well as the next available contract delivery month. The finer points of specifications and regulations can make or break cash-and-carry and reverse cash-and-carry operations because there are distinctions that influence the reverse transactions: The physical (actual securities) sold may not correspond identically with the purchased futures (forwards, options).

Deliveries

Deliveries have the most rigorous requirements for the actual physical transfer of ownership. When specific grades of coffee, cotton, corn, and so on must be delivered to satisfy the exchange regulations, any problem that is beyond the control of the short can impair his or her ability to make good delivery. For example, a transportation strike, a warehouse fire, pestilence, or excessive moisture can all influence the delivery. In part, the specification of certain grades and locations accounts for potential short-squeeze scenarios, yet the specification ties the futures to the underlying commodity. This connection is the rationale for convergence and explains the economic justification of the futures and options marketplaces.

Depending on exchange and futures contracts, there is a specific timetable that lists: position days, notice days, delivery days, and last trading days. These days may coincide or have precedence relative to one another, depending on the specific market. Typically, the sequence of these days and their associated events are: the position days establish who is most likely to receive a notice, the notice days are those days on which the notices may be issued, the delivery days are those when the underlying instrument (commodity) is transferred, and the last trading day is the final day of trading for the futures contract.

Position Days. The position days establish the longevity of the outstanding long positions. Also, they impart a sequential relationship to the delivery process, which can be an ongoing affair throughout the delivery period. Length of ownership is one of the criteria used to determine who is entitled to receive the to-be-issued notices. Usually, the oldest longs (not including rollovers) are first in line to receive the notices. In event of ties, random assignments are used to specify which long is to be presented with the notice.

Some exchanges consider three position days. These would refer to the previous session's intent by the short to issue (day 1), the actual issuance of the notice (day 2), and the final payment and delivery (day 3).

Notice Days. Notice days can be: first notice day, last notice day, or any intervening notice day. While a few futures contracts have only one notice day, which coincides with the first and last notice day, most permit a specified range of allowable days.

First notice days tend to occur near the first business day of the calendar month of the expiring futures delivery contract and continue for the proscribed period of time. These days represent the first day that a delivery notice can be issued.

The last notice day is the final day that a notice can be issued.

Intervening notice days are those business days that fall between the first and last notice days. These periods can run from two to three weeks. Some markets, however, have only one day, which is both first and last. (This is the case for cash settlement futures contracts.)

Generally, it is the position day's settlement price that is used for calculating the invoice settlement price to close out the contracts and complete the delivery process. In other words, when the long receives the notice, he or she would then know what was to be delivered in terms of maturities and coupons, or grades (fineness) and weights, and the price, which would be the prior session's settlement price, for the appropriate futures contract delivery month. This is the usual case. The night (day 1) before the short prepared the paper work for the intended delivery, the issued and received notice (day 2) to be priced, basis that settlement (day 1), and the long would then have the opportunity to prepare for final payment on the next business day (day 3) which would also be the delivery day.

Delivery Days. Delivery days are the days that deliveries are actually completed. The short presents the long with the allowable securities (commodity) and ownership is transferred and payment made. Depending on exchange and futures contract specifications, these deliveries can occur anytime during the delivery period, provided the other conditions are met. Chicago Board of Trade (CBOT) Treasury note and bond futures follow the format of three days: position, notice, and delivery, except for the final allowable delivery of the expiration month which is a two-day process.

Last Trading Day. Last trading day is the final day of trading for the futures contract. For options on the underlying futures, the option expiration day generally occurs in the preceding calendar month or coincides with the futures contract, but does not occur after the futures expires. The last trading day forces the decision of whether to offset the futures position by liquidation (or short covering), an EFP, or a delivery. In the case of cash-settled futures, the last trading day serves as the position, notice, and delivery days, except that there is no physical transfer, only a final fund reconciliation.

Purchase and Sale

Purchase and sale occur when the outstanding short seller makes the delivery of the particular commodity (security) and the outstanding long pays for and receives the particular commodity (security). On the day that the notice is issued and received, the short seller's open short-futures position is then closed by a purchase or journal entry long. Simultaneously, the open long-futures position is then closed out by the accounting entry of a sale, or receipt, of the delivered in commodity (security). These offsetting journal entries close out the P&S (purchase and sale) process. An exception to this is the wait-instructions hedge accounts, although they, too, will eventually be reconciled similarly. Wait-instruction accounts allow the matching of purchases and sales that are not predicated on a first-in first-out accounting. This matching may be necessary to identify positions for specific transactions or exact physical transfers.

A PHYSICAL DELIVERY

Gold deliveries highlight several concepts salient to most deliveries. There is a futures contract standard, weight allowance, grade (fineness) allowance, and payment procedure. These factors have corresponding ones for many financial futures contracts. Additionally these financial futures contracts provide for accrued interest, maturity and coupon (conversion factor), and specific type of bond. Figures 10.1 and 10.2 illustrate the flow of the delivery process.

Whereas the contract standard for COMEX gold futures is 100 ounces, and in a way perfect fineness, actual deliverable gold can be something else within exchange specifications. Consider an example in which one lot of gold is delivered: The short does not necessarily deliver one bar of gold that weighs exactly 100 ounces and has 1.000 fineness (meaning that it is 100 percent pure). The bar, instead, may weigh 98.234, 100.45, 103.25, or whatever other tolerable weight is permitted. Concurrently, the weight can be plus or minus 5 percent from the standard and the fineness may be .995, or higher. When the bars are less than standard weight (exactly 100 ounces), they are considered light, and when they are more than the standard, they are considered heavy. These variations in weights and fineness can influence the actual financial and material outcomes of these hedging transactions because more funding may be necessary or too much metal was received for the hedge.

The intended lot in this example weighs 99.5 ounces and has a fineness of .997. The settlement price on the position day (the trading session prior to the date of the received notice) was $497.20 per ounce.

Therefore, the settlement for invoice is computed as:

Weight × fineness × settlement price = gold invoice price, or

99.5 × .997   × $497.20   = $49,322.99

which differs from the standardized price of $49,720 (100 ounces × $497.20 = $49,720). The final part of the invoice settlement process is the

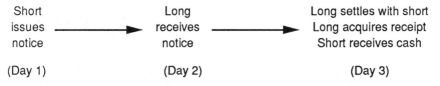

FIGURE 10.1   Flow of delivery process for gold.

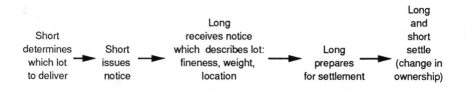

FIGURE 10.2   Flow of delivery process for gold.

allocation for storage charges. Depending on the depository, the monthly charges are approximately $7.00 per lot. The long would assume the storage charge and the short would be reimbursed; therefore, the final price for this one lot of gold would be adjusted by the storage charge as a credit for the short and a debit for the new long.

FINANCIAL FUTURES

The CBOT allows Treasury notes and bonds of various coupons and maturities to be delivered against the respective Treasury-note and Treasury-bond futures contracts. There are minimum maturity requirements that consist of regular maturity features or years remaining to call maturity features.

Because allowable issues for delivery vary in maturity as well as coupon, there must be a pricing mechanism that allows for variations in market price of these underlying securities. The primary device is the conversion factor. The conversion factor relates potential coupons and maturities to the contract standard of an 8-percent coupon, a 20-year maturity, and $100,000 par value. The conversion factor is less than one for coupons under the 8-percent standard, greater than one for coupons of more than 8 percent, and exactly equal to one for coupons equal to 8 percent because, in an 8-percent market, issues with 7¼ coupons would be trading at a discount, whereas in the same 8-percent market coupons of 14 percent would be trading at premiums. The conversion factor is also used for many basis analyses and arbitrage recognition programs.

Notice the similarity in invoice approaches used for gold and for the Treasury-bond futures contract. Weights are the heaviest consideration for precious metals deliveries, and the conversion factors are important for the bond delivery invoice. Fineness is accounted for by the 1,000 factor for bonds, since that represents the par value of these issues.

Conversion factor $\times$ 1,000 $\times$ futures settlement price $=$ Invoice for principal

Look at the 14-percent coupon of November 2006–11 again, and assume a futures settlement price of 88 16/32 or 88.50. All the calculation will be:

$$1.5633 \times 1,000 \times \$88.50 = \$138,352.05$$

The 7¼ coupon issue of May 2016 works out to:

$$.9171 \times 1,000 \times \$88.50 = \$81,163.35$$

In both cases, the principal invoice amounts (not including accrued interest) were different from the $100,000 par value standard. This conversion factor process relates the delivered securities to marketplace prices. Remember that with the passage of time, coupons less than 8 percent have an upward bias, while coupons greater than 8 percent have a downward bias in their conversion factor values—the conversion factors shift over time for specific issues. Only a coupon of exactly 8 percent would have a flat 1.0000 conversion factor. At this writing, there are no such deliverable instruments. The final invoice for our 14-percent bond is determined by:

Principal invoice $+$ accrued interest $=$ Final invoice amount

or, given 3 months accrual (.25 $\times$ $14,000 $=$ $3,500) the final amount would be $141,852.05 ($138,352.05 $+$ 3,500).

Figures 10.3 and 10.4 represent the flows involved in these financial futures deliveries. Again, the processes are similar for physical and financial futures.

REDELIVERIES

Futures contracts may allow for redeliveries or retenders of issued notices. For example, a long may receive a notice that was issued to him earlier than he expected or desired. Or, the delivered securities or physicals were not

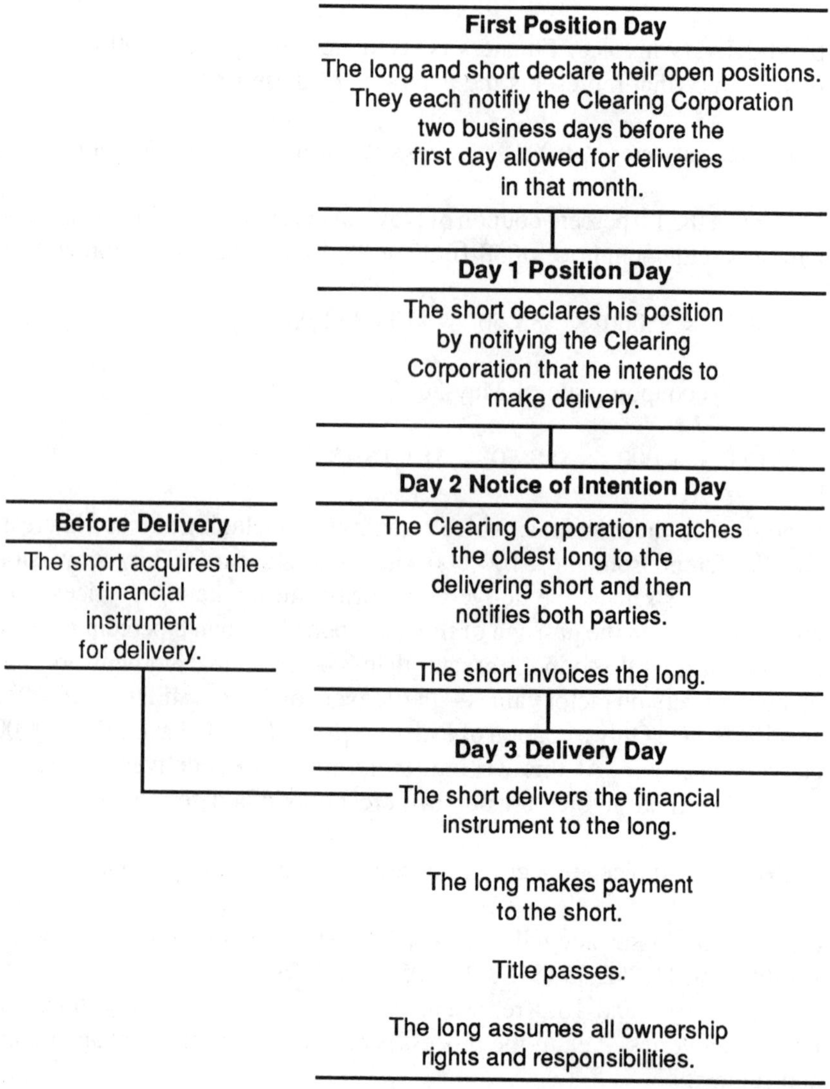

First Position Day
The long and short declare their open positions. They each notifiy the Clearing Corporation two business days before the first day allowed for deliveries in that month.

Day 1 Position Day
The short declares his position by notifying the Clearing Corporation that he intends to make delivery.

Before Delivery	**Day 2 Notice of Intention Day**
The short acquires the financial instrument for delivery.	The Clearing Corporation matches the oldest long to the delivering short and then notifies both parties.
	The short invoices the long.

Day 3 Delivery Day
The short delivers the financial instrument to the long.
The long makes payment to the short.
Title passes.
The long assumes all ownership rights and responsibilities.

SOURCE: © Chicago Board of Trade, *Understanding the Delivery Process in Financial Futures,* 1989.

FIGURE 10.3   Flow of delivery process for financial futures

Long	Clearing Corporation	Short

Process begins two businesss days prior to the named delivery month

	Long	Clearing Corporation	Short
First Position Day	By 8:00 p.m., two business days before the first day allowed for deliveries in that month, the long and short report all open positions to the Clearing Corporation by origin, house, or customer. They also must report any changes each day as they occur.		
Day 1 Position Day			By 8:00 p.m., the short notifies his clearing member that he intends to make delivery. The clearing member than files a Delivery Notice with the Board of Trade Clearing Corporaton. This cannot be canceled.
Day 2 Notice of Intention Day*	By 4:00 p.m., the long provides the short with the name and location of his bank.	By 8:30 a.m., the Clearing Corporation matches the oldest long to the short and then notifies both clearing members.	By 2:00 p.m., using calculations based on the Position Day settlement price, the short invoices the long through the BOTCC.
Day 2 Delivery Day	By 1:00 p.m., the long clearing member's bank has accepted Treasury bonds or notes by book-entry and, at the same time, paid the invoice amount via the "Fed system" to the short clearing member's account.		Short and long have until 9:30 a.m. to resolve invoice differences. By 10:00 a.m., the short deposits the bonds or notes to be delivered and instructs his bank to wire them to the long's account ("Versus Payment").

Process ends on the final business day of the named delivery month

All times refer to Central Standard Time.
*On the second to last business day of the delivery month, or last Notice of Intention Day, invoicing must occur by 3:00 p.m.

SOURCE: © Chicago Board of Trade, *Understanding the Delivery Process in Financial Futures*, 1989.

FIGURE 10.4 Flow of delivery process for financial futures

useful for the long's purposes. Rather than keeping these securities or physicals, the long can reissue the notice, although additional commissions and fees, when applicable, will be charged because it is another transaction.

There may be regulations that prevent a delivery from being retendered, particularly at a somewhat later date. For example, August pork bellies are not redeliverable against the subsequent February contract. Grain or livestock taken in one delivery may not be redeliverable due to infestation or sickness. Treasury bonds received may not have sufficient time left to maturity or first call date (15 years basis the delivery date), since the bonds were held from one futures contract delivery month to another. Or, there simply was no time left for the spot futures contract month and now the next futures delivery month became the nearby delivery month, and one will have to wait to redeliver the securities or commodities.

This has important ramifications for cash-and-carry type operations because wildcard traits are one-sided. The seller (the short) determines the exact security or weight and grade to be delivered within contractual provisions. The securities that were sold short may not identically match those that will be received against the open long position.

EXCHANGE-FOR-PHYSICALS

Although there can be actual physical exchanges or transfers of securities, these transactions are not considered deliveries in the strictest sense. Exchange-for-physicals is a technique that enables hedgers to predetermine what is to be transacted at what prices and/or what basis levels.

An important feature of exchange-for-physicals (EFPs) is that they are conducted outside the ring or pit. However, they are still recorded for exchange records and listed as physical exchanges in the exchange's terminology.

These transactions are permitted for bona fide hedging purposes (since a specific hedging operation is to take place). If these trades were conducted according to the ordinary public outcry procedure, then there would always be the risk that not all the lots would go to the appropriate parties at the desired prices. If a portfolio manager acquired securities from an investment house for a predetermined basis relationship, there would be no guarantee that the trade would be consummated because another broker acting on the behalf of his clients may have vigorously bid for the contracts.

This could also potentially affect the ultimate pricing for the hedging transaction. These transactions are permitted outside the ring because the two parties will complete an actual transfer and not a sham transaction— they are sometimes called ex-pit transactions (conducted outside the pit).

Depending on exchange and industry, these transactions are known as: Against Actuals (AAs), On call, or EFPs. Traditionally, AAs are used in agricultural markets, On call for textiles, and EFPs for energy, financials, and metals. On call provisions allow for buyer's call or seller's call. The buyer or seller designation effectively denotes who initiates the pricing (transaction). Depending on the contractual arrangement, the buyer may call the transaction and have the commodity (cotton) priced, or the seller may wait until the time is right, and then conclude the transaction, since the commodity is ready for physical transfer.

Wide latitude relative to contract delivery specifications is permitted for these EFPs. It may be that gold or silver of a required fineness is located outside an exchange-approved depository and the bars may not be of acceptable weight and shape (rather, the metal is for specific industrial purposes and smelted according to order). Note that this process can allow for hedging transactions that would not ordinarily be viewed as feasible for the futures and options markets: The futures contract grade is different from that which you use or produce; the bonds are too short in maturity and not deliverable against the contract; a firm needs flour and corn oil, not wheat, corn and soybean oil futures; a company needs jet fuel, not crude oil. These concerns and objections can be addressed via the exchange-for-physical mechanism.

CASH SETTLEMENTS

There are two parts to cash settlements: The imposition of initial margin and its maintenance (variation calls and removal of excess funds); and the final settlement. Given the stipulated settlement factors, the difference between the initiation price and the termination price means one final funds adjustment. If the long was imposed at lower prices, then one more payout would be forthcoming to the long and one more payout would be forthcoming from the short, relative to the prior session's status. This cash settlement mechanism removes uncertainties about availabilities for specific grades at particular points, given approved certification (assaying), transportation difficulties, and so on. It is an index and not one specific lot of a commodity or security.

Consider the CBOT municipal bond futures contract. Both the futures and the options contracts expire on the same day. The futures settlement is based on the Bond Buyer Index for municipal bonds (the index has its guidelines and procedures for computation). A hedger sold one contract of September municipal bond futures against his position at 88¹⁄₃₂ when the index was 89⁹⁄₃₂. The futures were at a 1¼-point discount relative to the index. If the actual position corresponded to the composition of the index (with all intervening adjustments), effectively holding the position would result in coverage, but at the cost of a convergence loss of 1¼ points ($1,250).

Table 10.1 illustrates the cash flow for the municipal bond futures contract. It shows variation changes on a day-to-day basis and the overall evaluation for both index and futures. Figure 10.5 illustrates the cash flow aspect of maintaining the short hedge with Table 10.1 data.

OTHER OFFSETS

AAs, On-call, EFPs, and deliveries are different ways to close out futures and options positions prior to expiration; another way is through simple offsetting transactions. For example, a hedger had an open long anticipatory hedge-futures position. The liquidation of that long prior to expiration or physical transfer would constitute an offset. Conversely, the buyback or covering of a sell hedge would offset that futures (options) hedge position. This highlights the flexibility of the hedging process when futures and options are used. Trades need not be carried until expiration or actual transfer. This is especially helpful when there has been a change in conditions, contractual agreements, strikes, delays, and other variables.

Alternative Delivery Procedure

The alternative delivery procedure (ADP) is a variation between an exchange-for-physicals and the standard delivery mechanism. It is permitted by the New York Mercantile Exchange for the energy complex. This alternative procedure allows for the ''delivery'' of products that would not

Table 10.1 Cash Settlement Scenario for Municipal Bonds

			Municipal Bonds			
Date	Cash index	Futures September	Index decimal equiva-lent	Futures decimal equiva-lent	Dollar change cash index	Dollar change futures
801	89.09	88.01	89.28	88.03		
802	89.18	88.16	89.56	88.50	281.25	468.75
803	89.19	88.14	89.59	88.44	31.25	−62.50
804	89.26	88.25	89.81	88.78	218.75	343.75
805	89.20	88.13	89.63	88.41	−187.50	−375.00
808	89.21	88.15	89.66	88.47	31.25	62.50
809	89.17	88.09	89.53	88.28	−125.00	−187.50
810	89.10	87.22	89.31	87.69	−218.75	−593.75
811	88.18	86.30	88.56	86.94	−750.00	−750.00
812	88.12	87.00	88.38	87.00	−187.50	62.50
815	88.10	86.29	88.31	86.91	−62.50	−93.75
816	88.10	87.07	88.31	87.22	0.00	312.50
817	88.10	87.05	88.31	87.16	0.00	−62.50
818	88.14	87.17	88.44	87.53	125.00	375.00
819	88.16	87.16	88.50	87.50	62.50	−31.25
822	88.15	87.15	88.47	87.47	−31.25	−31.25
823	88.18	87.24	88.56	87.75	93.75	281.25
824	88.23	88.01	88.72	88.03	156.25	281.25
825	88.16	87.28	88.50	87.88	−218.75	−156.25
826	88.20	88.03	88.63	88.09	125.00	218.75
829	88.26	88.16	88.81	88.50	187.50	406.25
830	88.28	88.14	88.88	88.44	62.50	−62.50
831	88.31	88.18	88.97	88.56	93.75	125.00
901	89.00	88.18	89.00	88.56	31.25	0.00
902	89.22	89.22	89.69	89.69	687.50	1125.00
906	89.22	89.24	89.69	89.75	0.00	62.50
907	90.00	89.25	90.00	89.78	312.50	31.25
908	89.31	89.25	89.97	89.78	−31.25	0.00
909	90.00	90.05	90.00	90.16	31.25	375.00
912	90.07	89.31	90.22	89.97	218.75	−187.50
913	90.07	90.01	90.22	90.03	0.00	62.50
914	90.19	90.14	90.59	90.44	375.00	406.25
915	90.20	90.13	90.63	90.41	31.25	−31.25
916	90.16	90.12	90.50	90.38	−125.00	−31.25
919	90.10	90.08	90.31	90.25	−187.50	−125.00
920	90.07	90.04	90.22	90.13	−93.75	−125.00
921	90.07	90.07	90.22	90.22	0.00	93.75
922	90.08		90.25	0.00	31.25	

NOTE: Dollar change for futures column must be multiplied by −1 to reflect short hedge cashflow.

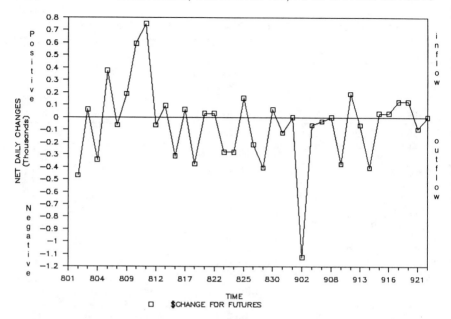

FIGURE 10.5   Cash flow for municipal bond example (short the futures).

ordinarily qualify for good delivery. It matches longs and shorts according to their submitted intentions presented to the exchange. The exchange then matches the parties.

TIMING OF FUNDING

Provisions must be made to make timely payment for delivery and the hedger must be familiar with the rules and have funds available for payment; otherwise, brokerage firms may charge for financing the transaction and impose other financial penalties in the event of a default, or credit sources must be tapped to secure the required financing to carry the inventory of securities or commodities. Most exchanges require the payment of cash on the next exchange business day after the delivery notice has been presented. This exchange business day may not be a business day for all banks, government offices, or other institutions. When payment is to be consummated by cash coming from a money market fund, depending on the location of the depository for that fund, the transfer may not be all that simple. For example, a firm may receive a notice on a Friday going into a long (three-day) weekend. The exchange is opened on Monday, as is the brokerage house, but the depository for the money market is not because of a state banking holiday (not a national holiday). Selling the money market fund would mean that interest would stop accruing to the portion that was sold, but funds would not be available until Tuesday which is unsatisfactory as a timely payment for good delivery. Besides, too many days of lost interest intervened. For typical trading-the-basis, arbitrage, or other narrowly margined financially motivated transactions, this slight incongruity is enough to turn a seemingly profitable transaction into a losing one.

A statewide closing of a main banking institution for a holiday can jeopardize a delivery both on the the receiving or making end, because funds may not flow out of or into the hedger/trader's bank on that day. Also, provision must be made for cash or next-day settlements of actual Treasury bills because the market may be thin or closed.

LIQUIDATION ONLY AND OTHER CONCERNS

Unusual market conditions may prompt changes in trading procedures and offsets. For example, futures contract transactions in the spot month may be limited to liquidation only and no new positions may be allowed. While aimed at curbing speculation, this mandate can preclude the hedging process. A firm may want to initiate new positions in the spot month to take advantage of very favorable basis relationships, but may be prevented from doing so. This temporary regulatory action can postpone market corrections because the pricing mechanism is no longer free to capitalize on situations for which it is geared. Sometimes these actions may be permitted for bona fide hedges, but when the hedging/trading strategy is complex, the hedger may be at a disadvantage.

11
Options

Options mean many things to many people. Some terms are accepted by many participants; however, there are terms that can be ambiguous. Even in the timeframe perspectives, such as day, intermediate, and position trading, there can be serious departures in meaning between what is to be expected and what is occurring. Each option has a role and similar objectives: to make money and to reduce risk. But, are all options on an equal footing?

Role of Options for Hedging

Options are an invaluable tool for placing, modifying, and tailoring protection for an organization. For cash-strapped companies or subsidiaries of tight parents, the payment of an option premium precludes additional financing in the form of variation margin calls. Market conditions, such as heightened volatility, can increase premiums. Yet under these conditions, a company can still implement a hedge program by choosing different strikes and delivery months. A hedger can reduce time value payments by engaging in a limited writes program, a strategy that alters the protective blanket but still gives the hedger choices: alternative modes of action. Hedgers can seek supplemental income and the associated protection that comes with premiums received; protection, however, is the primary focus for the purchase of options.

The implementation of options, futures, forwards, insurance policies, and other risk management techniques involves strategic planning and knowledgeable applications. One does not continually upgrade, downgrade, upgrade, and so on, life, property, casualty, and other coverages on a minute-to-minute or day-by-day basis. Parameters are determined, and adjustments are implemented when there are significant changes in or violations of these parameters. This approach is equally applicable to options for hedging programs.

Flexibility, income, protection, and strategic alternatives are but a few of the purposes a hedger may have when embarking on the application of options, either exclusively or in conjunction with other financial contracts and derivative products.

Terminal Value Perspective

One convention that expedites option analysis is terminal value. Terminal value means that the focus is on the premium value of the option at expiration. Some analysts go one step further and make the assumption that, at expiration, the option premium will be either zero or have some positive value. If it has positive value it is assumed to be entirely intrinsic. Time value no longer exists at that moment, because there is no longer any time. This is proven by multiplying the Black-Scholes model by zero whenever the t variable occurs, and it becomes evident, at that point, that there is only the potential for intrinsic value as the sole determinant of premium value.

Two key concepts for the valuation of options are volatility and terminal value, which relate to variance and location, respectively. Volatility is dispersion (not direction). The ultimate arbitrator of terminal value is the location of the underlying market in relation to the series of strikes, which defines the existence of intrinsic value. The emphasis on volatility is primarily symmetrical, in that the dispersion is considered similar about the mean, and this may not be true. It is obvious that a slight bias relative to the volatility statistics is more valuable and meaningful than larger, but always similar, displacements about stationary means.

When a market encounters a violent down draft and prices drop for ten days in a row, is the increase in volatility due to sharp fluctuations about a stationary mean? Or, is it due to a pronounced one-sided trading affair? Consider what is ultimately more valuable: a narrow trading range with an upward, downward, or even sideways bias? Or, a wide trading range with no bias? A slight trending bias is most valuable for options that are in-the-money and continue to become more so, rather than for at-the-money (ATM) options, and finally, even less so for the out-of-the-money options. This is portrayed by Figures 11.1 and 11.2, which illustrate the boundaries imposed about a mean or the volatility about the marketplace. Wider boundaries indicate higher volatilities. The slight movement in the slope of the lines dramatically dictates the valuation impact on an option. Consider the options starting on the at-the-money level—the next trade places them in- or out-of-the-money. (Similarly, the in-the-money options will have less associated time-value loss, and their dollar performance will be better.)

This analysis is significant for off-the-exchange options, which may have European characteristics and no readily available market to absorb changes in corporate expectations, objectives, and financial conditions. (In other words, the trader is in it until the end.) Then the problem becomes one of terminal-value expectations with a solution set that must consider potential outcomes and expected values, each with its own costs, benefits, and attributes.

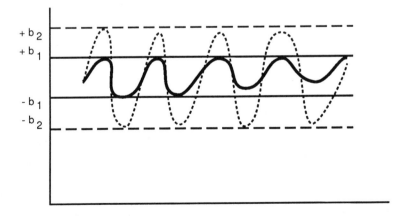

FIGURE 11.1 Stationary means and various boundaries.

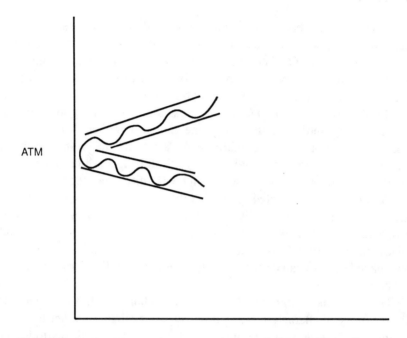

ATM

FIGURE 11.2   Nonstationary means and sloped boundaries.

TERMINOLOGY

This section defines terms that are important in the discussion of options. It is necessary to clarify volatility, which is the most popular variable under analysis. It is frequently viewed as symmetrical, not skewed; unconditional, not conditional; and precisely determinable, not shifting; and probably nonconverging.

Futures Contract Equivalent

Futures contract equivalent relates the status of the options, forwards, or cash positions to the pertinent futures positions. It mathematically defines the structure of these options or cash positions to the futures in order to better evaluate the needs, requirements, and constraints of the organization, relative to the futures benchmark. This is helpful in evaluating unprocessed raw materials against refined needs and products.

Option Types

There are two types of options: calls and puts. Both are considered unilateral contracts because the buyer acquires the right upon payment of the premium to the underlying position, while the seller incurs the obligation to satisfy that right upon an exercise.

Countless strategies, configurations, and related derivative products are based on these two types. Depending on how the positions are built, the hedger can arrive at bullish configurations with puts, bearish configurations with calls, and neutral or slightly biased strategies by using both types in various combinations.

Calls. Calls are the right and not the obligation to acquire the long-underlying-futures (physical) position upon exercise. If there is an exercise, the buyer of the call option receives the long-futures position for the specified delivery month priced at the strike price, regardless of where the underlying market is trading. Simultaneously, the writer of the call receives the offsetting short-futures position. Given this scenario, it is generally not in the interests of a long-call holder to exercise when the futures are below the strike, although this may occur (infrequently) because of late expiration and cash market considerations.

Only the buyer of an option can exercise. This feature is critically important to many strategies that seem to be lock-type situations, but that can result in loss or exposure from involuntary exercises. Conversions and reverse conversions are some of these vulnerable strategies that occur under particular market conditions.

The purchase of calls is usually a bullish position or, at the least, adds a bullish weight to the entire position. The sale of a call adds a bearish weight to the overall position. In a sale situation, potential income that also provides a degree of protection can be secured.

Puts. Puts are the right and not the obligation to secure a short-futures position upon exercise. If the purchaser of the put decides to exercise, then the long (buyer of the put) receives a short-futures position priced at the strike for the given delivery month, whereas the seller of the put receives the offsetting long-futures position priced at the strike price. Only the buyer or owner of a put option can exercise, and this leads to the potentially destabilizing condition known as *involuntary exercise,* which can drastically alter the granter's (writer's) overall position and risk posture. This is evident when market conditions are such that broad price jumps are occurring and adjustments are not smooth and not conducted at minimal costs.

The purchase of puts is usually a bearish position or, at the least, it adds a bearish weight to the overall position. In a sale situation, potential income that also provides a degree of protection can be secured.

Assignment of Signs

The assignment of plus or minus signs defines the bullish or bearish intent of purchased and sold options. The purchase of a call or the sale of a put, requires a plus sign. The sale of a call or the purchase of a put requires the imposition of a minus sign. By adding the assigned delta values, one can surmise the net delta effect and the degree of bullishness or bearishness for a given position at that particular moment (Figure 11.3). This cumulative perspective is useful for evaluating the degree of delta response, and the bullishness or bearishness for spreads, straddles, and synthetic positions.

Premiums

Premiums are the amount, or market value, of an option. Option valuation models compute theoretical or expected values that are not necessarily

	Calls	Puts
Bought	+	-
Sold	-	+

FIGURE 11.3 Assigning pluses and minuses to purchased and sold puts and calls.

those of the marketplace. At the outset, premiums are the amount that a buyer of an option pays a writer for the right of ownership. This right does not have to be exercised. Premiums consist of two parts: intrinsic and extrinsic values, or

PV = IV + EV
Premium value = PV
Intrinsic value = IV

where extrinsic value = time value (TV).

Exercise

Exercise is the right, and not the obligation, of a holder of a long position in options (whether they are puts or calls). Some options permit late exercise. Here, even though the particular option contract ceased trading earlier in the day, the holder nevertheless can still exercise within the exchanges' regulations that evening and, under certain mitigating circumstances, the next morning. Among these late exercise options are the popular Chicago Board of Trade CBOT Treasury note and bond options.

The payment of a premium by the purchaser of an option enables that owner to exercise the option into the underlying futures (physical) position. In the case of a long call, the owner, upon exercise, acquires a long-futures (physical) position priced at the strike for the specified delivery month. The grantor of the option (in this example, the seller of the call option) receives the short-futures position priced at the strike for the specified delivery month.

Involuntary Exercise

Exercise is the prerogative of the buyer of an option; consequently, the establishment of the underlying and offsetting position goes to the seller of the option. The involuntary exercise is not done at the request of the short, but rather at the initiative of the long. This element of involuntary action and effect is known as involuntary exercise and risk, and its occurrence can upset established strategies and require further adjustments and, perhaps, drastic realignments. Events beyond the control of the short have occurred and things have to be straightened out. The institutor of a strategy runs the genuine risk of having a leg of the strategy exercised away, depending on which option strategy was established, such as a conversion or reverse conversion. What had seemed to be a lock-type transaction actually emerged into something with considerably higher risk characteristics. The option that is exercised would present an underlying futures position that would probably be placed against the trend of the underlying marketplace. Otherwise, why would the exerciser have exercised? This form of risk can present unusual problems because the exercises could have occurred, the resulting futures positions imposed, and the underlying market could have moved substantially to impair the overall status of the writer, all overnight. Forced adjustments may not happen at an assumed (inconsequential) slight cost, and the actual response may not be an immediate one.

American-Style and European-Style Options

For American-style options, the buyer can exercise at any time up until expiration of the option contract. European exercise allows an exercise to occur only on the last day. The greater flexibility of the American-style option relative to the European-style option gives it an economic edge, and, hence, those premiums tend to be more expensive. The American-style option introduces the element of involuntary exercise.

Strike or Exercise Price

The level at which an option will be converted into the underlying futures or cash position is the strike price. The strike is the stipulated price at which the option gets priced upon exercise and, thus, is also known as the exercise price. Sometimes, options are exercised when they are apparently at- or out-of-the-money, but in these cases the underlying markets are such that the acquired futures position is expected to remain in a favorable relationship to the cash market. For example, a late afternoon capital market development can make T-bond out-of-the-money calls effectively be in-the-money because of a dramatic advance in the underlying government securities market. Options cease trading at 3:00 P.M. Chicago time, so developments can still influence whether or not those options are exercised because they have a late exercise provision. The more active options are those that are at and immediately around the at-the-money level.

Underlying Price

The underlying price refers to the market price of the underlying index, security, commodity, or futures contract. It helps to identify whether an option is in-, at-, or out-of-the-money.

For calls, when the underlying price is greater than the strike price (U>E), an option is in-the-money. An exercise of such an option will account for the intrinsic value while forfeiting any time value. Had the underlying price been less than the strike (U<E), then the option would have been out-of-the-money. Generally, exercising these relationships incurs additional financial losses for the owner of the options.

For puts, when the underlying price is less than the strike (U<E), then that option has intrinsic value. An underlying price that is greater than the exercise price (U>E) means that that particular put has no intrinsic value and is considered out-of-the-money. When the underlying price is equal to the exercise price (U = E) for either puts or calls, then that option is strictly at-the-money.

Expiration Month

Expiration month refers to the delivery month of the underlying futures contract. Options predicated on an underlying futures contract may expire in the calendar month prior to the futures delivery month contract. For example, the options on September Treasury bond futures will expire during August, and the options on December COMEX silver will expire during November. Other options have concurrent expiration features, particularly those based on an underlying index, such as the municipal bond options that expire when the underlying futures contract does. This applies to several stock index futures and options contracts as well.

Intrinsic Value

Intrinsic value is the first component of premium value. It is the ultimate determinant (from a terminal-value perspective) of whether an option will have residual value upon its expiration. If it is in-the-money, then it has intrinsic value. From a trading perspective, the ultimate determinant of value for a purchased option is whether it will expire in-the-money (especially if it starts out at- or out-of-the-money).

Extrinsic Value

Extrinsic value is the second component of premium value. All active options have extrinsic value, although they do not have to have intrinsic value. Extrinsic value accounts for the fact that at- and out-of-the-money options possess a chance of moving into the money during their lives. If there was little chance of this occurring, the extrinsic value, or time value, would reflect this slight possibility by imputing a small valuation for the extrinsic component. Options thrive on the possibility of fluctuations in price: In a static price structure there is no incentive to buy an option because the underlying position's price will remain flat over time.

An exception to this reasoning is the ability to lock in a supply or marketing alternative. By paying a premium, the purchaser of a call is in a position to buy the underlying commodity or security within the specified time span for a specified price. This payment is similar to a non-refundable deposit to hold a property: If there is a no exercise, the purchaser of the option forfeits the premium. This is useful to buy time in order to secure additional financing or to evaluate the marketplace further. Here, an initial payment of a comparatively small premium is preferable to immediate payment in full.

In-the-Money

In-the-money is the amount of intrinsic value and is the ultimate determinant of an option's value. Depending on exchange regulations, options that are in-the-money by specified minimum amounts at expiration will be exercised for the longs (owners) whether or not instructions to exercise were made. Options that are in-the-money directly benefit from continued favorable movements in the underlying position to the extent of their delta values. Conversely, if the underlying position's price movements were to reduce the intrinsic value of the option, then it can be expected that by the expiration day, that option's premium value will reflect the reduction in the intrinsic value and, of course, the dissipation of time value. Figures 11.4a

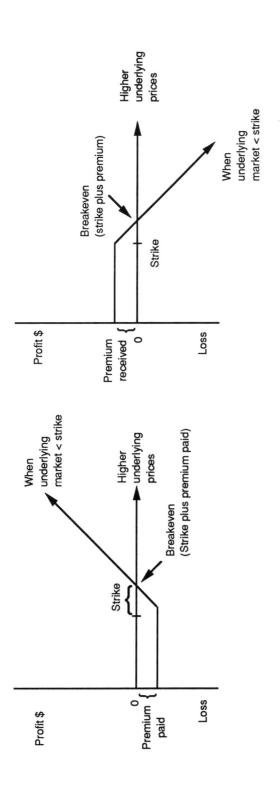

FIGURE 11.4a Purchased in-the-money call.

FIGURE 11.4b Sold in-the-money call.

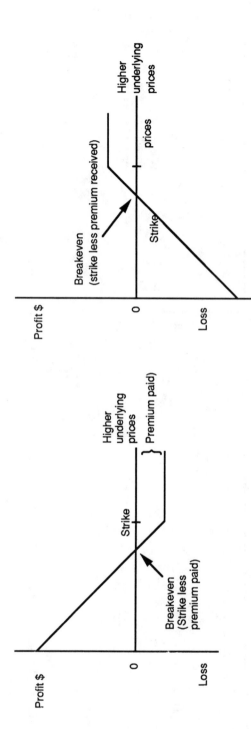

FIGURE 11.5b Sold in-the-money put.

FIGURE 11.5a Bought in-the-money put.

and b and 11.5a and b show call and put examples. They highlight the effects of a purchase or a sale of one option from a nonhedge perspective.

At-the-Money

Strictly speaking, the option with a strike price equal to the underlying position's price is considered at-the-money. For example, a Treasury note option with a strike price of 86-00 would be the at-the-money option if, and only if, the related futures position was trading exactly at 86-00. A tick more or less would mean that that option was in- or out-of-the-money by a small amount. For these slight differences, the options are considered either at-the-money (loose definition) or near-the-money.

This option level has maximum time value, but not premium value. In fact, all of its premium is attributable to time value. The next tick can very well dictate whether the option is in- or out-of-the-money in the strictest sense, which has dramatic ramifications for the eventual outcomes of the option's value, deltas, and adjustment processes. Figures 11.6a and b and 11.7a and b portray one contract example of purchased and sold calls and puts on a hedge perspective. By doing so, it emphasized time value paid as an "insurance" premium. These examples develop cap and floor and effective cap and floor concepts.

Out-of-the-Money

Options that have no intrinsic value and are not at-the-money are considered out-of-the-money. Theoretically, options that are out-of-the-money have an implied negative rate of return in that an exercise of these options results in an even larger financial loss because the newly acquired futures position (physical) would be priced at a level that is clearly disadvantageous to maintain. The exercise of an out-of-the-money call generates a long futures position that would be priced at a strike price that is higher than the underlying market. The position would have to be maintained for that disparity through the infusion of additional capital, or margin call. Figures 11.8a and b and 11.9a and b illustrate the shift in coverage and its cost due to different strike prices. Again, calls and puts are examined from purchase and sale perspectives.

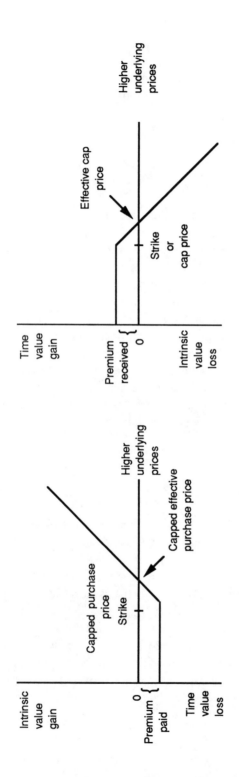

FIGURE 11.6b Sell at-the-money call as a hedge.

FIGURE 11.6a Purchase at-the-money call as a hedge.

304

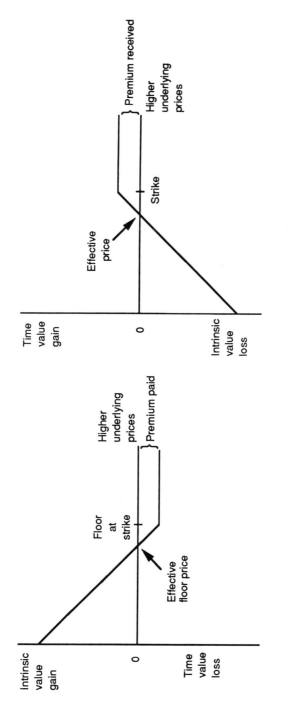

FIGURE 11.7a Bought an at-the-money put as a hedge.

FIGURE 11.7b Sold an at-the-money put as a hedge.

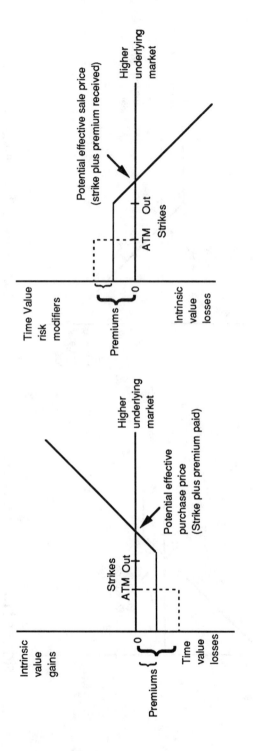

FIGURE 11.8a Bought an out-of-the-money call as a hedge.

FIGURE 11.8b Sold an out-of-the-money call as a hedge.

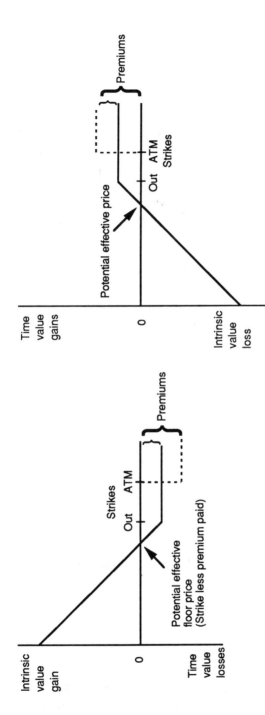

FIGURE 11.9a Bought an out-of-the-money put as a hedge.

FIGURE 11.9b Sold an out-of-the-money put as a hedge.

307

Futures versus Options Matrix

There are many aspects to the evaluation of futures versus options in addition to theoretical pricing models and premiums and futures prices themselves. A simple evaluation matrix illuminates the process at hand while offering alternative courses of action with their attendant benefits and costs. It is crucial to choose the better frameworks at the outset and then to search for and implement the appropriate adjustment mechanism rather than to decide on the adjustment mechanism and to be unsure or uncommitted to the basic framework. The fundamental framework will present alternative courses of action and movement that should account for the dominant portion of coverage rather than having the adjustment mechanism account for the fullness of coverage. For example, it makes a major difference if the program is to start delta neutral, maintain delta neutrality (regardless of costs), and terminate delta neutral. There can be circumstances that prefer, in a dominant sense, a process that starts with an expected terminal delta-neutral value.

Look at municipal bonds: How often should the hedger adjust? The options are dependent on a futures contract that is dependent on a cash index. The futures and options expire concurrently. Because the final settlement is absolute, there are fewer valuation problems than there are with the final settlement of a Treasury note or a bond contract that is subject to the vagaries of the seemingly cheapest-to-deliver concept of both the marketplace and each trading organization as well.

By applying favorable, neutral, and unfavorable circumstances against the framework we arrive at the potential solution set and not necessarily the one and only solution. The basic model is the special case of neutral/neutral with the expectation that the next outcome is just as likely to hit mean expected value as not. See Figure 11.10, which highlights the simple but representative horizon of different paths and effects for different conditions.

Even with municipal bonds, where the known convergence on expiration is zero, how the program arrived at its objective makes a big difference in performance.

Physical or Futures

Depending on contract specifications, the exercise of an option can generate the underlying futures position priced at the strike price for the

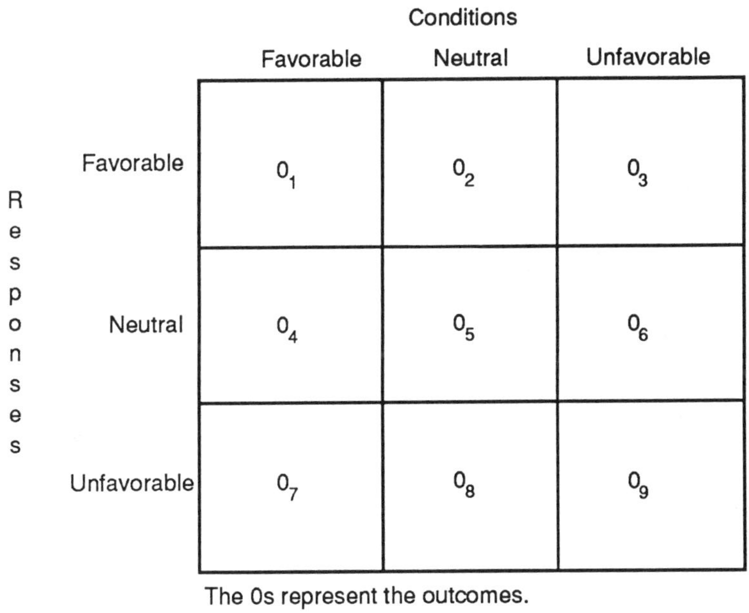

Conditions

	Favorable	Neutral	Unfavorable
Favorable	O_1	O_2	O_3
Neutral	O_4	O_5	O_6
Unfavorable	O_7	O_8	O_9

Responses

The Os represent the outcomes.

FIGURE 11.10 Favorable, neutral, and unfavorable responses versus favorable, neutral, and unfavorable conditions.

specified delivery month. Or, it can result in the actual delivery of a physical such as a foreign currency, a metal such as gold, or a security such as Treasury bonds.

Delta

Delta defines the degree of response between the underlying instrument and the specified option. When the underlying market moves $1.00 and the selected option moves 50 cents, then that option has a delta of .50. Similarly, if the underlying market moved $1.00 and the selected option moved 34 cents, then it has a delta of .34.

Its timeframe is very small, actually instantaneous. To assume that delta will remain the same over time is erroneous, except for the strike at-the-money level, with no change in underlying prices. The d1 statistic is the delta statistic.

Hedge Ratio. The hedge ratio is the reciprocal of delta. For example, a delta of .5 implies the placement of two such options in order to achieve unitary balance against futures contract equivalency. Similarly, a delta of .40 indicates 2½ options per futures contract equivalents. There can be objectives other than delta neutrality throughout the process that should be considered.

Delta Hedging. Delta hedging, which has several meanings, can refer to:

1. The use of a delta factor to estimate the number of options required to provide futures contract equivalent coverage according to the desired level of protection.
2. The focus of a basket of options that will, over the extremely short term, have financial offsetting properties so that the hedger from a dollar change basis would be indifferent about whether to use futures or options. Both of these alternatives, given the set assumptions, are (should be) identical in their compensatory movements.

These perspectives suggest that the deltas can add up, but the dollars do not have to. This can be understood by visualizing a basket of options contracts that has been implemented to generate offsetting financial flows. Under conditions of sharp and sustained price movements, the delta values for the series of options can still approximate the unitary case for the newly emerging in-, at-, and out-of-the-money options; however, the amount of intrinsic value would dominate the delta statistics. If there is no return or recovery, then those deltas will approach 1.00. The program under such unfavorable conditions will be seriously overhedged. This condition does not take months or weeks to develop—it can happen in a matter of days, or even hours. This can be understood by visualizing a basket of alternative hedging vehicles. The true costs of funding such alternatives versus their expected costs often are dispensed with by most models.

Basket of Options versus Futures, Forwards, or Actuals

There are important assumptions made during the presentation of option valuation models that include:

1. Ready and immediate access to fund flows generated by purchased options
2. No distinction between funding characteristics of purchased versus written options
3. The ability to make changes instantaneously, at no cost, on a continuous basis
4. Use of European-style options, although American-style are used often (this precludes involuntary exercise risks)
5. Minimal costs of implementing, maintaining, and realigning options accounts relative to their underlying positions, be they cash, forwards, or futures
6. The remote chance of large moves
7. Implicit belief that all hedgers will use identical models and variable values for their options-hedging programs (homogeneous expectations)
8. Luxury of multiple trials and errors
9. Implied replacement of lost funds
10. Resetting of decision-making process to initial conditions, regardless of success or failure

These points clarify the cost aspect of options and delta-oriented arrangements. How much does delta neutrality cost and what is its value? When options are used, it does make a practical difference whether they are purchased or sold, continuously realigned or monitored. Consider Figure 11.11, which pictorially reflects the relationship between the delta-geared hedging baskets. The passage of time grinds down premium values. Because of asymmetrical reward/risk characteristics of options, there are significant trading distinctions and hedging properties. Options can cost more for the same coverage relative to futures, although the latter choice is subject to marked-to-market margining provisions.

Consider gold, which has cash, futures, and options markets. If a trader bought the nearby futures and took delivery, then he owns the physical gold. To protect that position a put is purchased. This overall position would be a synthetic call. What happens now? The passage of time erodes the put premium value, as far as the extrinsic component is concerned. In a flat market, it makes no difference between holding the physical gold or the futures (aside from the implied carry), but it does make a difference for the option regardless of type. Options purchase plans are similar to insur-

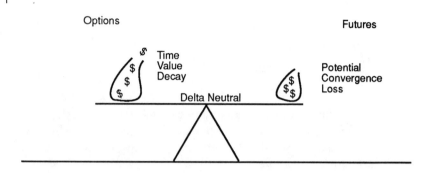

FIGURE 11.11   Illustration of bags balanced for delta neutrality.

ance in the sense that there is a forfeiture of premium if there is no catastrophic news. The coverage is adjusted by deductibles.

EVALUATION MODELS

There are several recognized option-valuation models. This text will examine the Black-Scholes model and then expand it to account for variable operating costs.

Many seminal works and models make the important assumptions of:

1. Small changes
2. Instantaneous changes
3. Continuous versus discrete distributions
4. Independence between observations
5. No costs for transactions (commissions, fees, and slippage)

These assumptions may not be accurate representations of the underlying distribution mechanism.

Black-Scholes Model

Fisher Black and Myron Scholes are commonly recognized as the postulators of option-valuation models. Professor Black applied the stock option-valuation mechanism to the commodity markets. The following is a presentation of that model as listed by John Labuszewski and Jeanne Cairns Sinquefield in *Inside the Commodity Option Markets*, published and reprinted by permission of John Wiley & Sons, Inc., copyright ©, 1985.

$$C = e^{-rt} [FN(d1) - SN(d2)]$$

$$d1 = \frac{\left[\ln \left(\frac{F}{S} \right) + \frac{ts^2}{2} \right]}{s\sqrt{t}}$$

$$d2 = d1 - s\sqrt{t}$$

where C = Theoretical call premium or its fair market value
        F = Futures price
        S = Strike price
        r = Interest rate
        t = Time until expiration expressed in years
        s = Standard deviation
        N = A normal cumulative probability distribution

and for puts the expression is:

$$P = -e^{-rt} [FN(-d1) - SN(-d2)]$$

where P = Theoretical put premium.

The use of natural logarithmic notation states a continuous pricing mechanism. The *ln* relative pricing transforms a time series into a lognormal one that dispenses with the probability of negative prices but not returns.

Time Value

Time value is a multiplicative factor depending on time left to expiration and volatility (a measure of dispersion). Time value is not proportional, in that premiums are double for twice the time outstanding, all other things being equal (market price, strike price, dispersion, interest rate), but rather more nearly an approximation of square root function. This is readily seen by examining the Black-Scholes model and focusing in on the t (time) variable and the ts^2 which represents time $\times$ variance. By taking the square root of the latter, we arrive at $s\sqrt{t}$. By substituting different values for time and volatility, the entire value of the expression will increase for the larger values of these two components and decrease for smaller values. This substitution stresses the interaction between time and dispersion. It alerts you to two potentially countervailing influences that would occur should volatility increase, but time comes rapidly to an end for the specified option.

Operationally, time and interest rates, in operation, are expressed as decimals and volatility as a percentage. Example 11.1 is the solution for the premium value of a gold option.

VOLATILITY

Most options valuation approaches consider volatility two-dimensional: historic and implied. We will consider three variations, each with its own trading and tracking qualities. They are: H(V), the historic volatility, I(V), the implied (current) volatility, and E(V), the expected volatility.

The implied volatility has characteristics similar to the current volatility. When models are unable to closely compute prevailing market premiums for a given volatility estimate (typically, historical in nature) then the solution "solves" for the volatility, given values for the other explanatory estimates.

In trading, whether it is futures, forwards, options, cash, real estate, or other property, it is the *expected* value and not the *fair* value that is crucial. A hedger does not sell a product or portfolio because it is fairly priced—the sale is consummated for the expectation of value received and how that is of benefit to the enterprise. Narrow fair value viewpoints assume that there is no economic advantage to either the purchase or sale of a particular item when it is fairly priced; therefore, one is indifferent about whether to buy or sell it at that particular level. Fair value is one dimension, market value another, and expected value still

$$C = e^{-rt} [FN(d_1) - SN(d_2)]$$

$$d1 = \frac{\ln\left(\frac{F}{S}\right) + \left[\left(\frac{s^2}{2}\right)(t)\right]}{s\sqrt{t}}$$

$$d_2 = d_1 - s\sqrt{t}$$

Substituting:

F = 440
E = 460
t = 73 days or .20 (73/365)
r = 10%
s = 15% or .15

then

$$d_1 = \frac{\ln\left(\frac{440}{460}\right) + \left[\left(\frac{.15^2}{2}\right)(.20)\right]}{.15 \sqrt{.20}} =$$

$$d_1 = -.6291$$

$$d_2 = -.6291 - (.15 \sqrt{.20})$$

$$d_2 = -.6962$$

$$ND_1 = .2676$$

$$ND_2 = .2451$$

$$C = e^{-(.10 \times .20)} [(440 \times .2676) - (460 \times .2451)]$$

$$C = 4.90 \text{ or } \$490 \text{ per option}$$

Example 11.1. Approximation solution for gold call option.

another. Fair value can better be described as a real estate or antique appraisal. It provides an indication of where an item (commodity, security) might transact—not where it will transact.

The role of fair value is to assist in the evaluation of an option, futures, or synthetic futures position or whatever is under consideration, given the values of important variables. As such, it is helpful in evaluating alternatives in order to isolate the optimum trading/hedging selections.

A subscript added to the volatility notations denotes a dynamic series. The three columns represent the historic, implied (current), and expected volatility values where V is volatility. This approach was applied earlier to the basis presentations.

$$
\begin{array}{lll}
H(V_n) & I(V_n) & E(V_n) \\
H(V_{n-1}) & I(V_{n-1}) & E(V_{n-1}) \\
H(V_{n-i}) & I(V_{n-i}) & E(V_{n-i}) \\
H(V_1) & I(V_1) & E(V_1) \\
H(V_0) & I(V_0) & E(V_0)
\end{array}
$$

The n subscript can refer to the 5th, 6th, 50th, 100th or whatever week, day, or hour. It is a reference point that anchors the time series. The o subscript refers to the last day, especially from an expiration point of view. This time flow state is diagrammed in Figure 11.12.

Variations among perceptions account for substantial differences in the estimated and expected values for options. Not all participants view the options identically. Even if all participants use only identical information, each participant's objectives can be different. For example, a producer looking for inventory or reserve valuation protection is more inclined to use purchased puts. Conversely, a user of product would be more concerned about protecting the input costs and would be inclined to a purchased call perspective. There are variations on these themes; however, they stress the sell-side and buy-side preoccupations of appropriate hedge programs.

These definitions for dispersion—volatility—are comparable to the basis and hedge account definitions. Arbitrage, trading the basis, and volatility transactions are dependent on the return to parity or movements away from the current to newer expectational levels.

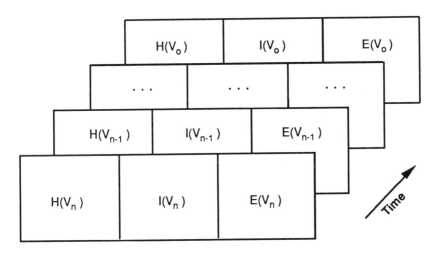

FIGURE 11.12   Time-adjusted matrix reflecting flow.

Historical Volatility

The dispersion statistic is computed for a specified time period, for example, the previous year, month, 20 days, 10 days, 5 days, or whatever timeframe is selected as convenient or representative. Typically, the dispersion statistic is the variance or its related statistic, the standard deviation. A major assumption of this statistic is that approximately 68 percent of the observations are expected to fall within 1 standard deviation of the mean. The complement to this argument is that only 32 percent, 16 percent on each side or tail, is expected to occur, given the one standard deviation about the mean volatility estimate. Some empirical results suggest that the outliers may be closer to 55 percent for the tails, and only 45 percent are expected to drop about the mean, given one level of dispersion. This has extremely dramatic consequences for the valuation of options and, in part, accounts for their seemingly cheap time values given normal oriented models for the in- and out-of-the-money categories and comparatively expensive price time value view for the at-the-money category. It should be recognized that trading the volatility arrangements implicitly assumes that volatility estimates do swing over time and even over specified timeframes, yet many programs explicitly assume that these swings will return toward some true convergence value. This empirical behavior is not an accurate description of a stable, normally related distribution.

Current Volatility

This concept refers to the prevailing level of the market's view of volatility. Sometimes, it is considered the implied volatility, usually when there has been a sudden movement in the underlying prices or options prices, and historical estimates yield option values that are significantly too little or too much. In such cases, the models tend to be solved by rearranging the terms for volatility, which then is viewed as the implied volatility estimate and not the historic volatility statistic. In these cases, the implied becomes the current volatility parameter.

Implied Volatility

When the historic volatility gives poor estimates to option premiums, then the hedger/analyst must take into account the prevailing market sentiment in order to provide a volatility estimate for subsequent option valuations. Distortions between theoretical and actual market prices is usually attributable to the variations between the historical and the implied volatilities. The shift in these values is due to changes in expectations and not to the pro forma posture of historical versus implied perceptions (estimates) in volatility.

Expected Volatility

Expected volatility is an important determinant of the pricing of options. It allows for skewness, conditional stacking, and rapid twisting of the probabilistic structure. When used in conjunction with a Bayesian modification approach, it has sound statistical underpinnings as well. It is the force behind the departures between the implied (current) and historical volatility. The sale of options, in order to capitalize on a shift between the historical and the implied, can be ill-timed due to this dominant factor. Consider an example of an agricultural freeze.

Suppose the Brazilian coffee crop was devastated by a harsh cold wave. It would be reasonable to assume that the jump in premium prices, particularly for calls, is due in part to the jump in the underlying futures (and cash) markets as well as to the higher value placed on the volatility statistic. The volatility estimate can continue to advance, however, and not immediately retreat from the overnight rise. In fact, as reports confirm large scale damage, one would look for the volatility to climb. It would seem that the market is somewhat more likely to advance than to decline and, thus, become skewed. Moreover, these reports can be confirmed by one's own analyses, given the duration and level of freezing temperatures for key growing areas and the resultant damage of plants. This is not speculation, but an educated statistical analysis of supply and its impact on prices. This does not preclude the potential occurrence of large downward moves or negative changes in prices, but it does suggest the likelihood of further advances in a much more broadly defined channel of price moves. Yes, volatility has increased, but more importantly, so has the expectation of higher prices over the investment horizon. The departure of implied to historic may not have fully discounted the entire move in one day—chances are that it did not. The departure can be expected to continue until a wave equilibrating mechanism or process takes hold. At that time, the overall probability distribution would take on a more symmetrical appearance than the skewed expected one.

For financials and currencies, this event-oriented analysis would reflect an important change in policies, if not immediately announced, definitely anticipated. For example, the expressed intent of the Federal Reserve to support the banking system given the events of October 19, 1987, was quickly reflected by the capital and money markets and, to a lesser extent, the stock market, since the Fed conducted transactions in the credit markets, not the equity markets. Figures 11.13, 11.14, and 11.15 illustrate that the follow-through in these markets shows an important statistical dependence.

Underlying to Strike Prices

Underlying to strike prices is often viewed as a given, but ultimately defines whether there is intrinsic value. At that termination point, options with intrinsic value will have some positive premium value. Otherwise they will

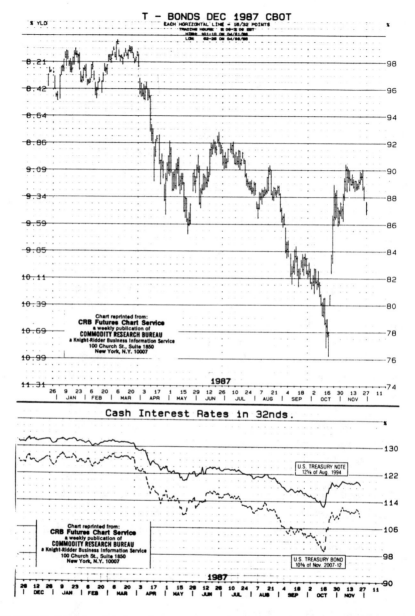

FIGURE 11.13 Major departure and expected volatility—Treasury bonds. (Reprinted from: CRB Futures Chart Service, a weekly publication of Commodity Research Bureau, a Knight-Ridder Business Information Service, 100 Church Street, Suite 1850, New York, NY 10007.)

FIGURE 11.14 Major departure and expected volatility—Treasury bills. (Chart reprinted from: CRB Futures Chart Service, a weekly publication of Commodity Research Bureau, a Knight-Ridder Business Information Service, 100 Church Street, Suite 1850, New York, New York 10007.)

not when the options lapse unexercised through the expiration and subsequent exercise timeframe. This underlying to strike relationship accounts for the greatest premium valuation, which can be seen when an option is in-the-money. The deeper the option goes in-the-money, the less attendant time value, but higher premium value, it will have. There is a transformation of component valuation parts—time and intrinsic values—that occurs when options move about their trading ranges. This moving about in conjunction with time value decay places premium values under stress, which will ultimately result in intrinsic or positive premium values or no value whatsoever past the unexercised expiration.

FIGURE 11.15 Major departure and expected volatility—stocks. (Chart reprinted from: CRB Futures Chart Service, a weekly publication of Commodity Research Bureau, a Knight-Ridder Business Information Service, 100 Church Street, Suite 1850, New York, New York 10007.)

Interest Rates

Interest rates have the connotation of opportunity costs, implied repo rates, or some short-term alternative. For financial futures contracts such as bonds and notes, the interest rate variable for the solution of the equation takes on the meaning of a short-term rate. Some traders use Treasury bill rates, Eurodollar rates, Libor, or a benchmark that represents their short-term opportunity costs. The question then shifts to whether the rate should be a one-day rate, such as federal funds, even though the option has seventy-eight days to expiration, a 78-day Eurodollar or Treasury bill rate, or whatever. Near-term, this variable does not have the same dramatic impact as shifts in dispersion or underlying to strike do on the valuation of an option. For long-term options, those exceeding a year, this variable takes on greater importance.

Time

Time refers to the amount of time remaining to expiration. Does an option have 1, 2, 3, 30, 90, 180 days between the present and its designated expiration? This aspect is not a linearly proportional factor (twice the time–twice the premium, all other things being equal); rather, it is better approximated by a square-root relationship. Subtleties for the valuation of options include the number of days in a year (360, 365, 366), the number of holidays and nontrading (nonbusiness) days in which market action cannot directly influence prices, although there may be overseas or off-exchange trading being transacted (this is akin to long weekends or a series of seasonal holidays during which the exchanges are closed and no exercises can be conducted).

Probabilities

Probabilities are, perhaps, the least understood variable of the entire evaluation process. Probabilities are often viewed as the N factor, and that is the extent of it, unless you look up the values of the standardized variates. Related features are the assumed strict continuity and independence that exist between observations, assumptions that are not necessarily so, particularly at important turning points or during explosive trends.

After the assumption of a normal distribution has been made and the distribution transformed into a lognormal one, this important variable tends to be overlooked. In part, this is due to very serious evaluation problems for establishing true estimates for the mean and dispersion parameters. A helpful property of the normal distribution is that the identification of these two moments, mean and variance (μ, σ^2) allows the specification of the curve. The application of volatility allows for greater dispersion about the mean. The function may not at all be stable, however, and still does not account for the empirical higher incidence in percentages of relatively large changes, whether they are up or down.

Consider two probability functions: the normal distribution and the cauchy distribution. Both have means and both have dispersion statistics. For the former distribution, the dispersion statistic is the variance (standard deviation). For the latter, the variance is considered infinite because that parameter does not converge towards a single value but, rather, may swing about in a nondampening manner. Nevertheless, estimates can be provided about how many observations can be expected at certain points along the curve, which, in part, describes dispersion.

Although parametric analytical techniques will assign a value for the variance, its reliability is suspect. It is prone to significant changes over time. Adjusting the lengths of the testing periods does not improve the estimates. Estimates can become more erratic. Curiously, this situation implies that the more observations, the poorer the estimate.

Since many options trading and hedging programs place considerable emphasis on volatility, it is very important to understand what is being assumed, what the limitations are, and what is being expected.

The assignment of a probabilistic structure is no different from the basic model, because both make assumptions about expected values and the critical probability distributions. The benefit of the direct imputation is the capacity to more readily account for potentially higher occurrences of large changes given one or two such large changes, the skewness of changes, or the potential for trends. As we shall see, the terminal viewpoint is particularly helpful. As expiration approaches, an option, even if it is only one tick in-the-money, will rapidly approach a delta of 1.00, whereas an option that is out-of-the-money by only one tick, will have a delta that rapidly approaches 0.00.

Need for Terminal Perspective

The ability of delta to approach zero if the component underlying position is out-of-the-money, approach 1.00 when the underlying option is in-the-money, and remain around .50 for the strict at-the-money option is very valuable information. It helps to minimize transactions to adjust for theta, vega, gamma, and delta risks. It provides insight into the mechanics and operations of the underlying processes as well as identifying and isolating the objectives of the program. We now extend the basic model to account for variable operating costs.

The evaluation model now becomes:

$$E(C) = e^{-rt} [N(d1)] - SN(d2)] + (q \times m)$$

where E(C) = Expected call premium value
   q = Expected cost per transaction in terms of fees, commissions, and slippage due to prevailing market conditions
   m = Random or imputed expected number of adjustments
   $(q \times m)$ = Total expected costs for adjustments

Similarly, the revised expressions for expectational put values becomes:

$$E(P) = -e^{-rt} [N(-d1) - SN(-d2)] + (q \times m)$$

where E(P) = Expected put premium value.

In both cases, all other terms are as defined earlier.

The introduction of the q cost term highlights the expense of the adjustment/realignment process and its importance to the eventual success or failure of a program. Adjustments can be very costly and difficult to implement during times when they are needed the most.

Consider overnight trading in Treasury bonds: If commissions and fees work out to $15.625 per roundturn and the expected slippage differential for placing an option trade is 1/64, the narrowest difference allowed (minimum tick for the T-bond option contract per CBOT) and its dollar value is $15.625, then the combined cost for a trade is $31.25, or one minimum tick per the T-bond futures contract. The 1/64 for the options slippage would be the prevailing spread differential for the quote say, 23/64 (bid) at 24/64 (offered). Much of the buying is done at the offer and the selling done at the bid since that is how a market functions: Go to the bid as a seller and go to the offer as a buyer.

By substituting $31.25 for the minimum daily charge and 20 days as the m factor, the typical monthly costs would be $625.00, and that is for but one futures-options contract equivalent. If this adjustment mechanism is extended over the course of a year, the total is $7,500 (12 × $625) per one futures contract equivalent. This is a high price to pay, considering the income stream from the standardized bond is $8,000 (8 percent coupon, $100,000 par).

The net expected value of the option, in this case a call, is found by rearranging some of the terms:

$$E(C) - (q \times m) = e^{-rt} [N(d1) - SN(d2)]$$

The equation shows that the net expected value of the option is inversely influenced by the number of expected adjustments. This is easy to visualize when conditions are such that there is only a slight wobble to the price (basis) series, yet adjustments are forthcoming. For other hedgers, the slight wobble would not have violated organizational guidelines. As many hedge plans favor the use of at-the-money options or ratio programs, costs rise with the same frequency of adjustments.

A useful guide for starting the evaluative process is to directly substitute previous cost experiences into the equation in order to determine the net expected value of the option (hedge). Otherwise, one can simulate the net expected values given different adjustment frequencies and q costs. An important advantage of this technique is that it guides the hedger on potential values from start to finish rather than letting the hedger be surprised along the way.

Adjustment Mechanisms

The selection of the adjustment mechanism is a key to the eventual success or failure of a program. The final selection comes down to expected values: Are multiple and slight changes more effective than fewer but more moderate ones, or a limited number of radical adjustments? The answer depends on the organization's costs and objectives.

DELTA NEUTRALITY

We will examine several delta neutral positions in which the only feature they have in common is the initial state of delta neutrality. Some start delta neutral and end delta neutral; others start delta neutral but do not terminate there. Depending on subsequent events, each strategy has its own traits that can lead to substantial and, occasionally, devastating results.

Delta neutrality does not tell the whole picture: These events are dramatized by no, moderate, and major departures from the initial states. Notice the financial effects, depending on how the position was initiated. Although the adjustment mechanism can restore a program to delta neutrality within minutes, hours, or the end of the day, the restoration of delta neutrality may not restore the financial loss due to the overhedge or underhedge.

Severe departures can require large scale adjustments (rolling up or rolling down basis the strikes and size of overall positions). Moreover, one may never get the opportunity to recover, at least immediately, because of the severity of the intervening action. Examine Tables 11.1–11.5, which capture the essence of buy/sell delta hedge programs. The straddle examples highlight collar applications. From one perspective, the written straddle would be comparable to selling a call against a long position and the sold put would partially immunize against an open short commitment. Remember that these tables reflect simple but representative cases.

Table 11.1   At-the-Money Options Scenario

Against Underlying Long Position—1 Futures Contract Equivalent							
Terminal	TIV long		TIV long		TIV short		TIV short	
Event	1 put	EP	2 puts	EP	1 call	EP	2 calls	EP
Major up 500	0	491.50	0	483.00	60	448.50	120	397.00
Moderate up 460	0	451.50	0	443.00	20	448.50	40	437.00
No up down 440	0	431.50	0	423.00	0	448.50	0	457.00
Moderate down 420	20	431.50	40	443.00	0	428.50	0	437.00
Major down 380	60	431.50	120	483.00	0	388.50	0	397.00

EP   = Effective price
TIV = Terminal intrinsic value
Premiums are assumed to be equal to $8.50 per ounce. This assumption is for both puts and calls.
1 contract programs reflect deltas of .50.
2 contract programs reflect deltas of 1.00.

Table 11.2 Illustrative One Adjustment—One Alternative Mechanism

	Long 1 put	EP	Long 2 Puts	EP	Short 1 Call	EP	Short 2 Calls	EP
After adjustment	+1P500	483.00	+2P500	466.00	−1C500	*	−2C500	*
Major up 500		491.50		483.00		448.50		397.00
Major down 380		431.50		443.00		388.50		397.00
After adjustment	+1P380	423.00	+2P380	426.00	−1C380	397.00	−2C380	414.00

EP = Effective Price

* These effective prices would vary depending on whether there was a timely rollover or the option was exercised.

+ 1P500 would indicate the purchase of one 500 strike put and −2C380 would indicate the sale of two 380 strike calls.

Table 11.3 Illustrative Synthetic Futures Equivalent Hedges

| | Synthetic Short Futures (−1.00) | | | | | | | Synthetic Long Futures (+1.00) | | | | | |
| | Buy 1 ATM Put (delta −.50) | | Sell 1 ATM Call (delta −.50) | | Net price effect | Net time value | | Buy 1 ATM Call (delta +.50) | | Sell 1 ATM Put (delta +.50) | | Net price effect |
	TV	TIV	TV	TIV				TV	TIV	TV	TIV	
Major up 500	−8.50	0	+8.50	60	−60	0		−8.50	60	+8.50	0	+60
Moderate up 460	−8.50	0	+8.50	20	−20	0		−8.50	20	+8.50	0	+20
No up–down	−8.50	0	+8.50	0	0	0		−8.50	0	+8.50	0	0
Moderate down 420	−8.50	20	+8.50	0	+20	0		−8.50	0	+8.50	20	−20
Major down 380	−8.50	60	+8.50	0	+60	0		−8.50	0	+8.50	60	−60

TV   = Time Value (+ received, − paid)
TIV = Terminal Intrinsic Value
ATM = At-the-money
NOTE: The synthetic positions mimic or replicate the underlying short (−1.00) or long (+1.00) futures contract equivalent.

Table 11.4   Illustrative Buy Straddle Effects

Illustrative Buy or Long Straddle—No Adjustments				
Buy 1 ATM put (−.50) TV	Buy 1 ATM call (+.50) TV	Total options TV	Total premium paid	Total options net TV
Major up 500	0	60	60	−17.00	+43.00
Moderate up 460	0	20	20	−17.00	+3.00
No up–down 440	0	0	0	−17.00	−17.00
Moderate down 420	20	0	20	−17.00	+3.00
Major down 380	60	0	60	−17.00	+43.00

TV = Terminal value
Note: Performance improves as market moves from initiating at-the-money (ATM) level. Performance is poorest at the at-the-money level.

Table 11.5   Illustrative Sell Straddle Effects

Illustrative Sell or Short Straddle—No Adjustments				
Sell 1 ATM put (+.50) TV	Sell 1 ATM call (−.50) TV	Total options TV	Total premium received	Total options net TV
Major up 500	0	60	60	+17.00	−43.00
Moderate up 460	0	20	20	+17.00	−3.00
No up–down 440	0	0	0	+17.00	+17.00
Moderate down 420	20	0	20	+17.00	−3.00
Major down 380	60	0	60	+17.00	−43.00

TV = Terminal value
NOTE: Performance deteriorates as market moves from initiating at-the-money (ATM) level. Performance is best at the at-the-money level.

Table 11.1 illustrates the hedge outcomes for major, moderate and no changes in the underlying market. This analysis viewed one (delta .50) and two (delta 1.00) contract alternatives when there are no adjustments. Table 11.2 illustrates the one adjustment situation for a major up and down move. Table 11.3 modifies the analysis from a combination perspective. Tables

11.1 and 11.2 viewed the hedge as either put or call strategies; now the focus is the combination of a put and a call. This gives rise to synthetic futures positions (here, the synthetic position is created by purchasing one type of option and selling the other type option). The two contract cases initially exhibit a delta neutral perspective against the underlying market position. Tables 11.4 and 11.5 examine the effects of combining the two option types (puts and calls) from buy and sell perspectives. That is, both option types are purchased or sold together. Table 11.4 lists the effective impact of buying or going long a straddle. From a trading viewpoint this would also be considered as "going long volatility." Either way, from a trading or hedging perspective the better results are achieved from departures about the central (at-the-money levels). Table 11.5 lists the impact of selling or going short a straddle-oriented strategy. From a trading perspective this would be viewed as "going short volatility" or "short time value." These five basic strategic orientations possessed similar delta attributes yet generated different results, given conditional market states and adjustment mechanisms.

The key factor is that all these strategies had comparable deltas. Some were considered delta neutral, yet there were significant differences among the outcomes.

Delta Behavior in the Absence of Market Movement

There are many adjustment plans devised to cope with fluctuating deltas and many attempts to restore those relationships to neutrality. A steady stream of multiple realignments misses the point of the initial hedge for many applications. Only if subsequent adjustments are done at zero cost with no slippage do the two approaches—many adjustments and few adjustments—remain at parity. As time passes, the emphasis on maintaining the basket of options and derivative products to generate instantaneous financial offsets cumulatively imbalances the program; and, at the least, requires considerable expenditures in terms of time and money.

This has significant bearing on determining whether to use in-, at-, or out-of-the-money options. In the absence of any subsequent market behavior in the underlying instrument, the delta for an option will approach zero, approach one, or remain at one-half for the strictly at-the-money option as that option approaches expiration. The importance of this cannot be overstressed. Knowing that options that are in- or out-of-the-money possess lower time value components helps in prepricing the cost of the hedge program. The greatest forfeiture for the purchase of an option for hedging is the full cost of the option itself. Subsequent events may cause a complete loss of that premium. In the case of an in-the-money option, both intrinsic and extrinsic values are lost. For the case of an out-of-the-money option the loss is only the extrinsic value, since it had no intrinsic value to begin with.

Initial Delta Condition

Delta will fluctuate or drift with a bias when there is no movement in the underlying position. Only for the strictly at-the-money level will the delta exhibit comparative stability of about one half (.5). The intent of maintaining coverage of .8 (a surrogate for 80 percent), .9 (a surrogate for 90 percent), or 1.00 (the delta neutral or 100 percent coverage) can be difficult. Particularly at those times when coverage is needed the most, results can be considerably less than desired.

A hedger may decide to start the process with a delta neutral perspective and stay with the initiating position come what may. This situation tends to be the case from a buy-side perspective of options whether they are puts or calls. This is not automatically the case for programs incorporating written options. Market moves may be of such extent and speed that the acquired coverage attributed to the premium received is considerably less than the valuation change in the underlying position. Moreover, there can easily be situations where the deltas fall into line and add up theoretically, yet the dollar flows were more substantial than ordinarily suspected. In such cases, there can be a substantial financing of intrinsic value that is far in excess of the premiums received. Figure 11.16 depicts a hypothetical delta hedge path against cumulative adjustment costs. Adjustments can be undertaken on each change, prespecified change or crossover. Even in any of these cases there is a cumulative cost (transaction and slippage) that weighs on the program. Notice the divergences between the paths and the cumulative cost effect of oscillating series and related adjustments.

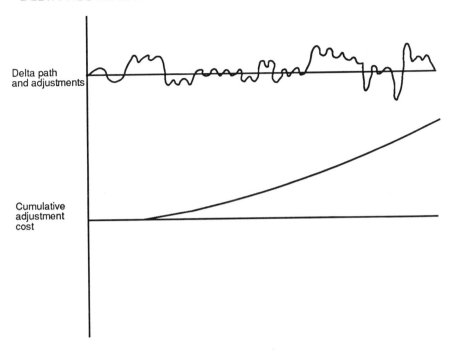

FIGURE 11.16   The depiction of oscillating delta hedge paths and cumulative costs due to adjustments.

In-, At-, and Out-of-the-Money Hedges

Tables 11.6, 11.7, and 11.8 highlight the differences for hedges for in-, at-, and out-of-the-money options from buy and sell perspectives. In the tables, the delta neutral condition was not instituted. Of particular interest is the effect of the time value on the effective hedge price. Table 11.6 shows that in-the-money options increase coverage when only 1 option is used. Table 11.7 shows the fulcrum and transitional case from options to synthetic short. Table 11.8 presents another synthetic short alternative. The boundaries, however, are wider because of the out-of-the-money options. This special position is called a *fence*.

These tables emphasize the need for the strategic overview against a scenario-oriented background. There are substantial financial differences depending on outcomes. Despite imperfect information, one can still tailor the protection to reduce excessive delta neutral hedging costs.

Table 11.6 In-the-Money Hedge

Start: Underlying @400, Option Premiums @22 ($2 Time Value)

Underlying market	TV long 420 put	TV short 380 call	Long put EP	Short call EP
340	80	0	398	362
360	60	0	398	382
380	40	0	398	402
400	20	20	398	402
420	0	40	398	402
440	0	60	418	402
460	0	80	438	402

EP = Effective Price
TV = Terminal Value
PV = Premium Value
Put EP = Cash + TV − PV
Call EP = Cash − TV + PV
Assumed cash and futures are equal and basis equal to zero.
Notice that the results change around the strike prices.

Table 11.7 At-the-Money Options as a Hedge

Start: Underlying @400, Option Premiums @7 ($7 Time Value)

Underlying market	TV long 400 put	TV short 400 call	Long put EP	Short call EP	Synthetic short EP
340	60	0	393	347	400
360	40	0	393	367	400
380	20	0	393	387	400
400	0	0	393	407	400
420	0	20	413	407	400
440	0	40	433	407	400
460	0	60	453	407	400

EP = Effective Price
TV = Terminal Value
PV = Premium Value
Put EP = Cash + TV − PV
Call EP = Cash − TV + PV
Synthetic Short EP = Cash + Option Residual Values + Net Premiums
Assumed cash and futures are equal and basis equal to zero. Strict synthetic short requires same strike and expiration for options. Synthetic short is long put and short call.

Notice that the synthetic short produces results identical to the actual short futures (given underlying assumptions).

Table 11.8   Out-of-the-Money Options as a Hedge

Start: Underlying @400, Option Premiums @5 ($5 Time Value)					
Underlying market	TV long 380 put	TV short 420 call	Long put EP	Short call EP	Synthetic short EP
340	40	0	375	345	380
360	20	0	375	365	380
380	0	0	375	385	380
400	0	0	395	405	400
420	0	0	415	425	420
440	0	20	435	425	420
460	0	40	455	425	420

EP = Effective Price   Put EP = Cash + TV − PV
TV = Terminal Value   Call EP = Cash − TV + PV
PV = Premium Value
Synthetic short EP = Cash + Option Residual Values + Net Premiums
Synthetic short here is also called a fence
Assumed cash and futures are equal and basis equal to zero. Strict synthetic short requires same strike and expiration for options. Synthetic short is long put and short call.
Notice that the synthetic short produces results identical to the actual short futures (given underlying assumptions).

Initial-to-End Delta Condition

The initial-to-end delta orientation is the special case of continuous, instantaneous adjustments, which can be modified to operate only when significant thresholds are violated. The initial-to-end delta perspective tends to remain the most costly. Despite a multitude of adjustments, it is vulnerable to important departures from the theoretical hedge account balances and the actual hedge position balances.

Terminal Delta Condition

The terminal delta perspective considers the financial significance of various strategies against a spectrum of outcomes. It initially evaluates the expected values for implementing strategies against their expected terminal value deltas. There can be only three outcomes: 1.00, .50, or 0.00, which represent the deltas for the in-, at-, and out-of-the-money options. These deltas will be the effective (moment before expiration) termination values for the host of options under consideration. It does not matter when the option expiration cycle is near its end that an option is 1, 10, 100 or more ticks in-the-money. It will still have a delta of approximately 1.00 because at that time it will reflect swings in the underlying option with minimal time value attached. Conversely, an option that is 1, 10, 100 or more ticks out-of-the-money will have a delta that is effectively zero because there is no intrinsic value, and time is rapidly expiring for that option (therefore collapsing any outstanding extrinsic value attached to that option). Tables 11.9, 11.10, and 11.11 represent cases of the in-, at-, and out-of-the-money options.

Notice that the passage of time would result in a serious overhedge for the in-the-money options if they were initiated as delta neutral versus the

Table 11.9 Terminal Delta View Given Initial in-the-Money Option

Illustrative 300 Ounces of Underlying Versus 4 and 3 Options Alternatives				
Start: Underlying @400, option premiums @23 (delta .75)				
Underlying market	TV long 4-420 put	TV long 3-420 put	Long 4 put EP	Long 3 put EP
340	320	240	416.00	397.00
360	240	180	409.33	397.00
380	160	120	402.67	397.00
400	80	60	396.00	397.00
420	0	0	389.33	397.00
440	0	0	409.33	417.00
460	0	0	429.33	437.00

EP = Effective Price   PV = Premium Value
TV = Terminal Value   Put EP = Adjusted (Cash + TV − PV)

Long 4 puts initiated at delta neutral, terminated on a decline as an overhedge of 1 futures contract equivalent.

Assumed cash and futures are equal and basis equal to zero.

Position of 4 puts was initiated as delta neutral (4 × .75) against three futures contract equivalent long position.

This process ending as an overhedge would also require additional premiums to initiate.

The purchase of 3 puts ended as delta neutral.

Table 11.10   At-the-Money Hedges

Start: Underlying @400, Option Premiums @10 (delta .50)				
Underlying market	TV long 1-400 put	TV long 2-400 put	Long 1 put EP	Long 2 put EP
340	60	120	390.00	440.00
360	40	80	390.00	420.00
380	20	40	390.00	400.00
400	0	0	390.00	380.00
420	0	0	410.00	400.00
440	0	0	430.00	420.00
460	0	0	450.00	440.00

EP = Effective Price   PV = Premium Value
TV = Terminal Value   Put EP = Adjusted (Cash + TV − PV)
Assumed cash and futures are equal and basis equal to zero.
The purchase of 2 at-the-money puts was initiated as a delta neutral position and would be twice as costly.
The purchase of 1 at-the-money put was only one-half delta netural at initiation. In the event of any down move it would eventually become delta neutral. Not so for the 2 put purchase. In the event of a down move it would eventually provide twice the required coverage.

Table 11.11   Out-of-the-Money Hedges

Dramatic Illustrative Example Sale of Calls Against Long Underlying Position				
Start: Underlying @400, option premiums @4 (delta .25)				
Underlying market	TV long 1-420 call	TV long 4-420 calls	Short 1 call EP	Short 4 calls EP
340	0	0	344.00	356.00
360	0	0	364.00	376.00
380	0	0	384.00	396.00
400	0	0	404.00	416.00
420	0	0	424.00	436.00
440	20	80	424.00	376.00
460	40	160	424.00	316.00

EP = Effective Price   PV = Premium Value
TV = Terminal Value   Put EP = Adjusted (Cash + TV − PV)
Assumed cash and futures are equal and basis equal to zero. The sale of one out-of-the-money call was not delta neutral at the initiation. When the market rallied beyond the strike of 420 from a terminal value perspective, the position was delta neutral. If the market collapsed the sale of one call only generated $4 of protection. The sale of the four out-of-the-money calls generated $16 of protection. However, the attendant risk was extraordinarily high. If the market rallied beyond the 420 strike the hedger effectively was overhedged by the extent of 3 additional futures contract equivalents. The effective hedge price dramatically declined.

coverage perspective. The cost overruns can be particularly expensive for delta neutral purchase programs for at-the-money options.

Compare Figures 11.17a, b, and c and Figures 11.18a, b, and c which illustrate the movement towards 1.00 or 0.00 for three different strikes for the in- and out-of-the-money options. Calls were illustrated here; the outcomes would be the same for puts. The at-the-money case and the two surrounding strikes are portrayed in Figure 11.19. Notice the constancy of the at-the-money option given the no-change environment for prices.

The application of options hedging strategies is virtually limitless, bounded only by one's creative prowess and constraints, because of the variation of strikes, months, interest rates, volatility estimates, and other variables. Options are adaptable and, in the hands of an experienced hedger, can provide custom-made coverage.

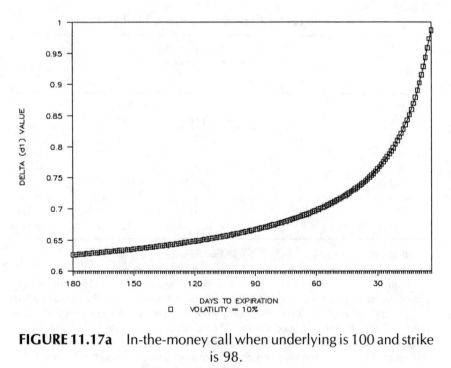

FIGURE 11.17a In-the-money call when underlying is 100 and strike is 98.

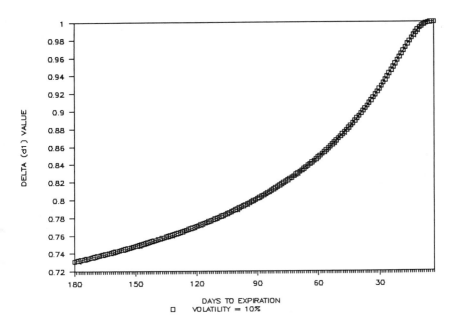

FIGURE 11.17b In-the-money call when underlying is 100 and exercise is 96.

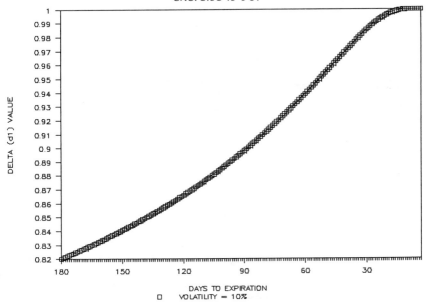

FIGURE 11.17c In-the-money call when underlying is 100 and exercise is 94.

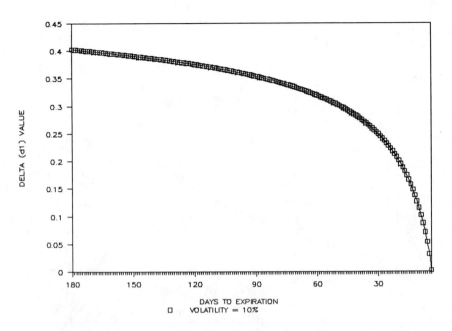

FIGURE 11.18a Out-of-the-money call when underlying is 100 and strike is 102.

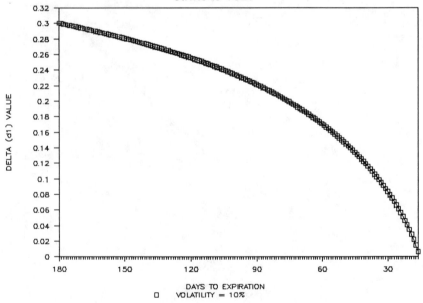

FIGURE 11.18b Out-of-the-money call when underlying is 100 and exercise is 104.

340

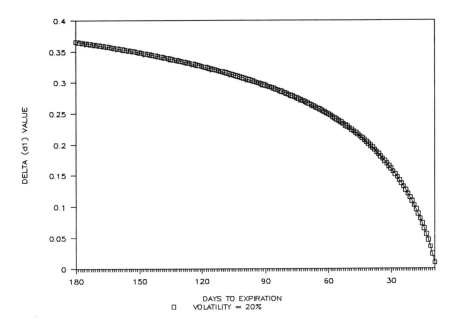

FIGURE 11.18c   Out-of-the-money call when underlying is 100 and strike is 106.

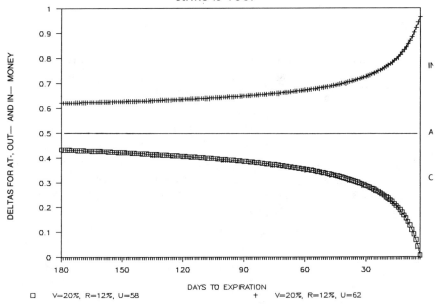

FIGURE 11.19   Simultaneous plotting of in-, at-, and out-of-the-money calls.

POSITIONS AND STRATEGIES

The construction of futures/options position against physicals can be accomplished in a variety of ways. Each has its own strategic importance. It does make a difference how the strategies are composed. Each strategy leaves its own trail as the program operates within the framework of fluctuating prices and basis relationships.

Consider Figure 11.20, which illustrates the strikes, expirations, and types. Similar diagrams will be used to conceptualize the construction of strategies dependent on these parts.

Synthetic-Long Futures Positions

The placement of a long call and a short put produces a synthetic-long futures position. This synthetic position will have the characteristics of a long underlying futures position (see Table 11.3). There will be a connection to marked-to-the-market margining via the sold put, the ability to capture any subsequent up move via the call, and the susceptibility to loss similar to the underlying futures if the market went down.

When this position consists of an at-the-money put and call, then it is strictly considered as the synthetic-long futures position. The position has the replicating characteristic of the underlying futures. An up move would be captured by the long call position and the put would eventually capture the premium. If the market remained the same, then the put would expire out-of-the-money and there would be an offsetting of time values, both paid and received, through the purchase of the calls and the sale of the puts. By applying the sign assignment principles to the deltas, the synthetic-long futures position at that point has a + .50 for the at-the-money call and another + .50 for the sold at-the-money put. Combining these deltas we arrive at a + 1.00. This is identical to being long the underlying futures position because the underlying long futures would have a delta of + 1.00. The capacity to modify the degree of bullishness is related to the strike price selection. In a relaxed sense, the position need not be composed strictly of at-the-money options, but rather a blending of appropriate strike prices. Because each strike has its own characteristics, a somewhat lower delta value for one of the parts would reduce the bullishness, whereas, a somewhat higher delta would impart a higher degree of bullishness.

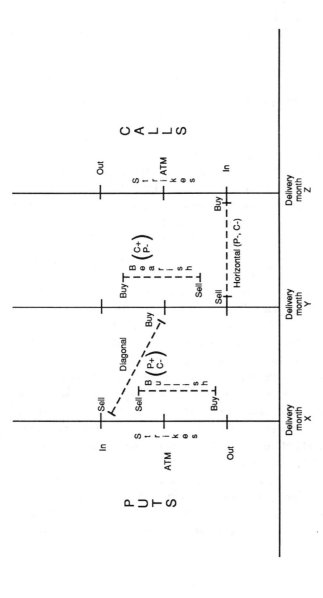

FIGURE 11.20 Illustrative spreads by types, expirations and strikes.

SOURCE: © 1989, Barkley International Inc.

NOTES:

1. Both legs are of the same type, i.e., buy 1 call and sell 1 call or buy 1 put and sell 1 put.
2. Relationship between strike prices on buy and sell legs defines bullish, neutral, or bearish configurations.
3. P = Puts, C = Calls.
4. Typically, + = Credit, − = Debit.

343

There is an operational problem that goes with all of this: The element of risk from the involuntary exercise of the put. This exercise could occur if the market collapsed abruptly and there was no intervening adjustment.

Synthetic-Short Futures Positions

The placement of a short call and a long put resembles being short the underlying futures (actuals) position. Strictly speaking this would occur at the at-the-money level for both the puts and the calls. The long put position would capture any down move and not run the risk of an involuntary exercise. Meanwhile the short call is vulnerable for variation margins in an advancing market scenario. By adjusting the strike prices, the architect of the position can adjust the relative degree of bearishness. This is because of the responsiveness of the various delta values associated with the different strikes for the different options. In the event of an advancing market, the placer of this position runs the risk of involuntary exercise. The call is jeopardized in that it may be prematurely exercised and thus disrupt the overall strategy. Once again there is a swapping effect of time values paid and received, for the puts purchased and the calls written. In essence, these two time values would be expected to cancel out. This gives rise to the situation of no time value payment or receipt on a net-net basis (see Table 11.3).

If there were disparities, then conversion and reverse conversions should be contemplated. These positions are geared to capturing imbalances in the time value components of puts and calls and hence give rise to call and put parities. The conversions and the reverse conversions are the epoxies that keep the options glued to the futures. These conversions and reverses must work out upon expiration, particularly for same day cash settled contracts such as stock index and municipal bond futures and options. This is due to the mandates of the exchange regulations and contract specifications.

Synthetic-Call Positions

The purchase of a put against a long futures, forwards, or cash position is considered a synthetic call since the resulting position has the characteristics of a long call. Table 11.12 demonstrates this for the crude oil market. Notice the way the purchased put injects a payment of time value into the holding which would be similar to that when an actual call is purchased. It has similar risk/reward characteristics. Significant differences lead to potentially arbitrageable situations.

Synthetic-Put Positions

The purchase of a call against the short forwards, futures, or cash position is a synthetic put. A long synthetic put has characteristics similar to a purchased-put option. Again, the payment of a time value is incurred, but here it is for a long call against a short underlying position. If significant departures occur between the synthetic put and the actual put option, then potentially exploitable conditions will have arisen. Table 11.13 shows a synthetic put example for crude oil.

The synthetic put is a useful strategy when it is difficult or expensive to rearrange a short position but modified coverage is desired. A call purchase may not entail large losses from time value decay when this strategy is applied to temporary situations. For example, an important OPEC meeting is upcoming and the outcome is questionable, but the resulting market action is expected to be large.

Downside protection is continued but there is a cap to the upside financial damage against a sharply advancing market, given an underlying short position. The trader is trading time value for information and the expectation of a better hedge mix.

Conversions and Reverse Conversions

Conversions and reverses hold the framework together in much the same way that spreads hold the futures and forwards together and the cash and carrys and reverse cash and carrys, and repo and reverse repos hold the cash and futures and cash and forwards together. Tables 11.14 and 11.15 show how the conversions and reverse conversions hold the futures and options markets together. Notice how variations in the constituent time values gave rise to these operations.

Table 11.12 Synthetic Calls for Crude Oil

	Long Synthetic Call Long Futures and Long Put				Short Synthetic Call Short Futures and Short Put			
Outcome	Net futures change	Financial value of put	Premium paid	Net effect	Net futures change	Financial value of put	Premium received	Net effect
Alt 19.25	2.00	0	−0.50	1.50	−2.00	0	0.50	−1.50
Alt 18.25	1.00	0	−0.50	0.50	−1.00	0	0.50	−0.50
Alt 17.25	0.00	0	−0.50	−0.50	0.00	0	0.50	0.50
Alt 16.25	−1.00	0.75	−0.50	−0.75	1.00	−0.75	0.50	0.75
Alt 15.25	−2.00	1.75	−0.50	−0.75	2.00	−1.75	0.50	0.75

These positions would replicate the actual option positions.

The synthetic long call would be similar to buying the in-the-money call when underlying is 17.25. The loss would have been 50 points due to time value decay. There would be a 25 point intrinsic value recovery.

The synthetic short call would be similar to selling the in-the-money call when underlying is 17.25. The gain would have been 50 points due to time value decay. For the actual call there would be a 25 point return of intrinsic value.

Table 11.13 Synthetic Puts for Crude Oil

	Long Synthetic Put Short Futures and Long Call				Short Synthetic Put Long Futures and Short Call			
Outcome	Net futures change	Financial value of call	Premium paid	Net effect	Net futures change	Financial value of call	Premium received	Net effect
Alt 19.25	−2.00	2.25	−0.75	−0.50	2.00	−2.25	0.75	0.50
Alt 18.25	−1.00	1.25	−0.75	−0.50	1.00	−1.25	0.75	0.50
Alt 17.25	0.00	0.25	−0.75	−0.50	0.00	−0.25	0.75	0.50
Alt 16.25	1.00	0	−0.75	0.25	−1.00	0	0.75	−0.25
Alt 15.25	2.00	0	−0.75	1.25	−2.00	0	0.75	−1.25

Alt = Alternative

These positions would replicate the actual option positions.

The synthetic long put would be similar to buying the out-of-the-money put when underlying is 17.25. The loss would have been 50 points due to time value decay. There would be no intrinsic value recovery.

The synthetic short put would be similar to selling the out-of-the-money put when underlying is 17.25. The gain would have been 50 points due to time value decay. For the actual put there would be no return of intrinsic value.

Table 11.14 Conversion for Crude Oil

Financial Impacts						
Actual Long		Synthetic Short				
Long futures (+1.00)	Futures change	Buy put (−.50) TPV and TIV	Sell call (−.50) TPV and TIV	Put premium paid	Call premium received	Net return
Initiated 17.25	Bought futures @17.25			Bought put @.50	Sold call @.85	
Alt 19.25	2.00	0	−2.25	−0.50	0.85	0.10
Alt 18.25	1.00	0	−1.25	−0.50	0.85	0.10
Alt 17.25	0.00	0	−0.25	−0.50	0.85	0.10
Alt 16.25	−1.00	0.75	0	−0.50	0.85	0.10
Alt 15.25	−2.00	1.75	0	−0.50	0.85	0.10

Alt = Alternative
TPV = Terminal Premium Value
TIV = Terminal Intrinsic Value
At expiration there is no time value only intrinsic value.
This technique exploits imbalances in time value components.
Time value for put started at 50 points and for call at 60 points.
Returns are computed by summing the rows.
Returns are the same for the different alternatives.
Option strike prices were 17 for put and call.

Synopsis of Synthetic Positions

Synthetic positions attempt to replicate the actual counterparts. If for the moment we set aside transaction costs, then these positions do have similar risk, reward, and behavioral characteristics.

Synthetic positions can replicate the underlying futures positions (synthetic long or short), the underlying option type (call or put), and various combinations such as straddles and strangles.

The synthetic options can be long or short. Also, the synthetic straddles and strangles can be bought and sold (long or short); therefore, the hedger can replicate underlying positions rapidly. Sometimes this is of the utmost importance. Using the rule-of-thumb delta of .5 for both the at-the-money

Table 11.15   Reverse Conversion for Crude Oil

			Financial Impacts			
Actual Short		Synthetic Long				
Short futures (+1.00)	Futures change	Sold put (+.50) TPV and TIV	Buy call (+.50) TPV and TIV	Put premium received	Call premium paid	Net return
Initiated 17.25	Sold futures @17.25			Sold put @.50	Bought call @.55	
Alt 19.25	−2.00	0	2.25	0.50	−0.55	0.20
Alt 18.25	−1.00	0	1.25	0.50	−0.55	0.20
Alt 17.25	0.00	0	0.25	0.50	−0.55	0.20
Alt 16.25	1.00	−0.75	0	0.50	−0.55	0.20
Alt 15.25	−2.00	−1.75	0	0.50	−0.55	0.20

Alt = Alternative
TPV = Terminal Premium Value
TIV = Terminal Intrinsic Value
At expiration there is no time value, only intrinsic value.
This technique exploits imbalances in time value components.
Time value for put started at 50 points and for call at 30 points.
Returns are computed by summing the rows.
Returns are the same for the different alternatives.
Option strike prices were 17 for put and call.

call and put, we can readily see the effects of synthetic positions in the listing. From the knowledge that purchased calls and sold puts are sign positive and sold calls and purchased puts are sign negative, the trader can determine the net delta impact of a synthetic position.

Synthetic positions, as their actual counterparts, can be long or short time value (or volatility). Table 11.16 describes the position, its components, delta characteristics, risk-reward attributes, and time value (volatility) properties.

Inverted versus Normal Market Structure

The market structure itself poses peculiar problems and requires different solutions. It boils down to what can be expected if nothing happens to the

Table 11.16 Synoptic Listing of Synthetic Positions

Underlying Position (Delta)	Long	Short	Delta
Futures (+1.00)	long 1 ATM call short 1 ATM put		(+.50 +.50 = +1.00)
Futures (−1.00)		short 1 ATM call long 1 ATM put	(−.50 −.50 = −1.00)
Call (+0.50)	long 1 futures long 1 ATM put		(+1.00 −.50 = +.50)
Call (−.50)		short 1 futures short 1 ATM put	(−1.00 +.50 = −.50)
Put (−.50)	short 1 futures long 1 ATM call		(−1.00 +.50 = −.50)
Put (+.50)		long 1 futures short 1 ATM call	(+1.00 −.50 = +.50)
Straddle (0.00)	long 1 ATM call long 1 ATM put		(+.50 −.50 = 0.00)
Straddle (0.00)		short 1 ATM call short 1 ATM put	(−.50 +.50 = 0.00)
Conversion (0.00)	long 1 actual futures	short 1 ATM call long 1 ATM put	(+1.0 −.5 −.5 = 0.00)
Reverse (0.00)	long 1 ATM call short 1 ATM put	short 1 actual futures	(+.5 +.5 −1.0 = 0.00)
Risk/reward characteristics	this column limited risk/ unlimited gain	this column unlimited risk/limited gain	
Volatility Postures	buying time value or volatility	selling time value or volatility	

NOTE: ATM values assumed to be .50.

underlying market (cash). Will the futures move down to cash or move up to cash? There are good reasons that the price structures have the appearance of an inverted structure. Two reasons are: administered prices or an acute shortage of supply relative to near-term demand. Not all of the buying is done at the highs and the selling at the lows. There is some sort of continuum, whereby hedging and trading occurs over the price series and not just two moments (peak and trough) in history. This partially explains why trading and hedging operations occur at what otherwise would seem to be uneconomic prices or basis levels. These apparently questionable transactions were part of an overall expected value strategy and not isolated actions.

Yield-curve analysis, intercrop analytical efforts, and fundamental assessments of the overall current and expected situations are used here.

Debits or Credits

Debit and credit strategies indicate the relative degree of the net premiums for an options program. In the case of debits, the options were strictly purchased; or when used in tandem with other legs, the purchase premiums were greater than the written premium, resulting in a net debit. Typically, the debit strategies entail no further financial commitment in terms of premiums or variation margins. This is not the case for credits: Often, the margin requirements are in excess of the premiums received, even though the potential loss can be less than the differences between the strikes.

SPREADS

The purchase and sale of the same type option as part of a strategy is a spread. For example, the purchase of a call and the sale of another call is a spread. Its posture (bullish or bearish) and classification is still indeterminate. It could be a vertical, diagonal, or horizontal spread. The implementation of a bullish vertical and a bearish vertical spread sharing the same intermediate strikes produces a *butterfly spread,* while two intermediate strikes produce a *condor spread.* Changing the expiration months for the same type of option stretches the characteristics over time and is known as a horizontal spread. Mixing strikes with different expiration months generates diagonal spreads. Figure 11.21 highlights relative degrees of

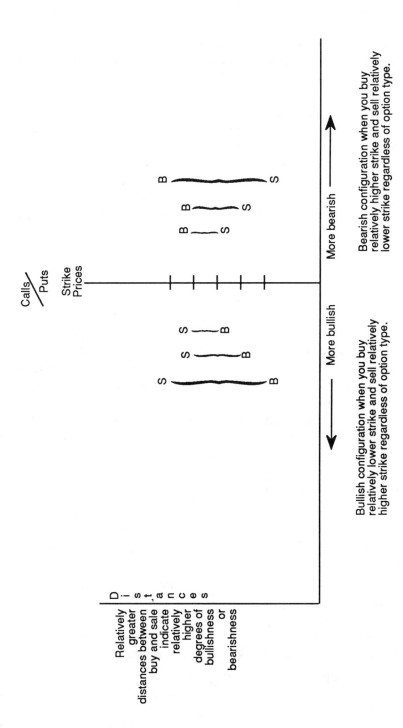

FIGURE 11.21 Degrees of bullishness/bearishness for one-to-one spreads.

351

bullishness or bearishness for vertical spreads.

Figure 11.21 relates the comparative impact of widening or narrowing the differences between two strikes. The greater the distance is, the higher the degree of bullishness or bearishness will be. Regardless of option type, it is the purchase of the comparatively lower strike and the sale of the higher strike that defines a bullish configuration. Conversely, the sale of the lower strike and the purchase of a higher strike is bearish. The vertical spreads relate different strike prices for the same type of option for the same delivery contract month; the horizontal spreads relate two different contract delivery months for the same strike prices and same type of option; and the diagonal spreads relate different strike prices and different contract delivery months for the same type of option (see Figure 11.22).

Vertical Spreads

An understanding of vertical spreads enables the hedger to construct strategies that are predicated on time value and its associated decay characteristics for options in-, at-, and out-of-the-money. A careful use of this strategy can assist in reducing premium dollar payments for buy-oriented type options programs. This capability is especially worthwhile during those times when market conditions cause premiums to increase dramatically from a substantial expansion in the time value components (this

SPREADS
either puts or calls

	VERTICAL	HORIZONTAL	DIAGONAL
STRIKE PRICES	different strikes	same strikes	different strikes
DELIVERY MONTHS	same expiration	different expirations	different expirations
EXPECTED SCENARIO	bullish or bearish	neutral market	bullish or bearish

Buy one type call (put) option and sell same type call (put).

FIGURE 11.22   Spread features and categories.

means that substantial premium forfeitures can be likely). For example, the market may stagnate or dampen over time, yet the trader has paid substantial premiums. These premiums were paid with the implied expectation that the market would not remain within a trading range, which is true for both hedging and trading programs.

Depending on expectations, vertical spreads can generate debits or credits and they have bullish or bearish configurations. Whenever the comparatively lower strike is bought and the higher strike is sold, then a bullish configuration vertical spread has been constructed, regardless of whether it was built with puts or calls. When the comparatively lower strike option is sold and the higher strike option is bought, then a bearish configuration is built regardless of whether this position was built with puts or calls.

The maximum loss for the spread position is limited to the extent of the net debit paid out, which is an attractive characteristic of these debit spread strategies. It is comparable to the maximum loss for a purchased put or call because the maximum loss would be the forfeiture of the paid premium. Unlike the single purchase of an option that can provide protection to the extent of the subsequent market move less the premium paid, that protective capacity is limited to the difference between the strike prices less the debit. For example, if the debit was $750 for two bond options of the same type, and the difference between their strikes was one strike interval, that is, an 84 versus an 86, then the value difference between the strikes would be $2,000 (since each point for T-bonds is worth $1,000), and the potential protection would be $2,000 − $750 = $1,250 per spread.

When credits are generated, the writer of the spread receives the net premium (credit), although margining frequently requires the financial capacity and responsibility to margin the position to the extent of the value difference between the strikes. For the previous example, the financial requirement is $2,000. The risk/reward characteristics are definable, and they would be the mirror image of the debit situation.

This strategy is worth considering when premium values appear to be quite expensive relative to the conditions at hand. Sometimes, insurance premiums become prohibitive, particularly in light of the policy limitations and the deductibles, plus the ability to demonstrate extent of loss. The situation is similar for hedging, particularly when the view of the market-place is of a three-conditional state (up, down, and sideways).

Horizontal Spreads

Horizontal, calendar, or time spreads are often synonymous. The motivating forces behind these trades, however, should be more than the single dimension of relative capture of time value. Typically, these spreads are placed in order to capture time value decay: Specifically, the nearby option is sold and the deferred bought. The premise for this position is that the nearby options exhibit the relatively fastest time-value decay.

Two delivery months are considered: The nearby has 30 days to expiration and the deferred has 120 days to expiration. When the nearbys come the end of the 30th day, they would (theoretically) have no time value, while the deferred option would still have 90 days of time value remaining. This aspect is very important for buy-versus sell-oriented hedge programs because premiums are predicated on two components: intrinsic and extrinsic value. By minimizing the cost of time value paid for, a hedger should be in a competitively stronger position relative to another hedger who frequently pays for time value in full. Figure 11.23 depicts comparative time value decays for different expirations.

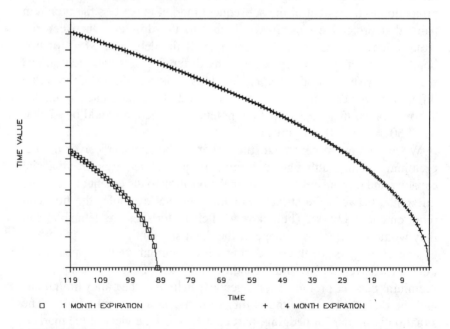

FIGURE 11.23 Comparative time value delays for two different expirations.

These spreads are also used to adjust for gyrations in the yield curve. This strategy can require the purchase of the nearby option and sale of the more deferred option because the dominant market force to reckon with at that particular time is the nearby rate.

Variations in fundamentals for intercrop-year commodities can dictate a more nearby focus for purchases relative to sales of options. This is to better accommodate different sets of fundamentals. Calendar spreading is not an automatic arrangement for capturing time value decay because the movements in the underlying market can dominate the pricing of the option in terms of intrinsic value. The hedger must also have funding prepared. Many futures markets have no limits on the spot month delivery contract, yet the more distant months may have price limits. This can dramatically influence funding requirements. It should also be noted that many options do not have price limits even though the underlying futures may. A final note on the attendant risks of doing calendar spreads is that for most markets, the nearby deliveries exhibit greater volatility or dispersion than the more forward months. Often market structure can change from normal carrying charges to an inverted arrangement (or vice versa). The driving months in these shifts in market structure are dominated by the nearby deliveries because they are the most sensitive to immediate supply/demand considerations.

Diagonal Spreads

Diagonal spreads are a hybrid between horizontal and vertical spreading arrangements. These spreads allow the hedger to modify relative time value decay characteristics and receive partial immunization. Benefits are achieved via the horizontal and vertical spread characteristics, respectively. These features assist in minimizing costs, improving performance, and adapting to a host of other concerns. The spreads have bullish or bearish configurations: They are established by the relationship between the purchased strike to the sold strike (similar to the vertical spreads operations).

Market Structure Analysis

Time value decay accelerates with the passage of time. The option with only 10 days remaining versus an option that has 40 days remaining will exhibit progressively faster decay with each passing day. On the 10th day, the first option will cease existing (therefore, no time value), while the other option will still have time value because it has 30 days remaining to its expiration. To visualize this concept, consider that the first option will lose 10 percent of its time value with the passage of only one day whereas the other option will lose only 2.5 percent of its time value with the passage of the same one day.

This characteristic of rapid time value decay is particularly helpful for sell-oriented programs. In the absence of any underlying movement, all the time value will accrue to the seller, while the buyer will forfeit the entire time value. Looking at this concept against the backdrop of in-, at-, and out-of-the-money options, the hedger can determine how expensive an insurance-buy oriented program is relative to one which attempts to capitalize on time value through its sale. A hedger who is aware of relative time value decay characteristics may prefer a more horizontally or diagonally structured hedge. Also, these variations allow the hedger to capitalize on time value, adjust for potential crop year or yield-curve moves, and be better prepared for recurring rollovers. It is crucial to assess the conditions influencing the structural shifts or maintenance of normal carrying charges (positive yield curves), flat markets, and inverted markets (negative yield curves).

Backspreading

A variation of ratio writes are reverse ratio spreads, positions which are also referred to as backspreads. Typically, a call is sold and more than one (a multiple) are bought at higher strike prices. This activity may produce credits, but the primary focus is the expectation of a dramatic market environment. Potential substitutions for the call sold at the lower price (focus on at-the-money level) are a short sale of futures or of the actual position. The latter position would approximate the call versus calls situation because of futures equivalency considerations and an implemented multiplier factor. Derivative products and other artificial positions can effectively behave as these backspreads would: The behavioral orientation looks for prospectively dramatic market movements.

COMBINATIONS

When the two types of options are combined, the result is a generic combination. The combinations can be: straddles, strangles, and synthetic futures positions.

Straddles

Straddle strategies are either bought or sold: They are not bullish or bearish, per se. A trader who goes long a straddle bought the at-the-money call and the at-the-money put. When this occurs, the position starts out delta neutral. The long call is equal to $+.50$ and the long put is equal to $-.50$, for a net effect of zero. Conversely, the sale of the at-the-money call (delta

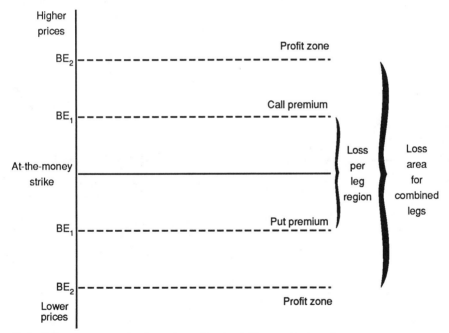

Note: At-the-money represents maximum loss level. Movements away from at-the-money level produce partial premium recovery.

BE₁ and BE₂ breakeven boundaries defined by individual and combined premiums paid.

FIGURE 11.24a Purchased (long) straddle—no adjustments.

−.50) and the at-the-money put (delta +.50) is also a delta-neutral position. Both straddles, long and short, however, have dramatic differences in overall characteristics, exposures, risk consequences, risk attributes, market expectations, and margining. Purchased straddles have limited risk (premiums paid), unlimited gain potential (less premium paid), and no additional margining or financing. Conversely, sold straddles have limited gain potential (premiums received), unlimited loss potential (adjusted for premiums received), and mark-to-market margining (see Figures 11.24a and b, and 11.25a and b).

BE₁ and BE₂ refer to the breakeven boundaries 1 and 2, respectively. They are defined by the premiums paid or received, depending on position. The absence of trends or diminution of volatility clearly favors the short straddle position, whereas a rapid and, particularly, early expansion of volatility or a sudden emergence of a sustainable trend favors the purchased straddle.

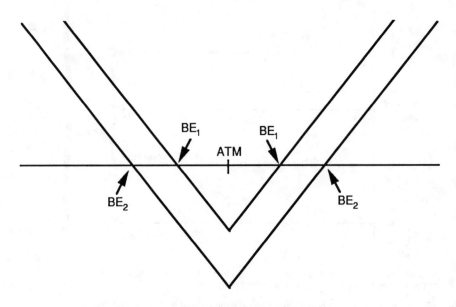

FIGURE 11.24b Purchased (long) straddle—no adjustments, breakeven analysis.

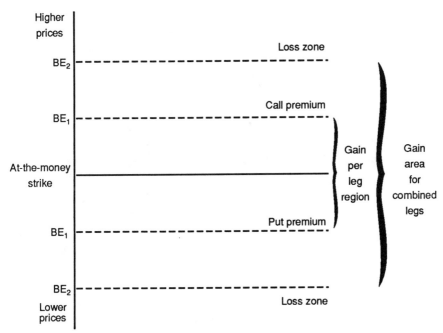

Note: At-the-money represents maximum profit level. Movements away from at-the-money reduce premium capture. Violations of boundaries produce losses.

BE₁ and BE₂ breakeven boundaries defined by individual and combined premiums received.

FIGURE 11.25a   Sold (short) straddle—no adjustments.

Strangles

Strangles are similar to the straddle presentation except that the strikes for the options are out-of-the-money ones and not in-, or at-the-money ones. Strangles allow for wider dispersion in the event of a sale (short the strangle), and require more of a move when purchased (long) in order to profit or receive risk reduction (protection) benefits from a terminal value point of view. Figures 11.26 and 11.27 numerically illustrate these concepts. Notice that Figures 11.26 and 11.27 have a range defined by two strikes, whereas Figures 11.24b and 11.25b each had one maximum point highlighted by peaked condition.

Sales of strangles provide maximum income and protection when the underlying market remains between the two strike prices. For strict

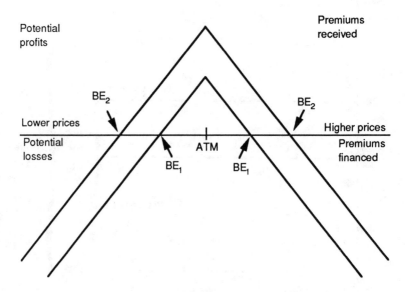

FIGURE 11.25b   Sold (short) straddle—no adjustments, breakeven analysis.

straddle writes, the maximum income point occurs when the underlying market is at the initiating at-the-money level for the written options at expiration.

Covered Writes

Covered writes is a common phrase with multiple meanings: It can refer to the sale of one in-, at-, or out-of-the-money call against one long futures position; or, it can refer to the sale of two at-the-money calls against the one futures position. Theoretically, three sold calls with a combined delta of approximately -1.00 (for example, 3 times $-.33333$) would constitute another covered write. Subsequent market moves in the underlying position will impact the prevailing delta status of the sold options. This behavior will potentially require adjustments: an increase in the number of options to be sold, a lowering (or rolling down) of strike prices, the covering or (rolling up) of strike prices, or a reduction in futures position, and so on to maintain

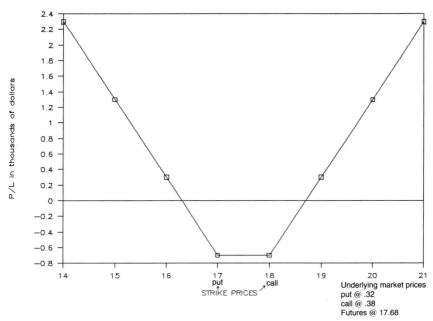

FIGURE 11.26 Purchased (long) strangle for crude oil.

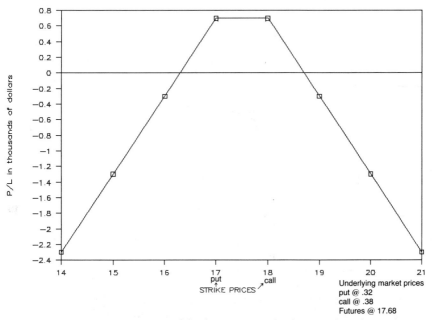

FIGURE 11.27 Sold (short) strangle for crude oil.

361

the elusive delta-neutral state. Table 11.17 presents different perspectives for covered writes using an underlying short position with puts.

The simple short two futures contract equivalents against the two short puts is viewed as a covered write for margining purposes. The sale of five puts is viewed as a delta-neutral write. Current margining rules view the other three short puts as being "naked."

Covered writes can also be against forwards, other options, physical positions, warehouse receipts or on cross hedging values.

Ratio Writes

Ratio writes or variable spreading (writing) programs are a variation of the covered write arrangement. Here, the emphasis is on doing a multiple number of options contracts relative to a single futures position as the benchmark. These strategies, by necessity, are most attuned to delta neutrality orientation. For the cases in which fewer than the proscribed number of options are written, the term *underwriting* emerges. When more than the computed number of options are written against the futures position, the concept of *overwrites* comes to the forefront.

Table 11.17 Covered Write for Futures and Puts

	Short 2 Futures	Short 2 Puts SP 90	Short 5 Puts SP 90	2 Puts Net $ Effect	5 Puts Net $ Effect
Start	90–30	2–14	5–35	0	0
Alt 1 88–00	$5,875.00	($2,125.00)	($4,453.12)	$3,750.00	$1,421.88
Alt 2 90–00	$1,875.00	$2,218.75	$5,546.88	$4,093.75	$7,421.88
Alt 3 90–30	0	$2,218.75	$5,546.88	$2,218.75	$5,546.88
Alt 4 92–00	($2,125.00)	$2,218.75	$5,546.88	$ 93.75	$3,421.88

SP = Strike or exercise price
Delta assumed to be .40 for these puts.
The Treasury note option premiums are quoted in 64ths.
By substituting an 8% coupon for the futures as a cash transaction, this operation would have been a covered write against short cash. More sophisticated analysis would factor in the amount of associated interest on short sale.

Table 11.18 illustrates several perspectives for ratio writes. It evaluates a one-to-one situation, a two-to-one situation, a three-to-one situation, and a four-to-one situation. These situations highlight delta neutrality and over and under cases. Notice that not all cases conformed to delta neutrality. This nonconformity is neither good nor bad in and of itself; rather, it reflects different expectations and probabilistic assignments or organizational requirements.

Caps

The purchase of a call places a ceiling or a cap on a formerly exposed position. The strike price dictates the level of the capped position. The strike, adjusted by the paid premium, indicates the net effect of the desired coverage. For example, the purchase of a 20-strike crude oil call in an 18.75 spot market indicates that crude oil protection has been acquired up until the expiration date of the option; this protection has

Table 11.18 Ratio Write Situation

		\multicolumn{4}{c}{Illustrative Ratio Writes—No Adjustments}			
		\multicolumn{4}{c}{Net Dollar Effects}			
	Long 1 futures	1:1 Short 1 call SP 92	2:1 Short 2 calls SP 92	3:1 Short 3 calls SP 92	4:1 Short 4 calls SP 92
Start	90–06	00–52	104/64	156/64	208/64
Alt 1 88–00	($2,187.50)	($1,375.00)	($562.50)	$250.00	$1,062.50
Alt 2 90–00	($187.50)	$625.00	$1,437.50	$2,250.00	$3,062.50
Alt 3 90–06	0.00	$812.50	$1,625.00	$2,437.50	$3,250.00
Alt 4 92–00	$1,812.50	$2,625.00	$3,437.50	$4,250.00	$5,062.50
Alt 5 94–00	$3,812.50	$2,625.00	$1,437.50	$250.00	($937.50)
Alt 6 96–00	$5,812.50	$2,625.00	($1,375.00)	($3,750.00)	($6,937.50)

SP = Strike or exercise price
Delta was assumed to be .333; therefore delta neutral would require 3 options.
1:1 Considered covered write for margining purposes.
2:1 Considered underwrite situation—initial delta condition.
3:1 Considered neutral situation—initial condition.
4:1 Considered overwrite situation—initial delta condition.

capped crude prices via the board at $20.00 per barrel. If the cost of the option was 45 points or 45 cents per barrel, then the adjusted cap price was effectively $20.45 per barrel to reflect the expense of the call. It is equally important to know both the level of the cap and its adjusted level.

Floors

The purchase of a put limits the downside decline of a portfolio, reserve, or inventory value. The strike price determines the floor level, and the expiration month determines the temporal extent of the coverage. The purchase of an 18-strike crude oil put in an 18.75 market means that downside price protection would (from a terminal value perspective) start at $18.00 per barrel. If the option were held until expiration, and the crude market subsequently declined to $18.01, the put would effectively be rendered worthless because it would have expired one tick out-of-the-money. If the cost of this option was 80 points, then the cost of the program would have been 80 cents per barrel for just that one time frame. This would have effectively protected inventories starting at the $18.00 level, but the net effect would be a protective level of $17.20 per barrel ($18.00 − .80 = $17.20). When placing floors and caps it is important to calculate expected maintenance costs as well. The rolling over of coverage can become prohibitively expensive unless alternative processes are established: Consider that the purchaser of the option did so only for the nearby month because it had the greatest liquidity. At this rate, multiplying the rollovers twelve times by this expected premium cost substantially alters the capped or floored levels and generates a substantial difference in overall profitability.

Collars

Collars are the simultaneous coverage provided by caps and floors, and they place boundaries about the underlying position. The critical issue is to determine a cost effective method of gaining such coverage, given the potential for multiple payments of time value even when such time value payments are reduced by using options that are not at-the-money.

Deductibles

Deductibles, like the caps and floors, arise as the differences between the underlying market and the options strike price. It is similar to insurance in the payment of a premium for coverage. What remains to be determined is: Whether the premium is economic or too expensive? What is at risk? Should one self-insure?

Trying to Recapture Basis Convergence Loss

Basis loss from convergence is a serious problem for hedgers, particularly for holders of bonds and notes. One response is to sell futures against bond holdings, thereby shortening the maturity (duration) into a short-term asset. Generally, this simple operation has a high price.

A progressive decline in futures prices from now to one year out, at quarterly intervals of approximately ¼, ½, and ¾ of a point, means 1 full point, 2 full points, and 3 full points of convergence loss if nothing unusual happens. This is a fat price to pay, given the 8 percent standardization of the note and bond futures contracts. One still must cope with basis-point response, yield-curve gyrations, shifts among the frontier of potentially cheapest to deliver, cost of financing, and the impact on repo and reverse repo operations—and that is just the beginning. By blending a mixture of futures and options, the hedger can, from an expected value perspective, attempt to reduce costs for the same coverage. Alternatively, the hedger can seek to enhance the level of coverage for the same amount of funding.

In Table 11.19, the four strategies have different outcomes. The four were: short futures, a synthetic short put (sale of calls), a synthetic long call (purchase of puts) and a synthetic short futures (fence). Notice that the synthetic futures position had a similar convergence loss, given no change in the underlying cash market. Also, if no adjustments were made, the options behaved more or less progressively than they did in their initial delta condition.

Complicating this situation is the fact that markets and the associated basis series fluctuate, and sometimes, quite dramatically. This calls for a strategy and not a blind application of a mechanical technique. It often does come down to paying time value or capturing time value.

Table 11.19   Comparative Analysis of Three Strategies

		Illustrative Net Effects		
Long cash @91-00	Sell 8 futures contracts	Sell 10 calls SP 92	Buy 10 puts SP 90	Buy 10 puts and sell 10 calls
Start	90-06	520/64cr	920/64db	400/64 net db
Alt 1 95–00	($6,500.00)	$10,125.00	$17,621.32	($4,253.68)
Alt 2 91–00	($6,500.00)	$8,125.00	($14,378.68)	($6,253.68)
Alt 3 87–00	($6,500.00)	($23,875.00)	($16,378.68)	($8,253.68)

cr = credit
db = debit
SP = Strike or exercise price
Assumption of perfect convergence on expiration day. That is, cash equals futures price (zero adjusted basis).
Here: Long $800,000 par value of 8% coupon securities.
The sale of calls and purchase of puts is a synthetic short position which is called a fence. The delta of the call option is .33 and the delta of the long option is .47. Therefore synthesized short has a combined delta of .80 or approximately the underlying short futures by .80 or four-fifths.
The purchase of 10 puts and the sale of 10 calls places this position at an initial delta neutral state (10 × −.80 = −8).

Consider a case in which a hedger has $800,000 or eight futures contracts. By changing the composition, the hedger can attempt to alleviate the burden of time value paid, or the convergence loss from selling futures. In fact, once the futures are placed, the verdict is known; it is just a matter of waiting it out for perfect convergence (cash settled) markets. By evaluating futures convergence losses against expected options effects, the costs and benefits of synthetic positions can be evaluated against the underlying futures and cash positions.

Consider a case in which there is no need for basis-point response adjustment. The tightest fit is via the futures, followed by options. Depending on the adjustment mechanism and the delta response, slight fluctuations in the underlying can generate the need for many small, but cumulatively costly, adjustments. Similar outcomes, although not as neat, occur for other futures-index markets. Convergence losses are substantial and quickly mount up over time, and that timeframe is not especially long. Table 11.20 presents rollovers of four times a year—any additional costs, such as commissions, fees, and slippage, are not included.

To alleviate these problems, optimal hedge mixes, which can require the blending of options (bought or sold) with futures or forwards, should be considered. Constructed payoff matrices inform the hedger of different outcomes for up, down, and sideways markets. Generally, the more transactions there are, the less efficient the program is, which implies that the initial specification of the problem may be inaccurate (because many adjustments are necessary). Optimal hedge mix approaches demonstrate the advantages, disadvantages, and costs for the program that may take different paths before it achieves its objectives. Figure 11.28 shows several alternatives for trying to minimize basis-point loss and enhance returns, given particular basis and market behaviors under favorable, unfavorable, and neutral conditions.

Paths and Price Diffusion

Paths give rise to a reproduction of a diffusion arrangement at each decision point. This can effectively be each moment in time, as

Table 11.20 Rollover and Convergence Loss Effects

	Cumulative Rollover Costs in Dollars 8 Futures Contract Equivalents			
	1 Rollover	2 Rollovers	3 Rollovers	4 Rollovers
¼ Point	$2,000.00	$4,000.00	$6,000.00	$8,000.00
½ Point	$4,000.00	$8,000.00	$12,000.00	$16,000.00
¾ Point	$6,000.00	$12,000.00	$18,000.00	$24,000.00
1 Point	$8,000.00	$16,000.00	$24,000.00	$32,000.00

Assumption of similar convergence loss on rollover.

The composition of convergence costs would be net time value or basis loss due to futures discount to cash.

Hedger must evaluate the comparative time value versus basis loss and associated financing costs as well as to determine an optimal hedge mix.

Categories

		Futures	Buy options	Sell options	Cumulative expected cost (benefit)
E n v i r o n m e n t s	Favorable	All Partial None	All Partial None	All Partial None	For various combinations
	Neutral	All Partial None	All Partial None	All Partial None	For various combinations
	Unfavorable	All Partial None	All Partial None	All Partial None	For various combinations

All = Total hedge consists of that particular category
Partial = Various percentages
None = Total hedge excludes that particular category

FIGURE 11.28 Hedge categories, environments, and alternative programs with associated expected cumulative costs-benefits.

illustrated in Figure 11.29. In practice, these curves change their shapes as the process tries to unravel itself. It is the elusive shape changing process that injects high risk and return into the system, which is comparable to rapidly changing actuarial tables. Some days, the expected life-span for the average male is 35 years, the next day 64 years, and for females 44 years, and then 94 years, and so on and so forth. Fortunately this widely fluctuating arrangement is not characteristic of mortality tables. Refinements bring improvements: By introducing conditional data, such as smoking versus nonsmoking, AIDS versus no AIDS and so on, risk groups can, to some extent, be identified. Figure 11.30 portrays conditional versus unconditional

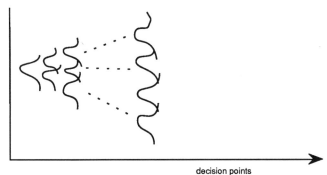

decision points
Each curve represents the probabilities at each decision point.
Cumulatively the sub curves conform to the entire process curve.

FIGURE 11.29 Paths and reproductive processes.

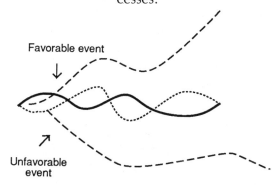

FIGURE 11.30 Conditional and unconditional paths.

pathing arrangements. It shows that a favorable or unfavorable event pushes the path onto a conditional route (heavy broken line). Otherwise the path oscillates about mean zero, acting in an unconditional manner.

Truth or Consequences

When the hedger elects to use particular models he or she is electing to believe the model's assumptions. Assumptions are artificial devices used to polish off or grind out troublesome operational facets. Occasionally, the most obvious features are overlooked and the difficulty of ascertaining "true" estimates for some variables, such as probability distributions, leaves hedgers prone to serious problems. This highlights the importance of a reasonable specification of the model. Accuracy versus practicality must be evaluated in terms of: What is at stake? How comfortable is the hedger with the program? Does the hedger know what makes the model tick?

Outliers

Outliers pose the highest risk/reward variables. Events during October 1987 brought international attention to this statistical phenomenon. The equity market experienced large rates of change followed by a progressive dampening effect, and the large ± changes occurred in proximity to one another. Essentially, in normal theory the drop of 508 points in one index (the Dow) or 80 points in another (the S&P) would be followed by a mean value of zero, or something close to it, as the most likely subsequent event. Empirically, it is not what happens.

Cauchy versus Normal Case Assumptions

The form and behavior of the underlying generating process can be the most important set of assumptions made. A primary and understandable reason that many of the models start and continue to remain (log) normally oriented is because of the vast body of statistical literature and applications software available for them. This is not so for many other distributive processes—some processes are so unstable that statistical frameworks are difficult to construct. Nevertheless, meaningful applications are possible, given a set of modified conditions.

Consider volatility: Do approximately 68 percent of the observations occur within one standard deviation of the mean? The normalcy assumption says yes. But what if only 45 percent occur within the inflection points of the curves? While these curves may have remarkable resemblances, they are substantially different in expectations and properties. In other words, is your model banking on expected values that should fall within an area bounded by one deviation, approximately 68 percent? Or, is your model attuned to the probability that less than half of the observations may fall within one dispersion statistic and more than half beyond this central tendency area?

Over the long run, they all may occasionally work out. But given a sequential testing format, you may never make it to the long run. A bankruptcy condition may be invoked, and a premature termination to the position or the firm can occur.

Analogies

Analogies are helpful tools for exploring probabilistic structures, and they have applications to options-pricing models regarding the N factor. In the following example, we will use marbles for an analogy. These familiar teaching tools highlight processes that appear during different market phases.

Net Changes

Think of net changes as marbles. Basic theory states that there are no significant differences among the distribution of marbles. The marbles are red and black and represent up and down changes. When you consider that trends exist in the marketplace, at times the red ones have greater weight (downside), and at other times the black ones have greater weight (upside), like marketplace trends. Seldom are they truly balanced; if they are, it is a trendless series. The number of up occurrences and down occurrences do not show statistical distinction over a relatively long period of time. They do stack up at important places, usually turning points and panic finales (up or down); in other words, they balance out for the period but not for the phase. This dependence in a time series can be seen by the application of Kendall's Trend Test or the Wallis and Moore Cycles Test, technically known as a "test for a series of ordered observations." Figures 11.31, 11.32, and 11.33 depict what happens at perfect balance and with slight shifts.

Empirically, it can be shown that there is a degree of affinity between large changes, both up and down. Also, small marbles (changes) favor other small marbles (changes). These conditions do not continue indefi-

— Changes
(Red)

+ Changes
(Black)

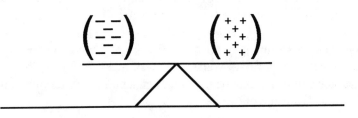

FIGURE 11.31 Fulcrum of red/black marbles that are
perfectly balanced.

— Changes
(Red)

+ Changes
(Black)

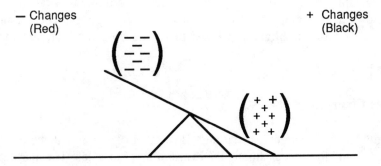

FIGURE 11.32 Fulcrum of red/black marbles that are
lopsided up.

— Changes
(Red)

+ Changes
(Black)

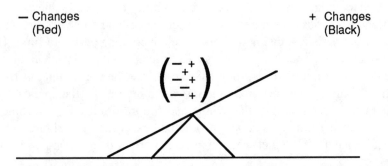

FIGURE 11.33 Fulcrum of red/black marbles that are lopsided down. (Here, the use of one urn reflects composite
process.)

nitely. Many times significant departures from these patterns of largeness or smallness suggest emerging equilibrium or trending behaviors. Another way to view this is to ask: With a 508 point drop in the blue chip index, would you expect the immediate subsequent changes to be comparatively large, not small (regardless of direction)? Effectively, many models strongly suggest little or no change (zero means) for subsequent observations whether they are immediate or distant. Figure 11.34 portrays absolute relative changes over time and shows that there is not an immediate return to little or no changes. By substituting volatility for these changes, it is recognizable that there is a dampening effect, but it takes time. Also, its mean or location value can be significantly farther away than the initial condition.

As trends develop or reverse direction, the relative size of the marbles changes, which is suggestive of a dynamically transforming probability distribution. Alternatively, the marbles may look the same size, but they have different weight; therefore, it is critical to use the proper statistical analysis tools to differentiate between the weights. Some methods assume that the same size means the same weight—if this were so, how could the

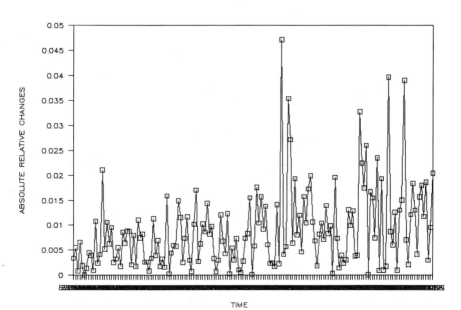

FIGURE 11.34 Absolute relative changes over time highlighting clustering effects.

trends or cyclical behavior of clusters or statistical dependence be explained?

Next, introduce white marbles, which reflect no change, or unchanged net results. These marbles are a demarcation line, and their expected value is the mean of the normal distribution with $\mu = 0$.

Figure 11.35 reflects an empirical approximation of the bell-shaped curve perspective. The slight shift about mean zero generated a substantial up trend in the underlying market (see Figure 11.36).

This principle of a slight shift or bias in the mean of the changes is equally applicable to down trending markets. Indeed, slight departures from mean zero are very important and, on a cumulative basis, strongly influence prices and basis levels. The subtle presence of one inordinately large marble or one of greater-than-accounted-for weight is sufficient to drive the mechanism into a trend situation or to a new equilibrium level. Many evaluation models depend on balance and independence among the ex-

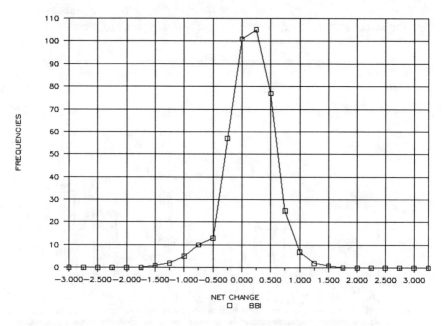

FIGURE 11.35 Empirical approximations to bell-shaped curve for net changes in municipal bond market. (Here, there was a slight positive bias.)

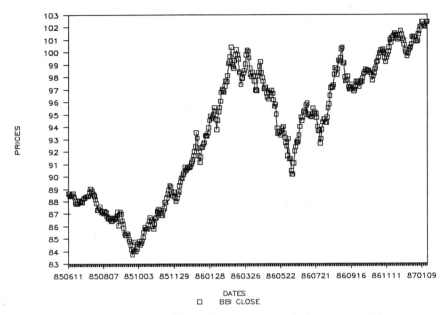

FIGURE 11.36   Municipal bond prices given slight positive bias to net changes. (see Figure 11.35).

pected changes. This special case is reflected by the probability distribution perched precariously on the fulcrum.

Delta

Delta is the expected change in premium for a small change in the underlying price for specified interest rates, strike prices, volatilities and expirations.

Gamma

Gamma is the expected change in delta, given a change in the underlying market. Gamma is most sensitive around the at-the-money level. Positive gamma is associated with the purchase of an option, negative gamma is associated with sale of an option. *Convexity* is a related concept that indicates an option's response to changes in the underlying instrument. The highest degree of convexity centers on the at-the-money level because that level is most sensitive to change. Convexity is viewed as favorable for option buyers and unfavorable for option sellers.

Theta

Theta measures the expected change in premium for a change in time—it is the risk attribute related to time. At-the-money options demonstrate increasingly faster rates of premium decline as the option approaches expiration. In- and out-of-the-money options experience time value decay, which is less responsive to the passage of time. Theta is viewed as positive for sellers of options. These sellers, or writers, expect to benefit by the associated amount of time value decay. Buyers of options are subject to negative theta or losses due to time value decay.

Vega

Vega measures the premium response to changes in volatility. (This derivative statistic is also known as omega or kappa.) Higher vega statistics indicate a higher price response given a one percent change in volatility. Generally, increases in volatility increase the delta values for out-of-the-money options, while decreasing the deltas for in-the-money options. Conversely, reductions in volatility enhance the in-the-money deltas and reduce the out-of-the-money deltas.

Rho

Rho measures the expected premium response to a change in the interest rate. Although this derivative is predicated on very small changes in the interest rate, it is frequently viewed from a change of a one-percent perspective.

Theoretical Values

Table 11.21 lists a call option's theoretical values for the derivative statistics of delta, gamma, theta, and vega. The trading date is March 1, the expiration date is March 19 (of the same year), the volatility is 15 percent, the interest rate is 5.5 percent, and the underlying futures price is 225.00. The strike prices are listed as 200.00 to 250.00 with 5.00 intervals.

The theoretical premium for this option for the 225 strike when the market is trading at 225.00 is 2.98. That 225 level is also the strict at-the-money level. Notice that delta is approximately 50 percent, which implies that if the underlying market were to move 1.00 (from 225 to 226 or to 224), then the premium would be expected to rise to 3.48 or decline to 2.48.

Hypothetical Call Option

Underlying Futures Price 225.00	Estimated Volatility 15.0%	Interest Rate 5.5%	Trading Date March 1	Expiration Date March 19
Exercise or Strike Price	Theoretical Premium	Theoretical Delta	Theoretical Gamma	Theoretical Theta	Theoretical Vega
250.00	0.00	0.1%	0.0%	0.001	0.001
245.00	0.01	0.6%	0.2%	0.003	0.008
240.00	0.08	2.7%	0.8%	0.013	0.031
235.00	0.34	9.8%	2.3%	0.036	0.087
230.00	1.16	25.9%	4.3%	0.067	0.162
225.00	2.98	50.5%	5.3%	0.083	0.199
220.00	6.09	75.3%	4.2%	0.065	0.157
215.00	10.26	91.4%	2.0%	0.032	0.077
210.00	15.01	97.9%	0.6%	0.009	0.022
205.00	20.00	99.5%	0.1%	0.002	0.004
200.00	25.00	99.7%	0.0%	0.000	0.000

NOTE: Deltas are sometimes presented as .505, .753, or .997 and not necessarily 50.5%, 75.3%, or 99.7%, respectively.

TABLE 11.21   Theoretical Derivative Statistics for a Hypothetical Call

The gamma associated with the 225 strike is 5.3, which provides an indication of delta's response to the same 1.00 change in the underlying price. If the market rallied to 226, then the delta would be expected to be 55.8. If the market declined to 224, then delta would be expected to drop from 50.5 to 45.2.

Theta is listed as .083 for the 225 exercise price. It implies that if there are no changes in the variables, with the exception of losing one day (it is now March 2), then the premium is expected to decline to 2.897 (2.980 − .083).

Vega (or kappa or omega) is listed as .199, which represents the expected change in the premium, given only a 1 percent change in volatility. If volatility were to increase to 16 percent, then the option's premium would be expected to advance to 3.179. If volatility were to decline to 14 percent, then the premium would be expected to fall to 2.781.

The gamma, theta, and vega statistics all show the highest degree of sensitivity for the at-the-money (near-the-money) strike prices. The associated statistics taper off as one examines options that move progressively deeper into- or out-of-the-money.

It should be noted that these statistics are actually in a state of flux because all of the variables are continually changing, even during very brief periods of time. It is very important for the hedger to understand the mechanics of his or her software to determine whether it rounds up, rounds down, or truncates. Slight alterations in the assumptions can produce major changes in the statistics and the computed premium values. Not all traders and hedgers use identical values for the variables, and significant departures from fair value can occur. When there is a consensus, then that is usually the fair value: When there are differences in estimation they can be due to expectations, or even errors.

EXCLUSIONARY PROGRAMS

When a hedger relies solely on options as the hedging instruments, the program is viewed as options to the exclusion of futures, forwards, and derivative products. Depending on corporate charters and external regulations, options-only programs may be implemented. Usually, these programs are buy-side only, and even the writing of options as part of spreads or other strategies can be expressly prohibited.

It is important for the hedger to understand that these constraints can drastically alter the solution set. This, in turn, can preclude actions that would ordinarily be preferred but are here prohibited.

COMPLEMENTARY PROGRAMS

Hedging programs that allow futures, options, and other derivative instruments are considered complementary. These instruments can be used together or separately, depending on the decisions of the hedging committee. Often these programs allow the writing of options as well. This inclusion is not only for protection or potential income purposes, but to reduce the costs of time value and allow the construction of other synthetic positions and arbitrage, or trading the basis, operations.

FINANCING AND MARGINING

The straightforward purchase of options precludes the need for additional financing in the form of variation margin calls. An exercise of the option, however, would subject the exerciser to prevailing futures margining requirements, and this must be considered. While the terms premium and margin are often used synonymously for the purchase of options, the terminology is incorrect for the writes. Writes generate premiums; however, the writer of the option may have to post additional funds to initiate and maintain the written options. These written positions are subject to mark-to-market margining rules.

Currently, each exchange has its own requirements and formulas. In addition, there is a movement toward common clearing facilities and delta-oriented margining. If the proposed changes become realities, then there will be access to funds generated by options appreciating in premium value, although not necessarily intrinsic value. This will level out the wrinkles between the basket of options versus futures-oriented trading–hedging arrangements.

FLEXIBILITY AND SUMMATION

The variety of strike prices, expiration months, arrangements of options, futures, forwards, and cash provide a broad horizon of hedging opportunities. One can modify the degree of a hedge program by the selection of options and futures. Funding capability, as well as opportunities for potential income, is enlarged because of the capitalization of rich premiums related to high volatilities. Even positions that would have resulted in over/under hedging conditions can now be more accurately hedged with options.

12
Designing and Implementing a Program

OVERVIEW

The principal facets of a hedge program are its objectives, constraints, risk management, opportunities, and operational management. All are inter-related and must be evaluated and implemented together. For organizations that intend to hedge but do not have a hedging operation online, the initial step is to name a hedging committee.

Hedging Committee

The hedging committee is a senior management group that determines the necessity of a hedge program. Once that happens, the following steps are taken:

1. Research and analyze hedgeable positions and conduct basis and other pertinent studies
2. Determine the degree of corporate commitment in terms of person-nel, resources, and capital
3. Establish guidelines, criteria, operational workflows, duties, and responsibilities

4. Contact divisions such as accounting, marketing, treasury, legal, and production and set up infrastructure and controls
5. Select and designate authorized traders to implement the actual transactions

Figure 12.1 shows interrelationships among the constituent groups for the hedging committee. The committee members are selected from divisions that will be directly involved in the process, and they establish the guidelines and scope for the hedge program.

Identification

One approach for the hedge committee in identifying the core risks, objectives, and constraints is to determine the core size of a hedge program.

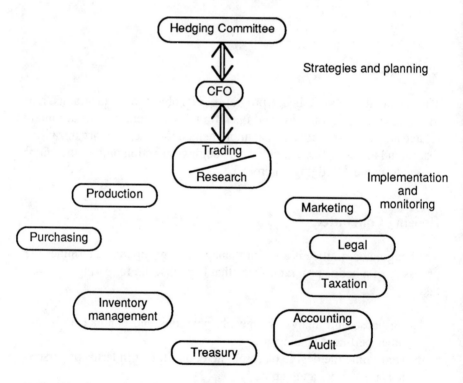

FIGURE 12.1   Flow from hedging committee to and among implementing groups.

Then they can start the evaluation process with futures and forwards around that area and make up the differences with options. This mixture of instruments can be helpful because it shifts contractual performance and financing risks away from the hedger and allows for the placement of hedges via options, which, when purchased, have asymmetrical properties. When puts are purchased against the long positions (expected production, reserves, inventories) the position is transformed into a synthetic call. The payment of time value can be very expensive if it is pursued on a continuous rollover basis during erratic markets; therefore it could be worthwhile to use options on a limited basis (buying perspective) to hold down costs while freeing the organization from delivery and other contractual performance constraints and obligations. If production suffers, the firm is partially protected against a dramatic event because the core portion of the hedge is maintained by futures, with the remainder accounted for through the placement of options. Although hedging is different from trading, both are decision making processes and the hedger, like the trader, can experience success or failure.

Legal Considerations

The corporation and its subsidiaries should be empowered to conduct hedging activities. Particularly, the charter must be examined to see whether all participating entities are permitted to use futures, forwards, and options markets and in what capacity. Sometimes, the parent may allow buy and write options programs but subsidiaries may be specifically excluded from granting options.

The organization must ascertain its regulatory constraints and make sure that filings are timely and complete and that other legal considerations are satisfied. Brokerage firms insist on being furnished with timely corporate resolutions, trading authorizations, and intended hedging papers (which, essentially, outline the markets, the expected maximum position size, and the expected average hedging position size). All of these are the discussion points for hedging programs. Each organization must pursue its legal grounds for establishing a hedge program as well as its economic need.

Objectives

Although each organization's goals may differ, risk management for the enterprise (in order to increase its longevity and performance) is a common element. To arrive at risk management solutions, questions must be asked, including:

1. Do all reserves have to be hedged?
2. Is it to be an annual, quarterly, monthly, weekly, daily, hourly, or moment-by-moment hedging process?
3. Are inventories, sales, and production to be treated similarly?
4. What about foreign exchange, asset and liability management, underwriting, and corporate portfolios?
5. Is the program limited to risk management or is it open to incremental income through premiums from options writing?

Each timeframe produces different solution sets, and the impact on constraints is substantial. Gross assets and liabilities, net exposure, partial exposure, and so on are variables that must be addressed. Even when risk management is chosen, there are many alternatives, such as forward contracting, futures, and options, that should be considered.

Constraints

There are two types of constraints, external and internal, both of which limit the actions of the hedger, but in different ways. The external constraints are imposed on the hedger. They can pose operational problems if large adjustments are necessary in a short period of time and can require the hedger to "shop around" for FCMs (futures commission merchants) willing and capable to carry positions. FCMs impose their own position limits, which can not exceed those of the exchanges. The credit department of an FCM may impose a 20-contract limit for one hedger and an 8,000-contract limit for another hedger, both in the same industry regardless of their corporate size, because of their creditworthiness, and not necessarily their need.

External. Among the external constraints is exchange position limits for futures and options positions. Although bona fide hedges can, in principal, be initiated and maintained without regard to size, position limits can occur after the organization petitions and receives exchange or other regulatory approval. While this approval usually is forthcoming, extraordinary factors can occur that may preclude it. For example, program trading that replicated baskets of securities against futures positions was temporarily denied permission to trade. Size was not the key issue, but rather, the concept of "mechanized" systems and strategies emerging in a highly erratic marketplace was. State insurance boards, banking commissions, federal agencies, and other outside organizations can influence the organization's capacity to implement hedges. Only partial hedging is allowed for some financial institutions including many insurance companies. Even brokerage houses may impose margin requirements or position, credit, or other financial limits for hedge programs. Banks and other lending institutions may modify their lending practices when positions are hedged. While the percentage of credit extended against positions may increase because that particular portfolio, inventory, reserve, or other item is hedged, the hedge program can be constrained not only by the limit of outstanding positions allowed, but by the amount of overall financing. For example, a bank may agree to the hedge of 1,250 contracts of silver or $36,000,000, whichever comes first. If additional financing is required in excess of $36,000,000 it can only come from other sources, if permitted; otherwise, the hedge would have to be modified to free up dollars by reducing the number of open contracts. This action can pose financial problems because such situations tend to occur at times when protection is most sought and less available. In early 1980, a preclusion of credit for the financing of metals occurred, and similar, though less drastic, measures were instituted against energy firms in the mid-1980s. This imposition of emergency measures against hedges can occur at any time and can be ruinous. For financials, if the Federal Reserve did not intervene on October 19, 1987, and for a period thereafter, the supply of capital to maintain (and not necessarily support) the capital markets would have been very slim. Specialist firms, bond houses, and stock arbitrage firms would have been caught in a liquidity trap in the sense that they would have been unable to finance their holdings and their only way of raising funds would have been further distress selling.

Internal. Although a firm may have complete hedging or core hedging as an objective, its management ability, financial capability, or competitive posture can severely limit the placement of a hedge program. It may take time for the desired program to be implemented in totality because funds may have to be freed (a corporation tottering near insolvency, not bankruptcy), production reestablished, assets freed from liens, a corporate charter modified to include hedging or different forms of hedging, and hedge instruments and processes as acceptable management functions. Broader powers are often required for writing hedges because corporate charters may specifically preclude them, or brokerage firms may insist that provisions be included within the documentation and corporate resolutions for the establishment of brokerage accounts for hedging purposes. Good business sense may not be enough to implement a program.

OPPORTUNITIES

Hedging programs can permit an expansion of an organization's business opportunity horizon. Hedges can substitute for some marketing functions, inventory management procedures, financing alternatives, acquisition choices, restructuring of corporate objectives and constraints, and so on. By selling deferred months in normal carrying charge structure markets, a hedger can attempt to capture the basis or lock in the implied carrying charges. These may be better or more attractive than those offered by the forwards or ordinary transactions marketplace. The sale of options can help reduce time value penalties or provide income alternatives while affording various degrees of hedge protection.

Trading Aspects

The implementation of hedges, adjustments, and their removal adds a new dimension to the program. Hedges do not always go on smoothly with tight quotes and smooth markets. Even when the marketplace is fairly liquid, trading conditions prevailing at the time when action is required can delay, speed up, or otherwise adjust the hedging arrangement. This may not be as problematic when trading against a fixed basis, since then the price level for the futures determines the final invoicing price for the set basis; but when one is trying to adjust the hedge program mix against changes in portfolios, assets, or liabilities, market conditions, both for the actuals and the futures and options, can be such that scale or limit orders may be off the mark by a substantial amount. There may be no immediate retracement or opportunity to place trades at what were optimal levels. One may have to settle for less-than-optimal levels that may provide adequate margins and good coverage, but at material differences from what was available only moments before. News items, trading conditions, and drastic realignments due to actual underlying business conditions all influence the transactional phase of the hedging process. Market orders, limit orders, stop orders, fill or kill, and other order variations can impact the successful performance of a hedge. Do you work an order or have it executed immediately? Do you give points or take points? Sometimes, the trades are simple enough: The futures are to be conducted on the close for the specified basis. Other times, you may require commodities such as wheat, oil, beans, or T-bonds but you were instructed to work the order over the next ten minutes, the hour, or the day. The latitude is given with the intention of reaping more favorable prices or basis levels. Sometimes averaging the process is desirable—the required amounts must be conducted at specified intervals during the day to try to achieve an average price rather than run the risk of the worst price. This method tends to be used by the firms concerned with moving the market too much, given the size of their operations. There is another school of thought about this: to do it all at once, or relatively quickly, to absorb all the favorable bids (offers) and, as the market recognizes and adjusts to the flow of orders and trends, the position your organization required will have been already established or liquidated.

Controls

It is essential for a program to have controls that can minimize loss from fraud, unauthorized trades, negligence, inaccurate write ups by the brokerage firm, the firm's traders, or the floor. Transaction reports should be confirmed immediately and often. A checking out at the cessation of the trading session is advisable because it gives all parties a chance to straighten out potential problems before they grow and make adjustments whenever possible via the cash or late-night markets or other feasible alternatives. Whether trading assistants or associates examine the tickets and positions, it is a good practice to institute.

Once the corporate charter has been approved or amended to permit hedging and trading-the-basis activities, it is necessary to designate authorized traders. These people do not necessarily trade in the ordinary sense of the word, but rather are empowered to act on behalf of the organization for the placement of orders.

Marketing, production, trading, and the accounting departments must receive copies of confirms and monthly statements in order to balance the books and closely monitor the positions. This is especially advisable for firms that have multiple traders for each operational area. Often, only the treasury department on a day-to-day basis may fathom the flow of funds in and out, while the other areas may not be aware of the overall posture of the organization. Additionally, sick leave or vacations can disturb the control process unless procedures were designed to account for many of these common contingencies. There should be contingency guidelines, and immediate access to senior management should be available during dramatic markets. It is important to have it laid out before hand and not after the fact. An elaborate system may not be necessary in small to moderate size organizations, though the principles should be followed. One error can be costly, since it may disrupt a firm's finances and alter its capacity to do business.

Taxation

The change in federal as well as state tax laws presents issues that are complex yet must be considered for hedging purposes. Inventory taxes and other property taxes can alter the tax consequences for hedgers. Unless otherwise instructed, brokerage firms process (P&S) positions, according to first-in, first-out (fifo) principles. This arrangement may not be satisfactory or representative for a hedger who may want to utilize last-in, first-out (lifo) guidelines or a matching of trades against actual positions, particularly for AAs and EFPs. By using *wait instructions* the accountability for such transactions is thus assured. This helps not only in evaluating the profitability of particular hedge activities, but assists in monitoring department positions and other concerns of the organization. Specific policies and recommendations must be forthcoming from professionals in these areas. A problematic spot is the differentiation between corporate trading versus hedging accounts. Depending on prevailing tax laws, this can mean substantial differences in the tax consequences for these activities, even if they are undertaken by the same party.

Production, Marketing, and Inventory Management

The isolation of trades and their economic impacts can often be best served by splitting the hedge process into distinct groups. Each area or subsidiary and its employees may share in the profits, while the ability to preserve the financial integrity of these groups is through multiple accounts.

Hedging does not mean one and only one account. Hedgers are permitted to maintain multiple accounts because accounts can be used by different groups for different purposes. Hedges established for physical exchanges can be one type, by an area such as production or marketing another type, and underwriting and house holdings can be still another listing. Each pertains to a hedgeable position, yet each refers to different circumstances and activities. A smelter may have an active acquisition group purchasing scrap metal throughout the day. The group may also sell scrap, given a satisfactory margin on the metal. This can happen if there is the ability to quickly use the scrap at certain locations.

A more sophisticated approach to hedging is derived from the area of inventory management: By assimilating all the distinct groups into one operation, the simple expected doubling in sales may not necessarily require the proportional doubling of anticipatory buy hedges. The rationale behind this is that inventories are more closely approximated by square root-related functions of sales, reordering costs, time lapses between orders and actual restocking, and carrying charges (interest rates). More nearly optimal decisions can be derived by taking this aspect into consideration. Should conditions become such that supplies are in jeopardy and projected deliveries into the firm are subject, then the solution set must become modified to place a higher priority on receiving critical inputs rather than exclusively relying on a financially oriented inventory management model which assumes that all conditions will be satisfied.

Import/export firms may seek to conduct the foreign exchange transactions in separate accounts in order to distinguish between the transactions for import as well as export. For multiple products it may be necessary for this decentralization because there are many transactions from new business, changes in orders, cancellations or additions to orders.

Financial firms may have to differentiate between trading/hedging activities and maintain separate accounts for multiple trading desks, portfolio operations, house investments, and underwriting. Market making for securities for narrow margins requires carrying positions overnight, yet it may be strongly recommended to do so on a hedged basis. Separate accounts may have to be established for different portfolios, cash and carrys (and reverses), and position trading accounts (or holding of inventories). Asset and liability management can require a different grouping of accounts, as can foreign operations to allow for foreign exchange consider-ations. This proliferation of accounts helps opening and closing transactions and allows autonomy to the different areas, but requires controls in order to evaluate the global and net impacts and exposures to the firm.

Rather than holding on-going meetings evaluating the natural hedge benefits between the marketing, production, and purchasing groups, the firm's hedge committee can provide guidelines given the *expected open exposure* of the different departments, in part and in total, and thus reduce the establishment of unnecessary hedges, which would duplicate natural hedge positions. Since hedges require time and funding resources, saving can be had by the knowledge of the firm's total current position and trading direction. There can be seasonal factors such as the buildup and depletion of heating oil and gasoline supplies throughout the year. Although refining may continue as an ongoing process, the different products may vary.

An informed hedge committee can make informed decisions. For the larger organizations, the hedge committee may consist of members of the board of directors and senior executives. However, the actual implemen-tation may fall on the shoulders of those authorized to act as traders on behalf of the organization. To keep the two groups in contact, a control and monitoring procedural process will have to be mapped out.

Accounting and Auditing

The outcomes of hedging transactions impact the income statement, while the items are primarily balance-sheet oriented. The deposit of warrants or Treasury securities or cash show up as assets, although their location may be different. If funding is forthcoming from lines of credit, then the liability side of the sheet must be viewed. For certain organizations, there is a required disclosure that is to be enclosed within financial statements: hedging transactions were used (although the precise size and transactional accounting is not presently required). The Financial Accounting Standards Board (FASB) provides guidelines for the recording and presentation of hedge transactions for many classifications such as currencies, physicals, and financials. The FASB publishes principles in determining the hedge status of trading programs as well.

TREASURY FUNCTIONS

The financing of hedge positions falls under the purview of the treasury area except for the smaller firms, in which the owner/manager or chief financial officer would be directly involved in the hedging program.

How are funds to be raised? Is it through the fed funds markets, the sale of certificates of deposit, or the lending institutions? Or, is it against securities owned, mortgaged properties, working inventories, processed or semi-processed goods, or receipts (warrants, or actuals)? The companies' cash position, consisting of demand deposits, short-term instruments, or Treasury bills, could be used for initial margin (except for the purchase of options).

Margining and Deliveries

The margining and dispositional outcomes of hedging decisions are financial and physical in nature. Margins can be satisfied by the placement of cash—effective but not very efficient. By choosing financial alternatives, a hedger can boost the performance of a program or, at the least, contain its costs. By collecting interest whenever possible on deposited collateral, a hedger is that much more ahead of what his position would have been and, perhaps, that much more ahead of his unenlightened competitors. Should Treasury bills be paying 7 percent, then the deposit of Treasury bills will improve that portion of the hedge by 7 percent on an annualized basis. If the Treasury bills are held by the firm's treasury as part of the cash position of current assets, then a simple journaling, or deposit of the required portion of the bills, would be a journal entry. This would not influence the composition of the firm's assets, only their location. The collateralization of the hedge accounts improves the financial posture of the firm (better than if it were maintained at a bank or other brokerage firm). In a sense, under these conditions, it could allow for a slight variation in the basis relationships because some positive interest is being generated off as part of the incentive to hold Treasury bills. More sophisticated approaches would entail playing the yield curve to get the better rates for Treasury bill holdings be they one month, three months, eight and one-half months, or a year out. Depending on each exchanges' regulations, Treasury instruments that have less than a year to maturity can be used, which means that notes or bonds that are to mature within a year can be used. There are times when these instruments offer slight yield advantages relative to comparable Treasury bills in terms of maturities.

Receipts received upon the completion of deliveries can be used (depending upon exchange) as marginable collateral because those very receipts can be redelivered against open-short positions. They represent the actual commodity underlying the futures-options contracts.

Funds can be wired in via fed funds or chips and, depending on the relationship with the brokerage firm, there is reciprocal treatment. For example, if you mail checks, they mail checks, if you wire funds, they wire funds, and so on. This equates the float on these transactions.

Exchange Memberships

The purchase of exchange memberships can offer financial benefits as well. Besides the privilege of being a member and voting on exchange matters, the possibility of having an employee on one of many committees in order to voice concerns and provide direction for better services, a membership allows the organization to save on exchange-imposed transactions fees that can be fifty cents, one dollar, or more per side. If the organization relies on futures or options contracts as hedging devices, this step can produce important savings. Additionally, NFA fees can be spared. While not large in and of themselves, savings of 20 to 24 cents per transaction represents savings of $20 to $24 per hundred, which assist in gaining a competitive edge for trading-the-basis programs.

Multiplying these figures out for an average of 100 contracts or 50 roundturns per day, which reflects only $10 million contract par value for bonds, can result in savings of $25,000 or more per year. Depending on the level of activity and the relevant fees, this commission and fee expense area can be more selectively controlled. Clearing member status can save additional charges because the organization need not pay clearing fees to others, although it must now have the capacity to clear its own trades. This next step opens up certain liabilities because the clearing house (and its membership) is the ultimate guarantor of all trades, and this may not be desirable for all hedgers, although many do take this step.

CONCLUSION

Hedging is a powerful risk management tool. There are four primary methods (contractual agreements, forward markets, futures, and options) to reduce risk and satisfy other organizational objectives. By transforming price- (yield-) level risk into the more manageable basis-level risk, a firm can improve its financial and operational efficiencies. Many times this risk transformation/reduction is substantial. The development, implementation, and monitoring of a hedge program generates residual benefits as well. A corporation can gain practical insight in coping with marketplace problems. By devising appropriate strategies, the firm can effectively respond and enhance its probability of attaining success.

Hedging is flexible. Often there are numerous potential solutions to accommodate a firm's particular objectives and constraints. By being familiar with the principles, practices, and development of strategies, a hedger can implement suitable plans of action.

Bibliography

Aaker, David A., ed., *Multivariate Analysis in Marketing: Theory and Application,* Wadsworth Publishing Co., Belmont, Calif., 1971.

Adams, F. Gerard and Jere R. Behrman, *Econometric Models of World Agricultural Markets,* Ballinger Publishing Co., Cambridge, Mass., 1976.

Alchian, A. A. and W. R. Allen, *Exchange and Production: Theory in Use,* Wadsworth, Belmont, Calif., 1969.

Alexander, S. S., "Price Movements in Speculative Markets: Trends or Random Walks," *Industrial Management Review* 2:7–26, May 1961.

Altman, Edward I., ed., *Financial Handbook,* 5th edition, Wiley, New York, 1981.

American Stock Exchange, *Interest Rate Options: Study Guide,* New York.

American Stock Exchange, *Stock Index Options: An Introduction to the Major Market Index,* New York, 1983.

Arthur Andersen & Co., *Accounting for Interest Rate Futures Transactions,* Chicago, 1982.

Arthur Andersen & Co., prepared by, *Interest Rate Futures Contracts: Accounting and Control Techniques for Banks,* Chicago Board of Trade and Chicago Mercantile Exchange, 1978.

Anderson, T. W., *The Statistical Analysis of Time Series,* Wiley, New York, 1971.

Angrist, Stanley W., *Sensible Speculating in Commodities: or, How to Profit in the Bellies, Bushels, and Bales Market,* Simon and Schuster, New York, 1972.

Archer, Stephen H. and J. C. Francis, *Portfolio Analysis,* Prentice-Hall, Englewood Cliffs, N.J., 1971.

Arrow, Kenneth J., *Essays in the Theory of Risk Bearing,* Markham Publishing Co., Chicago, 1971.

Arthur, Henry B., *Commodity Futures as a Business Management Tool,* President and Fellows of Harvard College, 1971.

Ash, Robert B., *Basic Probability Theory,* Wiley, New York, 1970.

Awad, Elias M. and Data Processing Management Association, *Automatic Data Processing: Principals and Procedures,* Prentice-Hall, Englewood Cliffs, N.J., 1966.

Bach, George Leland, *Economics: An Introduction to Analysis and Policy,* 5th edition, Prentice-Hall, Englewood Cliffs, N.J., 1966.

Barnes, Robert M., *Taming the Pits: A Technical Approach to Commodity Trading,* Wiley, New York, 1979.

Baratz, Morton S., ed., *Commodity Money Management Yearbook,* L.J.R., Inc., Columbia, Md., 1979–1987.

Baumol, W. J., "Speculation, Profitability and Stability," *Review of Economics and Statistics* 39:263–271, August 1957.

Baumol, William J., *Economic Theory and Operations Analysis,* 3rd edition, Prentice-Hall, Englewood Cliffs, N.J., 1961.

Bear, Robert M., "Margin Levels and the Behavior of Futures Prices," *Journal of Financial and Quantitative Analysis* 7(4):1970, September 1972.

Beckhard, Richard, *Organization Development: Strategies and Models,* Addison Wesley, Reading, Mass., 1969

Beckman, M. J., "On the Determination of Prices in Futures Markets." In M. J. Beckman, ed., *Patterns of Market Behavior: Essays in Honor of Philip Taft,* Providence, R.I., Brown University Press, 1965.

Berlin, Bruce S., *Corporate Use of Commodity Futures,* Conference Board Report No. 562, New York, 1972.

Bernstein, Jacob, *Cyclic Analysis in Futures Trading: Contemporary Methods & Procedures,* Wiley, New York, 1988.

Bernstein, Jacob, *The Handbook of Commodity Cycles: A Window on Time,* Wiley, New York, 1982.

Bernstein, Jacob, *The Investor's Quotient,* Wiley, New York, 1980.

Beyer, William H., Ph.D., *Handbook of Tables for Probability and Statistics,* 2nd edition, The Chemical Rubber Company, Cleveland, Ohio, 1968.

Black, Fischer, "The Pricing of Commodity Contracts," *Journal of Financial Economics* 3(1/2):167–179, January/March 1976.

Blackwell, David and M. A. Girshick, *Theory of Games and Statistical Decisions,* Dover, New York, 1954.

Commodity Trading Manual, 5th revised edition, Chicago Board of Trade, 1971.

Bogen, Jules I., Ph.D., ed., *Financial Handbook,* 4th edition, Ronald, New York, 1968.

Bookstaber, Richard M., *Option Pricing and Strategies in Investing,* Addison-Wesley, Reading, Mass., 1986.

Box, George E. P. and Gwilym M. Jenkins, *Time Series Analysis Forecasting and Control,* Holden-Day, San Francisco, Calif., 1970.

Brennan, M. J., "The Supply of Storage," *American Economic Review* 48:50–72, 1958.

Brigham, Eugene F. and Fred J. Weston, *Essentials of Managerial Finance,* Holt, Rinehart and Winston, New York, 1972.

Burkhead, C. E., R. C. Max, R. B. Karnes and E. Reid, *Usual Planting and Harvesting Dates,*, revised U.S.D.A., S.R.S., Agriculture Handbook No. 283, Washington, D.C., March, 1972.

Campbell, Donald T. and Julian C. Stanley, *Experimental and Quasi-Experimental Designs for Research,* Rand McNally, Chicago, 1963.

Cargill, Thomas F. and Gordon C. Rausser, "Temporal Price Behavior in Commodity Futures Markets," *Journal of Finance* 30:1043–1053, September 1975.

Cargill, Thomas F. and Gordon C. Rausser, "Time and Frequency Domain Representations of Futures Prices as a Stochastic Process," *Journal of the American Statistical Association* 67:23–30, March 1972.

Carleton, William T. and Eugene M. Lerner, *A Theory of Financial Analysis,* Harcourt, Brace & World, New York, 1966.

Chance, Don M., "Empirical Tests of the Pricing of Index Call Options," Working paper No. 48, *Working Paper Series,* Virginia Polytechnic Institute and State University, Blacksburg, Va., September 1985.

Chiang, Alpha C., *Fundamental Methods of Mathematical Economics,* McGraw-Hill, New York, 1967.

Chicago Board of Trade, *Action in the Marketplace,* Chicago, 1987.

Chicago Board of Trade, *Basic Spread Strategies: Using Options on Treasury Bond Futures to Capitalize on Changing Price Relationships,* Chicago, 1983.

Chicago Board of Trade, *CBOT Major Market Index Futures,* Chicago, 1984.

Chicago Board of Trade, *CBOT Options on U.S. Treasury Bond Futures,* Chicago, 1985.

Chicago Board of Trade, *CBOT Seminar: Strategies for Today's Markets. A Seminar for Institutional Investors and Account Executives,* Chicago.

Chicago Board of Trade, *The Chicago Board of Trade's Municipal Bond Futures Contract,* Chicago, 1985.

Chicago Board of Trade, *Commodity Futures Trading: Bibliography Cumulative through 1976,* Chicago.

Chicago Board of Trade, *Chicago Board of Trade Conversion Factors,* Chicago, 1985.

Chicago Board of Trade, *Contract Specifications and Vendor Guide,* Chicago, 1984.

Chicago Board of Trade, *The Delivery Process in Brief: Treasury Bond and Treasury Note Futures,* Chicago, 1987.

Chicago Board of Trade, *Domestic Certificate of Deposit Futures,* Chicago, 1981.

Chicago Board of Trade, *Domestic Certificate of Deposit Future: Price and Yield Calculator,* Chicago, 1982.

Chicago Board of Trade, *Financial Futures: The Delivery Process in Brief,* Chicago, 1982.

Chicago Board of Trade, *Financial Instruments Guide,* Chicago, 1987.

Chicago Board of Trade, developed by Jerome Lacey, *Financial Instruments Markets: An Advanced Study of Cash-Futures Relationships,* Chicago, 1986.

Chicago Board of Trade, *Financial Instruments Markets: Cash-Futures Relationships,* Chicago, 1980.

Chicago Board of Trade, *The Futures Market: Meet the Buyers and Sellers,* Chicago, 1976.

Chicago Board of Trade, *Gold Futures Trading on the Chicago Board of Trade,* Chicago, 1974.

Chicago Board of Trade, *GNMA Mortgage Interest Rate Futures*, Chicago, 1975.

Chicago Board of Trade, *GNMA Yield Calculator*, Chicago, 1981.

Chicago Board of Trade, *Grains*, Chicago, 1973.

Chicago Board of Trade, *A Guide to Financial Futures at the Chicago Board of Trade*, Chicago, 1982.

Chicago Board of Trade, *Hedging in GNMA Interest Rate Futures*, Chicago, 1976.

Chicago Board of Trade, *Hedging Workbook*, Chicago, 1972.

Chicago Board of Trade, *Institutional Index Futures*, Chicago, 1987.

Chicago Board of Trade, *Interest Rate Futures for Institutional Investors*, Chicago, 1986.

Chicago Board of Trade, *Introducing Options on Treasury Bond Futures*, Chicago, 1982.

Chicago Board of Trade, *Introduction to Corn Futures*, Chicago, 1970.

Chicago Board of Trade, *Introduction to Financial Futures*, Chicago, 1981.

Chicago Board of Trade, *An Introduction to the Interest Rate Futures Market*, Chicago, 1978.

Chicago Board of Trade, *Introduction to Hedging*, Chicago, 1972.

Chicago Board of Trade, *Introduction to the Wheat Futures Market*, Chicago.

Chicago Board of Trade, *July/December Corn Spread 1972–1987*, Vol. 1, No. 3, Chicago, 1987.

Chicago Board of Trade, *Long-Term Treasury Note Options*, Chicago, 1986.

Chicago Board of Trade, *Long-Term U.S. Treasury Bond Yield Calculator*, Chicago, 1982.

Chicago Board of Trade, *Major Market Index Futures*, Chicago, 1986.

Chicago Board of Trade, *Major Market Index Futures Special Research Report*, Chicago, July 1984.

Chicago Board of Trade, *Margins for Options on T-Bond & T-Note Futures*, Chicago, 1986.

Chicago Board of Trade, *Margins for Options on Treasury Bond Futures*, Chicago, 1983.

Chicago Board of Trade, *Municipal Bond Index Futures*, Chicago, 1986.

Chicago Board of Trade, *Municipal Bond Index Futures and Options*, Chicago, 1983.

Chicago Board of Trade, *NASDAQ-100 Futures: Trade Tomorrow's Winners Today*, Chicago, 1985.

Chicago Board of Trade, *Options on U.S. Treasury Bond Futures*, Chicago, 1986.

Chicago Board of Trade, *Options on U.S. Treasury Bond Futures for Institutional Investors*, Chicago, 1983.

Chicago Board of Trade, *Price Language of the Marketplace: A Grain Growers Guide*, Chicago.

Chicago Board of Trade, *Selected Writings of Holbrook Working*, Chicago, 1977.

Chicago Board of Trade, *Sources of Financial Futures Information: A Bibliography*, Chicago, 1980.

Chicago Board of Trade, *Sources of Financial Futures Information: A Bibliography, 1981 Supplement*, Chicago, 1981.

Chicago Board of Trade, *Speculating in Futures*, Chicago, 1973.

Chicago Board of Trade, *Strategies for Buying and Writing Options on Treasury Bond Futures*, Chicago, 1983.

Chicago Board of Trade, *Strategies for Today's Markets: Seminar for Financial Futures & Options*, Chicago.

Chicago Board of Trade, *Trading in Metals Futures,* Chicago, 1986.
Chicago Board of Trade, *Treasury Note Options Trading Strategies Booklet,* Chicago, 1986.
Chicago Board of Trade, *Understanding Commodity Futures Margins,* Chicago, 1980.
Chicago Board of Trade, *Understanding the Delivery Process in Financial Futures,* Chicago, 1980.
Chicago Board of Trade, *Understanding the MOB Spread,* Chicago, 1985.
Chicago Board of Trade, *U.S. Treasury Bond Futures,* Chicago, 1982.
Chicago Board of Trade, *U.S. Treasury Bond Futures,* Chicago, 1987.
Chicago Board of Trade, *Weather and the Corn Market,* Vol. 2, No. 3, Chicago, 1987.
Chicago Board of Trade, *Weather and the Soybean Market,* Vol. 2, No. 2, Chicago, 1987.
Chicago Board of Trade, *Weather and the Wheat Market,* Vol. 2, No. 1, Chicago, 1987.
Chicago Board of Trade, *Workings of the Market,* Chicago, 1976.
Chicago Board Options Exchange, *How to Make the Market Work for You without Buying a Single Stock: A Basic Guide to SPX,* Chicago, 1986.
Chicago Board Options Exchange, *S & P 100 Index Options: The Index Edge,* Chicago, 1984.
Chicago Board Options Exchange, *Understanding Options,* Chicago, 1984.
Chicago Board Options Exchange, *Writing Puts, Straddles, and Combinations,* Chicago, 1978.
Chicago Mercantile Exchange, *Bibliography and Information Source List,* Chicago, 1980.
Chicago Mercantile Exchange, *Cash Settlement for Feeder Cattle Futures,* Chicago, 1986.
Chicago Mercantile Exchange, *Chicago Mercantile Exchange: Tokyo,* Chicago, 1987.
Chicago Mercantile Exchange, *Feeder Cattle Options Fact Sheet,* Chicago, 1986.
Chicago Mercantile Exchange, *Fundamental Factors Affecting Feeder Cattle & Beef Cattle Futures,* Chicago.
Chicago Mercantile Exchange, *Futures and Options Trading for Pension Plans: The Regulatory Environment. CME White Paper Series Number 2: Regulatory Impact on Futures Trading Program,* Chicago, 1987.
Chicago Mercantile Exchange, *Futures Trading in Feeder Cattle,* Chicago, 1977.
Chicago Mercantile Exchange, *Futures Trading in Live Beef Cattle,* Chicago, 1976.
Chicago Mercantile Exchange, *A Guide to Margins for Options on Futures,* Chicago, 1985.
Chicago Mercantile Exchange, *Hedging: A Food Service Manager's Guide,* Chicago.
Chicago Mercantile Exchange, *Information Source List, 1986,* Chicago, 1986.
Chicago Mercantile Exchange, *An Introduction to ECU Futures,* Chicago, 1985.
Chicago Mercantile Exchange, *An Introduction to Livestock and Meat Options,* Chicago, 1986.
Chicago Mercantile Exchange, *Livestock Futures and Options: Contract Terms,* Chicago, 1987.
Chicago Mercantile Exchange, *The Merc at Work: A Guide to the Chicago Mercantile Exchange,* Chicago.
Chicago Mercantile Exchange, *Pork Belly Options Fact Sheet,* Chicago.
Chicago Mercantile Exchange, prepared by Robert C. Lower, *The Regulatory Environment: Futures Trading for Financial Institutions,* Chicago, 1982.

Chicago Mercantile Exchange, *A Self-Study Guide for Hedging with Livestock Futures*, Chicago, 1986.

Chicago Mercantile Exchange, *A Trader's Guide to Livestock Options*, Chicago, 1985.

Chicago Mercantile Exchange, *Using Currency Futures and Options*, Chicago, 1987.

Chicago Mercantile Exchange, *Using S&P 500 Stock Index Futures and Options*, Chicago, 1986.

Chou, Ya-lun, *Statistical Analysis with Business and Financial Applications*, Holt, Rinehart and Winston, New York, 1969.

Chow, Gregory C., *Analysis and Control of Dynamic Economic Systems*, Wiley, New York, 1975.

Citrus Associates of the New York Cotton Exchange, *FCOJ Futures*, New York, 1987.

Citrus Associates of the New York Cotton Exchange, *FCOJ Futures & Options: Trading Guide*, New York, 1988.

Citrus Associates of the New York Cotton Exchange, *Hedging FCOJ Futures*, New York, 1987.

Citrus Associates of the New York Cotton Exchange, *Introduction to Options on FCOJ Futures*, New York.

Clark, Peter K., "A Subordinate Stochastic Process Model with Finite Variance for Speculative Prices," with a discussion by B. Mandelbroit, *Econometrica* 41(1):135–155, January 1973.

Coffee, Sugar & Cocoa Exchange, *Guide*, New York.

Coffee, Sugar & Cocoa Exchange, *An Introduction & Strategy Guide: Options on Coffee Futures*, New York.

Coffee, Sugar & Cocoa Exchange, *Option Trading Strategies Handbook*, New York, 1983.

Coffee, Sugar & Cocoa Exchange, *Strategies for Buying and Selling Options on Cocoa Futures*, New York.

Coffee, Sugar & Cocoa Exchange, *Trading in Sugar Futures*, New York.

Coffee, Sugar & Cocoa Exchange, *Understanding Options on Futures*, New York.

Cohen, James B. and Sidney M. Robbins, *The Financial Manager*, Harper & Row, New York, 1966.

COMEX, *COMEX Aluminum Futures: A Guide for Hedgers*, New York.

COMEX, *COMEX Copper Futures*, New York.

COMEX, *COMEX Copper Futures: An Introduction*, New York.

COMEX, *COMEX Gold Futures*, New York.

COMEX, *COMEX Gold/Silver Ratio 1975–1987*, New York.

COMEX, *COMEX Gold Futures: An Introduction*, New York.

COMEX, prepared by Barkley International Inc., *Introduction to Hedging*, New York, 1988.

COMEX, prepared by Barkley International Inc., *Introduction to Hedging: A Seminar Manual*, New York, 1988.

COMEX, *COMEX Precious Metals Options: Strategies for the Investor*, New York.

COMEX, *COMEX: Option Master. Workbook*, New York.

COMEX, *COMEX Silver Futures*, New York.

COMEX, *COMEX Silver Futures: An Introduction*, New York.

COMEX, *Moody's Corporate Bond Index: Pocket Guide,* New York.

COMEX, *Options on COMEX Copper Futures: An Introduction,* New York.

COMEX, *Options on COMEX Gold Futures: An Introduction,* New York.

COMEX, *Options on COMEX Silver Futures: An Introduction,* New York.

Commerce Clearing House, *Commodity Exchange Act as Amended and Regulations Thereunder,* Commerce Clearing House, Chicago, 1987.

Commodity Research Bureau, *Understanding the Commodity Futures Markets,* New York, 1973.

Commodity Research Bureau, *Understanding the Commodity Futures Markets,* New York, 1981.

Compagnie des Commissionnaires Agrees Pres la Bourse de Commerce de Paris, *Paris Futures Markets,* Paris.

Cootner, Paul H., "Common Elements in Futures Markets for Commodities and Bonds," *American Economic Review Papers and Proceedings* 51:173–193, 1961.

Cootner, Paul H., ed., *The Random Character of Stock Market Prices,* revised edition, M.I.T., Cambridge, Mass., 1964.

Cootner, Paul H., *Speculation and Hedging,* Food Research Institute Studies 7, Supplement: 65–105, 1967.

Cox, Houston A., *A Common Sense Approach to Commodity Futures Trading,* Reynolds, 1972.

Cox, John C. and Mark Rubinstein, *Option Markets,* Prentice-Hall, Inc., Englewood Cliffs, N.J., 1985.

Dalrymple, Brent B., "Risk Analysis Applied to Commodity Speculation," *Journal of Finance* 26:790, June 1971.

Darst, David M., *The Handbook of the Bond and Money Markets,* McGraw-Hill, New York, 1981.

Dasse, Frank A., *Economic Impacts of Frozen Concentrated Orange Juice Futures Trading on the Florida Orange Industry,* unpublished dissertation, University of Florida, Fla., 1975.

Davis, James A., *Elementary Survey Analysis,* Prentice-Hall, Englewood Cliffs, N.J., 1971.

Dewey, Edward R., with Og Mandino, *Cycles, the Mysterious Forces That Trigger Events,* Hawthorn Books, Inc., New York, 1971.

Dippel, Gene, and William C. House, *Information Systems: Data Processing and Evaluation,* Scott, Foresman and Co., 1969.

Dobson, Edward D., *Commodity Spreads: A Historical Chart Perspective,* Greenville, S.C.

Doob, J. L., *Stochastic Processes,* Wiley, New York, 1953.

Dougall, Herbert E., *Capital Markets and Institutions,* 2nd edition, Prentice-Hall, Englewood Cliffs, N.J., 1970.

Dougall, Herbert E., Ph.D., and Harry G. Guthman, Ph.D., *Corporate Financial Policy,* Prentice-Hall, Englewood Cliffs, N.J., 1962.

Drexel Burnham Lambert, *At Last, There's a Way to Reduce Rollover Risk and Control Your Borrowing Costs . . . ,* New York, 1984.

Drexel Burnham Lambert, *The Bottom Line Benefits of Interest Rate Swaps,* New York, 1985.

Drexel Burnham Lambert, *Options Hedging and Trading Techniques for the Petroleum Industry,* New York, 1985.

Drucker, Peter F., *Men, Ideas, and Politics,* Harper & Row, New York, 1971.

Dusak, Katherine, "Futures Trading and Investor Returns—An Investigation of Commodity Market Risk Premiums," *Journal of Political Economy* 81(6):1387–1406, November/December 1973.

Edwards, Robert D., and John Magee, *Technical Analysis of Stock Trends,* Springfield, Mass., 1966.

Ehrich, Rollo L., "Cash-Futures Price Relationships for Live Beef Cattle," *American Journal of Agricultural Economics* 51:26–40, February 1969.

Ellsworth, P. T., *The International Economy,* 4th edition, Macmillan, New York, 1969.

Elton, Edwin J. and Martin J. Gruber, eds., *Security Evaluation and Portfolio Analysis,* Prentice-Hall, Englewood Cliffs, N.J., 1972.

Engel, Louis, *How to Buy Stocks,* 4th revised edition, Bantam Books, New York, 1967.

Fama, Eugene F., "The Behavior of Stock Market Prices," *Journal of Business* (38):34–105, January 1965.

Federal Reserve Bank of Richmond, *Instruments of the Money Market,* Richmond, Va., 1968.

Federal Reserve Bank of Richmond, *Keys for Business Forecasting,* Richmond, Va., 1969.

Federal Reserve Bank of St. Louis, *U.S. Financial Data,* St. Louis, Mo.

Financial Accounting Standards Board, *Statement of Financial Accounting Standards No. 52: Foreign Currency Translation,* Stamford, Conn., December 1981.

Financial Accounting Standards Board, *Statement of Financial Accounting Standards No.80: Accounting for Futures Contracts,* Stamford, Conn., August 1984.

FINEX, *Five-Year U.S. Treasury Note Futures. FYTR: An Introduction,* FINEX, a division of the New York Cotton Exchange, New York, 1987.

FINEX, *U.S. Dollar Index Futures,* FINEX, a division of the New York Cotton Exchange, New York.

Fong, H. Gifford and Frank J. Fabozzi, *Fixed Income Portfolio Management,* Dow Jones-Irwin, Homewood, Ill., 1985.

Fox, Karl A. and William C. Merrill, *An Introduction to Economic Statistics,* Wiley, New York, 1970.

Freund, John E., *College Mathematics with Business Applications,* Prentice-Hall, Englewood Cliffs, N.J., 1969.

Freund, John E. and Frank J. Williams, *Elementary Business Statistics: the Modern Approach,* Prentice-Hall, Englewood Cliffs, N.J., 1964.

Frey, T. D., "Forecasting Prices for Industrial Commodity Markets," *Journal of Marketing* 34:28–32, April 1970.

Friedman, Milton, *A Program for Monetary Stability,* Fordham University Press, New York, 1969.

Friedman, Milton, *A Theory of the Consumption Function,* Princeton University Press, Princeton, N.J., 1971.

Friedman, Milton, *Dollars and Deficits,* Prentice-Hall, Englewood Cliffs, N.J., 1968.

Friedman, Milton, *Essays in Positive Economics,* University of Chicago Press, Chicago, 1966.

Friedman, Milton, ed., *Studies in the Quantity Theory of Money,* University of Chicago Press, Chicago, 1965.

Frost, Alfred J. and Robert R. Prechter, Jr., *Elliott Wave Principle: Key to Stock Market Profits,* New Classics Library, Chappaqua, N.Y., 1978.

Fuller, Leonard E., *Basic Matrix Theory,* Prentice-Hall, Englewood Cliffs, N.J., 1962.

Gann, W. D., *How To Make Profits Trading in Commodities,* Lambert-Gann Publishing Co., Pomeroy, Wash., 1976.

Gann, William D., *Truth of the Stock Tape,* Lambert-Gann Publishing Co., Pomeroy, Wash., 1976.

Gann, William D., *45 Years in Wall Street,* Lambert-Gann Publishing Co., Pomeroy, Wash., 1976.

Gastineau, Gary, *The Stock Options Manual,* McGraw-Hill, New York, 1979.

Gnugnoli, Giuliano and Herbert Maisel, *Simulation of Discrete Stochastic Systems,* Simulation Science Research Associates, Chicago, 1972.

Gold, Gerald, *Modern Commodity Futures Trading,* Commodity Research Bureau, New York, 1959.

Goldberg, Ray A., *Agribusiness Coordination,* The President and Fellows of Harvard College, Boston, Mass., 1968.

Gordon, Robert A., *Business Fluctuations,* 2nd edition, Harper & Row, New York, 1961.

Gould, Dr. Bruce G., *How to Make Money in Commodities,* Bruce Gould Publications, Seattle, Wash., 1980.

Granville, Joseph E., *A Strategy of Daily Stock Market Timing for Maximum Profit,* Prentice-Hall, Englewood Cliffs, N.J., 1960.

Granville, Joseph E., *Granville's New Key to Stock Market Profits,* Prentice-Hall, Englewood Cliffs, N.J., 1969.

Gray, Roger W., "Risk Management in Commodities and Financial Markets," *American Journal of Agricultural Economics,* 58(2):280–285, 296–304, May 1976.

Green, J. R., "Temporary General Equilibrium in a Sequential Trading Model with Spot and Futures Transactions," *Econometrica* 41:1103–1123, November 1973.

Gross, Alan E., Barry E. Collins and James M. Bryan, *An Introduction to Research in Social Psychology,* Wiley, New York, 1972.

Grushcow, Jack and Courtney Smith, *Profits Through Seasonal Trading,* Ronald, New York, 1980.

Haimann, Theo and William G. Scott, *Management in the Modern Organization,* Houghton Mifflin, Boston, 1970.

Hare, Van Court, Jr., *Systems Analysis: A Diagnostic Approach,* Harcourt, Brace & World, New York, 1967.

Harlow, Charles V., Herbert L. Stone and Richard J. Teweles, *The Commodity Futures Game,* McGraw-Hill, New York, 1974.

Hester, Donald D. and James Tobin, eds., *Financial Markets and Economic Activity,* Wiley, New York, 1971.

Hieronymus, Thomas A., *Economics of Futures Trading*, Commodity Research Bureau, New York, 1971.

Hoel, Paul G., *An Introduction to Mathematical Statistics*, Wiley, New York, 1971.

Hogg, Robert V. and Allen T. Craig, *Introduction to Mathematical Statistics*, 3rd edition, Macmillan, New York, 1970.

Houthakker, H. S., "Can Speculators Forecast Prices?," *Review of Economic Statistics*, 39:143–151, May 1957.

Houthakker, H. S., *Commodity Futures IV: An Empirical Test of the Theory of Normal Backwardation*, Cowles Commission Discussion Paper, Economics No. 2124, 22 June 1955.

Houthakker, H. S., "Normal Backwardation." In J. N. Wolfe, ed., *Value, Capital, and Growth: Papers in Honour of Sir John Hicks*, Edinburgh, Edinburgh University Press, 1968.

Houthakker, H. S., "Restatement of the Theory of Normal Backwardation," Cowles Foundation Discussion Paper, No.44, 18 December 1957.

Houthakker, H. S., "Systematic and Random Elements in Short-term Price Movements," *American Economic Review Papers and Proceedings* 51:164–172, 1961.

Houthakker, H. S. and L. G. Telser, "Commodity Futures II: Gains and Losses of Hedgers and Future Speculators," Cowles Commission Discussion Paper, Economics No. 2090, December 1952.

Hurst, J. M., *The Profit Magic of Stock Transaction Timing*, Prentice-Hall, Englewood Cliffs, N.J., 1970.

Index and Option Market, *Inside S&P 500 Stock Index Futures*, Index and Option Market, a division of Chicago Mercantile Exchange, Chicago.

Index and Option Market, *Opportunities in Stock Futures: Standard & Poor's 500 Stock Index Futures Contracts*, Index and Option Market, a division of Chicago Mercantile Exchange, Chicago.

International Monetary Market, *Gold Futures Trading for Bullion Dealers*, International Monetary Market, a division of Chicago Mercantile Exchange, Chicago, 1982.

International Monetary Market, *The International Monetary Market*, International Monetary Market, a division of Chicago Mercantile Exchange, Chicago, 1981.

International Monetary Market, *The International Monetary Market. Price and Yield Calculator: Eurodollar TD Futures, Treasury Bill Futures, and Domestic CD Futures*, International Monetary Market, a division of Chicago Mercantile Exchange, Chicago.

International Monetary Market, *91-Day U.S. Treasury Bills*, International Monetary Market, a division of Chicago Mercantile Exchange, Chicago.

International Monetary Market, *Understanding Futures in Foreign Exchange*, International Monetary Market, a division of Chicago Mercantile Exchange, Chicago, 1979.

International Petroleum Exchange, *Historical Price Comparison Charts 3*, London.

International Petroleum Exchange, *An Introductory Guide to Oil Futures Trading on the International Petroleum Exchange*, London.

International Petroleum Exchange, *IPE Fuel Oil Contract and the Shipping Industry*, London, 1987.

International Petroleum Exchange, *IPE Gas Oil Traded Options*, London.

International Petroleum Exchange, *The IPE Oil Products Contracts. Gas Oil. Heaby Fuel Oil,* London, 1987.

International Petroleum Exchange, *Techniques of Basis Trading,* London, 1987.

Jaedicke, Robert K. and Robert T. Sprouse, *Accounting Flows: Income, Funds, and Cash,* Prentice-Hall, Englewood Cliffs, N.J., 1965.

Jensen, Michael C., ed., *Studies in the Theory of Capital Markets,* Praeger Publishers, New York, 1972.

Jiler, Harry, ed., *Guide to Commodity Price Forecasting,* Commodity Research Bureau, Inc., New York, 1971.

Johnson, Lynwood A. and Douglas C. Montgomery, *Forecasting and Time Series Analysis,* McGraw-Hill, New York, 1976.

Johnson, Norman I. and Samuel Kotz, *Continuous Univariate Distributions, Volume 1,* Houghton Mifflin, Boston, 1970.

Jones, Claude L., *Theory of Hedging on the Beef Futures Market,* Review of Economic Studies 27(9):139–151, June 1960.

Kansas City Board of Trade, *The Future is Here: Value Line Average Stock Index Futures,* Kansas City, Mo., 1982.

Kansas City Board of Trade, *Futures Trading and Hard Winter Wheat,* Kansas City, Mo., 1982.

Kansas City Board of Trade, *Using Stock Index Futures to Reduce Market Risk,* Kansas City, Mo.

Kaufman, P. J., *Commodity Trading Systems and Methods,* Wiley, New York, 1978.

Kaufman, P. J., *Handbook of Futures Markets: Commodity, Financial, Stock Index, and Options,* Wiley, New York, 1984.

Kendall, Sir Maurice, *Time Series,* 2nd edition, Hafner Press, New York, 1976.

Kenyon, David E., *Farmers' Guide to Trading Agricultural Commodity Options,* USDA, Washington, D.C., April 1984.

Kerekes, Gabriel T. and Frank H. Zarb, eds., *The Stock Market Handbook,* Dow Jones-Irwin, Inc., Homewood, Ill., 1970.

Koziol, Joseph D., *A Handbook for Professional Futures and Options Traders,* Wiley, New York, 1987.

Kroll, Stanley and Irwin Shisko, *The Commodity Futures Market Guide,* Harper & Row, New York, 1972.

Labuszewski, John and John E. Nyhoff, *Trading Financial Futures: Markets, Methods, Strategies, and Tactics,* Wiley, New York, 1988.

Labuszewski, John and John E. Nyhoff, *Trading Options on Futures: Markets, Methods, Strategies, and Tactics,* Wiley, New York, 1988.

Labuszewski, John and Jeanne Cairns Sinquefield, *Inside the Commodity Option Markets,* Wiley, New York, 1984.

Labys, Walter C., *Quantitative Models of Commodity Markets,* Ballinger, Cambridge, Mass., 1975.

Labys, Walter C. and C. W. J. Granger, *Speculation, Hedging and Commodity Price Forecasts,* Heath Lexington Books, Lexington, Mass., 1970.

Lancaster, Kelvin, *Mathematical Economics,* Macmillan, New York, 1970.

Larson, Arnold B., "Estimation of Hedging and Speculative Positions in Futures Markets," *Food Research Institute Studies* 2:203–212, 1961.

Leuthold, Raymond M., "Random-Walk and Price Trends—The Live Cattle Futures Market," *Journal of Finance* 27(4):879–889, September 1972.

Levin, Richard I. and Rudolph P. Lamone, *Quantitative Disciplines in Management Decisions*, Dickenson Publishing, Belmont, Calif., 1969.

Levy, Robert A., *The Relative Strength Concept of Common Stock Forecasting*, Investors Intelligence, New York, 1968.

Lietaer, Bernard A., *Financial Management of Foreign Exchange*, The M.I.T. Press, Cambridge, Mass., 1971.

Lindow, Wesley, *Inside the Money Market*, Random House, New York, 1972.

Loosigan, Allan M., *Interest Rate Futures*, Dow Jones Books, Princeton, N.J., 1980.

Luskin, Donald L., ed., *Index Options & Futures: The Complete Guide*, Wiley, New York, 1987.

Luskin, Donald L., ed., *Portfolio Insurance: A Guide to Dynamic Hedging*, Wiley, New York, 1988.

Mandelbroit, B., "Forecasts of Futures Prices, Unbiased Markets, and Martingale Models," *Journal of Business* 39:242–255, January 1966.

Mandelbroit, B., "The Variation of Certain Speculative Prices," *Journal of Business* 36(4):394–419, October 1963.

Mandelbroit, B., "The Variation of Some Other Speculative Prices," *Journal of Business* 40:393–413, October 1967.

Mao, James C. T., *Quantitative Analysis of Financial Decisions*, Macmillan, New York, 1969.

Markowitz, Harry M., *Portfolio Selection*, Yale University Press, New Haven, 1969.

Martell, Terrence F. and George C. Philippatos, "Adaptation, Information and Dependence in Commodity Markets," *Journal of Finance*, 29:493–498, May 1974.

Mass, Nathaniel J., *Economic Cycles: An Analysis of Underlying Causes*, Wright-Allen Press, Inc., Cambridge, Mass., 1975.

McMillan, Lawrence G., *Options as a Strategic Investment*, New York Institute of Finance, Prentice-Hall, New York, 1986.

Merrill Lynch Pierce Fenner & Smith, *How to Hedge Commodities*, New York, 1965.

Merrill Lynch Pierce Fenner & Smith, *The Impact of PIK (Payment-in-Kind)*, New York, 1983.

Merrill Lynch Pierce Fenner & Smith, *The London Metal Exchange: An Introduction to Hedging*, London, 1979.

MidAmerica Commodity Exchange, *$500,000 U.S. Treasury Bill Futures*, Chicago, 1981.

MidAmerica Commodity Exchange, *Opportunities in Domestic Refined Sugar Futures*, Chicago, 1982.

Minneapolis Grain Exchange, *Eliminate the Risk of Leading an Uneventful Life*, Minneapolis, Minn.

Minneapolis Grain Exchange, *Spring Wheat Futures*, Minneapolis, Minn.

Minneapolis Grain Exchange, *Spring Wheat Options*, Minneapolis, Minn.

Mitchell, Wesley C., *Business Cycles and Their Causes,* University of California Press, Berkeley and Los Angeles, 1963.

Morganstern, Oskar and John Von Neumann, *Theory of Games and Economic Behavior,* Wiley, New York, 1976.

Murphy, John J., *Technical Analysis of the Futures Markets: A Comprehensive Guide to Trading Methods and Applications,* New York Institute of Finance, Prentice-Hall, New York, 1986.

National Futures Association, *Buying Options on Futures Contracts: A Guide to Their Uses and Risks,* Chicago, 1988.

National Futures Association, *Glossary of Futures Terms,* Chicago, 1988.

National Futures Association, *Understanding Opportunities and Risks in Futures Trading,* Chicago, 1986.

New York Coffee and Sugar Exchange, *Sugar Futures Contracts,* New York.

New York Cotton Exchange, *Cotton Deliverer's and Receiver's Guide,* New York.

New York Cotton Exchange, *Cotton Futures,* New York.

New York Cotton Exchange, *An Introduction to Hedging Cotton Futures,* New York.

New York Cotton Exchange, *An Introduction to Options on Cotton Futures (for hedgers),* New York.

New York Cotton Exchange, *An Introduction to Cotton Futures Options (for investors),* New York.

New York Cotton Exchange, *Trading Guide—Cotton Futures and Options Contract Specifications,* New York.

New York Futures Exchange, *"The Long and Short of It." Foreign Exchange Contracts,* New York.

New York Futures Exchange, *"The Market Will Fluctuate . . ." Introducing New York Stock Exchange Index Futures,* New York.

New York Mercantile Exchange, *The Crack Spread Handbook,* New York, 1984.

New York Mercantile Exchange, *Energy Futures Complex: Heating Oil, Gasoline, Crude Oil,* New York, 1986.

New York Mercantile Exchange, *New York Mercantile Exchange Guide,* New York.

New York Mercantile Exchange, *NYMEX Energy Complex, Information Kit,* New York, 1987.

New York Mercantile Exchange, *NYMEX Energy Complex. Introduction: Propane Futures,* New York, 1987.

New York Mercantile Exchange, *NYMEX Energy Options: Strategies at a Glance,* New York, 1987.

New York Mercantile Exchange, *NYMEX Hi-Tech Metals: Platinum, Palladium,* New York, 1987.

New York Mercantile Exchange, *Perspectives on NYMEX 1986–87,* New York.

New York Mercantile Exchange, *Petroleum Futures Information Kit,* New York.

New York Mercantile Exchange, *Petroleum Products Futures. Information and Rules in Brief: No. 2 Heating Oil, No. 6 Industrial Fuel Oil,* New York, 1980.

New York Stock Exchange, *Fast Answers to Questions about Options on OTC Stocks,* New York.

New York Stock Exchange, *NYSE Beta-Index Options: To Cushion the Risk of a Volatile Portfolio*, New York, 1986.

New York Stock Exchange, *Options on the Market*, New York, 1986.

Options Clearing Corporation, *Characteristics and Risks of Standardized Options*, Chicago.

Orgler, Yair E., *Cash Management: Methods and Models*, Wadsworth Publishing, Belmont, Calif., 1970.

Patel, Charles, *Technical Trading Systems for Commodities and Stocks*, Trading Systems Research, Walnut Creek, Calif., 1980.

Patinkin, Don, *Money, Interest and Prices*, 2nd edition, Harper & Row, New York, 1965.

Paul, Allen B., "Treatment of Hedging in Commodity Market Regulation," *Technical Bulletin No. 1538*, ERS-USDA, Washington, D.C., April 1976.

Peck, A. E., ed., *Selected Writings on Futures Markets*, Chicago Board of Trade, Chicago, 1977.

Peck, A. E., ed., *Views from the Trade*, Book 3, Chicago Board of Trade, Chicago, 1978.

Philadelphia Stock Exchange, *ECU Option: Options on the European Currency Unit*, Philadelphia.

Philadelphia Stock Exchange, *The National Over-the-Counter Index: Options and Futures*, Philadelphia.

Philadelphia Stock Exchange, *Options on the Value Line Composite Index*, Philadelphia.

Philadelphia Stock Exchange, *Understanding Foreign Exchange Options: The Third Dimension to Foreign Exchange*, Philadelphia.

Platt, Robert B., *Controlling Interest Rate Risk: New Techniques and Applications for Money Management*, Wiley, New York, 1986.

Prechter, Robert R., Jr., ed., *The Major Works of R. N. Elliott*, New Classics Library, Chappaqua, New York, 1980.

Pring, Martin J., *Technical Analysis Explained: An Illustrative Guide for the Investor*, McGraw-Hill, New York, 1980.

Reinach, Anthony M., *The Fastest Game in Town*, Random House, New York, 1973.

Riehl, Heinz, and Rita M. Roderiguez, *Foreign Exchange Markets*, McGraw-Hill, New York, 1977.

Ritter, Lawrence S. and William L. Silber, *Money*, Basic Books, New York, 1970.

Rivett, Patrick, *Model Building for Decision Analysis*, Wiley, Chichester, 1980.

Robbins, Sidney, *The Securities Market*, The Free Press, New York, 1966.

Robichek, Alexander A. and Stewart C. Myers, *Optimal Financing Decisions*, Prentice-Hall, Englewood Cliffs, N.J., 1965.

Roll, Richard, *The Behavior of Interest Rates*, Basic Books, 1970.

Rose, Joy and Leon Rose, eds., *Commodity Money Management Yearbooks*, L.J.R. Inc., Columbia, Md., 1980.

Rosen, Lawrence R., *The Dow Jones-Irwin Guide to Interest*, Dow Jones-Irwin, Inc., Homewood, Ill., 1974.

Rudolf Wolff & Co., *An Introduction to the London Metal Exchange and the London Commodity Markets*, Rudolf Wolff & Co., London.

Schein, Edgar H., *Process Consultation: Its Role in Organization Development*, Addison Wesley, Reading, Mass., 1969.

Schlaifer, Robert, *Probability and Statistics for Business Decisions*, McGraw-Hill, New York, 1959.

Schwager, Jack D., *A Complete Guide to the Futures Markets: Fundamental Analysis, Technical Analysis, Trading, Spreads & Options*, Wiley, New York, 1984.

Schwartz, Edward W., *How to Use Interest Rate Futures Contracts*, Dow Jones-Irwin, Inc., Homewood, Ill., 1979.

Selby, Samuel M., Ph.D., ed., *Standard Mathematical Tables*, 21st edition, The Chemical Rubber Company, Cleveland, Ohio, 1973.

Shell, Karl and Giorgio P. Szego, eds., *Mathematical Methods in Investment and Finance*, North Holland Publishing Co., Amsterdam, 1972.

Siegel, Sidney, *Nonparametric Statistics*, McGraw-Hill, New York, 1956.

Silvey, S. D., *Statistical Inference*, Penguin Books, Baltimore, Md., 1970.

Sklarew, Arthur, *Techniques of a Professional Commodity Chart Analyst*, Commodity Research Bureau, New York, 1980.

Sloan, Harold S., and Arnold J. Zurcher, *A Dictionary of Economics*, 4th edition revised, Barnes & Noble, New York, 1968.

Solomon, Ezra, *The Theory of Financial Management*, Columbia University Press, New York, 1963.

Spencer, Milton H., Ph.D., *Managerial Economics*, 3rd edition, Richard D. Irwin, Inc., Homewood, Ill., 1968.

Sprinkel, Beryl W., Ph.D., *Money and Markets*, Richard D. Irwin, Inc., Homewood, Ill., 1971.

Sprinkel, Beryl W., Ph.D., *Money and Stock Prices*, Richard D. Irwin, Inc., Homewood, Ill., 1964.

Stalnaker, Ashford W. and Bevan K. Youse, *Calculus*, International Textbook Co., Scranton, Pa., 1969.

Stapleton, R. C., *The Theory of Corporate Finance*, George G. Harrap, London, 1970.

Starr, Martin K., *Management: A Modern Approach*, Harcourt Brace Jovanovich, New York, 1971.

Statistical Reporting Service, USDA, "Scope and Methods of the Statistical Reporting Service," Miscellaneous Publication No. 1308, U.S. Government Printing Office, Washington, D.C., July 1975.

Steinbeck, George and Rosemary Erickson, *The Futures Markets Dictionary*, New York Institute of Finance, Simon and Schuster, 1988.

Stigler, George J., *The Theory of Price*, 3rd edition, Macmillan, New York, 1966.

Sveshnikov, A. A., *Problems in Probability Theory: Mathematical Statistics and Theory of Random Functions*, Dover, New York, 1978.

Swiss Bank Corporation, *Foreign Exchange and Money Market Operations*, 1978.

Teichroew, Daniel, *An Introduction to Management Science*, Wiley, New York, 1964.

Telser, L. G., "Futures Trading and the Storage of Cotton and Wheat," *Journal of Political Economy*, 66:233–255, 1958.

Teweles, Richard J., Charles V. Harlow and Herbert L. Stone, *The Commodity Futures Game. Who Wins? Who Loses? Why?*, McGraw-Hill, New York, 1974.

Theodore, Chris A., Ph.D., *Applied Mathematics: An Introduction*, Richard D. Irwin, Inc., Homewood, Ill., 1965.

Tintner, Gerhard, *Econometrics*, Wiley, New York, 1967.

Toronto Stock Exchange, *Toronto 35 Options for the Individual*, Toronto, 1987.

United States Department of Agriculture, "Conversion Factors and Weights and Measures," Statistical Bulletin No. 362, ERS-USDA, Washington, D.C.

United States Department of Agriculture, *Corn Production*, Agricultural Handbook No. 322, Agricultural Research Service, U.S.D.A., in cooperation with Minnesota Agricultural Experiment Station, Washington, D.C., March 1975.

United States Department of Agriculture, *Major World Crop Areas and Climatic Profiles*, U.S.D.A., Washington, D.C., September 1981.

Vancil, Richard F., ed., *Financial Executive's Handbook*, Dow Jones-Irwin, Inc., Homewood, Ill., 1970.

Van Horne, James C., *Function and Analysis of Capital Market Rates*, Prentice-Hall, Englewood Cliffs, N.J., 1970.

Wagner, Harvey M., *Principles of Operations Research*, Prentice-Hall, Englewood Cliffs, N.J., 1969.

Wald, Abraham, *Sequential Analysis*, Dover, New York, 1973.

Wallis, W. Allen and Geoffrey H. Moore, "A Significance Test for Time Series and Other Ordered Observations. Technical Paper 1: September 1941," National Bureau of Economic Research, New York, 1941.

Walsh, Myles E., *Understanding Computers: What Managers and Users Need to Know*, Wiley, New York, 1981.

Ward, Richard, *International Finance*, Prentice-Hall, Englewood Cliffs, N.J., 1965.

Ward, Ronald W., *FCOJ Futures Market to Reduce Price Uncertainty*, Florida Agricultural Experiment Station, Report No. 5666, Gainesville, Fla., November 1974.

Ward, Ronald W., "Market Liquidity in the FCOJ Futures Market," *American Journal of Agricultural Economics* 56(1):150–154, February 1974.

Ward, Ronald W., "Measuring Market Liquidity: Case Study of FCOJ Futures," *Commodity Journal* 10(1)33–40, January/February 1975.

Ward, Ronald W. and Frank A. Dasse, "Empirical Contributions to Basis Theory: The Case of Citrus Futures," *American Journal of Agricultural Economics* 59(1):72–80, February 1977.

Wilder, J. Welles, Jr., *New Concepts in Technical Trading Systems*, Trend Research, Greensboro, N.C., 1978.

Wiley, Robert J., *Real Estate Accounting and Mathematics Handbook*, Wiley, New York, 1980.

Williams, Larry R., *How I Made One Million Dollars in the Commodity Market Last Year*, Conceptual Management, Carmel Valley, Calif., 1974.

The Winnipeg Commodity Exchange, *The Winnipeg Commodity Exchange: The Canadian Financial Futures Market*, Winnipeg.

Wonnacott, Ronald J. and Thomas H. Wonnacott, *Econometrics*, Wiley, New York, 1970.

Working, Holbrook, "Futures Trading and Hedging," *American Economic Review* 43:314–343, 1953.

Working, Holbrook, "Speculation on Hedging Markets," *Food Research Institute Studies* 1:185–220, 1960.

Working, Holbrook, "The Theory of Price of Storage," *American Economic Review* 39:1254–1262, 1949.

Working, Holbrook, "Theory of the Inverse Carrying Charge in Futures Markets," *Journal of Farm Economics* 30:1–28, 1948.

Woy, J. B., *Commodity Futures Trading: A Bibliographic Guide,* R. L. Bowker, New York, 1976.

Zellner, Arnold, *An Introduction to Bayesian Inference in Econometrics,* Wiley, New York, 1971.

Zweig, Martin E., Ph.D., *The ABC's of Market Forecasting: How to Use BARRON'S Market Laboratory Pages,* Dow Jones, Chicopee, Mass., 1980.

Zweig, Martin E., Ph.D., *Understanding Technical Forecasting: How to Use BARRON'S Market Laboratory Pages,* Dow Jones, Chicopee, Mass., 1978.

Periodical References

Barrons, Dow Jones, New York.
The Bond Buyer, New York.
Business Week, New York.
Chicago Board of Trade, *Interest Rate Futures Statistical Annual,* Chicago.
Chicago Board of Trade, *Statistical Annual Cash and Futures Data,* Chicago.
Broker News, Chicago Mercantile Exchange, Chicago.
CME Futures & Options Review, Chicago Mercantile Exchange, Chicago.
Statistical Yearbook: Metals Data, COMEX, New York.
Statistical Yearbook: Options Data, COMEX, New York.
Commodity Futures Professional, Chicago Board of Trade, Chicago.
Commodity Perspective, Knight-Ridder Business Information Service, Chicago.
Commodity Research Bureau Chart Service, New York.
Commodity Research Bureau *Yearbooks,* New York.
Consensus, Kansas City, Mo.
U.S. Financial Data, Federal Reserve of St. Louis, St. Louis, Mo.
Financial Futures, Data Lab, Niles, Ill.
Financial Futures Professional, Chicago Board of Trade, Chicago.
Forbes, New York.
Fortune, New York.
Futures Charts, Commodity Trend Service, North Palm Beach, Florida.
In the Money: Livestock Option Letter, Chicago Mercantile Exchange, Chicago.
International Economic Conditions, Federal Reserve of St. Louis, St. Louis, Mo.
Kansas City Board of Trade, *Statistical Report,* Kansas City, Mo.
Lotus Information Network, San Mateo, Calif.

Market Perspectives: Topics on Options and Financial Futures, Chicago Mercantile Exchange, Chicago.

New York Mercantile Exchange, *Energy in the News,* New York.

Municipal Market Data, Boston, Mass.

Outlook: NYSE Options, NYSE, New York.

Review, Federal Reserve of St. Louis, St. Louis, Mo.

Strategist, Barkley International Inc., Bedford, N.Y.

Trading Trends, Minneapolis Grain Exchange, Minneapolis, Minn.

The Wall Street Journal, Dow Jones, Chicopee, Mass.

Index